The SSCP® Prep Guide
Mastering the Seven Key Areas of System Security

Debra S. Isaac
Michael J. Isaac

Ronald D. Krutz, Consulting Editor

Wiley Publishing, Inc.

Publisher: Robert Ipsen
Executive Editor: Carol Long
Assistant Developmental Editor: Scott Amerman
Editorial Manager: Kathryn A. Malm
Managing Editor: Angela Smith
Text Composition: John Wiley Composition Services

This book is printed on acid-free paper. ∞

Wiley also publishes its books in a variety of electronic formats. Some content that appears in print may not be available in electronic books.

Library of Congress Cataloging-in-Publication Data:

ISBN: 0-471-27351-1

Printed in the United States of America

10 9 8 7 6 5 4 3 2 1

Contents

Introduction

Progress, far from consisting in change, depends on retentiveness. Those who cannot remember the past are condemned to repeat it.

George Santayana

When we agreed to write this book, we had two objectives in mind:

1. To provide system/network administrators or other operational staff study material on the system security field in preparation for the (ISC)^2 *System Security Certified Practitioner* (SSCP) certification exam

2. To provide quality background and general information on information system security so that others can learn about this field and the profession can grow

We believe that we have accomplished both objectives. We hope that you find the tools and the information that you need to become proficient in systems security within the covers of this book.

The (ISC)^2 Organization

The *International Information System Security Certification Consortium* (ISC)^2 is a nonprofit organization that has been working diligently for more than a decade to professionalize the *information system security* (ISS) field. Early on, (ISC)^2 tapped into the knowledge of senior ISS professionals and, by pooling international resources, developed a common body of knowledge and certification testing program for two different types of certifications:

1. The SSCP certification (technical) for which this text is prepared

2. The *Certified Information System Security Professional* (CISSP), which is targeted at a more senior (management) professional

The fields are distinct, and the certifications are intended to show the distinction.

The Common Body of Knowledge (CBK)

The SSCP *Common Body of Knowledge* (CBK) is a compilation and refining of pertinent security information from around the globe. The CBK was developed after it was discovered that no industry standards were in existence, nor was there an organization to maintain such information. To successfully become certified as an SSCP, you must have a working knowledge in the seven domains of the SSCP CBK:

- Access controls
- Administration
- Audit and monitoring
- Risk, response, and recovery
- Cryptography
- Data communications
- Malicious code/malware

The following is a description of each domain, and you should know the definitions:

Access controls.   The access controls area includes the mechanisms that enable a system manager to specify user and process rights; which resources they can access, and what operations they can perform.

Administration.   The administration area encompasses the security principles, policies, standards, procedures, and guidelines used to identify, classify, and ensure the confidentiality, integrity, and availability of an organization's information assets. It also includes roles and responsibilities, configuration management, change control, security awareness, and the application of accepted industry practices.

Audit and monitoring.   The audit function provides the capability to determine whether the system is being operated in accordance with accepted industry practices and in compliance with specific organizational policies, standards, and procedures. It also provides a mechanism to document accountability. The monitoring area includes those mechanisms, tools, and facilities used to identify, classify, prioritize, respond to, and report on security events and vulnerabilities. This area supports the accountability principle of system security.

Risk, response, and recovery.   The risk, response, and recovery area encompasses the roles of a security administrator in the risk analysis, emergency response, disaster recovery, and business continuity processes, including the assessment of system vulnerabilities, the selection and testing of safeguards, and the testing of recovery plans and procedures. It also addresses the knowledge of incident handling to include the proper acquisition, protection, and storage of evidence. This area supports the availability and integrity principles of system security.

Cryptography.   The cryptography area addresses the principles, means, and methods used to disguise information to ensure its integrity, confidentiality, authenticity, and non-repudiation.

Data communications.   The data communications area encompasses the structures, transmission methods, transport formats, and security measures used to provide integrity, availability, authentication, and confidentiality for data transmitted over private and public communications paths.

Malicious code.   The malicious code area encompasses the principles, means, and methods used by programs, applications, and code segments to infect, abuse, or otherwise impact the proper operation of an information processing system or network.

The Exam

The examination for SSCP certification covers the seven domains of knowledge from the SSCP CBK. The SSCP examination and certification are focused on the areas of security most closely associated with the technical staff. The examination is given throughout the world and consists of 125 multiple-choice questions, taking up to four hours. The (ISC)^2 Web site can be used to search for locations where the examination is being held. You can also register online for the examination at www.isc2.org.

How the Book Is Organized

The authors are both SSCP certified and CISSP certified through (ISC)^2. Our experiences with study guides on the market were less than enthusiastic, however. When we were approached about writing the book by our technical editor, Dr. Ron Krutz, we knew how we would organize the material. What we noticed missing in many other books relating to system security was any history or frame of reference for the readers. By providing this additional information, we feel that we have a book that is a single, high-quality reference for the serious SSCP student and that will suit the general population interested in system security.

The text is organized as follows:

Chapter 1—The Journey Toward Information System Security

Chapter 2—Domain 1: Access Controls

Chapter 3—Domain 2: Administration

Chapter 4—Domain 3: Audit and Monitoring

Chapter 5—Domain 4: Risk, Response, and Recovery

Chapter 6—Domain 5: Cryptography

Chapter 7—Domain 6: Data Communications

Chapter 8—Domain 7: Malicious Code

Appendix A—Glossary

Appendix B—Testing Tools

Appendix C—References for Further Study

Appendix D—Answers to Sample Questions

Who Should Read This Book?

Because this book is written to have the broadest audience, there are at least three categories of readers:

1. Candidates for the SSCP examination who are studying on their own or with a group and who wish to determine whether they have the knowledge and skills necessary to pass the SSCP examination. The student will find this comprehensive guide to the examination full of valuable information. In addition, with the sample questions for each domain included, the student will get a real feel for the type and level of detail of the questions as well as provide reinforcement for the current knowledge of the student.

2. Students who have or are going to attend a seminar or class to prepare for the SSCP examination. For the same reasons listed earlier, this single text is an invaluable asset in preparing for the examination.

3. Anyone who has an interest in system security.

Summary

Back in the days when we, the authors, learned about system security, there was almost no written material. As technology has produced point solutions, more and more material is being written regarding the specific solution and security or the specific software and its security. Even today, there is not a wealth of knowledge documented and available for the person who wants to pursue systems security. Instead of purchasing hundreds of books, journals, and so on, this book provides that "one-stop-shop." To have this type of environment available for system security, written by two professionals with more than 40 years of combined experience in this field, is to have access to a wealth of knowledge.

Acknowledgments

We would like to thank:

All our friends and family for their love and support

Dr. Ron Krutz, who requested that we write this book

Wiley Publishing for supporting us through the entire process

The U.S. *National Institute for Standards and Technology* (NIST) for their kind permission to include many new NIST Publications in this book

About the Authors

Debra Isaac has 19 years of Automated Information Systems management and operations experience and 13 years of automated information system security and information assurance (IA) program management for the federal government. She also has five years of U.S. Federal Government department-level policy development and program implementation. She is a *System Security Certified Practitioner* (SSCP), a *Certified Information System Security Professional* (CISSP), and has a certification in the *INFOSEC Assessment Methodology* (IAM) through the *National Security Agency* (NSA). Ms. Isaac holds a *Bachelor of Science* (BS) degree and a *Master of Science* (MS) degree in the computer field from the University of Maryland. She is an Edison Fellow. She has two daughters, Phaedra and Nichelle, and lives with her husband (and best friend) in Maryland.

Michael Isaac has more than 22 consecutive years of extensive computer experience in systems administration, *information security* (INFOSEC), the management of data resources, database design, and data administration ranging from mainframes to personal computers. He is a *System Security Certified Practitioner* (SSCP), a *Certified Information System Security Professional* (CISSP), and a member of the IEEE. He has two daughters, Phaedra and Nichelle, and lives with his loving wife of 24 years in Maryland.

Michael and Debra Isaac currently work for Corbett Technologies, Inc., located in Virginia. Michael is a senior systems engineer and provides direct support to federal clients. Debra is the vice-president responsible for strategic direction and new solutions.

CHAPTER 1

The Journey Toward Information Security: An Overview

Many terms or phrases can describe the concept of protecting important information that typically resides in a computer system: computer security, system security, information security, operations security, data security, COMPUSEC, INFOSEC, asset protection, risk management, information assurance, Internet security, network security, and *information system* (IS) security.

Few find it surprising that the name quagmire plagues this discipline, which has continuously evolved since the middle of the last century. The importance of protecting information, regardless of the container in which it resides, was evident since that moment in prehistory when someone realized that there was value in preventing someone else from knowing what they knew. More recently, information system security evolved from an informal function—part of the internal *electronic data processing* (EDP) function—to a formal, separate profession within the business environment. Parallel with this evolution, the language of system security—the lexicon—has moved from the provincial lexicon of a minority subculture (the computer savvy of the late 1960s, 1970s, and 1980s) to be included within the business world's lexicon of today. Regardless of how long we discuss this topic here, the lexicon is still confusing to say the least. Here, in the first years of the twenty-first century, we face a deluge of misnomers and misinterpretations regarding, what we will call through the remainder of this book, the field of information system security and the security practitioner of such a system.

For you to study for and successfully pass the specific (ISC)^2 examination for *System Security Certified Practitioner* (SSCP), you must understand the lexicon of this field of study. Each of the terms associated with information system security originally had a specific definition. As time passes, however, and the further removed from the field a person is, the less understanding there is regarding the lexicon. Therefore, if you intend to be a security professional, you need to have an overall understanding of the lexicon, its history, and how information system security supports an organization's mission.

Information system security is a vital function within the mainstream business environment today. You support (the system administrator or network/systems specialist) the organization you work for in many ways. The SSCP-certified individual has the basic knowledge to help the organization achieve its security mission and vision.

Five Essentials for Making the Journey

For you or your organization to successfully have secure, protected, and trusted information systems, you have to be actively on the journey toward information system security. How do you start that journey? What tools do you need? Which direction do you go? We hope that we address these questions in this chapter and throughout the remainder of this book. To make this journey toward information security, you will need the following items:

- A *map*, which we call a roadmap, to describe the terrain, obstacles, and distances and shows the destination.
- A *strategy* for following the map.
- Navigational *tools* to keep you on the right track and going in the correct direction.
- *Resources* that enable you to progress along the path that the map defines.
- *Time* for planning and execution.

We will now discuss these items in more detail.

Roadmap for Information System Security

Most people have used a map at one time or another. Typically, we rely on a map when the terrain is unfamiliar, the destination is new, or the course that we wish to take does not seem clear. The same situation holds true for the security of your systems. We need to develop and use a map to direct our journey toward information system security.

A rudimentary map has existed for information system security for many years, but we cannot rely on it alone, anymore. The world has changed (the systems are more advanced and complex), and there are new and faster roads available (security services and security mechanisms that did not exist previously). We must use that rudimentary map as a starting point because it gives great insight and help in defining our own map. The map that already exists contains the three general areas that you must traverse. These areas include the fundamental security objectives of information system security: *Confidentiality, Integrity, and Availability* (CIA). So, that rudimentary map looks something like Figure 1.1. Just like an out-of-date city map, not all roads are depicted, many roads lead to the same place, and not all obstacles are shown. But the map does point out that there are three areas. To provide security for your systems, you must travel to each security objective: CIA. How you get there, how long you stay there, and what you will do while there are the elements of the map you must develop yourself.

Now that you know the out-of-date map exists, we need to develop your version for your system by adding some detail. We understand pretty well the terrain of the basic map; it consists of the fundamental security objectives, CIA (sometimes referred to as the security TRIAD).

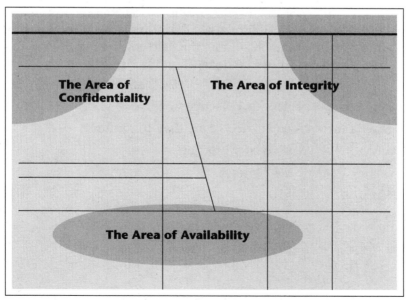

Figure 1.1 The rudimentary map is a starting point.

Security Objectives

Throughout the evolution of information system security, the basics, fundamental principles, and objectives have not changed—confidentiality, integrity, and availability (see Figure 1.2). While we have referred to these basics as a TRIAD for several years, we do not mean them to be considered as an equilateral triangle. On the contrary, every implementation has to have a primary focus. You and your organization's needs determine whether that primary focus is on confidentiality, integrity, or availability. While the three objectives should exist for all systems, a primary focus is necessary for risk management. Confidentiality is the objective that information is not disclosed to unauthorized persons, processes, or devices. Integrity is the objective that supports sameness of the information. Availability is the objective of timely, reliable access to data and services for authorized users (including restoration).

Security objectives are the essence of all information system security. All information system security policies, controls, safeguards, countermeasures, and even threats, vulnerabilities, and security processes can and should be considered within the framework of the security objectives. When you measure the effectiveness of controls, are you trying to determine how well the objectives of confidentiality, integrity, and availability are supported? Of course you are.

Many academic and philosophical discussions have occurred regarding the nature of the objectives of security, and many still continue today. You need to realize that there are differing opinions within the field concerning most security topics. For example, there would be dozens, hundreds, or perhaps thousands of opinions expressed in response to the following questions:

- Are the desired results principles, objectives, or goals?
- Are the desired outcomes end states, or are they continuums?
- Can you ever achieve 100 percent protection?

Figure 1.2 The objectives of security—the TRIAD.

These are just some of the topics that we could raise. Today, there are no totally correct answers to some questions. You need to recognize that this young profession has as much give and take as there is in the law or even in medical professions. Room still exists in the field for great research and major contributions.

As mentioned, the following are the three main objectives of system security:

Confidentiality. The confidentiality objective applies to both data and system information and is sometimes referred to as the secrecy objective. This objective's intent is to provide protection from unauthorized disclosure. Confidentiality applies to data in storage, during processing, and while in transit.

Availability. The objective of availability (of systems and data) is to provide protection from *denial of service* (DoS) of the *information technology* (IT) resource (system or data). Availability considers both the existence of the data or information and the ability to gain access to it, including the restoration of service, system, and data.

Integrity. Integrity (of system and data) is the objective that the system resources must be protected from unauthorized, unanticipated, or unintentional modification. This objective can apply to data and to the system. Data integrity is the property that data has not been altered in an unauthorized manner while in storage, during processing, or while in transit. Integrity can also refer to system integrity—the quality that a system has when it performs its intended function in an unimpaired manner—free from unauthorized manipulation.

In recent years, the integrity objective has evolved to include subelements. This area is one where the evolution of a concept has resulted in three new terms. These additional concepts stand on their own as security objectives in many policies, organizations, and books. For the SSCP, it is important to understand that the following three subelements are not additional objectives; rather, they are subelements of the integrity objective:

Authenticity. Authenticity provides assurance to the identity of someone or something. When an object (someone or something) claims to have a particular identity (normally a username or coded ID), the objective of authenticity is to provide a means to confirm the claim.

Non-repudiation. Non-repudiation ensures the availability of irrefutable evidence that supports the speedy resolution to any disagreement. In general, disagreements occur regarding whether a particular event occurred, when it occurred, what parties were involved with that event, and what information was associated with that event.

Accountability.   The purpose of accountability as a security sub-objective is to provide a level of assurance that the system can uniquely identify and determine the actions and behavior of a single individual within that system.

Security Services

Security services are how, in general, the objectives of CIA are manifested. Another way to look at it is that a security service is the instantiation of the security objective. For example, if the security objective you desire to implement is authenticity, you locate a security service that provides authenticity. That service is normally wrapped within a mechanism, several mechanisms, or a procedure.

Each objective is implemented by using an appropriate security service or set of services. The services enable the requisite functionality through the specified mechanisms providing the service that supports the intended policy. This set of objectives, services, and mechanisms select those solutions that will implement the defined policies.

Finally, because security services come in a variety of forms, we need to use security mechanisms to implement the security services because the mechanism determines the robustness of the security service.

Security Mechanisms

Security mechanisms are those solutions, technologies, policies, and procedures that we can implement on a system or in an enterprise. Where do the security services and most of the non-technical mechanisms of information system security come from? They originate from the totality of security disciplines that exist. Most security disciplines are much older than information system security, and their value has been well documented. Information system security draws guidance from the technical, operational, and managerial security disciplines (their robust functions, activities, and tasks) and applies them to information systems. Table 1.1 shows the relationship between objectives, services, and mechanisms and describes how the objectives of CIA decompose into the security services and security mechanisms. This table also shows how several security services support each objective, how the security services are implemented, and how they all work together to ensure that the policy that established the security objective is enforced.

GETTING FROM OBJECTIVE TO MECHANISMS: AN EXAMPLE

We determine that our system needs to have protection from being viewed by those who are not authorized. (The confidentiality objective.)

So, we require the use of security services to enforce the protection of the system and the data. To illustrate this concept, we will use the security services of access control, *identification and authentication* (I&A), and audit.

We have many security mechanisms from which to choose for the purpose of achieving confidentiality. We choose the security mechanisms of *access control lists* (ACLs) on directories and files; we will use the I&A mechanism to explicitly grant access to the system and data; and we will maintain I&A and access information in audit logs to periodically validate that all is working as it should.

Table 1.1   Decomposition of Objectives into Their Services and Mechanisms

OBJECTIVE	SECURITY SERVICE	MECHANISM
Confidentiality	Personnel security	Security clearance, training, rules of behavior
	I&A	User ID, password, token
	Access controls	Access control lists (ACLs), physical access control devices
	Labeling	Manual procedures
	Secure disposal	Policy stating requirements for labeling of documents Policy stating that all paper products are shredded
Integrity	Accountability	User id and password
	I&A	PKI (SSI authentication)
	Audit	Client audit
	Least privilege	Client and enterprise server
	Object reuse	Auditing
	IV&V	External contractor, independent element in organization
	Training	Online training, new employee training
Availability	Physical security	Site specific
	Risk management	Monitoring and tracking activities
	CP	Off-site backup and hot site procedures

Security mechanisms change and expand with emerging technologies. You should check the state of the market whenever you are in need of implementing new security mechanisms. Security services change much less often. Security objectives seem to never change, although occasionally someone will suggest that the CIA TRIAD should also contain other objectives such as non-repudiation, or "N." This situation is simply another of those cases we described earlier where the newer entrants to the field do not know the lexicon well enough to understand that non-repudiation is a subelement of the integrity objective.

As with any map, in order to use it correctly you must determine where you are, then where your destination is located on the map, and finally choose your course. In the world of information system security, the same approach applies (see Figure 1.3).

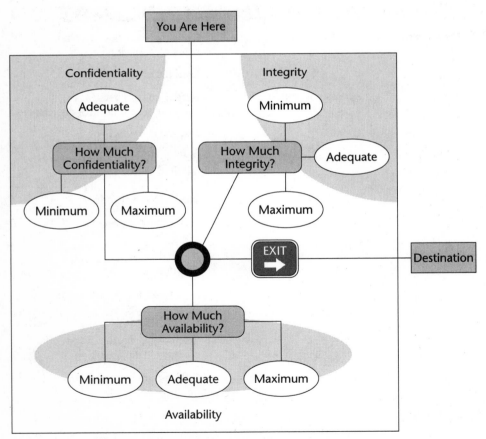

Figure 1.3   Positioning yourself on the map.

First, you determine where you are today (with respect to providing adequate security for your systems.) You can accomplish this task on a single system, as an organization, or as an enterprise. Once you have determined where you are, document that place. See the "You Are Here" block in Figure 1.3.

Second, you must determine where you want to be—where your final destination is located. To do that, you need to decide what amount and type of security/protection your system needs, is required to have, or you want it to have. Figure 1.4 shows graphically how you might make that decision. When you have identified that, document that place as "Destination X." When determining your destination, include how to protect the information as well as the fact that it must be protected (see Table 1.2). Some things for you to consider when determining your destination are as follows:

- You cannot protect everything from everyone.
- There are not enough resources and money in the world to totally mitigate all risks.
- Focus on protecting the most important information first, that which must be protected, and that with the highest risk.

Third, develop the course for the map that gets you to your destination while going through all the areas that you need to go through. Identify potential obstacles and bumps in the road. Identify resources that are necessary to accomplish the plan. The course that you develop is unique because your specific organization has different requirements and needs than the company next door:

- Develop policy based on the protection needs and your valued information.
- Implement policy with people, technology, and processes.
- Support these resources using money and time.

Table 1.2 Types of Information to Keep in Mind

DATA REQUIREMENTS	SECURITY SERVICES NEEDED TO FULFILL DATA REQUIREMENTS
1. Must protect due to legislative requirements	How to protect it (need to know), physical separation, and so on
2. Must protect due to agency requirements	How to protect it (need to know), physical separation, and so on
3. Should protect to prevent embarrassment, lawsuits, and so on	How to protect it (need to know), physical separation, and so on
4. No real need to protect	No protection schema defined

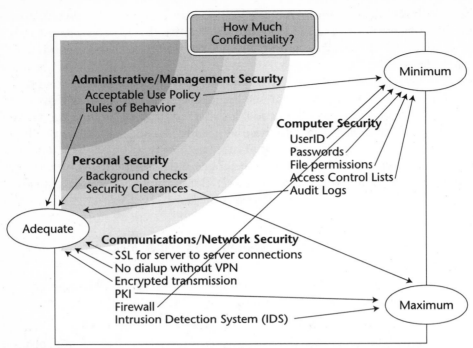

Figure 1.4 Select the types and quantities of mechanisms to support the robustness of the objectives.

Once you have completed these steps, you have a map (a plan of action) that you can implement. So, now we follow the map.

Because we all want to develop and follow the roadmap toward information system security, let's look at the specific details necessary to accomplish these steps.

Strategy for Achieving Information Security

Developing a strategy for achieving information system security is important. A strategy generally is the high-level plan that shows the general direction you wish to take, the priorities, who will accomplish what tasks, and with what resources.

In the field of information system security, a security architecture accomplishes the same goal. A security architecture provides the security framework for an organization or system and describes the objectives, services, and mechanisms that have been determined and that reflect the security policy and technology of the organization, enterprise, or system. The security architecture is a design, or plan, that specifies what security services—such as authentication, authorization, auditing, and intrusion detection—that security mechanisms need to address.

The security architecture is not effective without policies and procedures, assignment of roles and responsibilities, commitment of resources, training of critical personnel (for example, users and system administrators), and personal accountability. This architecture includes the establishment of physical security and personnel security measures to control and monitor access to facilities and critical elements of the IT enterprise.

The most effective strategy today is layered protection. The U.S. Department of Defense calls this same strategy defense in depth. This strategy ensures that systems maximize their resistance to attacks and minimize the probability of a security breach due to a weakness in any single security mechanism.

This strategy is based on developing layers, or rings, of protection around your system or enterprise (see Figure 1.5). As you pass through each ring, additional security mechanisms are in place to thwart an intruder and minimize his or her ability to gain access to important assets. The intent of the layered protection is to provide a combination of security mechanisms and technical solutions that is broad enough to address all the security requirements and deep enough to provide adequate security, preventing any single security breach from causing a major impact. This description does not suggest that a single focused effort against an organization will never succeed, but it is much less likely if enough appropriate security mechanisms are in place.

As shown in Figure 1.6, the outermost layer—represented here by protection ring 4—represents the initial boundary between an enterprise, organization, or single information system and the big, bad world (such as the Internet). At this layer, your security mechanisms might include *public key infrastructure* (PKI), firewalls, *Virtual Private Networks* (VPNs), and authentication for routers and *domain name service* (DNS). Protection ring 3 sets up the barriers between the individual system and its network and might include PKI, firewalls, and/or VPNs.

The next protection layer, ring 2, places mechanisms to support the CIA requirements at the system level. This layer might include workstations, servers (NT and/or Unix), and mainframes. The operating systems must have all known holes and weaknesses fixed.

The innermost layer, protection ring 1, protects the actual information or data that resides on a system. The security mechanisms might include application-level access controls such as additional passwords, data access controls such as ACLs, and the encryption of data/files, digital signatures, and auditing.

By applying a focused, knowledgable implementation of security mechanisms in this manner, you can realize cost savings and improved security.

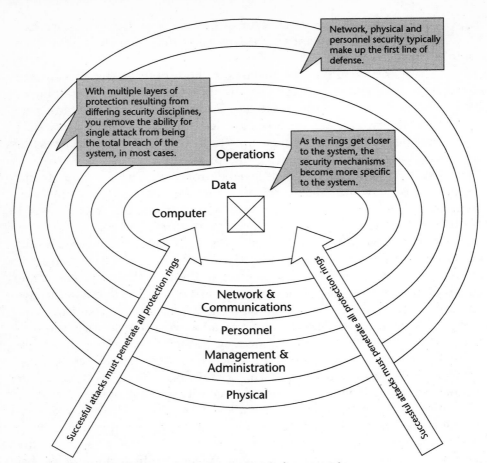

Figure 1.5 The application of security services in layers, or rings.

Once you have determined what your strategy will be and what general direction you wish to take, you need to assign priorities to the various activities that you must accomplish. At this point, you need to outline the resources required to implement and maintain your path. It is important to understand the level of effort required to accomplish this journey.

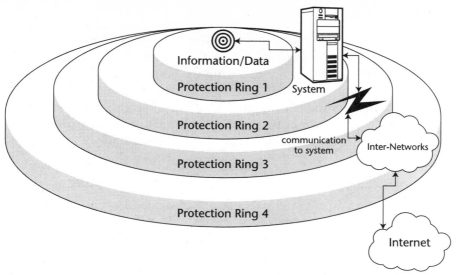

Figure 1.6 Protection rings in a focused, knowledgable implementation of security mechanisms.

Navigational Tools for Achieving Information Security

Recall that we are discussing what you must have to make that journey toward information security. We have discussed the roadmap. We have discussed the strategy, and now we will discuss the navigational tools that will keep you on the right track and going in the correct direction once you have started. Let's look at the map again. How much is the minimum? What are the elements that make up adequate integrity? We do not yet have enough information. We need to decompose this map, so let's get to it.

First, we need to understand what tools are available. Our navigational tools are the various security disciplines that we draw upon to provide measures of protection and layers of security for our information and information system. The security professional uses various combinations of these security disciplines to assist him or her with following the necessary course. An information system security practitioner or professional might be viewed as one who can demonstrate his or her knowledge in these areas, skills in the details of application within these fields, and ability to assess their effectiveness for any specific information system.

Computer Security

Traditionally, computer security deals with the actual computer system and networks and their internal abilities to provide security. The Common Criteria's protection profiles and the TCSEC's orange book represent examples of computer security. Protection of information systems against unauthorized access to or modification of information, whether in storage, processing, or transit, and against DoS to authorized users, including those measures necessary to detect, document, and counter such threats, are as follows:

- Measures and controls that ensure confidentiality, integrity, and availability of the information processed and stored by a computer
- All of the technological safeguards and managerial procedures established and applied to computer hardware, software, and data in order to ensure the protection of organizational assets and individual privacy

Data/Information Security

We often refer to this traditional security discipline as classification management. This discipline exists, as do most of these disciplines, outside the context of information systems security. This security discipline is focused on providing the correct level of protection for the information regardless of state (electronic, paper, and so on). The basis of data/information security is:

Protection of data from unauthorized (accidental or intentional) modification, destruction, or disclosure.

Communications/Network Security

Communications security was a separate security discipline that focused on the protection of communications of voice and facsimiles as well as computers when they were connected by using hardware encryption devices. As networks replaced dedicated lines and encryption became less cumbersome, these two areas blended together—and rightly so. The networks of today carry everything and more organizations other than just the military require encryption.

Measures and controls are taken to deny unauthorized persons information derived from telecommunications and to ensure the authenticity of such telecommunications. Communications/network security includes the following:

Cryptosecurity.   Cryptosecurity involves those measures used to minimize or prevent encrypted information from being deciphered by an unauthorized recipient (can include protecting the source of the encryption itself).

Transmission security.   Transmission security involves those measures used to prevent unauthorized recipients from receiving information during the transmission.

Emission security.   Emission security involves those measures used to prevent unauthorized recipients from deriving intelligent information from the study of any electromagnetic (radiated or conducted) emanations.

Physical security.   Physical security involves those measures used to control physical access to the network, system, and data.

Administrative/Management Security

The administrative/management security discipline typically covers all the issues that arise that the other security disciplines cannot handle (for example, minimum requirements for the protection of information and systems in your organization, policies and procedures for access to systems, rules of behavior, or the development and implementation of a personnel vetting process for system administrators or security personnel).

Administrative/management security includes the following:

- The management constraints and supplemental controls established to provide an acceptable level of protection for data

- The management constraints and operational, administrative, and accountability procedures and supplemental controls established to provide an acceptable level of protection for data (also known as procedural security)

Personnel Security

Personnel security is present in some organizations more than in others, depending on the need. If there are security clearance processes, personnel will perform the vetting of individuals.

Personnel security includes the following:

- The procedures established to ensure that all personnel who have access to sensitive information have the required authority as well as appropriate clearances

- The means or procedures such as selective investigations, record checks, personal interviews, and supervisory controls designed to provide reasonable assurance that persons being considered for, or granted access to, classified information are loyal and trustworthy

OPSEC EXAMPLE

The staff at a local pizza chain was the first (non-military) to know of the impending declaration of war on Iraq (The Persian Gulf War). Why? No one told them directly, but because the command and control centers in the Pentagon went on 24-hour high alert, all of the staffers were ordering pizza around the clock. Within two days, the United States declared war.

Operations Security

The *operations security* (OPSEC) discipline deals with denying information about capabilities and/or intentions by identifying, controlling, and protecting generally unclassified evidence of the planning and execution of sensitive activities from potential adversaries. We can also use OPSEC when protecting people.

For the SSCP in particular, operations security is also a synonym for system administration security. In that context, operations security refers to the act of understanding the threats to and vulnerabilities of computer operations in order to routinely support operational activities that enable computer systems to function correctly. Operations security also refers to the implementation of security controls for normal transaction processing, system administration tasks, and critical external support operations.

Resources for Achieving Information Security

Now, we will discuss the resources that you require to be successful in your journey. The resources you need are primarily people, technology, and processes—each of which are described in the paragraphs that follow.

People

A number of different people are instrumental in following the roadmap toward system security. The SSCP is certainly at the forefront. But the SSCP cannot do it alone. As we discussed in the navigational tools, many other security disciplines and professionals have specific knowledge in other areas that are required to reach the goal. These professionals include SSCPs, additional security specialists (possibly CISSP certified), security auditors, systems administrators, and security managers.

Technology

Technology (technical security solutions) is a supporting role in information system security, not the total solution. If you are technology oriented, you might find this concept difficult to understand and accept. Let's repeat it: Technology plays a supporting role, not the only role. Systems need to have security technology integrated as much as possible to support the security objectives. These technologies are varied and contain different capabilities, some of which are incompatible or could require many additional resources to implement and maintain. Also, keep in mind that every new technology introduced will have its own vulnerabilities. Technological solutions should be evaluated to ensure that future changes to the architecture are not severely impacted in migrating to new (and sometimes unpredictable) technologies.

Processes

Processes must be included in the resources used to achieve information system security. Processes are formalized, documented, repeatable methods of accomplishing a task. Processes include many specific procedures used to achieve certain end results, such as the following:

- Organizational and system-specific policy
- The chain of reporting for security incidents
- Backup and restoration procedures for systems, databases, and the like in support of contingency planning
- Clearance for new employees in differing positions
- Training of users, administrators, and management in policy, procedures, and ethics
- Adding new, removing old, and deactivating users on a system

You can imagine that the number of processes in use is not trivial. Documented processes are important in all businesses to consistently achieve the desired result. This situation is the same for those who are in the process of achieving a consistent level of security.

You should use the resources described previously together to achieve information system security in an organization or system. Generally, organizational policy is the driving force, directs efforts, and should be instrumental in any organization—or the course toward our destination is foggy and not clear. Policy drives the implementation of people and technologies to meet goals set in these policies; if there is no goal, we cannot arrive at our destination.

Time

This element is absolutely essential. Too many times, we (the authors) have seen managers demand that system security become a priority today and that everything should be accomplished by this time next month. Just so you know, 99 percent of the time, attaining that goal is not possible. Large organizations (more than 1,000 systems) can expect to have a three- to five-year roadmap for implementing information system security (plan of action). The reason is quite simple: Like the baby and the woman analogy, one woman can have a baby in nine months, but nine women cannot have a baby in one month. This scenario just does not work. The plan has to be developed, the money and human resources have to be identified, and the policies and procedures must be developed and at least partially institutionalized or else they will not work. The technology has to be identified and tested and so on. It does not matter how important your company is or how skilled you are as a security practitioner; having an adequate security system in place cannot happen without adequate time.

How the System Security Certified Practitioner Participates

The SSCP should be able to participate in many of the activities required for initially setting up a system's security and providing security expertise. He or she will most likely participate daily in following the map for information system security. The SSCP will apply and maintain security services and security mechanisms in several areas, such as 1) operating the system in a way that is consistent with the underlying objectives of security, 2) providing effective implementation of security mechanisms for the systems, and 3) recommending and implementing security technology to maintain an acceptable level of security for the system.

Conclusion

It is an exciting time for system security practitioners. Technology changes so rapidly that you are the first line of defense. Your personal knowledge and the ability for you to transform the system(s) you support to protect the entire organization. You are needed and wanted in almost every organization in the world. We hope that this book will provide you with the necessary information to enhance your knowledge and skills and that you join us in the ranks of the System Security Certified Practitioner.

Domain 1: Access Controls

The system security practitioner should understand the details associated with access control systems, their capability to provide protection, their inherent vulnerabilities, and how they support overall security objectives. Access controls are security services that are implemented through security mechanisms by using people, technology, and processes. Access controls, when properly used, support a proactive security approach. The proactive approach is cyclical in that you are always in one of the three cycles: prevention, detection, or reaction. The proactive approach by a security professional greatly increases protection and minimizes an adversary's chances of a successful attack.

Our Goals

For each of the seven domains, our goal is to provide you with three things:

1. Enough information about the domain so that you will be prepared to sit for the SSCP examination.

2. An understanding of how the overall system or enterprise security objectives, CIA, are carried through to the services and mechanisms within this domain.

3. An understanding of how the services and mechanisms of this domain provide security through one or more of the protection, detection, and reaction aspects of system security.

We do not believe you need to be taught the basics of each security service and/or security mechanism. You know your job as a system administrator or network administrator. What we intend to do is provide you with the connections and concepts that bring those isolated technical and administrative processes that you perform into the bigger picture: system security practice.

Domain Definition

According to the (ISC)^2 study guide, "Access control permits management to specify what users can do, which resources they can access, and what operations they can perform on a system. Access control provides system managers with the ability to limit and monitor who has access to a system and to restrain or influence the user's behavior on that system. Access control systems define what level of access that individual has to the information contained within that system based upon predefined conditions as authority level or group membership. Access control systems are based upon varying technologies including passwords, hardware tokens, biometrics, and certificates, to name just a few. Each access control system offers different levels of confidentiality, integrity, and availability to the user, system, and stored information."

The access control domain includes all of the mechanisms that enable a system manager to specify what users and processes can do, which resources they can access, and which operations they can perform. Access controls have a varied and broad application for the security practitioner. There are physical access controls such as locks, doors, gates, guards, cardkeys, and biometrics; administrative access controls such as procedures, acceptable use policies, and training; and then there are logical access controls such as user IDs, passwords, smart cards, *access control lists* (ACLs), group policies, file accesses, and roles. The security practitioner requires a thorough understanding of all three types of access controls (physical, administrative, and logical) and should be accomplished at using them in combination to support the layered security approach. We cover administrative controls in Chapter 3, "Administration."

> **NOTE** Information system security is not just technical point solutions implemented on a system. Any realistic security solution consists of many security mechanisms from the various security disciplines, woven into layers of security around a system or enterprise—all in support of the confidentiality, integrity, and availability needs of the information and system. If you throw technology or point solutions (as they are called these days) at a system, you might be missing the big picture and/or receiving a false sense of security. You have a roadmap; remember to follow it.

Why Control Access?

Controlling access is vital to the wellness of the systems and networks under your care. With access to your system, an adversary can do almost anything. Without access to your system, an adversary can do nothing. Just as important is that access controls place a level of accountability on authorized users.

Although access controls are fundamentally an easy concept, a fully integrated solution of complementary access control techniques is often difficult to achieve. They must be consistent with your organization's policy, minimize the likelihood of unauthorized access, disclosure, and modification, and be user-friendly enough so that authorized users do not seek to circumvent them.

We often use the comparison of a house to a system or network to illustrate the principles of access controls. The controls on the house (see Figure 2.1) provide a measure of security but not complete protection. For example, we rely on the lock on our door to keep burglars out, but reality shows us that if they really wanted to gain access, they would not use the door with the big lock—they would break a window. Or (if there were a security alarm system on the windows), they could just cut through the wall. A large number of mid-price range homes are constructed of sheet rock (or drywall), and the construction guys cut the material with a packing knife.

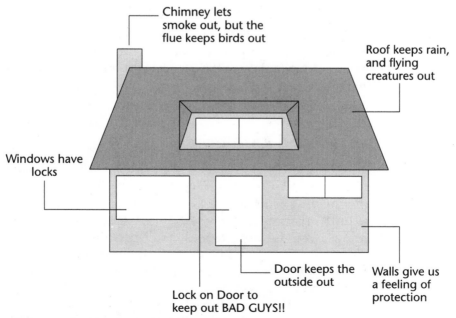

Chimney lets smoke out, but the flue keeps birds out

Roof keeps rain, and flying creatures out

Windows have locks

Door keeps the outside out

Walls give us a feeling of protection

Lock on Door to keep out BAD GUYS!!

Figure 2.1 The access controls principle.

What is important to remember is that there are things inside your network or system (house) that require protection from multiple sources, and the sources can gain access in many ways.

Access controls include all the mechanisms that enable a system manager to specify what users and processes can do, which resources they can access, and what operations they can perform. There are physical access controls such as locks, doors, gates, guards, cardkeys, and biometrics, and then there are logical access controls such as user IDs, passwords, smart cards (uses both physical and logical), ACLs, group policies, file accesses, and roles.

We control access to our system or enterprise through the focused application of security services and mechanisms. We also control access to hold authorized users accountable for their actions and to prevent access from unauthorized entities. When we understand the uses of access controls (including encryption as an access prevention mechanism), we can minimize attacks from adversaries such as DoS and DDoS, brute force, spoofing, and man-in-the-middle attacks.

Access controls support all three of the security objectives:

Confidentiality.   Through controls that protect access based on authorization

Integrity.   Through access controls to the data and processes

Availability.   Through the proper implementation and administration of controls so that they do not deny service to authorized users

Without a policy that provides protection for all information, a system access control policy will do little to provide security for an organization's valuable assets. Policies must include a method for determining what must be protected and to what extent. It should also delineate handling, marking, and disposal procedures for *all* information.

Protection of Assets and Resources

Let's image a system—a really big system located in an expansive computer facility. It has a supercomputer, a CRAY, as its centerpiece for computation. It has IBM mainframes providing controlling and scheduling, access, peripheral management, and so on. The facility has wonderful user space—cubicles with soft chairs, low lighting, awesome workstations, and fiber connections to all workstations. Let's continue to imagine that there is no external connectivity of any type—no network connections, no modems, and no external communication lines. The owners also want to protect its information (and the system itself because of the costs), so they have hired a concrete company to build a concrete building around the facility. Now, the computers sit inside a big concrete box. The door is barred and locked, and the key is thrown away. This system has the ultimate access control, but to what end? Who does this setup benefit? How useful is this level of protection? The owners did provide access control, but it was unacceptable. No one, even legitimate users, can get to the system.

Now, let's discuss how you can really use access controls as part of an acceptable security solution. Access controls perform two major functions: They provide accountability for legitimate users with access and they prevent (hopefully) non-legitimate users from gaining access. We must consider, implement, and maintain all of the security services and mechanisms that we discuss in this book with the destination (recall the journey) always in mind.

Assurance of Accountability

Accountability is the integrity objective subelement that provides the system security practitioner with the ability to know who has been on the system and what they did. When systems are set up with unique identification and authentication for users (and logging is enabled), the users can be held accountable for their actions while logged onto the system. Accountability also provides a way to detect whether an attack has taken place. If your users understand that they are responsible for their actions, they will be forthcoming with abnormal activity regarding their accounts.

SECURITY IN ACTION: AN EXAMPLE

Bob, who regularly grumbles about the long logon process, logs on every morning while drinking his first cup of coffee. He thinks Mondays are the worst days. He has to wait for the system to tell him it has been two days since his last logon. No kidding! This past Monday, however, the message on the screen caught his eye: "It's been 1 day since your last logon." He stared at the screen. After several minutes, he called the system help desk to report the strange display.

Prevention of Unauthorized Access

When authorized users (people or programs) gain access to a system, they might pass through several types of access controls. When the person (or program) trying to gain access is unauthorized, access controls can minimize and even prevent most attacks.

Several types of methods are commonly used for attacking a system. We describe the most common in the following paragraphs as well as means of preventing the attacks from happening.

DoS/DDoS Attacks

A *denial of service* (DoS) or *distributed denial of service* (DDoS) attack is an attempt by an adversary to prevent authorized access to a system or to the system resources or to delay the system's operations. A common method of launching a DoS attack is by flooding. Flooding attempts to cause a failure in a computer system or other data processing entity by providing more input than the entity can process properly. DoS is the act of denying service on a system or network (by whatever means). DDoS is a specific type of DoS attack that initiates from multiple sources to attack a common system or network with enough traffic to disallow the legitimate use of this resource:

- We saw examples of DDoS attacks in the commercial environment early in 2000 with eBay, Amazon, CNN, and others losing their Web-based businesses for several hours. Attackers used compromised computers throughout the Internet to mount attacks on various Web sites.

- Microsoft MSN, Carpoint, Expedia, and other Web services became victims of a DDoS attack in 2001.

- *Gibson Research Corporation's* Internet connection was brought down two years in a row. In 2001, a 13-year-old hacker using Windows zombies (Windows workstations that have been taken over by attackers and used as puppets in an attack) attacked it. Again in 2002, the company was hit, this time by a Distributed Reflection Denial of Service, where network traffic was generated that routed through many paths, generating additional traffic at each point, and converged at the point of attack.

If someone within your network launches Mstream, a DoS tool, and floods a target network, it fills caches used in some router configurations to speed routing decisions. Mstream spoofs source addresses, and because the cache treats each source and destination address pair as a cache entry, it quickly fills with junk entries.

So, what can we do to prevent, detect, and react to such attacks? For publicly accessible Web sites, it is impossible to implement access controls that deny access based on a list of approved users (all potential users have default access). Detecting DoS attacks is easy from the forensic analysis of the network and system audit trails. Forensic analysis refers to the examination of data packets traveling through the network. This analysis can show the specific techniques used to create the attack and enable the creation of appropriate filters to eliminate this traffic. Analysis can also determine the cause and point to the source of the attack.See Chapter 4 for further information on forensics. Reaction to attacks of this sort requires cooperation and is not always easily accomplished with complete success.The contingency plan and incident response capability (see Chapter 5) should address your processes for dealing with this type of attack. You can prevent attacks originating internal to your network by filtering against source address spoofing at all layers of your network.

Table 2.1 depicts the protection, detection, and reaction strategies recommended by CERT for system administrators. This strategy enables the evolution of protection mechanisms. Current technology enables various methods to provide these services, and you can provide many at multiple levels within a network.

Table 2.1 Suggestions for Security Administrators

IMMEDIATELY (< 30 DAYS)	
Protection	■ Apply anti-spoofing rules at the network boundary (which makes your site a less appealing target for intruders).
	■ Keep systems up to date on patches.
	■ Follow CERT/CC and SANS best practices.
	■ Review boundary security policy to ensure that outbound and inbound packets are restricted appropriately.
Detection	■ Look for evidence of intrusions in logs and so on.
	■ Look for distributed tool footprints as described in documents from the CERT/CC or your incident response team.
	■ Enable the detection of unsolicited ICMP echo replies and unusually high traffic levels.
Reaction	■ Report to a predefined list of contacts approved by management.
	■ Establish detailed, written, management-approved plans for communicating with Incident Response Teams, *Internet service providers* (ISPs), and law enforcement.
	■ Obtain training and experience in forensic techniques required to analyze compromised systems and identify other hosts involved, such as the master hosts on a distributed network.
NEAR TERM (30-180 DAYS)	
Protection	■ Establish reference systems using cryptographic checksum tools such as Tripwire.
	■ Scan your network periodically for systems with well-known vulnerabilities, and correct problems that you find.
	■ Evaluate and (possibly) deploy an *intrusion detection system* (IDS).

(continued)

Table 2.1   *(continued)*

NEAR TERM (30-180 DAYS)	
Detection	■ Periodically compare systems to your reference system by using cryptographic checksum tools such as Tripwire. ■ Run host-based software to detect vulnerabilities and intrusions.
Reaction	■ Ensure the ability to capture, analyze, and collect forensic evidence accurately and quickly by developing a "forensic toolkit" of tools and programs to assist with forensic analysis. ■ Work with your ISP to establish a good business relationship with service level agreements that identify the ISP's responsibilities in tracking and blocking traffic during DoS attacks.
LONG TERM (> 6 MONTHS)	
Protection	■ Identify a system administrator who has responsibility for each system and the authority, training, and resources to secure the system. ■ Deploy resources for host-based intrusion detection. ■ Provide security training for users. ■ If you do not have sufficient resources or support to effectively protect systems, lobby for them.
Detection	■ Develop a system for profiling traffic flows and detecting anomalies suitable for real-time detection and prevention. ■ Create and practice a response plan.
Reaction	■ Work with management to ensure that policies are in place that enable appropriate measures against suspect systems. ■ Work with your ISP to implement improved security requirements and capabilities in your service-level agreement.

Source: Taken from Results of the Distributed-Systems Intruder Tools Workshop held in Pittsburgh, PA November 2-4, 1999.

Spamming

Spamming can also be considered a DoS attack. To spam is to indiscriminately send unsolicited, unwanted, irrelevant, or inappropriate messages. This problem has become a real concern in commercial advertising over the Internet. The worst spammers do not even use a valid domain name in the sender's name. They also tend to originate from compromised systems on the intranet.

The DoS caused by spamming includes the time wasted reading and sorting through the numerous unsolicited emails to determine what is solicited, the storage resources used, and the time used for processing such unwanted mail. Spamming can be considered trespassing, a theft of private resources, and harassment.

The mechanisms used to limit spamming include mail filters, the notification of service providers, and involving law enforcement. Mail filters can be implemented at the mail server or at border points on a network. Filters can limit mail based on a specific list or rule set of spamming sites. Be aware that some spamming is spoofed and could appear to be from one site but in reality is from another. Some occurrences of spamming are initiated from compromised mail servers unknown by their administrators (who are not security conscious). Additional mechanisms include the use of Internet Web sites for notification and additional information regarding the fight against spamming. One such organization is the *Coalition Against Unsolicited Commercial Email* (CAUCE).

Brute Force Attacks

The brute force approach to gaining access to a system involves beating on the known doors of the system until it gives in. Technically speaking, this process involves launching password cracking programs against the password file, trying known vendor back doors, and searching for accounts without passwords.

The protection of resources is vital to the security of a system. The password file in old UNIX systems contained the encrypted form of a user's password. Anyone could download this password file and use a password-cracking program to extract any weak passwords to valid accounts. Newer implementations of the *identification and authorization* (I&A) mechanism in UNIX include the use of a shadow file, which now contains user passwords (encrypted) and is set to be inaccessible to anyone other than the I&A process and the administrator.

This particular security mechanism ensures that password cracking becomes harder to do now that the files are inaccessible to all except those that require them. That does not mean, however, that you can become complacent. If an intruder gains administrative access to your system, then the file is accessible. Users inadvertently provide tremendous support to adversaries trying brute force attacks. If your users do not use good passwords, you have a huge vulnerability.

Masquerade Attacks

In a masquerade attack (also known as a spoof), the adversary (a person or a program) gains information that enables him or her to gain legitimate access to the system by "posing." Posing is the term used for the act of impersonating an authorized person, program, file, or system. A form of masquerade attack can be executed by sending an email that contains an attachment that has a well-known file extension that the mail client automatically executes. This attachment could appear to be a picture and is actually a disguised program that executes, performing any actions that the writer intended (or coded correctly). This type of attack can be extremely damaging. Once a knowledgeable adversary has any type of legitimate access, the adversary can easily get whatever information is available to the legitimate user (or administrator), damage the integrity of information, or leave a Trojan behind.

Man-in-the-Middle Attacks

A man-in-the-middle attack occurs during a communication transmission. It works like this: Information is prepared for transmission by the sender. The information is transmitted. Before the intended receiver receives the information, an interloper intercepts the transmission. With the true information in hand, the interloper may change or redirect the information before sending the transmission on to its intended receiver. The receiver is unaware of the interception and any changes that may have occurred. There are several ways to minimize this type of attack. Using a message authentication code (MAC) or encryption of the message are the most common countermeasures.

Self-Inflicted DoS

Too much access control can self-inflict a DoS on the resource being protected, as in the case of our *very* secure facility described previously. DoS can also be inflicted by the administrator locking user accounts after a number of unsuccessful attempts, when a user actually needs access and cannot remember their new password. This access could occur on a weekend when no administration activities can be performed immediately to unlock the account. The user might desperately need access but is denied by access controls until an administrator can be available to unlock the account and reset the user's password. Typically, self-inflicted DoS has a limited impact. An example where this situation is not true is when a malicious person attempts to lock all users' accounts by automating the process of attempting logon to all known accounts with invalid passwords, thereby denying access to a large number of legitimate users until manual methods are used to unlock accounts. There is also no certainty that this situation will not occur again. Other methods of remediation should be applied in this instance.

Types of Access Controls

Three general types of access controls exist: physical, logical, and administrative. From a security standpoint, all access controls should be applied based on the principle of Exclude All-Include by Exception. This method is how a typical physical access control mechanism works. Let's consider that the security mechanism is a locked door. When the door is locked, it excludes all except those who were given a key. Also consider a military base that puts up a fence with a gate and guards. That base excludes all except those that have been granted access and who display the proper credentials. This technique is how biometric access devices function. The vast majority of persons cannot gain access through a biometric keypad—only those who have been authorized and who had their prints recorded. This idea of exclude all—include by exception is useful because those exceptions are closely monitored and approved based on a person's need and an authorization from someone on the inside—someone with the permission to sponsor him. The disadvantage of biometrics comes from the time it takes to register a person originally for access to a specific system.

Physical Controls

The concept of physical access control has been around since the beginning of time. In *The Book of Genesis*, God denied physical access to the Garden of Eden. Medieval times introduced and refined many concepts of physical security. How did medieval landholders build their dwellings? (See Figure 2.2.) They used what we continue to refer to in this book as layers or rings of protection. For example, the following were often in place for protection:

- Landholders normally located the dwelling in a location where they could easily view adversaries approaching.
- A moat, not really very deep, was wide enough to prevent crossing without tremendous difficulty (most people did not swim then).
- Sometimes human-eating creatures dwelled in the moat.
- A drawbridge allowed no access, except when open.
- Walls were built high without windows or outcrops within easy reach.
- Guard stations were positioned along the walls, in windows, and at doors.
- Thick walls and strong doors prevented brute force attacks.
- Procedures existed to challenge prospective entrants. (What is the password?)
- Procedures were created to ensure that guards were changed frequently to prevent inattention (they were killed if caught asleep while on guard).

Figure 2.2   Physical access controls in the Middle Ages.

These physical security access controls prevented many attacks but limited the mobility of the occupants. Most of the time it kept the bad people out, but sometimes it gave a resolute force the ability to prevent supplies, transmissions, and reinforcements from exiting or entering the dwelling.

Physical security is known in many groups as "guns, gates, and guards." It describes the approach and the techniques for using physical controls. Physical controls are functionally independent of hardware, software, and communication links, and how much and where you implement physical controls depends on your protection requirements.

Using physical controls to prevent access to physical components of the system such as communications circuits, telephone closets, processors, and servers decreases the possibility of unauthorized access. The appropriate approach for implementing physical access controls is (again) the layered rings approach combined with other security mechanisms, as described in Chapter 1, "The Journey Toward Information Security."

Logical Controls

The concept of logical access control is much newer. Logical access controls are those that are applied within the enterprise or system itself as opposed to the physical environment.

The best approach for using access controls is to combine the use of physical and logical restraints in a way that is most appropriate for your organization and the data to be protected.

PHYSICAL VERSUS LOGICAL CONTROLS: AN EXAMPLE

A cardkey access card that allows you into the computer room is an example of physical access control while permission on a file that allows you to update it is an example of a logical access control.

Referring to our general approach to security, protection rings, we need to visualize the concepts of protection for the castle for an information system. We would need to have the following:

- An intrusion detection system enabling us to notice whether adversaries draw too near

- Access to our enterprise from outside through a properly configured firewall

- Publicly accessible Web servers outside our system perimeter isolated in a demilitarized zone (DMZ) where, if they get attacked, the attack cannot easily spread to the rest of the organization

- Accessibility enforced through strong I&A, using tokens as well as passwords

- Strict procedures regarding modem use

- A network with one I&A and the individual systems with separate I&A

You need to place controls on the data, on the users, on the system, on the network, and at the perimeter of the network.

Administrative Controls

The concept of administrative controls includes administration of security in all phases of the system life cycle. These are the management policy and procedures the organization has put in place to provide access control to resources.

Access Control Mechanisms

We have discussed guns, gates, and guards enough. We understand by now that physical access controls either prevent or permit access to the physical components of a system or enterprise. The rest of this section deals with access controls that provide access and authentication to the system or enterprise. There are three generally accepted methods for performing user authentication, based on:

- Something the user *possesses* (such as a card/badge, called *tokens*)

- Something the user *is* (a physical characteristic, or *biometric*, such as a fingerprint)
- Something the user *knows* (such as a *password*)

Token-Based Access Controls

Token-based access controls are used everywhere, not only to control information systems access. The following are tokens that you might see in the course of your day:

- Elevator key
- Metro passes
- Door keycard
- Smart Card
- Fortezza cards

Characteristics-Based Access Controls

In access control, automated methods of verifying or recognizing a person based upon a physical or behavioral characteristic are referred to as biometrics. Biometric techniques can be classified on the basis of some passive attribute of an individual (for example, fingerprint, eye retina pattern, or speech pattern) or some unique manner in which an individual performs a task (for example, writing a signature or typing):

Retina.   Demonstrated to be more accurate than fingerprints, facial geometry, hand prints, iris maps, or voice dynamics. Retinal scanning is uniquely well suited to securing access to buildings, transportation centers, government and military assets, computer networks, and medical and financial information.

Iris.   Identification relies on the unique color, texture, and pattern of the iris (the colored part of your eye).

Fingerprint or thumbprint.   For a finger imaging system, one or more fingerprints are scanned one or more times using a finger image scanner device, and the resulting digital fingerprint image is used to generate a Finger Image Identifier Record. Although there is constant discussion regarding the state-of-the-art in biometrics, this type of recognition is the most widely implemented.

Facial recognition system.   All or part of the face is "photographed" using a video or other type of camera. One or more images might be required. These images are used to generate the template(s) that might contain either extracted feature information or digital image data.

Hand geometry systems.   The size and shape of the hand and fingers are used to verify identity.

Speech pattern.   Voice verification uses bass and treble tones, vibration in the larynx, and throat and nasal tones to verify identity.

System Level Access Controls

The first types of access controls that we will discuss here are *Discretionary Access Control* (DAC) and *Mandatory Access Control* (MAC). In the corporate world as well as in governments, information is categorized based on its importance or value to the organization. In order to establish appropriate access controls for the entire system and all its information, you have to start with an understanding of the requirements for protection of the information. Most specially categorized information has specific access requirements. There are many types of categorizations, as you can see in Table 2.2.

When you implement DAC, you restrict access to *objects* (files, data, and programs) based on the identity of the *subject* (user or program). This method works because the subject has certain characteristics and permissions assigned to it. It is called discretionary because in its implementation, many system processes (as well as administrators) can bypass the restriction. This level, however, is the absolute, bottom-of-the-barrel minimum that you would ever want for access control.

When you implement MAC, you still restrict access to *objects* (files, data, and programs) based on the identity of the *subject* (user or program), but this time there is also a formal authorization required. (Remember the Exclude All—Include by Exception rule? Here it is implemented inside a system.) Further, it *must always occur* and cannot be bypassed, even by privileged subjects such as processes or admin-level users. In order for this level of access control to work in most environments, all data sets must be labeled as to their sensitivity.

Table 2.2   Categories of Information That Might Require Access Control

SOME SENSITIVITY CATEGORIES	
Medical Information	Secret
Top Secret	Confidential
Competitive Sensitive	Unclassified
Confidential	Sensitive
Personnel	Company Confidential
Privacy Data	*Freedom of Information Act* (FOIA)
Financial Staff Only	Privacy Act

SYSTEM LEVEL ACCESS CONTROL: AN EXAMPLE

A user operates on a trusted system that utilizes MAC. This system also supports users who have differing access privileges based upon need-to-know restrictions, security clearance, or other discriminators. If the user wants to share a file or grant access to another user, the second user must meet the access credentials required of the file or the system will deny access.

Typically, the primary distinction between MAC and DAC is that the subject (user or process) is limited by the enforcement mechanism in granting access to or sharing the objects that it owns. MAC is traditionally enforced by the system, often called a trusted system, and uses security labels attached to the objects to implement the security policy. A system, in this sense, is said to have a *Trusted Computing Base* (TCB)—the protected part of the operating system, the security kernel that manages the security policy (see Figure 2.3).

Security kernel.   The hardware, firmware, and software elements of a trusted computing base that implement the reference monitor concept.

Reference monitor.   The abstract machine that must mediate all access of subjects to objects. As part of the TCB, it must mediate all access, be protected from modification, be verifiable as correct, and always invoked.

Both the DAC and MAC approaches to security, however, rely on the principle of least privilege. Least privilege is the principle that each subject is authorized for the minimum amount of privileges or access needed to perform its tasks. This principle helps to assure that each user receives only that information to which he or she is authorized access.

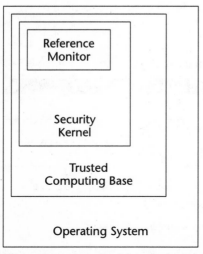

Figure 2.3   A *Trusted Computing Base* (TCB).

Account-Level Access Controls

While system-level access controls are absolutely critical; system-level access controls are broad and give only the basic levels of protection. Since information systems typically have several types of applications, information, and users, a more defined level of access control is normally required. To accommodate this further need for control, account-level access controls are used.

Privileged Accounts

Privileged accounts represent a special access control concern. Privileged users possess the ability to bypass most access control schemes and are capable of modifying most, if not all, system objects. It is important that you establish and administer all privileged user accounts in accordance with a role-based access scheme that organizes all system and network privileges into roles (for example, key management, network, system administration, database administration, and Web administration). Privileged users (commonly known as the super user or administrator) should (system capabilities permitting) be required to log on using a unique, unprivileged user account before assuming a privileged role. You should closely monitor privileged role authorization, assignments, and usage.

Individual and Group I&A Controls

I&A are necessary to ensure that users are associated with the proper security attributes, such as identity, protection level, or location. In addition, without I&A there can be no accountability. Normally, I&A is provided through combined user ID and password mechanisms. User IDs are used for identification only (they are afforded no protection). Normally, they are stored and transmitted in the clear because their purpose is not to authenticate but only to identify. That is why for so many years we have put the two (user ID and password) together when we discuss them. But realistically, additional controls such as biometrics or smart cards can and should be used. Why? User IDs and passwords have been around since the 1960s. When we worked on mainframes in the 1970s, the method of password generation and delivery was more complex than many schemes today. User IDs and passwords are a 40-year-old solution. Let's see if we can put this situation into perspective. Would you rely on hospital equipment or a telephone that was 40 years old? It's not just 40 years, either—we are talking 40 technology years. Human beings had not yet been to the moon when passwords were used as the primary authentication mechanism.

Along with being possibly the oldest logical access control, passwords represent the greatest number of violations of policy when we perform *security test and evaluations* (ST&Es) or penetration testing. If you decide to rely on passwords, then there must be strong management guidance for the development and use of them. We have provided some guidance in the following discussion.

Group identification and authorization is not recommended. We recognize that this method is quite common in some areas of industry, but there is no ability to control access if multiple people have the same identification. Group I&A completely undermines the whole intent (unless your intent is to allow access to everyone without control). On the other hand, group accounts for system or network access represent an easy method of user administration. Access control techniques for group accounts that should be used to maintain accountability include using group IDs only in conjunction with an individual user ID and authentication mechanism (password).

Some movement has occurred in the area of password updating. The following list provides you with an up-to-date look at kinds of passwords that are currently in use. What we have already discussed is still the norm, however:

One-Time Passwords **(OTPs).**   One-time passwords are a security mechanism set up on many Unix or Linux systems. In a normal system, a person would type in his or her user ID and password when prompted, but the one-time password asks you to enter a different password every time you log in according to the code that it has given you.

OPIE.   *One-Time Passwords in Everything* (OPIE) is a freely redistributable kit that will drop into most Unix systems and replace your login and *file transfer protocol* (FTP) daemon with versions that use OTP for user authentication. It also includes an OTP generator and a library to make it easy to add OTP authentication to existing clients and servers.

Single Sign-On (SSO).   An access control mechanism that provides brokering access to files, applications, and so on (each user has one authentication point for all authorized uses).

Kerberos.   Kerberos is a network authentication protocol that uses secret-key cryptography. The Kerberos protocol is used in a client/server environment to authenticate the client to the server and the server to the client. After authenticating client/server identity, you can use Kerberos to encrypt data. Kerberos does not send any data that might enable an impersonation of a legitimate user.

Password Management and Policy

What should the minimum length of a password be in order to be effective at preventing access? Should it be four characters? No one believes a four-character password is acceptable anymore. Should it be six characters? Current U.S. government policy—specifically, the *National Institute of Standards and Technology* (NIST)—calls for six characters alphanumeric plus a special character. Microsoft has six listed on its knowledge base. Should it be eight characters, however? We took a quick scan on the Internet and discovered that most of the universities with published password policies had eight characters alphanumeric plus a special character as their minimum. The Pittsburgh Supercomputer Center, medical centers, and the U.S. military require eight alphanumeric characters plus a special character. Operating and database systems may have different recommended password lengths and acceptable character sets. Obviously, the security industry still has not figured out how to handle this authorization mechanism. That does not stop us, however, from sharing with you what we believe (along with most of the real world) to be acceptable password guidance (see Table 2.3).

Table 2.3 Bad Passwords versus Good Passwords

BAD PASSWORD	REASON(S) WHY IT IS BAD	GOOD VERSION
ICECUBE	You should not use a dictionary word (any language). In this case, do not use two dictionary words together. Password cracking programs do not actually crack your password; they use the same algorithm to mask (encrypt) dictionary words and combinations and then compare the two (your encrypted password with the dictionary-encrypted word). When they find a match, they have cracked the password.	1Ce*CUb3 Replace letters for numbers that appear similar, and use special characters and case changes.
Personal information (name, dog's name, kids' names, license plate number, and so on)	Information that is known about you is easily derived through social engineering or guessing.	UMUC*I995 A combination of personal information with something that cannot be guessed using the concepts in example 1. In this example, the school and year you graduated are combined with special characters.

(continued)

Table 2.3   *(continued)*

BAD PASSWORD	REASON(S) WHY IT IS BAD	GOOD VERSION
Password	This password is better than *no* password at all, but is the first one guessed.	
Appledumpling9	Cracking programs also typically try several variations of comparisons. The programs strip the first and last positions of the password off, removing any prefix or suffix numbers added to dictionary words.	App1E$Dumpl1ng
Longliverockandroll	This password uses a combination of dictionary words, so the password can be easily guessed.	LngLv-100-RckNdRll Remove all vowels and use mixed case with numbers and special characters.
iliketoeat	This password uses dictionary words, so the password can be easily guessed.	Il2e-duyu Create an acronym from your phrase, misspell some words, and use numeric and special characters.

- The length should be eight characters, containing alpha/numeric and special characters with no beginning number or ending number. Determining a password is not complicated; use the guide shown in Table 2.3 for doing so.

- In addition to ensuring that passwords are selected properly, initial requests for a password should include authorization by a supervisor and should be done in person.

- Enforce the expiration of passwords (automatic when possible) and prevent password reuse for at least five increments.

- Change policy should be a factor of the sensitivity and criticality of your system and data. Passwords used with privileged user accounts should be changed more frequently than those of regular system user accounts, but typically administrators bypass the requirement for change and almost *never* change their password. System administration account passwords should be stronger than normal user accounts require due to the level of access allowed.

Our recommendation for password treatment is shown in Table 2.4.

Table 2.4 Recommended Password Treatment

Password length	Eight or longer (longer for administrators)
Password change	Every 90 days, privileged users (administrators) more often
Password authorization	Written authorization by supervisor
Password reuse	Cannot reuse the previous five passwords

Role-Based Access Controls

Another way to control access at the account level is through the use of *role-based access controls* (RBACs). RBACs are a means of assigning users the ability to create, modify, and review information and transactions for which they are responsible, based on their functional role. This function is another method of applying the least-privilege principle. RBAC can be implemented within a user's organization but is very often associated with alternate system administrators for small systems and *local area networks* (LANs). A specific user's account can be designated, in addition to his or her functional job, as a backup operator. This function is role-based access control. Permissions for these types of accounts must be closely administered.

Session-Level Access Controls

Session controls are an additional layer of access control that many systems activate to provide an additional layer of protection (recall the protection rings in Chapter 1). The following list identifies several commonly implemented session-level controls:

Multiple Logon Control.   When the system supports multiple logon sessions for each user ID or account, that security mechanism should be used to limit this functionality. It provides control over the number of logon sessions for each user ID, account, or for a specific port of entry. The information system should always have the default set to a single logon session.

User Inactivity.   Another control, when the system supports it, is the detection of user inactivity over a period of time, such as no keyboard entries. If the system supports this session-level access control, it should disable any future user activity until the user re-establishes the correct identity by entering his or her authentication information.

Logon Notification.   If the system provides the capability, the user should be notified upon successful logon of the date and time of the user's last logon, the location of the user (as can best be determined) at last logon, and the number of unsuccessful logon attempts using this user ID since the last successful logon. This notice should require some action on the user's part, such as clicking an OK button to remove it from the screen.

Data-Level Access Controls

Data (or information) has three states: processed, transmitted, or stored. The access controls for each state differ, and many types of systems provide data-level access controls. There are controls for the data within the programs that manage it (transactions), controls for data that have confidentiality or privacy concerns or are being transmitted, and controls for handling and storing that data when outside the system in human-readable format (hard copy) or removable media.

Transaction-Level Data Access Control

These controls are more readily seen within applications such as *database management systems* (DBMS) or financial programs. This level of control is normally used when the integrity of the information is critical. There is a trail (through audit logs) of who did what and when. Access control mechanisms also exist to ensure that data is accessed and changed only by those who are authorized. Access and changes to the data are recorded in transaction logs, which should be reviewed periodically; and immediately upon indication of a system security event.

ACLs are used by some major applications to provide access controls to the data that the application manages. Typically, ACLs contain the identity and access authority for every user. In some systems, *Read, Write, Execute* (RWX) is defined. ACLs are used by most firewalls to provide the basis for the rules that they enforce.

When computers share physical connections to transmit information packets, a set of MAC protocols are used to enable information to flow smoothly through the network. An efficient MAC protocol ensures that the transmission medium is not idle if computers have information to transmit. It also prevents collisions due to simultaneous transmission that would waste media capacity. MAC protocols also give different computers fair access to the medium.

Encryption

We will discuss encryption in detail in Chapter 6, "Cryptography," but will highlight some of the issues here. Encryption can be used to provide access control to information within a system, and it can be used to provide access controls to information in transit. When there are issues of privacy regarding a portion of the information on your system, it is easy to provide encryption for those data files, directories, and so on. That additional layer of security is normally all the additional protection required for sensitive files that have special restrictions on access. When you use encryption as we just described, almost any algorithm will do nicely, such as *Pretty Good Privacy* (PGP) or the encryption that is internal to many software applications today.

Encryption can also be used to provide excellent access control to information in transit. In 2003, no one should send anything unencrypted through the wires or over the airways. Corporations and government agencies should be applying the energy and resources they need to accomplish this goal now. It is so easy to capture information in transit that you should seriously consider encryption a requirement for any security roadmap. It absolutely fills the need for confidentiality and integrity most of the time. If you add a digital certificate to that, you have the best implementation of the confidentiality and integrity objectives that you could want. Depending on your cryptographic algorithm selection (and its implementation), you could protect an email, a bank transaction, or a national secret.

Handling and Storing Output and Media

Access controls to physical output and media are normally categorized as handling and storage procedures. Corporate information that has been identified as requiring any type of security should be physically marked and then treated according to the procedures associated with that category. Sensitive information should never be tossed out with the trash. It is a good idea to have a separate trash bin for sensitive documents, papers, and diskettes. The contents of this bin should be destroyed periodically.

If you recycle corporate documents, they should be shredded first. What type of shredder should your company use? How small should the chad be? Your approach to shredding requires common sense. If you can still read a document after it has been shredded, there was no point to shredding. Table 2.5 shows the common shredder types and the levels of security that they provide.

Table 2.5 Common Shredder Types and the Levels of Security Provided

1/2-inch strips	You might choose this setting for normal trash, but reconstitution is simple.
1/4-inch strips	This setting is the better choice for least-sensitive information.
1/32" x 7/16" cross-cut	This setting provides an increased security level and is known as a high-security shredder (no ability to reconstitute documents).

Computer-related media should have handling and destruction procedures as well. A good procedure for all media is to make certain that they are labeled. The label should disclose its sensitivity level. Then, when the media is no longer needed, never throw it in the trash bin but instead destroy it.

All computer-related media are written to via electrical impulses. With disks (hard drives, floppies, and so on), the electricity produces a magnetic field. The magnetic field generates pulses with different patterns representing positive and negative currents. These pulses are recorded on the surface of the disk as on/off or binary 0,1. Magnetic tape is also written to in this manner. CDs and other optical media take the electricity and produce a laser with varying degrees of intensity. The laser pits the optical medium to varying degrees. Because of the complex method of writing to media, it is important to understand how to remove or destroy the data when it is no longer needed. Coercivity is the property of magnetic material that describes the amount of a magnetic field that is required to reduce the media from its current state (containing data) to a true zeroized condition (from a recorded state to an unrecorded state). Coercivity is measured in oersteds (Oe), and the media's Oe number is available from the manufacturers. As shown in Table 2.7, it is important to know the Oe value of your media in order to properly eradicate it. Table 2.6 shows example media types and an acceptable method for destroying them.

While most people recognize the need to do something with media, rarely do they realize the need to have procedures for handling system components such as those described in Table 2.7.

Table 2.6   Media Types and Means for Destroying Them

TYPE OF MEDIA	MEANS OF ERADICATION*
Magnetic tape:	
DAT, VHS, et al.	Use a high-security degausser
Magnetic disk:	
Floppy, superdisks, diskpacks, CDs, DVDs	Use a high-security degausser
Removable hard disks	Use a high-security degausser
Optical Disk:	
Read Many, Write Many	Destroy
Read Only	Destroy
Write Once, Read Many (Worm)	Destroy

*Media need to be eradicated so that data cannot be reconstituted.

Table 2.7 Procedures for Handling Eradication from System Components

SYSTEM COMPONENT	MEANS FOR ERADICATION*
Random Access Memory (RAM)(Volatile)	Remove all power, including batteries and capacitor power supplies, from the RAM circuit board.
Electronically Alterable PROM (EAPROM)	Pulse all gates. If extremely sensitive, then overwrite all locations with a character, its complement, and then a random character.
Electronically Erasable PROM (EEPROM)	Perform a full chip erase (see the manufacturer's data sheet). If extremely sensitive, then overwrite all locations with a character, its complement, and then a random character.
Erasable Programmable ROM (EPROM)	Perform an ultraviolet erase according to manufacturer's recommendations. If extremely sensitive, then overwrite all locations with a character, its complement, and then a random character.
Flash EPROM (FEPROM)	Perform a full chip erase (see the manufacturer's data sheet). If extremely sensitive, then overwrite all locations with a character, its complement, and then a random character.
Programmable ROM (PROM)	Destroy if extremely sensitive.
Magnetic Bubble Memory	Degauss with a high-security degausser.
Magnetic Core Memory	Degauss with a high-security degausser.
Magnetic Resistive Memory	Degauss with a high-security degausser.
Magnetic-Plated Wire	Overwrite all locations with a character, its complement, and then with a random character. If extremely sensitive, leave each overwrite in memory for a period longer than the sensitive data resided.
Nonvolatile RAM (NOVRAM)	Some NOVRAM are backed up by a battery or capacitor power source. Remove all power, including batteries and capacitor power supplies. Some NOVRAM are backed up by EEPROM; perform a full chip erase (see the manufacturer's data sheet). Then, if extremely sensitive, overwrite all locations with a character, its complement, and then a random character.
Read-Only Memory (ROM)	Destroy if extremely sensitive.

*Removal is necessary so that data cannot be reconstituted.

NOTE Type I magnetic tape has a coercivity of 350 oersteds or less; Type II has a coercivity between 351 and 750 oersteds; and Type III has a coercivity greater than 750 oersteds. Today, almost all magnetic media is greater than 750 oersteds. It is important for you to purchase and use only degaussers that are approved for eradication greater than 750 oersteds. The United Kingdom has developed a standard for degaussers that takes much of the guesswork out of this process: the SEAP 8500 degaussing standard. Any products that meet the SEAP 8500 Type II (high) ensures an erasure depth of at least -90dB and will adequately degauss any media up to 1644 oersteds.

Sample Questions

1. A user providing a password to a system is involved with:
   a. Evaluation
   b. Identification
   c. Authentication
   d. Authorization

2. The proactive approach to access control emphasizes which one of the following triples?
   a. Prevention, detection, confirmation
   b. Detection, correction, identification
   c. Prevention, detection, authentication
   d. Prevention, detection, reaction

3. Kerberos is an authentication scheme that uses which of the following technologies?
   a. Public key cryptography
   b. Digital signatures
   c. Private key cryptography
   d. Factoring of large numbers

4. A *denial of service* (DoS) attack can be implemented by:
   a. Trying all possible combinations of words to break a password
   b. Sending large amounts of unsolicited messages
   c. Overwhelming the input of an information system to the point where it can no longer properly process the data
   d. Posing as a known, trusted source

5. The number of times that a password should be changed is a function of:
   a. The critical nature of the information to be protected
   b. The user's memory
   c. The strength of the user's cryptography
   d. The type of workstation used

6. The three standard means of access control are:

   a. Physical, preventive, and logical (technical)

   b. Administrative, physical, and mandatory

   c. Administrative, logical (technical), and discretionary

   d. Physical, logical (technical), and administrative

7. A database View operation implements the principle of:

   a. Least privilege

   b. Separation of duties

   c. Entity integrity

   d. Referential integrity

8. A synchronous password generator:

   a. Generates a password that must be used within a variable time interval

   b. Generates a password that must be used within a fixed time interval

   c. Generates a password that is not dependent on time

   d. Generates a password that is of variable length

9. Access control is concerned with:

   a. Threats, assets, and objectives

   b. Vulnerabilities, secret keys, and exposures

   c. Threats, vulnerabilities, and risks

   d. Exposures, threats, and countermeasures

10. The type of access control that is used in local, dynamic situations where subjects have the ability to specify what resources certain users can access is called:

    a. Mandatory access control

    b. Rule-based access control

    c. Sensitivity-based access control

    d. Discretionary access control

11. Which of the following types of access control is preferred when there are frequent personnel changes in an organization?

    a. Mandatory

    b. Role-based

    c. Rules-based

    d. User-based

12. Using symmetric key cryptography, Kerberos authenticates clients to other entities on a network and facilitates communications through the assignment of:

    a. Public keys

    b. Session keys

    c. Passwords

    d. Tokens

13. In a relational database, data access security is provided through:

    a. Domain

    b. Views

    c. Pointers

    d. Attributes

14. In a biometric system, the time that it takes to register with the system by providing samples of a biometric characteristic is called:

    a. Setup time

    b. Login time

    c. Enrollment time

    d. Throughput time

15. Which one of the following statements is TRUE concerning *Terminal Access Controller Access Control System* (TACACS) and TACACS+?

    a. TACACS supports prompting for a password change.

    b. TACACS+ employs tokens for two-factor, dynamic password authentication.

    c. TACACS+ employs a user ID and static password.

    d. TACACS employs tokens for two-factor, dynamic password authentication.

16. An attack that can be perpetrated against call forwarding is which of the following types of access controls?

    a. Time stamping

    b. Digital certificate

    c. Timeout

    d. Callback

17. In biometrics, a "one-to-one" search to verify an individual's claim of an identity is called:

    a. Authentication

    b. Audit trail review

    c. Accountability

    d. Aggregation

18. Which one of the following is a goal of integrity?

    a. Accountability of responsible individuals

    b. Prevention of the modification of information by unauthorized users

    c. Prevention of the unauthorized disclosure of information

    d. Preservation of internal and external consistency

19. A security kernel is:

    a. An abstract machine that mediates all accesses of subjects to objects

    b. The hardware, firmware, and software elements of a trusted computing base that implement the reference monitor concept

    c. The protected part of the operating system

    d. A means of controlling the administration of a database

20. Users who possess the ability to bypass most access controls are:

    a. Anonymous users

    b. Privileged users

    c. Guest users

    d. Trusted users

21. In finger scan technology:

    a. The full fingerprint is stored.

    b. Features extracted from the fingerprint are stored.

    c. More storage is required than in fingerprint technology.

    d. The technology is applicable to large, one-to-many database searches.

22. Mandatory access control uses which of the following pairs to authorize access to information?

    a. Roles and identity

    b. Clearances and roles

    c. Classification and clearances

    d. Identity and roles

23. An example of two-factor authentication is:

    a. A password and an ID

    b. An ID and a PIN

    c. A PIN and an ATM card

    d. A fingerprint

24. The *Crossover Error Rate* (CER) refers to which one of the following technologies?

    a. Employee history

    b. Databases

    c. Cryptography

    d. Biometrics

25. Biometrics is used for authentication in the logical controls and for identification in the:

    a. Detective controls

    b. Physical controls

    c. Preventive controls

    d. Corrective controls

26. Which of the following is NOT an assumption of the basic Kerberos paradigm?

    a. Client computers are not secured and are easily accessible.

    b. Cabling is not secure.

    c. Messages are not secure from interception.

    d. Specific servers and locations cannot be secured.

27. Logon notification, detection of user inactivity, and multiple logon control are examples of what level of access control?

    a. System level

    b. Account level

    c. Data level

    d. Session level

28. A dynamic password is one that:

    a. Is the same for each logon

    b. Is a long word or phrase that is converted by the system to a password

    c. Changes at each logon

    d. Is unverifiable

29. Procedures that ensure that the access control mechanisms correctly implement the security policy for the entire life cycle of an information system are known as:

    a. Accountability procedures

    b. Authentication procedures

    c. Assurance procedures

    d. Trustworthy procedures

30. CHAP is:

    a. A protocol for establishing the authenticity of remote users

    b. A protocol for establishing the authenticity of palm prints

    c. A protocol for establishing the authenticity of Kerberos exchanges

    d. A protocol for establishing TCP/IP connections

CHAPTER

3

Domain 2: Administration

Security administration is a vital function of any system's operation. Many if not all of the activities of a security administrator have been performed for decades in large, centralized mainframe environments. The rationale for performing these activities, however, is not because of the size of the system but the importance of the information. These activities should be performed at various levels in an organization—but system administrators and/or network administrators should ensure that they understand each element and provide support and recommendations for resources for which they have responsibility.

Our Goals

For each of the seven domains, our goal is to provide you with three things:

1. Enough information about the domain so that you will be prepared to sit for the SSCP examination.

2. An understanding of how the overall system or enterprise security objectives, CIA, are carried through to the services and mechanisms within this domain.

3. An understanding of how the services and mechanisms of this domain provide security through one or more of the protection, detection, and reaction aspects of system security.

We do not believe you need to be taught the basics of each security service and/or security mechanism. You know your job as a system administrator or network administrator. What we intend to do is provide you with the connections and concepts that bring those isolated technical and administrative processes that you perform into the bigger picture: system security practice.

What Is Security Administration?

According to (ISC)^2, security administration "encompasses the security principles, policies, standards, procedures and guidelines used to identify, classify and ensure the confidentiality, integrity and availability of an organization's information assets. It also includes roles and responsibilities, configuration management, change control, security awareness, and the application of accepted industry practices."

Security administration is where the rubber hits the road. Security administration is the name for the functions and activities related to the security of a system or enterprise that are typically performed by a security administrator, security officer, or security manager. While some of the specific activities are in actuality performed by the system and network administrators, the responsibility for them resides with the security administrator. But security administration sometimes requires more than assuming duties that someone else has been performing. Many security administration functions in organizations are handled by various personnel (personnel security, physical security, and so on), or in many instances they include functions that are *not* being accomplished at all (audit review, verification of user account holders, and so on). It is the responsibility of all SSCP-certified individuals to ensure that systems security is maintained and that all efforts to mediate and repair security flaws are taken. Remember that it is all in the name of the TRIAD—*Confidentiality, Integrity, and Availability* (CIA). See Figure 3.1.

Security administration—proper security administration—provides the effectiveness for the security mechanisms that are in place to enforce the CIA objectives within the system. For more detailed information about the TRIAD (CIA), see *Roadmap for Information System Security* in Chapter 1, "The Journey Toward Information Security: An Overview."

Figure 3.1   The objectives of security: the Triad.

We can break down security administration into three functions:

1. Developing or refining the roadmap toward information security for your system or enterprise.

2. Implementing, or making certain that someone implements, the security roadmap.

3. Administering the implementation for the operational system or enterprise.

We will discuss each of these three functions in detail later in the chapter. But first, we need to examine the concepts and processes under which security administration operates.

Security Administration Concepts and Principles

A security administrator cannot administer something that does not exist. While we do not assume that you do not have a security roadmap, we want to provide you with the concepts and principles that you should be familiar with if you need to build one (so that you can administer it). Planning is a crucial element in all administration functions, whether they are security, system, network, corporate, or any other type. Without planning, you accomplish very little. Many times, lack of planning can result in the expenditure of funds, which leads to mild to disastrous consequences. Planning is also critical for meeting goals and supporting any request for funding in an organization. If banks do not give loans to individuals starting businesses without proof of planning and guidance, then why should computer security administration be any different?

Many of these concepts and processes will be familiar to you. Some might not, however, because they are from different security disciplines. So, let's cover those issues and concepts now.

Security Equation

Security administrators must understand the reason why security is included in their systems and enterprises. The central issue of system security is *risk*. We live in an uncertain world, but risk is not something to be worried about—we should *manage* it. Risk management is the process of identifying, measuring, and controlling risks. We cover this topic in detail in Chapter 5, "Risk, Response, and Recovery." The following is the description we use in the system security field to identify risk:

> *Risk is a function of the likelihood of a given threat agent (or threat source) exploiting a particular vulnerability, and the resulting impact of that adverse event on the organization.*

Risk management is an area of study unto itself, so we will not dwell on it here other than to repeat that security administration activities contribute significantly to identifying, measuring, and controlling risks. The *National Institute of Standards and Technology* (NIST) has developed a new method of risk management (refer to the document on the accompanying CD-ROM titled, "Risk Management Guide for Information Technology Systems").

System Life Cycle

Large and complex systems and enterprises cannot be purchased from a catalog and delivered next week, used for a year, and then tossed into the closet. There is considerable time and resources applied to developing a large system (see Figure 3.2). The system is developed in phases, and the system life cycle can be viewed as the process of developmental changes through which a system passes from its conception to the termination of its usefulness and its disposal. Figure 3.2 illustrates a generic systems development life cycle that many organizations use.

You need to have an understanding of system and software development life cycles because, as the administrator for security, you might participate in these development efforts. You should address security at every phase of the development life cycle.

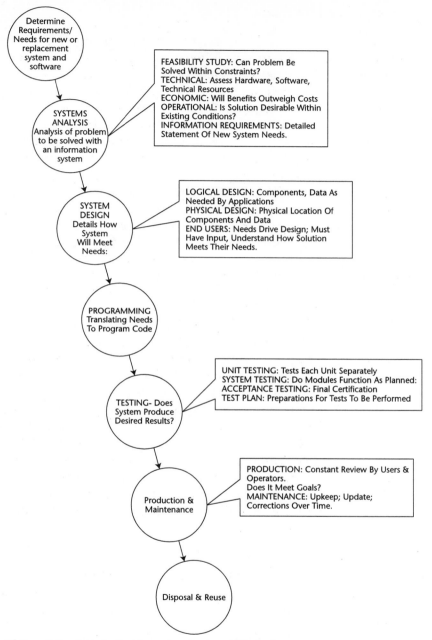

Figure 3.2 A typical system development life cycle.

Security Development Life Cycle

The security development life cycle overlays conventional development processes to reflect activities conducted on behalf of security personnel to ensure compliance with operational and security requirements, policy, and best practices. Security mechanisms can pertain to anything from an application to the entire network infrastructure. Those mechanisms implemented throughout an organization can be used to provide protection for a number of components, such as *public key infrastructure* (PKI) or encryption. These type mechanisms should be leveraged within an organization so that their protection covers the widest number of resources. Other security mechanisms might present challenges to new systems' operational capabilities. Changes might be required throughout the infrastructure of networks (open ports on firewalls, router ACLs, and so on) that might be necessary to meet operational requirements. Research, cooperation, and planning by all interested parties must be accomplished to ensure success in any life cycle process.

In the following sections, we discuss activities within the security life cycle phases.

Conceptual Analysis Phase

This phase determines security requirements and occurs in concert with the analysis of program requirements. To include security mechanisms that meet the requirements, some work must be done in defining the security requirements necessary for the particular system. If this data is personal or medical, it might need the protection required by legislation. Other requirements are levied on financial systems. Security requirements for Internet-connected systems must meet other requirements. These types of requirements must be included so that the system that is designed meets these requirements. A security policy is developed for the system at this time, and this phase includes activities such as a risk analysis and the strategy and plans necessary to complete certification of the system for operation. Other activities can include the following:

- Developing a security strategy and schedule
- Determining the security inputs for the system *test and evaluation master plan* (TEMP)
- Performing user/owner analysis
- Performing data and asset analysis
- Determining security mode of operations
- Performing law/statute/regulation/analysis
- Performing threat analysis

- Performing vulnerability analysis
- Performing risk assessment/analysis
- Determining security policy
- Determining a certification strategy and plan
- Compiling system security requirements
- Developing a controls list (security mechanisms)

System Design Phase

During the design phase of system development, system security controls are designed to develop a security architecture that meets requirements specified in the previous phase. Processes are designed to ensure the continued success of the program. These processes support the security objectives and include a concept of operations, a contingency plan, reporting structures, and so on. Agreements with *Internet service providers* (ISPs), data providers, and other network-connected resources should be established. These agreements define the terms of the connectivity of resources such as whom to contact for support, availability of resources, and service responsibilities. The following are steps in this phase:

1. Select controls (security mechanisms).
2. Develop a security concept of operations.
3. Review/validate system security requirements.
4. Obtain required connectivity agreements: a *Memorandum of Agreement* (MOA), *Memorandum of Understanding* (MOU), *Service Level Agreement* (SLA), *Service Interface Agreement* (SIA), and so on.
5. Develop a contingency plan.
6. Review/revise the configuration management plan.
7. Develop a security users guide.
8. Develop a security administration guide.
9. Develop a security training and awareness program.
10. Ensure/establish a security reporting structure.
11. Develop security architecture.

Programming (Building) Phase

During the programming phase of system development, the security activities include planning the implementation of the security architecture. Security mechanisms within an application must be programmed to meet requirements identified in the design phase. The following are steps in this phase:

1. Perform liaison activities with the programming community.
2. Obtain facility information.
3. Develop a security architecture implementation plan.

Test Phase

To evaluate the effectiveness of security controls, tests are generally developed. These tests are written to perform activities (such as observe, interview, review or test) that can be used to determine whether security mechanisms are implemented correctly. These tests are then performed and a report is produced that details the results of these tests. This report is used to support a recommendation to either fix and retest any critical failure or to place the system in operation. The following are steps in this phase:

1. Develop security test procedures.
2. Perform a security test.
3. Develop a security test report.
4. Obtain a certifying official recommendation to deploy.
5. Finalize documentation and forward to the approving authority.

Production and Maintenance Phase

When a system is being prepared for use, initial security training should be conducted as well as operational training. Periodic security reviews should be done to ensure the continued protection of system resources and data. These reviews should occur whenever a system is changed (such as when software or hardware is upgraded) or when security has been compromised. The following are steps in this phase:

1. Perform initial security training.
2. Establish/participate in periodic reviews.
3. Establish field operations maintenance.
4. Perform periodic security training.

Security professionals should be included in many activities when a system is being developed. This list is long and is not intended to fit all organizations. Your organization might require additional (or fewer) steps to achieve the same goal: the protection of resources. An example of a security process overlaying a development process can be found at: www.dmso.mil/public/library/projects/hla/guidelines/fsp1.2-final.pdf.

If you have any system development activity starting in your organization, you (or someone) need to be involved in every phase of developing the roadmap for security. It is much easier to build security into a system than it is to retrofit security into an existing network infrastructure or application.

Data/Information Storage

Data is stored in many different ways within an information system. In order to administer the security of a system, the security administrator should understand how data is stored. When data is stored within a computer system, it is stored in a repository called memory. When data is stored external to a computer system, it is called storage. There is short-term and long-term storage. Data storage is measured in kilobytes (1,024 bytes), megabytes (1,024 kilobytes), gigabytes (1,024 megabytes), and terabytes (1,024 gigabytes). Mass storage is sometimes called auxiliary storage.

The main types of mass storage devices are as follows:

Floppy disks. These disks are relatively slow and have a small capacity, but they are portable, inexpensive, and universal.

Hard disks. These disks are very fast and have more capacity than floppy disks, but they are also more expensive. Some hard disk systems are portable (removable cartridges), but most are not.

Optical disks. Unlike floppy and hard disks, which use electromagnetism to encode data, optical disk systems use a laser to read and write data. Optical disks have very large storage capacity, but they are not as fast as hard disks. In addition, the original optical disk drives were write-once/ read-only. *Read/write* (R/W) varieties are more expensive. *Digital Video Disk* (DVD) writers exist for home use but are an emerging technology (for home use) and are not as common as *Compact Disk* (CD) R/W.

Magnetic tapes. This means of storage is relatively inexpensive. Tapes can have very large storage capacities and can only be accessed sequentially. Tapes are one of the slowest methods in use today but were initially used in mainframe environments as a replacement for punched cards and perforated tapes.

The term *memory* identifies data storage that comes in the form of chips, and the word *storage* is used for memory that exists on tapes or disks. The term "memory" is usually used to refer to physical memory, which refers to the actual chips that are capable of holding data. Some computers also use virtual memory, which expands physical memory onto a hard disk.

Primary Storage

A somewhat dated term for main memory, primary storage refers to the storage that is directly accessible by the *central processing unit* (CPU) without mechanical assistance (such as is used in tapes or disks). Main memory is volatile (loses stored values when power is removed).

Secondary Storage

Secondary storage refers to mass storage devices, such as disk drives and tapes. Mass storage refers to various techniques and devices for storing large amounts of data. The earliest storage devices were punched paper cards, which were used as early as 1804 to control silk weaving looms. Modern mass storage devices include all types of disk drives and tape drives. Mass storage is distinct from *memory*, which refers to temporary storage areas within the computer. Unlike main memory, mass storage devices retain data even when the computer is turned off.

Real (Physical) Memory

Real memory refers to internal storage areas in the computer (see the previous section, "Primary Storage").

Every computer comes with a certain amount of physical memory, usually referred to as main memory or *random-access memory* (RAM), which is used as the primary storage device. You can think of main memory as an array of boxes, each of which can hold a single character (byte) of information. A computer that has 1MB of (physical) memory, therefore, can hold and access about 1 million bytes of information.

Volatile Memory

Volatile memory is memory that loses its contents when the power is turned off. All RAM except the CMOS RAM used for the BIOS is volatile. ROM, on the other hand, is nonvolatile.

The following list shows the several different types of volatile memory:

RAM (random-access memory).   RAM is the same as main memory. When used by itself, the term RAM refers to read and write memory, meaning that you can both write data into RAM and read data from RAM. This term contrasts with ROM, which permits you only to read data. Most RAM is volatile, which means that it requires a steady flow of electricity to maintain its contents. As soon as the power is turned off, whatever data was in RAM is lost.

ROM (read-only memory). Computers almost always contain a small amount of ROM that holds instructions for starting up the computer. Unlike RAM, ROM cannot be written to, only read.

PROM (programmable read-only memory). A memory chip on which you can store a program. But once the PROM has been used, you cannot wipe it clean and use it to store something else. Like ROMs, PROMs are non-volatile.

EPROM (erasable programmable read-only memory). A special type of PROM that can be erased by exposing it to ultraviolet light. This function enables reprogramming and reuse by the manufacturer.

EEPROM (electrically erasable programmable read-only memory). A special type of PROM that can be erased by exposing it to an electrical charge. This function enables systems administrators the capability to set options used to boot a system (or perform other functions) by using computer programs that are specifically created by each vendor.

Virtual Memory

Virtual memory is an imaginary memory area supported by some operating systems and is implemented in conjunction with the hardware. You can think of virtual memory as an alternate set of memory addresses. Programs use these virtual addresses rather than real addresses to store instructions and data that are not currently being used by the program in control. See Figure 3.3 for a graphic representation.

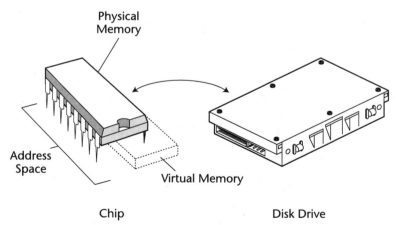

Figure 3.3 Virtual memory swapping/paging.

Operating systems control the function of swapping of data to/from memory/disk when needed and controls tables that define where paged data is kept and how to restore it when needed:

- Virtual memory is memory that cannot be addressed by the CPU (fake memory).
- Swapping is the process of shifting memory to/from disk.
- Paging is how memory is divided and managed when swapping in and out from disk.

The copying of virtual pages from disk to main memory is known as *paging* or *swapping*.

Storage Access Methods

Access to any form of data can be classified generically as sequential or random. Each process provides benefits and drawbacks. Some programming languages and operating systems distinguish between sequential-access data files and random-access data files, allowing you to choose between the two types. Devices can also be classified as sequential access or random access. (See Figure 3.4.) We will discuss each in the following paragraphs.

Sequential Access

Sequential access refers to reading or writing data records in sequential order, that is, one record after the other. To read record 10, for example, you would first need to read records 1 through 9.

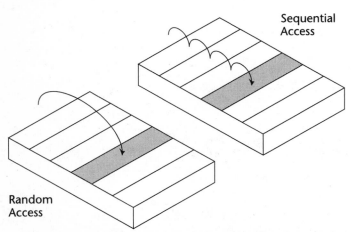

Figure 3.4 A simple representation of access methods.

In a sequential-access file, you can only read and write information sequentially, starting from the beginning of the file. Sequential access files are faster if you always access records in the same order.

For example, a tape drive is a sequential access device—because to get to point Q on the tape, the drive needs to pass through points A through P.

Random Access

Random access refers to the ability to access data at random. Unlike sequential access systems, to get to point Q in a random access system, you can jump directly to point Q. A disk drive is a random access device: The drive can access any point on the disk without passing through all intervening points. Disks are random access media, whereas tapes are sequential access media.

The terms "random access" and "sequential access" often describe data files in storage. A random access data file enables you to read or write information anywhere in the file. Random-access files are faster if you need to read or write records in a random order. A good example would be a data file such as a corporate employee phone directory, where names are added, changed, or deleted frequently. In this example, you could manipulate a file containing pointers to data to enable random access by following the appropriate pointer. Random access is sometimes also called direct access.

Both types of files have advantages and disadvantages. If you are always accessing information in the same order, a sequential access file is faster. If you tend to access information randomly, however, random access is better.

Policies and Practices

Every organization, regardless of size, has policies and practices that direct the organization's business and personnel. The following paragraphs discuss some of the types of policies and practices that affect systems security.

Employment Policies

Every employer has either explicit policies and practices regarding employee hiring, termination, and acceptable behavior—or they have an implicit policy and practice. As the security professional, you need to make it your business to understand those policies and practices. Is there a background check for employees as a requisite for hiring? Does your company have a minimum standard for acceptable criminal activity as a prerequisite for hiring? Is there a security clearance process?

The following are some items to locate when you are pulling together the information you need concerning your organization's employment policies:

- New employee orientation material that includes employees' overall security responsibilities regarding systems use

- Job descriptions and performance objectives that contain security-related elements

- A description of the process for employees receiving authorization and access to systems

- Information about how employee terminations (voluntary or involuntary) are handled, especially information regarding their system access and accounts

Hiring practices and prerequisites regarding past criminal behavior can be a strong personnel security mechanism to consider when providing the detail for your roadmap. To further support any human resources policies and procedures, an acceptable-use (of corporate systems) policy that employees read, understand, and sign assists in providing awareness to the organization of the importance placed on system security:

Position definition.   Early in the process of defining a position, security issues should be identified and addressed. Once a position has been broadly defined, the responsible supervisor should determine the type of computer access needed for the position. Two general security rules apply when granting access: the separation of duties and least privilege.

Separation of duties.   This term refers to dividing roles and responsibilities so that a single individual cannot subvert a critical process. For example, in financial systems no single individual should normally be given authority to issue checks. Rather, one person initiates a request for a payment and another authorizes that same payment.

Least privilege.   This term refers to the security objective of granting users only those accesses that they need to perform their official duties. Data entry clerks, for example, might not have any need to run analysis reports of their database.

In addition to employer/employee policies, there are typically policies regarding the control and protection of all corporate assets—of which information systems is one.

If you are fortunate enough to have located and compiled all those policies and procedures, learn them. If your organization does not have them, your responsibility is to write them—at least from a security perspective. Distribution and training in the implementation of policy and procedures is a critical aspect of security administration.

Security Policies

Policy exists at several levels in system security. See Figure 3.5 for an illustration of the layers of policy. We give further descriptions of the levels of policy in the following paragraphs.

Organizational Policy

We can view this level of policy as a statement of commitment, buy-in, support, or concern for the topic (in this case, anything relating to security and information.) These types of statements are very important and need to be in place in order for the lower levels of an organization to obtain the funding and other resources required to implement the "vision" of the senior management and those responsible for the security of its resources. The following is an example of this level of policy:

> *Company X recognizes that our product is knowledge, and that our knowledge provides value to our customers. We must provide adequate protection for our intellectual property, our product lines and our corporate internal data. That protection will include protecting the privacy (confidentiality), the integrity and the availability of our information resources.*

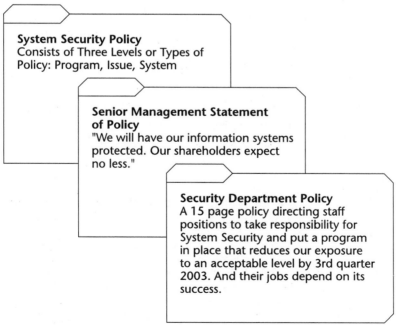

Figure 3.5 Policy existing at various levels of an organization.

Overall Security Policy

This level of policy concerns the development and implementation of the vision and direction identified by the organization's policy. Typically, we cover information system security along with the overall IT policy or with the asset protection or physical security policy. Information system security is still a subordinate function, however. Examples of this level of policy are as follows:

Acceptable use for corporate systems.   This policy identifies those activities that are not approved for corporate asset use. This policy might include Internet surfing for other than work-related support, downloading inappropriate material, music, ordering personal products over the Internet, using the workstation for personal business, or using email for personal purposes.

Password policy.   This concept delineates that all users will have unique user IDs and passwords and that no sharing of passwords or group user IDs is authorized.

New user training.   This policy identifies when, how, and what will be provided to new users before they are given access to the systems.

System-Level Policy

System-level policy is the enforcement of the security policy defined previously, using the people, processes, and technologies associated with your system. The system-level policy is more refined and exact. If we use the acceptable use policy identified in the previous section, the system level policy should state how that policy will be enforced. For example, your system-level policy might include the following:

External firewalls will have filters set to deny incoming .mpeg files or files over 4MB. Specific addresses known for inappropriate material will be blocked. Periodic scanning will be performed on the network for unauthorized activity. Email storage space will be limited to 10MB, after which, it will be removed from the server and archived.

Depending on the nature of the policy, it can be a broadly stated issue or specific orders—but in all cases that we know of, policy is considered mandatory within any organization.

One example of a policy that covers all three levels is the separation of duties, which is essential to the integrity of any organization and should be enforced. These checks and balances ensure that no abuse of privilege is allowed. Personnel are assigned responsibility for various duties as defined by corporate policy.

EXAMPLE OF SEPARATION OF DUTIES

◆ **The clerk who authorizes payment does not also produce the check.**

◆ **The person who reviews all security-related logs does not also have normal control (administration) of the system.**

Standards

In the early years of computing, each manufacturer of computer systems built proprietary systems. The hardware and the software of each manufacturer were distinct from other manufacturers—not like they are today, but secretly distinct. They did not provide details on how the systems were built to anyone. This approach forced many companies that relied on computers to remain with one manufacturer exclusively. While the manufacturers had a pretty sweet deal, everyone (computer manufacturers included) recognized that this approach reduced competition and innovation. Software companies could not build software for more than one hardware company, because how that software was built depended on how the system for which it was being designed worked. Cabling companies could not make a cable that connected the peripheral devices of more than one brand of peripherals. Standards had existed in other industries for many years. In the 1970s, the concept of standards-based systems started moving into the computer industry. They have been developed collectively by those in the industry, have gone through an industry adoption process, and now are quasi-mandatory. Many examples are meant to provide for interconnection (as in interfaces) of electrical connections, network protocols, and system components. The following are examples of standards:

IEEE 802.11. This standard is the Wireless Ethernet LAN standard established by the *Institute of Electrical and Electronics Engineers* (IEEE).

EIA RS-232-C. This standard is the serial cabling standard that specifies cable and protocol requirements, and is typically used in modem and printer communications.

CCITT V.35. This standard is used to connect digital services over phone lines to routers or gateways.

A set of standards should be established within your organization whenever possible. A good example is a baseline of security mechanisms that is adopted as an organizational standard. If your organization can specify a uniform, technical baseline applicable across the enterprise, that baseline can be institutionalized and become the standard. Standards are intended to be mandatory.

Guidelines

Many organizations and societies have knowledge and experience in various aspects of information systems and system security. Although a few of these organizations might have actual responsibility and authority for providing direction (see our discussion of policy), many others desire to improve the state of information systems and system security. When a body (society, organization, agency, and so on) has no explicit authority or responsibility to provide mandatory policy but does provide direction, we refer to that direction as guidance. Guidance, or guidelines, is normally provided to direct and clarify how policy should be followed in an organization. The following are examples of guidelines:

- Establishing and maintaining a *demilitarized zone* (DMZ)
- Securing a Windows 2000 top-level domain controller
- Password management guidelines

Procedures

Procedures are detailed steps that lead the reader through whatever process is defined. They are the set of instructions for performing a specific task. *Merriam-Webster's Collegiate Dictionary* defines procedures as "a series of steps followed in a regular definite order <legal *procedure*> <a surgical *procedure*> b : a series of instructions for a computer that has a name by which it can be called into action." Specific tasks can be started, worked, and completed by using a procedure. The following are examples of procedures:

- Establishing and terminating user accounts
- All standard operating procedures
- Email management
- Reporting procedures
- Training
- Operations logbook
- Physical security management
- Configuration management procedures
- Backup procedures
- Restore procedures

For an example, see the sidebar titled "Backup Procedures for the Server," which explains the procedures for backing up a server that is running Windows NT.

BACKUP PROCEDURES FOR THE SERVER

The server will be backed up nightly. Minimum requirements are once a week for a full backup and daily incremental backups. A backup log will be maintained, and all media will be clearly labeled and stored in the tape safe. The rotation for tapes will be a new tape each night for 15 days; then, reuse them in order but do not overwrite—append to the end. When the tapes are full, store them in off-site storage for one year.

1. Log on to the server with an account that has backup permission.

2. Select Start ➪ Programs ➪ Administrative Tools (Common) ➪ Backup.

3. Choose Windows from Menu Choices and Select Drives under the Windows Menu.

4. Check by clicking the box beside the drive icon for drives C, D, and F.

5. Check boxes for: Verify after Backup; Backup Local Registry; and Restrict Access to Owner or Administrator.

6. For Operation Type, select Replace.

7. For Backup Type, select either Incremental or Normal.

8. Press OK.

Remember, the backup tapes are complete copies of the files on the system and contain company-sensitive information. They must be protected.

Information Classification

We hear about information being classified all the time in the news. Governments have it and corporations have it, but what is it? Simply put, to classify information is to place it in separate categories containing other information requiring the same type and level of protection.

Does your corporation need to develop a classification system? Most do just so that they can keep certain information from being released to the public. This information can be financial status, credit card accounts, personnel data (such as Social Security number), or just about anything that the corporation values. Some organizations separate classifications based on the type of data, such as financial, personal, or institutional secrets. Classifications are basically the naming convention used to denote that certain information requires additional protections. A standard approach to developing a classification system is to define a classification scheme. A classification scheme is a logical, uniform system for the arrangement of information or knowledge. A fully developed classification scheme specifies categories and provides the means to relate the categories to each other. You should define specific standards for the assignment and administration of each classification. The following outline provides an example classification scheme and how this hierarchy lays out. Most organizations use as few levels of classification as possible to provide the necessary protection for each. The scheme used by the U.S. military is hierarchical, with each level requiring additional protections (Unclassified, Sensitive but Unclassified, Confidential, Secret, and Top Secret). Each level is defined to have more serious consequences if it is not protected according to the classification level assigned:

OUTLINE FOR A CLASSIFICATION SYSTEM

1. CLASSIFICATION STANDARDS
2. CLASSIFICATION LEVELS
3. CLASSIFICATION AUTHORITY
4. CLASSIFICATION CATEGORIES
   a. Duration of Classification
   b. Identification and Markings
   c. Classification Prohibitions and Limitations
5. DECLASSIFICATION AND DOWNGRADING
   a. Authority for Declassification
   b. Schedule for Declassification
   c. Transferred Information
6. SAFEGUARDING
   a. General Restrictions on Access
   b. Distribution Controls
7. PROGRAM DIRECTION
   a. General Responsibilities
   b. Sanctions

The security programs management organization will assist you and provide appropriate policy defining security of the organizational resources, including financial, contracting, planning, physical, and personnel data. Talk to financial, personnel, medical, or other departmental personnel to determine the specific requirements of each. If all else fails, many resources can be consulted that provide best practices—and many more provide direct support for very specific areas. Many times, good common sense enhances planning and is required when determining security services and mechanisms that are necessary and appropriate.

If you do not have a system of classification, an alternative approach to deciding what protection and how much is to conduct some type of *analysis* that will determine the worth or value of your information and system resources. Table 3.1 describes what you should look for in your analysis. A *Business Impact Analysis* (BIA) produces that same type of result. In the system security arena, this type of analysis is normally conducted within a formal *certification process.*

If needed, a BIA can assist you with allocating security resources. Ron Krutz and Russ Vines provide a good discussion of BIA in their book, *The CISSP Prep Guide: Gold Edition* (Wiley, 2003).

A good rule of thumb is to provide security mechanisms based on the value of what you are protecting. While many organizations rely on the formalized impact defined in their classification systems, there are other ways to determine value. You could assess the impact of the loss or disclosure of the data, the cost of replacement, or the amount of embarrassment that its disclosure or loss could produce. Then, place a higher value on the more serious impacts. The higher the value, the more protection required. The lower the value, the less protection is needed.

To keep yourself on track, keep the following points in mind when assessing the level of security in your organization:

- You cannot protect everything from everyone.
- There are not enough resources and money in the world to totally mitigate all risks.
- Focus on protecting the most important information first: that which must be protected and that with the highest risk.

Many other items should be considered so that protection mechanisms are sufficient and do not create any unwanted impact within an organization. Common sense is a definite plus.

Table 3.1   Pointers for Determining Information Protection

LEVEL OF PROTECTION	PROTECTION SCHEMA
1. Must protect due to legislative requirements	How to protect it (need-to-know), physical separation, and so on
2. Must protect due to agency requirements	How to protect it (need-to-know), physical separation, and so on
3. Should protect to prevent embarrassment, lawsuits, and so on	How to protect it (need-to-know), physical separation, and so on
4. No real need to protect	No protection schema defined

Security Modes of Operation

Security modes of operation refer to how the users relate to the information that the system processes. By defining a system in terms of its mode of operation, it is easier to determine the risk exposure from insiders. The following definitions are from the *National Information System Security Glossary*. Security modes of operation are the description of the conditions under which an *information system* (IS) operates based on the sensitivity of information processed and the clearance levels, formal access approvals, and need-to-know of its users. Four modes of operation are authorized for processing or transmitting information:

- Dedicated mode
- System high mode
- Compartmented/partitioned mode
- Multilevel mode

Each of these modes of operation is discussed in the following paragraphs.

Dedicated Mode

In this IS security mode of operation, each user who has direct or indirect access to the system, its peripherals, remote terminals, or remote hosts has all of the following: (a) valid security clearance for all information within the system;(b) formal access approval and signed nondisclosure agreements for all the information stored and/or processed (including all compartments, subcompartments, and/or special access programs); and (c) a valid need to know for all information contained within the IS.

When in dedicated security mode, a system is specifically and exclusively dedicated to and controlled for the processing of one particular type or classification of information, either for full-time operation or for a specified period of time (period of processing).

System High Mode

In this IS security mode of operation, each user who has direct or indirect access to the IS, its peripherals, remote terminals, or remote hosts has all of the following: (a) valid security clearance for all information within an IS; (b) formal access approval and signed nondisclosure agreements for all the information stored and/or processed (including all compartments, subcompartments, and/or special access programs).

Compartmented Mode

In this mode of operation, each user who has direct or indirect access to a system, its peripherals, remote terminals, or remote hosts has all of the following: (a) valid security clearance for the most restricted information processed in the system; (b) formal access approval and signed nondisclosure agreements for information to which a user is to have access; and (c) a valid need to know for information for which a user is to have access.

Partitioned Security Mode

In this IS security mode of operation, all personnel have the clearance but not necessarily formal access approval and need-to-know information for all information handled by an IS.

Multilevel Mode

In this mode of operation, all the following statements are satisfied concerning the users who have direct or indirect access to the system, its peripherals, remote terminals, or remote hosts: (a) Some users do not have a valid security clearance for all the information processed in the IS; (b) all users have the proper security clearance and appropriate formal access approval for that information to which they have access; and (c) all users have a valid need to know only for information to which they have access.

Trusted Computing Base (TCB)

The following definitions are taken from DOD 5200.28-STD. The totality of protection mechanisms within a computer system—including hardware, firmware, and software—is responsible for enforcing a security policy. A *trusted computing base* (TCB) consists of one or more components that together enforce a unified security policy over a product or system. The capability of a trusted computing base to correctly enforce a security policy depends solely on the mechanisms within the TCB and on the correct input by system administrative personnel of parameters (for example, a user's clearance) related to the security policy.

Security Kernel

The security kernel is the hardware, firmware, and software elements of a TCB that implement the reference monitor concept. It must mediate all accesses, be protected from modification, and be verifiable as correct.

Reference Monitor

The reference monitor is an access control concept that refers to an abstract machine that mediates all accesses to objects by subjects.

Process Isolation

Process isolation is the concept that each running program maintains its own address space for operation and data storage. This function prevents one program from accessing or changing data or programs stored in memory that the other program controls.

Traffic Analysis

Traffic analysis is performed to determine whether patterns of data are being used to undermine the confidentiality, integrity, or availability of system resources or data. This analysis can be done in real time but is typically done after collecting historical data to show baselines, minimum/maximum values, and so on of collected information. In security, we are interested in all aspects of traffic flow, from the capability to record all activity throughout a network to the usage of certain protocols over (possibly publicly available) network segments.

OSI 7 Layer Model

The reference model for *Open Systems Interconnection* (OSI) is a standard (see the section on standards for concept discussion) reference model for communications between two end users on a network. The model defines seven layers, each of which are defined in the following paragraphs. The brief OSI model discussion focuses on understanding how computer systems communicate across a network.

Layer 1, the Physical Layer.   This layer represents the actual physical communication hardware and media. As an example, you can see from Figure 3.6 that the physical representation defines whether *fiber distributed data interchange* (FDDI), or twisted pair, is the physical medium for communication over this network.

Layer 2, the Data Link Layer.   This layer provides error control by receiving and resending every bit. It also provides framing of the data stream and the address of the network nodes.

Layer 3, the Network Layer.   This layer provides routing. On the Internet, Layer 3 addresses are referred to as *Internet Protocol* (IP) addresses. The addresses are normally unique, but in circumstances involving *Network*

Address Translation (NAT), it is possible that multiple physical systems are represented by a single Layer 3 IP address.

TIP These three lower-level layers (layers 1-3) work together to perform the communication bridge over which the actual communication takes place.

Layer 4, the Transport Layer.   This layer divides the message into packets at the sender's end and reassembles them at the receiving host. Protocols used at this layer include UDP and TCP.

Layer 5, the Session Layer.   This layer establishes, manages, and terminates the connections between the processes over the network.

Layer 6, Presentation.   The presentation layer transforms data into a mutually agreed-upon format that each application can understand. Data encryption is performed here. As an example, if the sender's file was an EBCDIC-coded text file and the receiver had to receive an ASCII-coded file, the translation would occur at this layer.

Layer 7, Application.   This layer determines which services are available to the user, such as file transfer, the World Wide Web, or remote login.

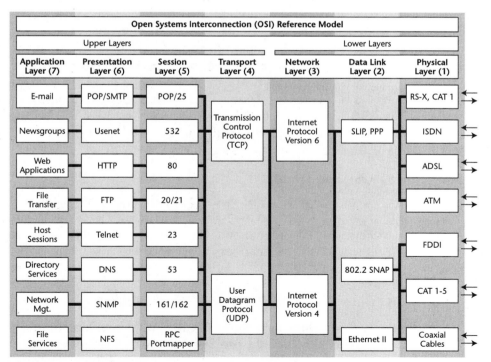

Figure 3.6 The OSI model.

TIP The top four layers are known as end-to-end layers because they do not engage the in-between hosts through which they might pass.

Configuration Management

Configuration management (CM) is the process of identifying, analyzing, and controlling the software and hardware of a system. A CM process contains a process for change—an authority to authorize change. Without a formal process in place, the temptation to buy equipment and place it on the system to see what happens is overwhelming to systems staff and users. New printers, *personal digital assistants* (PDAs), personal tax programs, and other equipment and software end up connected to the system. What is wrong with this approach is that the organization's resources, including mass storage, network bandwidth, and help desk support, cannot properly plan for and manage these additional activities. For example, let's say that you install a PDA email converter on your desktop. The next time you turn on your system, your corporate email will not initiate. You call the help desk; they cannot figure it out. The help desk spends six hours trying to fix a problem you should not have had. You find that the software you installed is not compatible with the corporate network, but because there was no configuration management process in place, you did not know it. Now, you might find that your entire desktop is frozen up and has to be reinstalled. All this effort takes place just because you wanted to install some software that does not apply to work at all but that you thought would be productive. CM is not just for users who have a desire for new toys. Upgrading a system's software should never be done just because a newer version is out or a patch is released. Even changing out hardware for a newer version is not a good practice without first providing adequate vetting through testing. When you work in a continuously operational environment, the implications of changing a system are significant.

Configuration Control Board (CCB)

The *Configuration Control Board* (CCB) is the authorizing agent in the CM process. Its job is to provide a method of review to ensure that certain software (and hardware) changes are considered both from the operational perspective and for security implications *before* changes are approved for use.

Process for Change

The following is the process for hardware or software configuration changes:

1. A proposed *configuration change request* (CCR) should be filled out in detail (see Figure 3.7). Include the proposed change, a justification for change, and all security and operational issues that must be addressed as a result of this proposed change.

```
CONFIGURATION CHANGE REQUEST

Date:

CIRCLE ONE: HARDWARE / SOFTWARE

DETAIL OF CHANGE REQUESTED:




OPERATIONAL AND SECURITY CONCERNS:


CCB NOTES:



CCB APPROVAL DATE          CCB DISAPPROVAL DATE
```

Figure 3.7   A sample configuration change request.

2. Submit the CCR to the CCB.

3. The CCB will review and decide based on both operational and security concerns. The CCB will respond with a written approval or disapproval for any CCR, and a copy of all CCRs will be kept and added to the hardware configuration management plan.

Building Your Roadmap

Now that we have managed to give you a glimpse of the breadth of diverse knowledge you need to perform your job as a security administrator, we will try to make this information fit together.

As we mentioned at the beginning of this chapter, security administration sometimes requires more than assuming duties that someone else has been performing. In this field, that is extremely unlikely. There might be parts and pieces that are accomplished, sometimes by various individuals or groups, but rarely is the whole security administration function performed. So, we will not assume that any person other than the security administrator for a system performs other unrelated functions. We will discuss how you will build your security operation so you can administer it when it is built.

Developing the roadmap of system security is where most of the work gets accomplished in order to ensure that you have a system with adequate protection. As you recall from our first chapter, we need to have a roadmap to follow. Normally in an organization, the enterprise security manager develops the roadmap and provides it to the systems staff. If it exists, use it. If it does not, you need to do it yourself as a security administrator.

Starting with Policy

The basis for the roadmap is current policy and best practices that have been bought into by and been approved by senior management. How the roadmap is implemented is typically up to the individual security administrators based on the criticality of the information and its sensitivity.

If the roadmap is given to you, that is great. If you have to develop your own, however, you need to know how to do so. There has to be input into this process of developing or refining your roadmap. That input might come from other parts of the organization and should include at least the following:

- Organizational policies such as:
  - Personnel security
  - Physical security
  - Asset protection
  - Information protection
  - Personnel hiring and termination
  - Employee responsibilities
- The security architecture (if one exists). By security architecture, we mean a description of security principles and an overall approach for complying with the principles that drive the system design—guidelines on the placement and implementation of specific security services within various distributed computing environments.
- System security best practices

- Security rules of behavior
- The system life cycle development process
- System acquisition process
- A manual for writing policies
- Process for policy and standards approval
- Anything else that might provide insight

All of these policies and procedures are necessary because they will be instrumental in providing layers of protection for your system. The rules of the organization can be implemented in the system through technical, administrative, or physical controls. When the policies are vague or are not available, you need to document the approach you want to see in the systems and then apply for approval as appropriate. You, as security administrator, need to complete your roadmap with the existing policies and procedures as best you can.

Let's take a break and look at a picture we saw earlier in Chapter 1, "The Journey Toward Information Security: An Overview" (see Figure 3.8).

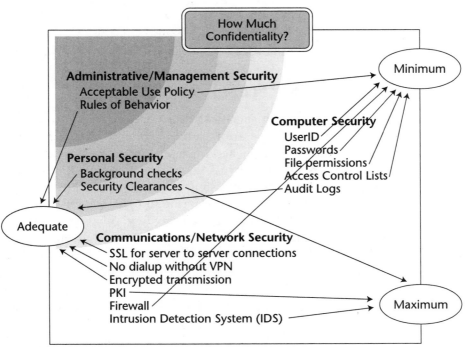

Figure 3.8 Security mechanism choices.

Do you know how much is enough? Do you know what security objective is most important to the information you are preparing to protect? Just keep in mind that we cannot accomplish everything in one day. (Chapter 5, "Domain 4: Risk, Response, and Recovery," explains the risk analysis approach, and has methods for determining asset value and sensitivity.)

Defining Specific Requirements

Now that you have your arms around all the internal policies, document the policies as a requirement statement (see Table 3.2). These become the security requirements that you need to implement within your system. Then, use industry best practices, government-published guidelines, and other reputable sources to define other practices that help complete the decomposition. What you have now are the requirements (and best practices) that, when implemented, will provide layered rings of protection around your information systems or enterprise.

You should create a table of your own with all the specific requirements showing mechanisms and services to be provided. Your selection of security services and security mechanisms must be based on the value of the assets you are protecting. The value will have two results: a criticality amount and a sensitivity level. As shown in the sample table, this chart provides an easy way to visualize what services and mechanisms are needed.

Implementing Security Mechanisms

Now that we have a roadmap built specifically for your organization, we can implement it. Change is not always appreciated in organizational cultures, however. Some organizations willingly accept change, and others fight it. You need to work within the organization to get your security roadmap accepted, even as you start making changes to the system and its environment.

The roadmap is very flexible and has the information you need to prepare a *plan of action and milestones* (POA&M) for the security of your system. You will need the POA&M to seek funding, additional people, or other resources. You will need your POA&M to schedule the implementation by priority so that interdependent security services and mechanisms can be implemented in the proper order.

For the changes that are going to take place, the security administrator needs to be a champion of the cause.

Common Technology-Based Security Mechanisms

The following paragraphs discuss several common security mechanisms: firewalls, DMZs, and *virtual private networks* (VPNs).

Firewalls

Firewalls are designed to prevent unauthorized access to or from a private network. Firewalls can be implemented in both hardware and software (or a combination of both) and are normally used to prevent unauthorized external users from accessing private networks connected to the Internet. All traffic entering or leaving the internal network passes through the firewall. The firewall examines each message and blocks those that do not meet the specified security criteria. The following are several types of firewall techniques:

Packet filter.   Looks at each packet entering or leaving the network and accepts or rejects it based on user-defined rules. Packet filtering is fairly effective and transparent to users, but it is difficult to configure. In addition, it is susceptible to IP spoofing.

Application gateway.   Applies security mechanisms to specific applications, such as *File Transfer Protocol* (FTP) and Telnet servers. This technique is very effective, but it can impose performance degradation.

Circuit-level gateway.   Applies security mechanisms when a TCP or *User Datagram Protocol* (UDP) connection is established. Once the connection has been made, packets can flow between the hosts without further checking.

Proxy server.   Intercepts all messages entering and leaving the network. The proxy server effectively hides the true network addresses.

In practice, many firewalls use two or more of these techniques in concert. A firewall is considered a first line of defense in protecting private information. The following sections provide recommendations to help you create technically sound and maintainable policies that address major security concerns and firewall issues. These have been extracted from NIST's SP 800-41, "Guidelines on Firewalls and Firewall Policy."

Virtual Private Networks (VPNs)

A VPN is a network that is constructed by using public wires to connect nodes. For example, there are a number of systems that enable you to create networks using the Internet as the medium for transporting data. These systems use encryption and other security mechanisms to ensure that only authorized users can access the network and that the data confidentiality and integrity are maintained.

Table 3.2   Instantiating Policy into Requirements

REQUIREMENT	SECURITY SERVICE	SECURITY MECHANISM IN PLACE	UNDER DEVELOPMENT	FUNDED	PLANNED	PRIORITY
Confidentiality						
1. All Web-based transactions will be protected.	Encryption SSL PKI LDAP&ACL					
2. Passwords will be protected from view by all.	Administrative procedures Shadow the password file or use encrypted passwords.					
Integrity						
1. Corporate users will be held accountable for their actions.	I&A User ID and passwords Audit Logging all relevant activity					

Table 3.2 *(continued)*

REQUIREMENT	SECURITY SERVICE	SECURITY MECHANISM IN PLACE	UNDER DEVELOPMENT	FUNDED	PLANNED	PRIORITY
Availability						
1. There will be adequate procedures in place for performing critical functions during normal service disruptions.	Contingency planning SLA MOAs Back up communications line UPS					

Another valuable use for firewalls and firewall environments is the construction of VPNs. A VPN is constructed on top of existing network media and protocols by using additional protocols (and usually encryption). If the VPN is encrypted, it can be used as an extension of the inner, protected network.

In most cases, VPNs are used to provide secure network links across networks that are not trusted (see Figure 3.9). For example, VPN technology is increasingly used in the area of providing remote user access to organizational networks via the global Internet. This particular application is increasing in popularity due to the expenses associated with implementing private remote access facilities, such as modem pools. By using VPN technology, an organization purchases a single connection to the global Internet, and that connection is used to provide remote users with access to otherwise private networks and resources. This single Internet connection can also be used to provide many other types of services. As a result, this mechanism is considered to be cost-effective when secure remote network communications is required.

You can use several different protocols on a modern virtual private network. The first and perhaps the most currently used is a set of protocols known as IPSec (Internet Protocol Security). The IPSec standards consist of IPv6 security features ported to IPv4, which is the version of IP in use today on the Internet. Other current VPN protocols include PPTP (Point-to-Point Tunneling Protocol), a Microsoft standard, and the *Layer 2 Tunneling Protocol* (L2TP).

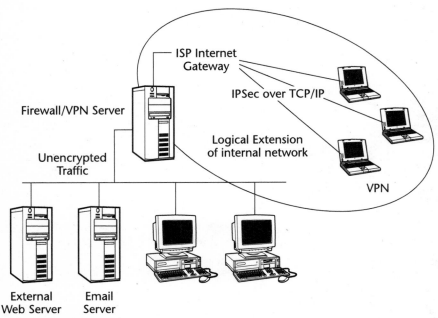

Figure 3.9 VPNs support secure networks.

Intranets

An intranet is a network that employs the same types of services, applications, and protocols present in an Internet implementation without involving unrestricted external connectivity. For example, an enterprise network employing the TCP/IP protocol suite, along with HTTP for information dissemination, would be considered an intranet. In Figure 3.9, the internal protected networks are examples of intranet configurations.

Most organizations currently employ some type of intranet, although they might not refer to the network as such. Within the internal network (intranet), many smaller intranets can be created by using internal firewalls. As an example, an organization might protect its personnel network with an internal firewall, and the resultant protected network might be referred to as the personnel office intranet.

Because intranets utilize the same protocols and application services present on the Internet, many of the security issues inherent in Internet implementations are also present in intranet implementations. Therefore, intranets are typically implemented behind firewall environments.

Extranets

Extranets are extensions of corporate resources that enable collaboration and secure communications between partners. These are typically implemented within a layered protection scheme that provides protection of this extension to the network. These networks enable an organization to control data content presented to the user. Corporate partners might wish to collaborate on a new system design, and each wants to ensure that no other corporation can steal their work. They also do not want to share all the corporate resources with their partner—only those necessary to accomplish their collaborative design effort.

Demilitarized Zone (DMZ)

A company that wants to host its own Internet services without sacrificing unauthorized access to its private network can use a DMZ. The DMZ sits between the Internet and an internal network and provides a defense position, usually through a combination of firewalls and *bastion hosts*. Typically, the DMZ contains devices accessible to Internet traffic, such as Web (HTTP) servers, FTP servers, SMTP (email) servers, and DNS servers.

The most common firewall environment implementation is the DMZ network, which exists between two firewalls. Each firewall is connected to either the internal or external network. The firewalls can be configured to allow specific traffic at each point to pass (or be restricted), which enables many services to be contained within a DMZ.

DMZ networks serve as attachment points for computer systems and resources that need to be accessible either externally or internally but that should not be placed on internal, protected networks. For example, an organization could employ a boundary router firewall and two internal firewalls and place all externally accessible servers on the outer or external DMZ between the router and the first firewall. The boundary router would filter packets and provide protection for the servers, and the first firewall would provide access control and protection from the servers in case they were attacked. The organization could locate other internally accessible servers on the internal DMZ located between the two internal firewalls; the firewalls could provide protection and access control for the servers, protecting them both from external and internal attack. This environment is represented in Figure 3.10.

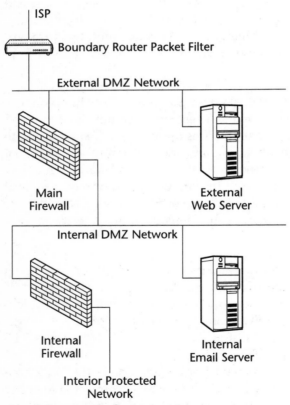

Figure 3.10 A DMZ firewall environment.

DMZ networks are typically implemented as network switches that sit between two firewalls or between a firewall and a boundary router. Given the special nature of DMZ networks, they typically serve as attachment points for systems that require or foster external connectivity. For example, it is often a good idea to place remote access servers and VPN endpoints on DMZ networks. Placing these systems on DMZ networks reduces the likelihood that remote attackers will be able to use them as vectors to enter private networks. In addition, placing these servers in DMZ networks enables the firewalls to serve as additional means for controlling the access rights of users who connect to these systems.

One DMZ network configuration is the so-called service leg (see Figure 3.11). In the service leg configuration, a firewall is constructed with three different network interfaces. One network interface attaches to the boundary router; another network interface attaches to an internal connection point, such as a network switch; and the third network interface forms the DMZ network. This configuration subjects the firewall to an increased risk of service degradation during a *denial-of-service* (DOS) attack aimed at servers located on the DMZ. In a standard DMZ network configuration, a DoS attack against a DMZ-attached resource such as a Web server will likely impact only that target resource. In a service leg DMZ network configuration, the firewall bears the brunt of any DoS attack because it must examine any network traffic before the traffic reaches the DMZ-attached resource. This action can impact organizational traffic if, for example, the organization's popular Web server is under attack.

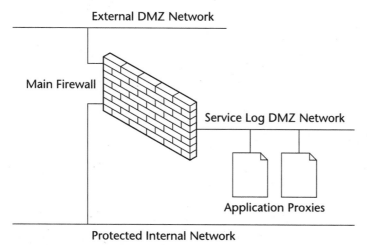

Figure 3.11   A service leg implementation.

Much material exists describing which product is better at what functions, so be aware that it is a buyer-beware environment in the computer industry. The World Wide Web is so much a part of our lives now that we recommend you go to reputable sources for the most up-to-date product lines. It is easy to buy less than you need, and it is just as easy to buy more than you could ever use.

Administering Security in an Operational System or Enterprise

Security administration, as you have seen, is not just about setting passwords on the network or monitoring the IDS system logs. Yes, those are activities that must be accomplished—but security administration involves understanding the underlying concepts of how all the resources of the organization work together to provide security to the information you are protecting.

Administration, once it is all set up, is a pretty straightforward function. It just takes a tremendous amount of time to do it correctly. The main tasks are as follows:

- Maintaining the security mechanisms in their security configuration
- Keeping a close watch on operational changes (they all have some security impact)
- Conducting reviews to make certain that everything is still working properly
- Keeping one eye on the market for better ways to provide security to our customers
- Responding to incidents
- Performing all the other functions identified in this book

Because the role that firewalls play today is so critical in our environment, we thought that we would offer further recommendations from NIST.

Access to the Firewall Platform

The most common method for breaking into a firewall is to take advantage of the resources made available for the remote management of the firewall, which typically involves exploiting access to the operating system console or access to a graphic management interface.

For this reason, access to the operating system console and any graphic management interface must be carefully controlled. The most popular method for controlling access is through the use of encryption and/or strong user authentication and restricting access by IP address. Most graphic interfaces for firewall management incorporate some form of internal encryption. Those that do not can usually be secured using *Secure Sockets Layer* (SSL) encryption. SSL will usually be an option for those graphic management interfaces that rely on the *Hypertext Transport Protocol* (HTTP) for interface presentation. If neither internal encryption nor SSL are available, tunneling solutions such as the *secure shell* (ssh) are usually appropriate.

For user authentication, several options exist. First, most firewall management interfaces incorporate some form of internal authentication, which in many cases involves an individual user ID and password that must be entered to gain access to the interface. In other cases, this process can involve a single administration account and its corresponding password. In still other cases, some firewalls can support token-based authentication or other forms of strong authentication. These secondary forms of authentication typically encompass centralized authentication servers such as RADIUS and TACACS/TACACS+. Both RADIUS and TACACS/TACACS+ provide external user accounting and authentication services to network infrastructure components and computer systems. RADIUS and TACACS/TACACS+ can also be integrated with token-based solutions to better enhance administration security.

Firewall Platform Operating System Builds

Another key factor in successful firewall environment management is platform consistency. Firewall platforms should be implemented on systems containing operating system builds that have been stripped down and hardened for security applications (in other words, a bastion host). Firewalls should never be placed on systems that are built with all possible installation options.

Firewall operating system builds should be based upon minimal feature sets, and all unnecessary operating system features should be removed from the build prior to firewall implementation (especially compilers). All appropriate operating system patches should be applied before any installation of firewall components. The operating system build should not rely strictly on modifications made by the firewall installation process. Firewall installation programs rely on a lowest common denominator approach; extraneous software packages or modules might not be removed or disabled during the installation process. The hardening procedure used during installation should be tailored to the specific operating system undergoing hardening. Some often-overlooked issues include the following:

Any unused networking protocols should be removed from the firewall operating system build.   Unused networking protocols can potentially be used to bypass or damage the firewall environment. Finally, disabling unused protocols ensures that attacks on the firewall utilizing protocol encapsulation techniques will not be effective.

Any unused network services or applications should be removed or disabled.   Unused applications are often used to attack firewalls because many administrators neglect to implement default-restrictive firewall access controls. In addition, unused network services and applications are likely to run using default configurations, which are usually much less secure than production-ready application or service configurations.

Any unused user or system accounts should be removed or disabled. This particular issue is operating system specific, because all operating systems vary in terms of which accounts are present by default as well as how accounts can be removed or disabled.

Applying all relevant operating system patches is also critical.   Because patches and hot fixes are normally released to address security-related issues, they should be integrated into the firewall build process. Patches should always be tested on a non-production system prior to rollout to any production systems as well. This pre-rollout testing should include several specific events:

- A change of the system time (minute by minute and hour by hour)
- A change of the system date (both natural and manual)
- Adding and deleting appropriate system users and groups
- Startup and shutdown of the operating system
- Startup and shutdown of the firewall software itself
- System backups
- Unused physical network interfaces physically disabled or removed from the server chassis

Logging Functionality

Nearly all firewall systems provide some sort of advanced logging functionality. The generally accepted common denominator for logging is the Unix syslog application. Unix syslog provides for centralized logging as well as multiple options for examining and parsing logs. This logging program or daemon is available for nearly all major operating systems, including Windows NT, Windows 2000 and XP, and all Unix and Linux variants.

Once a set of firewall logs has been passed to a centralized logging server, quite a few software packages are available to examine those logs. Syslog-based logging environments can also provide inputs to intrusion detection and forensic analysis packages. Solaris provides the *Basic Security Module* (BSM) that enables very detailed and selective logging of nearly all system events.

Those firewalls that do not support any syslog interface must use their own internal logging functionality. Depending on the firewall platform, there are numerous third-party tools for log maintenance and parsing.

Firewall Selection

Organizations should examine carefully which firewall and firewall environment is best suited to their needs. Assistance is available from a number of commercial sites that deal with firewall selection and analysis. At the back of the book, we have also provided a list of *Uniform Resource Locators* (URLs) to help you identify products and implementations. A firewall environment should be employed to perform the following general functions:

- Filtering packets and protocols
- Performing stateful inspection of connections
- Performing proxy operations on selected applications
- Logging traffic allowed and denied by the firewall
- Providing authentication to users using a form of authentication that does not rely on static, reusable passwords that can be sniffed

The firewall should be capable of filtering packets based on the following characteristics:

- Protocol; for example, Internet Protocol (IP) and Internet Control Message Protocol (ICMP)
- Source and destination IP addresses
- Source and destination ports (that identify the applications in use)
- Interface of the firewall that the packet entered

The proxy operations should, at a minimum, operate on the content of *Simple Mail Transfer Protocol* (SMTP), FTP, and HTTP protocol traffic. Organizations and agencies might find that they need several firewalls to accomplish these tasks.

Firewall Environment

A boundary router or other firewall should be used at the Internet connection to create an external demilitarized zone, or DMZ (see the section titled *Demilitarized Zone (DMZ)* in this chapter). Web servers and other publicly accessible servers should be placed on the DMZ so that they can be accessible as needed and still have some protections provided by the firewall. Internal users should be protected with an additional firewall. This example is one implementation of a layered approach to security.

Figure 3.12 shows a general picture of a firewall environment. For remote users, a VPN (see the section titled *Virtual Private Network* in Chapter 7) is preferable.

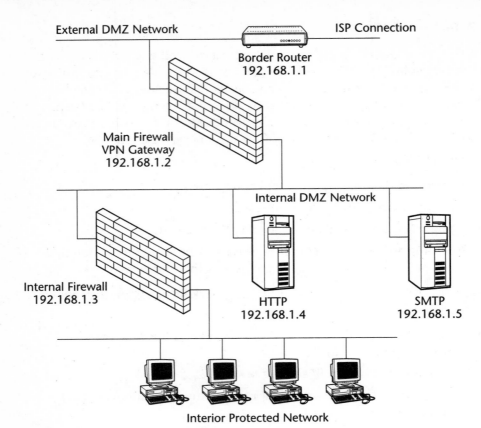

Figure 3.12   A sample firewall environment.

While a dial-in server could be located behind a firewall, a more secure approach would be to combine it with a VPN server located at the firewall or external to the firewall so that remote connections can be securely authenticated and encrypted. Intrusion detection is recommended as an additional safeguard against attacks. Figure 3.13 shows a network-based *intrusion detection system* (IDS). A host-based IDS could be used on systems where high-speed throughput is not an issue (for example, with email servers). Network address translation and split DNS are recommended to hide internal system names and addresses from external networks. Remote users should use personal firewalls or firewall appliances when connecting to ISPs regardless of whether dial-in or higher-speed connections are used.

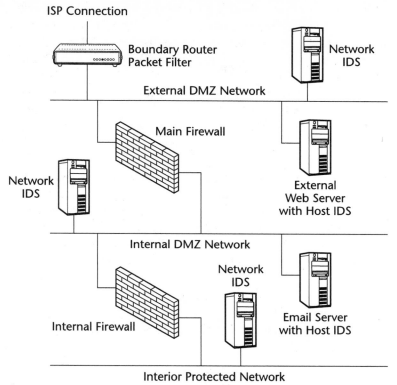

ISP Connection

Boundary Router
Packet Filter

Network
IDS

External DMZ Network

Main Firewall

Network
IDS

External
Web Server
with Host IDS

Internal DMZ Network

Network
IDS

Internal Firewall

Email Server
with Host IDS

Interior Protected Network

Figure 3.13   A sample of a network with firewalls, DMZ, and IDS.

Firewall Policy

You should perform a general risk assessment and a cost-benefit analysis on the network applications that the organization or agency has chosen to use. This analysis should result in a list of the network applications and the methods that will be used to secure the applications.

A firewall policy should be written to include a network applications matrix (or similar specification). This policy should be maintained and updated frequently as new attacks or vulnerabilities arise or as the organization's needs in terms of network applications change. This policy should make the process of creating the firewall rule set less error-prone and more verifiable because the rule set can be compared to the applications matrix.

All firewall and security policies should be audited and verified at least quarterly. The default policy for the firewall when handling inbound traffic should be to block all packets and connections unless the traffic type and connections have been specifically permitted. This approach is more secure than another approach that is used often: permitting all connections and traffic by default and then blocking specific traffic and connections. No default policy for handling outbound traffic is included here; organizations should consider using outbound traffic filtering as a technique for further securing their networks and reducing the likelihood of internally based attacks.

As a general rule, any protocol and traffic that is not necessary (in other words, not used or needed by the organization and/or denied by policy) should be blocked via the use of a boundary router and packet-filtering technology. This action will result in a reduced risk of attack and will create a network environment that has less traffic and is thus easier to monitor.

Proxy applications should be used for outbound HTTP connections and for inbound/outbound email and should be capable of the following operations:

- Blocking Java applets and applications
- ActiveX and JavaScript filtering
- Blocking specific Multipurpose Internet Mail Extensions (MIME)
- Scanning for viruses

NOTE We are not recommending that you *enable* the blocking of active Web content; just be capable of blocking if necessary. The decision to block active content, excluding viruses, should be weighed carefully, because blocking active content will render many Web sites unusable or difficult to use. Executable files in email attachments that could be blocked include the following:

.ade .cmd .eml .ins .mdb .mst .reg .url .wsf

.adp .com .exe .isp .mde .pcd .scr .vb .wsh

.bas .cpl .hlp .js .msc .pif .sct .vbe

.bat .crt .hta .jse .msi .pl .scx .vbs

.chm .dll .inf .lnk .msp .pot .shs .wsc

Organizations should not rely solely on the firewall proxies to remove content. Web browsers should be set to appropriate security levels, and antivirus software should be used on personal computers.

As stated previously, the overall policy of the firewall should be to block all inbound traffic unless that traffic is explicitly permitted. Table 3.3 shows the services and applications traffic ports that should be blocked when inbound connections are requested by that policy, with exceptions noted.

Table 3.3   Summary of Ports/Protocols to Block

APPLICATION	PORT NUMBERS	ACTION
Login services	telnet - 23/tcp	Restrict w/ strong authentication
	SSH - 22/tcp	Restrict to specific systems
	FTP - 21/tcp	Restrict w/ strong authentication
	NetBIOS - 139/tcp Always block	
	r services - 512/tcp - 514/tcp	Always block
RPC and NFS	Portmap/rpcbind - 111/tcp/udp	Always block
	NFS - 2049/tcp/udp	Always block
	lockd - 4045/tcp/udp	Always block
NetBIOS in Windows NT	135/tcp/udp	Always block
	137/udp	Always block
	138/udp	Always block
	139/tcp	Always block
	445/tcp/udp in Windows 2000	Always block
X Windows	6000/tcp - 6255/tcp	Always block
Naming services	DNS - 53 udp	Restrict to external DNS servers
	DNS zone transfers - 53/tcp	Block unless external secondary
	LDAP .389/tcp/udp	Always block

(continued)

Table 3.3 *(continued)*

APPLICATION	PORT NUMBERS	ACTION
Mail	SMTP - 25/tcp	Block unless external mail relays
	POP - 109/tcp and 11/tcp	Always block
	IMAP - 143/tcp	Always block
Web	HTTP - 80/tcp and SSL 443/tcp	Block unless to public Web servers; may also want to block common high-order HTTP port choices - 8000/tcp, 8080/tcp, 8888/tcp, etc.
Small Services	Ports below 20/tcp/udp	Always block
	time - 37/tcp/udp	Always block
Miscellaneous	TFTP - 69/udp	Always block
	finger - 79/tcp	Always block
	NNTP . 119/tcp	Always block
	NTP - 123/tcp	Always block
	LPD - 515/tcp	Always block
	syslog . 514/udp	Always block
	SNMP - 161/tcp/udp, 162/tcp/udp	Always block
	BGP - 179/tcp	Always block
	SOCKS - 1080/tcp	Always block

Table 3.3 *(continued)*

APPLICATION	PORT NUMBERS	ACTION
	ICMP	Block incoming echo request (ping and Windows traceroute); block outgoing echo replies, time exceeded, and destination unreachable messages except "packet too big" messages (type 3, code 4). This item assumes that you are willing to forego the legitimate uses of ICMP echo request to block some known malicious uses.

Consideration must be given to the usage of various ports and securing them by using additional mechanisms to provide the required security coverage when you require them to operate. The following types of network traffic should always be blocked:

- Inbound traffic from a nonauthenticated source system with a destination address of the firewall system itself

- Inbound traffic with a source address indicating that the packet originated on a network behind the firewall

- Inbound traffic from a system using a source address that falls within the address ranges set aside in RFC 1918 as being reserved for private networks

- Inbound traffic from a nonauthenticated source system containing *Simple Network Management Protocol* (SNMP) traffic

- Inbound traffic containing IP source routing information

- Inbound or outbound network traffic containing a source or destination address of 127.0.0.1 (localhost)

- Inbound or outbound network traffic containing a source or destination address of 0.0.0.0

- Inbound or outbound traffic containing directed broadcast addresses

Recommendations for Firewall Administration

If the firewall is implemented on a vendor operating system (for example, Unix or Windows), the operating system should be stripped of unnecessary applications and should be hardened against attack. All patches should be applied in a timely manner. Firewall backups should be performed via an internally situated backup mechanism (for example, a tape drive). Firewall backups should not be written to any backup servers located on protected networks, because this action might open a potential security hole to that network. Firewalls should log activity, and firewall administrators should examine the logs daily. The *Network Time Protocol* (NTP) or another appropriate mechanism should be used to synchronize the logs with other logging systems such as intrusion detection so that events occurring on different systems can be correlated.

An organization should be prepared to handle incidents that might be inevitable despite the protections afforded by the firewall environment. An incident response team should be created to assist the recovery from and analysis of any incidents. All personnel should understand how to use the incident reporting procedures for them to be effective in an organization.

Placement of VPN Servers

In most cases, placing the VPN server at the firewall is the best location for this function. Placing it behind the firewall would require that VPN traffic be passed outbound through the firewall (encrypted) and that the firewall is then unable to inspect the traffic, inbound or outbound, and perform access control, logging, or scanning for viruses, and so on. Figure 3.14 shows a VPN that is terminated by the firewall, providing a logical extension of the internal protected network. The firewall employs IPSec between the remote laptop systems and would pass the decrypted traffic between the firewall and the internal network.

Advanced VPN functionality comes with a price, however. For example, if VPN traffic is encrypted, there will be a decrease in performance commensurate with (a) the amount of traffic flowing across the VPN and (b) the type/length of encryption being used. Performing encryption in hardware will significantly increase performance, however. For some DMZ environments, the added traffic associated with VPNs might require additional capacity planning and resources.

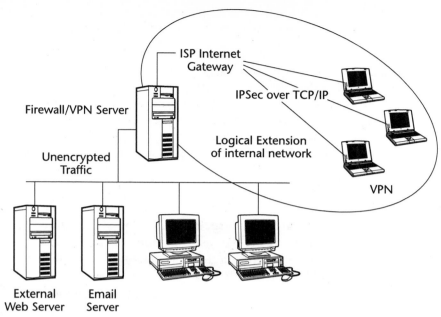

Figure 3.14 A VPN terminated by a firewall.

Security Awareness Training

Three groups are recognized as needing security training in an organization: users, management, and executives. The focus for each of these groups should be on their relationship with the information systems. How they interact with the systems, what they use them for, and what (if any) benefits the system provides them are all important considerations. All three groups should cover their responsibilities with regard to system security, and each group should have specific training developed with their needs in mind. Each group's training should have a unique focus and a different level of technical and security information, and the delivery method should vary.

Users

Users need security training in the following areas:

Focus. Legitimate, well-meaning users have potentially caused more loss of information systems assets than all other groups of threats. It is imperative, according to Kevin Mitnick in his book *The Art of Deception* (Wiley; 2002), that users of your systems be well educated against security threats such as social engineering.

Users should be given information to help them make good decisions regarding their use of the systems in their daily activities.

Level of information. Their training should consist of the basics of information system security as it applies to the system they work on and the environment in which they work. It should include the practices that they should exercise, such as good password protection, avoiding giving information over the phone, and reporting suspicious activity as well as how to protect their data and workstations when accessing external sites, such as the Internet. They should be taught about threats and vulnerabilities and the risks to their information and their systems. The only way to effectively implement a system security program is to have the users supporting the security program.

Delivery method. We recommend instructor-based training for users. While occasional awareness presentations (short messages or slides provided by e-delivery or computer-based training, known as CBT) delivered electronically to their desktops might function as incremental updates in order to appeal to their sense of responsibility for their own information. Personal contact works best.

Frequency. Users need security training at least once a year. While this sounds very time consuming and possibly expensive, the changes in the technology that users have access to changes too rapidly to not keep them up to date on the security implications.

Management

Management needs training in the following areas:

Focus. Management's function is to get the company's product out the door and to the customer for as little cost as possible. Whether you like it or not, their eye is always on the scale—balancing the additional cost of security versus the additional profitability if they do not do it. If you allow them to believe that security is an overhead function that provides no increase to the bottom line (the profitability), then you have not done an adequate job in training them.

Level of information. To make your case for security, the training managers' need is significantly different from that of the users. Management has to be shown the business case for security. They should be participatory in determining how much security is needed and knowledgeable to base security on the value of their assets. They also need to know why, from a business perspective, it is important for them to support it and when necessary provide funding. They should be responsible for making security work in their organization, and they need to understand the impacts to their business unit if their system's security fails. They need to understand how simple it is for that security to fail. Their responsibility for providing protection to their business line is something they are familiar with implementing. It is called business risk management.

Delivery method.   We have briefed managers and executives for many years, and our experience tells us that you should deliver this type of training in three parts: Develop a point paper (a short, directly to the point document of no more than four pages) that discusses what we covered earlier and state that the intent is to get in front of them in a small group to brief them on the specifics of their system security program. Second, develop a formal briefing and be prepared to answer questions. Discuss the overall program, the current status of system security, their responsibilities, and what else is needed for you to continue (or start) a good program. The third part of this delivery method is to follow up with a written memo or letter that highlights the first and second steps, and remind them again of their responsibilities.

Frequency.   Once a year is often enough for management training, but managers are users, too, and should attend user training as well.

Executives

Executives need training in the following areas:

Focus.   Executives, in most companies, are held personally responsible by their shareholders or investors for the success of the company. The focus for executives then, is to show them how information system security will improve the successfulness of the company.

Level of information.   The company executives should be made aware of what information system security is all about at a general level— in other words, how it affects their organization (positively and negatively—including shareholder-perceived value if you get attacked), where should it be done, why it should be done, and how it is getting or not getting done.

Delivery method.   Short written briefs of one to two pages are as much as you can expect them to read. If it is more than that, the chances are it will not get read until the very urgent, immediate, for your eyes only, and all the other important documents are reviewed. If you want to get to your executives, you should keep this document brief and to the point.

Frequency.   Give training as needed. The company executives are not executives because they do not pay attention to what is important. If you have made them understand system security, you will know. You will see it rise in importance within the organization.

Sample Questions

1. In the CIA triad, the tenet of confidentiality guarantees that:
   a. The data will not be altered by unauthorized means.
   b. The data will not be seen by unauthorized eyes.
   c. The data will be available to those who will need it.
   d. The data will be protected from lower security levels.

2. The concept of data integrity assures that:
   a. The information will not be seen by those with a lower security clearance.
   b. The information will not be lost or destroyed.
   c. The information will be protected from fraudulent accounting.
   d. The information will be protected from unintentional or unauthorized alteration.

3. In a system life cycle, information security controls should be:
   a. Part of the feasibility phase
   b. Implemented prior to validation
   c. Designed during the product implementation phase
   d. Specified after the coding phase

4. The software maintenance phase controls consist of:
   a. Request control, configuration control, and change control
   b. Request control, change control, and release control
   c. Request control, release control, and access control
   d. Change control, security control, and access control

5. Place the following four information classification levels in their proper order, from the most-sensitive classification to the least sensitive:
   a. Top secret
   b. Unclassified
   c. SBU
   d. Secret

6. Place the following general information classification procedures in their proper order:

   a. Publicize awareness of the classification controls.

   b. Classify the data.

   c. Specify the controls.

   d. Specify the classification criteria.

7. Which statement below describes "separation of duties?"

   a. Each user is granted the lowest clearance required for their tasks.

   b. Helps ensure that no single individual (acting alone) can compromise security controls.

   c. Requires that the operator have the minimum knowledge of the system to perform his task.

   d. Limits the time an operator performs a task.

8. Which choice below is NOT considered a defined role for information classification purposes?

   a. Data owner

   b. Data object

   c. Data user

   d. Data custodian

9. Place the organizational data classification scheme in order from the most secure to the least:

   a. Private

   b. Sensitive

   c. Confidential

   d. Public

10. What does the data encapsulation in the OSI model do?

    a. Creates seven distinct layers

    b. Wraps data from one layer around a data packet from an adjoining layer

    c. Provides "best effort" delivery of a data packet

    d. Makes the network transmission deterministic

11. Place the five system security life cycle phases in order of procedure:

    a. Development/acquisition phase

    b. Initiation phase

    c. Implementation phase

    d. Disposal phase

    e. Operation/maintenance phase

12. Which term below describes the concept of separation of privilege?

    a. A formal separation of command, program, and interface functions.

    b. Active monitoring of facility entry access points.

    c. Each user is granted the lowest clearance required for their tasks.

    d. A combination of classification and categories that represents the sensitivity of information.

13. What is a *programmable logic device* (PLD)?

    a. A program resident on disk memory that executes a specific function

    b. An integrated circuit with connections or internal logic gates that can be changed through a programming process

    c. *Random access memory* (RAM) that contains the software to perform specific tasks

    d. A volatile device

14. Random access memory is:

    a. Nonvolatile

    b. Volatile

    c. Programmed by using fusible links

    d. Sequentially addressable

15. Which choice MOST accurately describes the difference between the role of a data owner versus the role of a data custodian?

    a. The custodian makes the initial information classification assignments, and the operations manager implements the scheme.

    b. The custodian implements the information classification scheme after the initial assignment by the owner.

    c. The custodian implements the information classification scheme after the initial assignment by the operations manager.

    d. The data owner implements the information classification scheme after the initial assignment by the custodian.

16. Primary storage is the:

    a. Memory that provides non-volatile storage, such as floppy disks

    b. Memory where information must be obtained by searching sequentially from the beginning of the memory space

    c. Memory for the storage of instructions and data that are associated with the program being executed and directly addressable by the CPU

    d. Memory used in conjunction with real memory to present a CPU with a larger, apparent address space

17. What is a control packet sent around a Token Ring network called?

    a. Secondary storage

    b. A computer bus

    c. A token

    d. A field in object-oriented programming

18. Which of the following is NOT a VPN standard or protocol?

    a. UTP

    b. PPTP

    c. L2TP

    d. IPSec

19. Which choice below describes the process of data destruction?

    a. Overwriting of data media intended to be reused in the same organization or area

    b. Degaussing or thoroughly overwriting media intended to be removed from the control of the organization or area

    c. Complete physical destruction of the media

    d. Reusing data storage media after its initial use

20. Which choice below is NOT an accurate statement about standards?

    a. Standards specify the use of specific technologies in a uniform way.

    b. Standards are not the first element created in an effective security policy program.

    c. Standards help describe how policies will be implemented within an organization.

    d. Standards are senior management's directives to create a computer security program.

21. Which TCP/IP protocol below operates at the application layer?

    a. IP

    b. FTP

    c. UDP

    d. TCP

22. What is the Data Link Layer of the OSI reference model primarily responsible for?

    a. Internetwork packet routing

    b. LAN bridging

    c. SMTP Gateway services

    d. Signal regeneration and repeating

23. Which choice below incorrectly describes the organization's responsibilities during an unfriendly termination?

    a. System access should be removed as quickly as possible after termination.

    b. The employee should be given time to remove whatever files he needs from the network.

    c. Cryptographic keys in the employee's property must be returned.

    d. Briefing on the continuing responsibilities for confidentiality and privacy.

24. Which of the following is NOT a property of a packet filtering firewall?

    a. Uses ACLs

    b. Susceptible to IP spoofing

    c. Intercepts all messages entering and leaving the network

    d. Examines the source and destination addresses of the incoming packet

25. Configuration management control refers to:

    a. The use of privileged-entity controls for system administrator functions

    b. The concept of "least control" in operations

    c. Implementing resource protection schemes for hardware control

    d. Ensuring that changes to the system do not unintentionally diminish security

26. Which is NOT a layer in the OSI architecture model?

    a. Session

    b. Data Link

    c. Host-to-host

    d. Transport

27. What choice below is an example of a guideline?

    a. A recommendation for procedural controls.

    b. The instructions on how to perform a Quantitative Risk Analysis.

    c. Statements that indicate a senior management's intention to support InfoSec.

    d. Step-by-step procedures on how to implement a safeguard.

28. Which of the choices below is an OSI reference model Presentation Layer protocol, standard, or interface?

    a. *Structured Query Language* (SQL)

    b. *Remote Procedure Call* (RPC)

    c. *AppleTalk Session Protocol* (ASP)

    d. *Musical Instrument Digital Interface* (MIDI)

29. What is the definition of configuration identification?

    a. Identifying and documenting the functional and physical characteristics of each configuration item

    b. Controlling changes to the configuration items and issuing versions of configuration items from the software library

    c. Recording the processing of changes

    d. Controlling the quality of the configuration management procedures

30. Which of the following terms is NOT associated with a *Read-Only Memory* (ROM)?

    a. Firmware

    b. *Static RAM* (SRAM)

    c. *Field Programmable Gate Array* (FPGA)

    d. Flash memory

CHAPTER

4

Domain 3: Auditing and Monitoring

Auditing and monitoring are the primary tools available to the security practitioner for accomplishing two things: (1) determining what has gone on *before* (auditing) and (2) determining what is going on *now* (monitoring). We will cover both topics in this single domain and also cover computer forensics basics.

Outside organizations periodically require an auditor to review your system to ensure compliance with industry-specified policies and governmental laws. In this chapter, we also cover functions relating to the audit of computer systems.

Our Goals

For each of the seven domains, our goal is to provide you with three things:

1. Enough information about the domain so that you will be prepared to sit for the SSCP examination.

2. An understanding of how the overall system or enterprise security objectives, CIA, are carried through to the services and mechanisms within this domain.

3. An understanding of how the services and mechanisms of this domain provide security through one or more of the protection, detection, and reaction aspects of system security.

We do not believe you need to be taught the basics of each security service and/or security mechanism. You know your job as a system administrator or network administrator. What we intend to do is provide you with the connections and concepts that bring those isolated technical and administrative processes that you perform into the bigger picture: system security practice.

Domain Definition

According to (ISC)[2], "The monitoring area includes those mechanisms, tools and facilities used to identify, classify, prioritize, respond to, and report on security events and vulnerabilities. The audit function provides the ability to determine if the system is being operated in accordance with accepted industry practices, and in compliance with specific organizational policies, standards, and procedures."

Auditing is one of the fundamentals of system security and has been around for decades. Yet, no one seems to have internalized the need for turning logs on, reviewing the logs, saving the logs, and protecting them.

Suppose that one day you come to work and your system has a message on the screen that says, "Help! Someone I don't know has done something very bad to me." That scenario is not likely to happen. If this method is how you deal with auditing, you are in for a rude awakening. Threats to networks include not only those that are readily apparent but also those that are covert. These covert actions are meant to be hidden and can be used to perform information gathering and other activities. The only way to save your systems and networks is to be proactive and put in the time and develop your course of action now. There are two tools you have that can assist in preventing, detecting, and reacting to an event: *auditing* and *monitoring*. They go together like a team; they are complementary capabilities.

The auditing process captures current activity on system assets such as servers, workstations, routers, firewalls, and the like. Audit files (sometimes called logs) are intended to be held for posterity or until needed. Monitoring views current activity on the actual network, usually watching IP traffic, but is a passive activity that does not retain data (unless the program has combined audit and monitoring functions, as many commercial products have done). It is real time (or near real time), and once the data has gone through the monitor, you cannot recover it.

These two are two halves to a whole—they provide an entire picture of your system/network before, during, and after an event. We will discuss these concepts in detail.

Auditing

Auditing refers to either 1) the examination of the system or 2) the act of performing the examination. An audit trail is a historical record of events. We examine and discuss these concepts in more detail and discuss their interrelationships in the following sections.

Audit Characteristics

The term *audit* carries two meanings in the information system security field:

1. To collect, store, and review system logs in order to gain an understanding of what has occurred (audit logs/audit trails).

2. To conduct a review of the security of your system (that is, to audit your system).

In the majority of this chapter, we will address the first instance of the term *audit*. Toward the end of the chapter, we provide a "how to conduct a review" (audit) of your system's security. System security auditing is the act of collecting, storing, and reviewing the actions of persons, programs, and/or processes that relate to the operations and security of the system in order to ascertain whether there was a breach in the system's security. A commonly accepted practice to ensure that the amount of data collected is adequate is to log all activity that could be an indication that something is abnormal or is going haywire.

Many systems provide some level of auditing, and many provide a number of auditing choices. Auditing could include the capture of all network traffic, login failures, and so on. Organizations should require a defined auditing standard using metrics, which specify the most critical audit requirements and those that are less critical. What those metrics are, exactly, is open to interpretation; but we, your authors, are sticking with the most traditional security perspective: audit until it hurts and then back off just a bit. Automated tools greatly assist with the reduction of audit data into comprehensible information. As security professionals, we audit for a number of reasons. Some security-related reasons for why we audit are as follows:

- To identify a potential breach in security
- To reconstruct the events that led to a security breach
- To reconstitute the activities performed during the breach
- To prove that something has happened (we will address forensics at the end of this chapter)

In our world of layers of protection (see Chapter 1), auditing exists at the network protection layer, at any subnet gateway, at the servers (email, database management systems, firewalls, routers, file, applications, and so on), within the applications, and at the users' workstations whenever possible.

Components to Audit

Because the commonly accepted practice is to audit everything that has the capability to log events, let's discuss the specific components on which we want to run audit logs within the protection layers.

External/Internal Network Boundary Auditing

Regardless of whether you have established a DMZ, you need to audit the components at the outer edge of your perimeter. At that point, either a dedicated firewall or a high-assurance guard needs to be in place. The auditing of this device (or devices if you have a DMZ established) should be performed based on the policies you have documented in your roadmap toward security. This strategy is your first line of defense. If you do not make a huge effort to get this part correct, you will be forever cleaning up messes on the inside of your system.

A good example of how to show the relationship of your policies and requirements to your system component capability is shown in Table 4.1. The table shows services and their policy implementation at the firewalls, both internal and external.

For example, your organization might have an FTP service requirement. If so, you want to make certain that no anonymous FTP actions take place by rejecting all anonymous requests. You want to allow FTP services to users inside the internal firewall but only with a user ID and password or if they are using SSH. But even authorized users will not be able to FTP through the external firewall, because all FTP requests are denied.

Nearly all firewall systems provide some type of advanced logging functionality. Logging output from application-proxy gateway firewalls tends to be much more comprehensive than similar output from packet filter or stateful inspection packet filter firewalls. Application-proxy gateway firewalls are aware of a much larger portion of the OSI model.

The generally accepted common denominator for logging functionality is the Unix syslog application. Unix syslog provides for centralized logging as well as multiple options for examining and parsing logs. This logging program or daemon is available for nearly all major operating systems, including

Windows NT, Windows 2000 and XP, and all Unix and Linux variants. Those firewalls that do not support any syslog interface must use their own internal logging functionality. Depending on the firewall platform, there are numerous third-party tools for log maintenance and parsing.

Another extremely important activity that must be maintained once you start to implement audit is time. The *Network Time Protocol* (NTP) or another appropriate mechanism must be used to synchronize the logs across the various components and with any intrusion detection system you have installed. Without a synchronized time, your ability to locate, track, correlate, and determine activity is severely impacted.

A word about the technology is in order, so we will tell you how components should be installed to support security. Then, we will describe audit capabilities. We are sharing a sample firewall topology and rule set courtesy of NIST, based on the following requirements:

- All internal network traffic permitted outbound to all sites through both firewalls and the boundary router

- Inbound SMTP (email) permitted to the main firewall, where it is passed to a proxy server and then to internal email clients

- Outbound HTTP (Web) traffic permitted to the internal firewall, where it is passed to an HTTP proxy server and then onto external Web sites

- Inbound connections from remote systems permitted to the firewall's VPN port, where it is passed to internal systems

- All other inbound traffic blocked

In reality, this list would be longer and more specific. In this example, however, the HTTP application proxy could cache Web pages for performance reasons, and it could also filter active content such as Java, JavaScript, or ActiveX controls and log outbound connections. The SMTP application proxy would examine all email attachments or inline content for viruses and quarantine the infected code as necessary.

The firewall environment for this network is shown in Figure 4.1. An external DMZ network would connect to the Internet via a packet filter serving as a boundary router. The main firewall would incorporate a VPN port for remote users, and such users would need VPN client software to connect to the firewall. Email inbound would connect to the main firewall first, which would pass it on to an application proxy server located on an internal DMZ. Outbound Web traffic would connect to the internal firewall, which would pass it on to an HTTP application proxy located on the internal DMZ.

Table 4.1   System Security Policy Implementation at Firewalls

TCP/IP APPLICATION SERVICE	LOCATION	INTERNAL HOST TYPE	INTERNAL HOST SECURITY POLICY	FIREWALL SECURITY POLICY (INTERNAL)	FIREWALL SECURITY POLICY (EXTERNAL)
Finger	Any	Unix	TCP Wrapper	Permit	Reject
"	Any	PC–TCP/IP	None	Permit	Permit
FTP	any	Unix	No Anonymous; UserID/Password; Secure Shell (SSH)	Permit	Application proxy with user authentication
"	any	PC–TCP/IP	Client only; anti-virus	Permit	Application proxy with user authentication
TFTP	Any	Unix server with diskless clients only	Secure mode; permit TFTP to limited directories	Permit only local domain; reject other	Reject
"	Any	Unix–all other	Disable	Reject	Reject
"	Any	PC–TCP/IP	Disable	Reject	Reject
Telnet	Any	Unix	Secure shell	Permit	Application proxy with user authentication
"	Any	PC–TRP/IP	Client only	Permit	Application proxy with user authentication

Table 4.1 (continued)

TCP/IP APPLICATION SERVICE	LOCATION	INTERNAL HOST TYPE	INTERNAL HOST SECURITY POLICY	FIREWALL SECURITY POLICY (INTERNAL)	FIREWALL SECURITY POLICY (EXTERNAL)
"	Any	Router/firewall	Two password layers' token authentication	Token authentication	Reject
NFS	Any	Unix	Limit exports; host /groups (granular access)	Reject all, except by written authorization	Reject
"	Any	PC–TCP/IP	Client only	Reject	Reject
NetBIOS over TCP/IP	Any	Windows NT/95/WFW	Limit access to shares	Permit local domain only; reject others	Reject

This table and the portions of this section are provided courtesy of the *National Institute of Standards and Technology* (NIST). For more information, visit www.nist.gov.

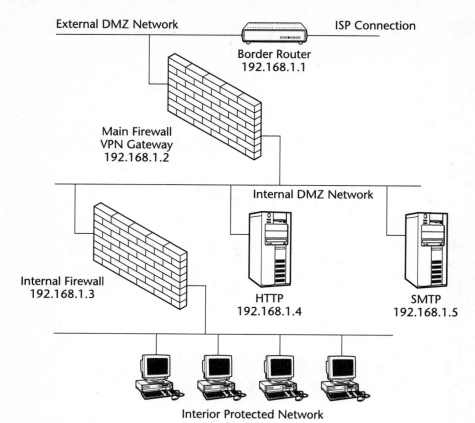

Figure 4.1 A sample firewall environment.

A rule set for the boundary router would look similar to Table 4.2. Note, however, that this rule set is greatly simplified; a real example would involve vendor-specific (Cisco, 3Com, and so on) conventions and other details.

Rule 1 enables return packets from established connections to return to the source systems. (Note that if the boundary router were a hybrid, stateful firewall, rule 1 would not be necessary.) Rule 3 permits inbound connections to the main firewall's VPN port; rules 4 and 5 tell the router to pass SMTP and HTTP traffic to the main firewall, which will send the traffic to the respective application proxies. Rule 8 then denies all other inbound connections to the main firewall (or any other systems possibly located on the external DMZ).

Table 4.2   A Sample Rule Set for a Boundary Router

RULE	SOURCE ADDRESS	SOURCE PORT	DESTINATION ADDRESS	DESTINATION PORT	ACTION	DESCRIPTION
1	Any	Any	192.168.1.0	>1023	Allow	Rule to allow return TCP connections to internal subnet.
2	192.168.1.1	Any	Any	Any	Deny	Prevent the firewall system itself from directly connecting to anything.
3	Any	Any	192.168.1.2	VPN	Allow	Allow external users to connect to the VPN server.
4	Any	Any	192.168.1.2	SMTP	Allow	Allow external users to send email to the proxy.
5	Any	Any	192.168.1.2	HTTP	Allow S	End inbound HTTP to proxy
6	Any	Any	192.168.1.1	Any	Deny	Prevent external users from directly accessing the firewall system.
7	192.168.1.0	Any	Any	Any	Allow	Internal users can access external servers.
8	Any	Any	Any	Any	Deny	The "catch-all" rule—Everything not previously allowed is explicitly denied.

The main and internal firewalls would employ stateful inspection technology and could also include application-proxy capability, although this method is not used in this example. The main firewall would perform the following actions:

- Allow external users to connect to the VPN server, where they would be authenticated.

- Pass internally bound SMTP connections and data to the proxy server, where the data can be filtered and delivered to destination systems.

- Route outbound HTTP traffic from the HTTP proxy and outbound SMTP traffic from the SMTP proxy.

- Subsequently deny other outbound HTTP and SMTP traffic.

- Subsequently allow other outbound traffic.

In order to audit the firewall and/or routers we have discussed, we would log all activities that were violations of the policies we established. The process for establishing the audit trail is as follows:

1. Use your roadmap to determine what security mechanisms you need to provide.

2. Develop a rule set matrix showing what you will implement and where. See Tables 4.1 and 4.2 for example matrices for rules.

3. Turn on those logs/audit functions that document (sometimes set off alarms) the exceptions to the rule set.

4. Turn on those logs/audit functions that document (sometimes set off alarms) the violations.

5. Refer back to the tables to help determine the rules for user or service behavior. Refer back to Chapter 1 for defining your security services and mechanisms.

Internal/Subnet Boundary Auditing

We are still using the sample topology in Figure 4.1. As shown in Table 4.1, the internal firewall would accept inbound traffic from only the main firewall and the two application proxies. Furthermore, it would accept SMTP and HTTP traffic from the proxies only, not from the main firewall. Lastly, it would permit all outbound connections from internal systems. If you need a more robust security front line, you can consider changing the firewall rules to the following:

- Internal and external DNS servers could be added to hide internal systems.

- *Port* address translation (PAT) and *network address translation* (NAT) could be used to further hide internal systems.

- Outbound traffic from internal systems could be filtered, possibly including traffic to questionable sites or for services whose legality is questionable or because of management policies.

- Multiple firewalls could be employed for failsafe performance.

Server Audit

The majority of major functions in a system are distributed across several hosts that provide dedicated or quasi-dedicated support for that major application, often referred to as servers. For example, there are domain controllers, mail servers, file servers, Web servers, database servers, print servers, and so on. Keep in mind that we are discussing servers.

Auditing will depend on the specific operating system you are using and the capabilities of the application itself. There are specific administrator manuals for configuring both. We will try to give you the generic requirements for configuring the audit functions, but you will need to refer to your own administration manual for the specifics.

Server logs must be capable of collecting and storing adequate data to assist you in any number of activities. You should once again go back to your fundamentals:

1. Use your roadmap to determine what security mechanisms you need to provide.

2. Develop a rule set matrix showing what you will implement and where.

3. Turn on those logs/audit functions that document (sometimes set off alarms) the exceptions to the rule set.

4. Turn on those logs/audit functions that document (sometimes set off alarms) the violations.

We use a relational database server to show what functions to audit. This general approach can be used on any server type and is implemented differently in each. Databases are an ever-increasing concern, and the best approach to auditing databases is to use the internal audit capabilities of the software, then complement that with server-level auditing. The following database activities should be logged:

- Creation, alteration, or dropping of a database
- Creation, alteration, management, or dropping of a table space or segment
- Creation, alteration, or dropping of any database table
- Creation, alteration, or dropping of a database index
- Enabling and disabling of the audit functionality
- Granting and revoking of database system type privileges
- Any user statement that returns an error message because the object referenced does not exist
- Any user statement that renames a database object
- Database startup, shutdown, online backup, and archiving
- Database performance statistics collection

The rationale for auditing this level of database activity is straightforward: You cannot tell what has occurred and by whom without it.

User Workstations

Audit functions exist on workstations at differing levels according to the operating system being used. So that we can be more specific, we have selected to demonstrate a Microsoft Windows 2000 workstation. Auditing on a Windows 2000 workstation is implemented at two levels: the server (we discussed server audit earlier) and locally on the workstation. Windows 2000 workstation has significant auditing capability, and for that reason we continue to emphasize that you follow your roadmap, document your needs in the matrix, and then set out to implement it. What type of auditing do you need at a user workstation? It will depend on what auditing is being performed at the servers and what your objectives are.

Local auditing is set for a workstation by accessing the control panel (see Figure 4.2).

When you open the control panel (Start | Settings | Control Panel), you have a tool folder labeled Administrative Tools. Double-click the folder, and you will see a window that looks like Figure 4.3.

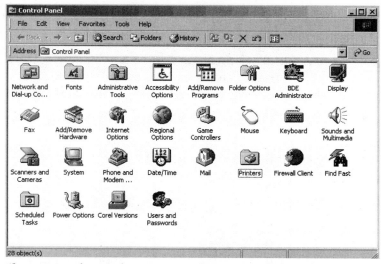

Figure 4.2   The Windows 2000 workstation control panel.

Figure 4.3   Windows 2000 Workstation Admin Tool Folder.

There are two folders of interest regarding audit in this location: Event Viewer and Local Security Policy. The first, Event Viewer, is used by the system administrator to manage and review logs about program, security, and system activity on the workstation. While all users can review the application and system logs, only a system administrator can review the security log files. The event viewer shows the logs in a reviewable manner. For each type of log, the following information exists about every event:

- Date and time
- Source of the event (program, process, or user)
- Type of event
- Category
- Event
- User ID
- Account
- Computer name

Windows 2000 workstation, as installed, has system and administration turned on and security logs turned off. You must set this command yourself. To view, add, or change the audit function (located within the security area), open the Local Security Setting folder from the Administrative Tools menu (see Figure 4.4). You can also set auditing policies within the registry; see your Windows 2000 administration manual.

As you can see, once you are inside the Local Security Settings you can configure several policies, accounts, and the public key at the local system level. As we are setting the audit policies, open Local Policies and see Figure 4.5.

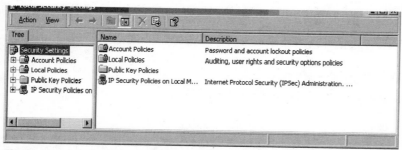

Figure 4.4 The Windows 2000 Workstation Security Settings folder.

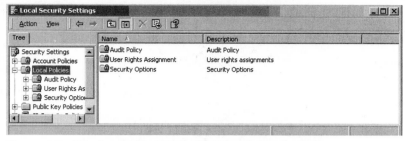

Figure 4.5   Windows 2000 Workstation Local Security Policy.

From this view, you can easily see the audit policy folder. Open the audit policy folder and select among the many options for auditing, as shown in Figure 4.6.

For this demonstration, we have selected audit process tracking. At this point, we see in Figure 4.6 that the audit process tracking local setting is set to no auditing. We open the file by double clicking. When the window opens, you have the options of setting successful attempts to be audited, unsuccessful attempts to be audited, or both, as shown in Figure 4.7. We selected both.

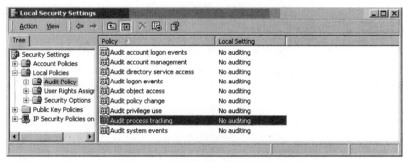

Figure 4.6   Windows 2000 Workstation Audit Policy Selection.

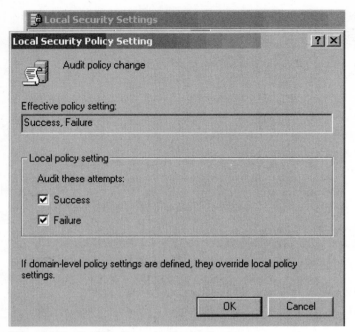

Figure 4.7 Audit policy selection options.

Now close the window and take another look at the local audit policy change in Figure 4.8. We have changed it to record all process activity. Auditing in Windows 2000 systems must go hand in hand with the selection of security policies on the workstation or else there will be little of auditing that can function.

Just a note here: There are also similar activities to be performed on a Windows 2000 server that will implement (sometimes overriding) policies. Then, any changes you make on the local system will augment what was set at the server level.

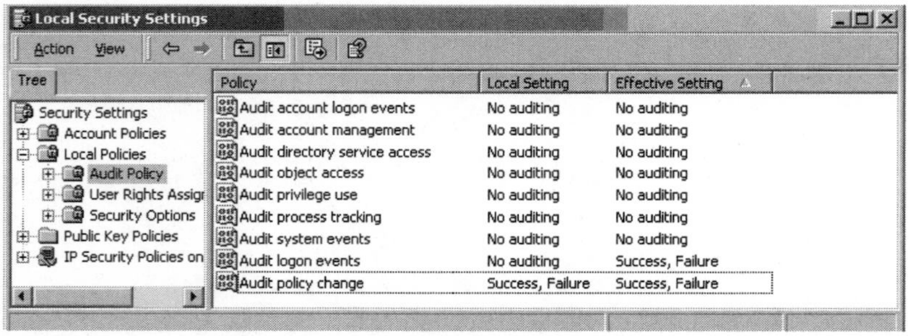

Figure 4.8 The audit policy setting has changed.

NOTE Be aware that you can also modify the effective setting by mismatching and overriding certain features. Watch the effective settings column on the policy editor screens.

This point is where most system staffs come to blows with the security administrator. When the technology exists, you should audit firewalls, routers, and other network devices, systems, accounts, and sensitive files. While each component has its own set of audit capabilities, there is always concern for the resources. Resources that are impacted by audit are as follows:

- Systems (sometimes dedicated) for collecting, processing, and storing

- Human resources to analyze the data and turn it into information through some type of heuristic approach once received

- Offline storage for saving logs for a prescribed period of time

The cost of hardware and storage media has so drastically changed over the past two decades that it almost seems as if hardware is free. Money will solve the resource issues 1 and 3, but dealing with the second resource issue is not trivial. Reviewing and providing context to all of the audit data, from different sources and possibly different formats, is not simple. In the past few years, several solutions have been offered to provide help in the area of reviewing log files from diverse components. You can standardize a baseline by using syslog, as we mentioned earlier, or several automated programs could be used to correlate audit data from firewalls, databases, servers, and the like. Although reviewing the logs is good practice and can overwhelm administrators, you should use an automated tool to help. Automated tools provide added value because they can perform trend analyses and anomaly analyses as well as quickly and accurately determine patterns of behavior and violations of policy documented in the logs. Detailed logs are normally retained and reviewed in the forensic analysis process to determine very specific information about an event.

While we are discussing what to audit, we need to remember that system security has other security disciplines upon which it can rely. Not all auditing needs to be internal to the system or needs to be performed in an automated fashion. Recording any operational status, activity, or abnormality (such as what time backups are performed) or system maintenance activities can and should be documented in a logbook. Again, the correlation is needed across several layers of protection to be certain a violation or other event has occurred.

Data to Collect During an Audit

In the previous section, we provided some information about the components to audit and showed examples of how to audit. Generally, you need to be certain of your policy, develop your rule set, and include—as a minimum—the collection of audit data pertaining to the following events:

EVENTS

- Login
- Logout
- Use of privileged commands
- Application and session initiation
- Use of print command
- All permission modification
- Export to removable media (successful)
- Unauthorized access attempts to files (unsuccessful)
- Attempts to access security files
- System startup and shutdown

For each event, the following data should be collected:

- Date and time of each event
- User ID
- If possible, the origin of the request (for example, terminal ID)
- Type of event
- Success or failure of the event, except as noted earlier
- Denial of Service (DoS) due to lockout resulting from excessive number of logon attempts
- Blocking or blacklisting a user ID, terminal, or access port and the reason for the action
- Privileged activities and other system level access
- Activities that might modify, bypass, or negate safeguards controlled by the system
- All system admin functions
- Disconnects and outages of devices (especially remote devices)
- Unauthorized attempt to log on, access files, start processes, and so on
- Program anomalies and process/program aborts
- Additions, deletions, and maintenance of system hardware and software

Making Sense of Data

There is a lot of resistance to reviewing log files and maintaining the required level of auditing on systems due to the (potential) quantities of available audit data. The complexity of systems, even small ones, combined with the quantity and speed of data communications leaves us few options; we must rely heavily on automation for data correlation and data reduction. This new group of tools used to assist in reviewing audit logs and identifying anomalies is absolutely required. Data must be managed and correlated to become useful information to the security specialist.

Data/Information Management

The following are concerns about management of this data:

How long to keep it.   Our experience tells us that 30 days is never long enough. While six months seems to be the norm, recent espionage cases have used audit data that was more than 10 years old. This situation is always tricky. Too short, and you have no ability to recreate an event or group of events over time; but long-term storage requires more backup media, a continuously larger space, and so on. Balance is the key.

Where to store it.   The audit data can be stored with the whole system backups, so when an event requires reconstitution, you have all the data of the system available. So you store it with the system backup. Then the question is where to store the system backups? A local copy is always needed to quickly restore a system. In addition, a backup copy should be stored offsite. The issues regarding storage are typically: What is offsite? Does it mean out of the system area, or out of the building, or out of town? How often should that offsite backup be refreshed? There are no cut-and-dry answers. These issues should be addressed in your roadmap, and the decisions should be made based on the value of the information you are protecting.

How to protect it.   Many people do not consider how to protect audit data. If it is stored on magnetic media, it should be protected from environmental extremes, fire, and electromagnetic disturbances that might destroy the data.

What and to whom do you report?   Again, this question should be documented in your roadmap. If it isn't, you can start by reporting to your direct supervisor, the owner of the system, and the CIO.

Report formats.   Most security organizations have a reporting format for incidents. Try to use those in existence, or locate one that has been used successfully in the past. Try the CERT/CC at www.cert.org.

- Different audit data in varying formats should be retained for periods that cover what is required by an organization. Many organizations are required to retain audit information to support backup/recovery/restoral processes while others are legally required to retain financial (and other) information for specified amounts of time.

- Organizational policy and governmental laws dictate the protection requirements for many types of audit data. Short and long-term audit record storage should be implemented. Short-term storage should support immediate requirements when current events are being reconstructed, but long-term storage is required to support historical events.

- Audit data should be protected from alteration and destruction in storage and during transmission. This action is intended to retain the integrity of any audit data collected.

- Every organization should define those incidents that require reporting and to whom to report what information. This goal is usually accomplished by using written (or email) notification of events and then taking a response. Management of these (incident response) activities should be sufficiently documented.

- The format of reports of audit incidents varies and should be detailed enough to define the event and associated actions to enable decision-making and fulfill organizational requirements.

Conducting a Security Review (Audit)

An audit of your system requires planning, purposefulness, and some skills. We want to provide you with a roadmap for conducting an audit of your system, whether it is a complete audit of all components or a focused audit of a single host or firewall.

Planning Stage

What are you going to audit? You have to know that first, and the planning stage prepares you for a security review. Specific results should be determined in any audit, and ensuring that sufficient testing is conducted requires planning.

Prepare your audit toolbox. What type of equipment will you need? The audit toolbox should contain sufficient resources to allow examination of security mechanisms to determine compliance with policy.

The Policies

Remember that all security-related system components are on the system to enforce some aspect of the policies. You will need to have the decomposition of security objectives into security services and security mechanisms if there is one. You will need to build it if there is not one, because this device will be your major metric for determining how well your system is protected.

Automated Tools

You will need standard, automated tools to make the job go more quickly and consistently. These tools include the hardware and software that will be required to connect to and evaluate systems, such as the following:

HARDWARE

- Laptop with network interface(s)
- Sniffer
- Wireless network scanner

SOFTWARE

- Vulnerability scanner (ISS Internet Scanner, Nessus, and so on)
- Standard network utilities such as Telnet, rsh, ping, traceroute, and so on
- Network mapping utilities (NMap, WhatsUp, and so on)
- Port scanner
- Wireless scanner software
- Operating system (Windows, Unix, Mac, and so on); each has its own specific network capabilities (such as Microsoft Networking)
- Reporting software (Crystal Reports, Word, and so on)

This list covers a broad variety of automated auditing tools. The tools chosen should reflect the result to be achieved in performing the audit.

Discovery Tools

We group collection and discovery tools together because they overlap a great deal. Discovery tools are used to assist the auditor in identifying the system assets that the auditor must audit, such as the hosts and other network resources. These types of tools collect considerable information about the net-worked-based resources. This undertaking is usually conducted because topology maps and architecture drawings are out of date. This discovery or collection process supported with tools provides a new baseline of the system that can be used for future security updates and security enhancements to the network.

Documentation Tools

Auditing a system requires documenting what you have learned, which will give you a baseline against which you can make audits at later times—making each subsequent one less painful. These tools can include word processors, databases, and report writers.

Audit Reduction Tools

Many software packages are available (some are even free) that can manipulate the audit files from several component types. You will need this type of tool to review the audit logs for events and to make certain they are being collected. You will still need to determine whether they are being reviewed and stored as defined by organizational policies.

Analysis Tools

Analysis tools are known as vulnerability tools or penetration tools by many. Tools such as Ice-Pick, SATAN, cyberCOP, Internet Scanner, Nessus, and others, however, are absolutely necessary in today's environment. These tools can be located at commercial, military, open source, and other Web sites including:

Internet Security Systems, Inc.	www.iss.net
Nessus	www.nessus.org
Network Associates	www.nai.com
SAINT Corporation	www.saintcorporation.com
Axent	enterprisesecurity.symantec.com

When launched against a target system, they assess the vulnerability of that system from hundreds or even thousands of threats. These programs have rule sets that contain common vulnerabilities in systems (default passwords, sendmail port open, and so on). The programs act as an adversary and try to gain access to your system based on the rule set it contains. They produce detailed reports and some offer technical recommendations for remediation.

Reporting Requirements

If you do not know what you need to report, how will you know whether you have collected it, considered it, or analyzed it? Reporting within an organization is required to provide a documented account of any event that requires an action. Security issue reporting should not be any different from other organizational reporting. Reporting should start with an immediate verbal communication of the event, and documentation should be immediately started that captures events and actions to include who, what, and when. Who reported the call, to whom was the call reported, what is the nature of the event, what was done to respond to the event, when did the event occur, when were actions taken in response to the event—these and other information must be collected to properly document any event. Written reports are periodically required to inform management and security personnel of events and to keep them informed as to the progress made to repair and prevent future events from occurring. Initial written reports are typically required after a period of a couple days to a week after the event to enable the collection and analyzing of data that is required to address any event.

Reporting procedures should keep in mind any network connections that might also be affected by the event. Agreements made prior to connecting systems should exist that delineate the reporting procedures for events that could impact the interconnected systems. Procedures should also be in place to address any possible event.

The following elements should be addressed when reporting security incidents:

- Date/time of report
- Date/time of event
- Name and phone number of the point of contact
- Location where the incident occurred
- Description of the hardware, operating system, and software involved and the number of affected systems
- A brief description of the sensitivity and type of information on the systems affected
- A detailed account of the event
- For virus infections, include the method of detection, the software used to remove the virus, the type of virus, and the source of the virus
- Corrective actions taken to contain the incident, clean or dispose of contaminated media, educate users, and any measures taken to prevent a similar incident
- A detailed account of the loss, theft, damage, destruction, or denial of service caused by the security event, including the estimated cost of the event and how it affects the safety of individuals, the security of organizational information, and the security of the organizational resources affected by the event

Implementation Stage

1. Review policies.
   - Are they complete?
   - Are they comprehensive?
2. Develop a security matrix.
3. Review security documentation
   - Include system-related documentation.
   - What are the security features of all major components?
4. Review audit capability and use.
   - Are the security features of all major components utilized?
   - Compare the security features utilized to the matrix. Do they match?
   - Is the audit trail complete enough to reconstruct an event?
5. Review security patches and update releases for all components.
   - Compare releases to the current configuration.
6. Run analysis tools.
   - Host based if auditing a host
   - Network based
   - Database based
   - Do known security holes exist?
   - Are exploits of the organization's assets possible, probable, or likely?
7. Correlate all information.
8. Develop a report.
9. Make recommendations to correct problems.

Monitoring

When our phone rings, we answer it. This action is a form of monitoring. The phone will accept calls destined to it and will ring to indicate that a call is ready to be received. You hear the ring and pick up the phone, completing the call. If you are not monitoring the phone, you might not hear it ring. The same holds true for monitoring information systems. If you are not prepared for an event, you might not provide the proper protection and miss important events.

Monitoring has really taken off in this new millennium, and the field has solidified the concept of proactive network and host monitoring. The most current thoughts regarding this area are to combine the network monitoring, host, and other component auditing with anti-virus program management and incident response and a new term is born: security operations.

Monitoring Characteristics

Monitoring, unlike auditing, is typically performed in real or near real-time. Monitoring can be viewed as the proactive version of audit reviewing. As we have matured in our information systems technology, we have learned that to identify and reconstruct incidents of any type, reviewing audit trails alone is inadequate. Waiting until after a security incident has occurred is no longer the only option. We must be proactive and identify the potential attack as it begins or as it is occurring. In order to assist with performing this level of monitoring, many automated tools have been developed.

Components to Monitor

Zeros and ones and bits and bytes are what we want to monitor, and monitoring the network simply means monitoring the traffic on the network. Network traffic consists entirely of zeros and ones and bits and bytes traveling from one point to another through many routes. Monitoring is not limited to network monitoring, however; there are three types of monitoring we need to discuss: network monitoring, security monitoring, and keystroke monitoring.

Network Monitoring

Network monitoring is a function of the systems and network administrators. These activities include monitoring collision rates, throughput speed, bandwidth utilization, and the like. Network monitoring supports the operational readiness of a collection of systems.

Security Monitoring

Security monitoring is a function of the security administrator. Constantly looking for security breaches requires that all allowed and disallowed activity is monitored for proper usage. Improper usage can be an indication of a security event that requires additional research, which can include watching for traffic to/from specific addresses, unsuccessful logon attempts, and successful logon attempts from unknown locations or at times that do not match standard work hours.

Keystroke Monitoring

This process involves viewing or recording the actual keystrokes transmitted by a user and the destination computer's response. Keystroke monitoring is normally performed as part of a network-based security breach investigation. This type of monitoring is very powerful if you are tracking during an attack; however, it is very important that you realize in the United States there is some uncertainty whether or not keystroke monitoring equals a wiretap. If it does, then to perform keystroke monitoring is a criminal offense—the same as an illegal wiretap. Our recommendation is to seek professional law enforcement support (get a warrant) if you need to collect this level of data.

Intrusion Detection Systems (IDSs)

In addition to the bits and bytes traversing the network, an intrusion detection system would help you with correlating the state of the network. An *intrusion detection system* (IDS) works as follows: You locate sensors at various locations throughout the network. Those sensors provide data back to the main software system, and network devices are also available that provide IDS services such as routers, switches, and firewalls.

Types of IDSs

NIDS

NIDS are network-based IDSs that typically consist of a number of selectively deployed sensors that report findings to a central console. These sensors should be placed at locations on the network so that all data transmissions are able to be monitored at some point. Collections of data can be analyzed to produce information that is critical for intrusion detection and subsequent remediation. The central console can also be used to direct actions to be taken as a result of network sensor findings (these actions can be to modify an ACL to deny access to a detected intrusion source or to provide configuration of network deployed sensors).

Types of NIDS include Snort, Real Secure, Secure Intrusion Detection System (formerly NetRanger), NFR NID, and Cyber Cop. These can be obtained from the following Internet resources:

Snort	www.snort.org
Real Secure	www.iss.net
NFR NID	www.nfr.net
Secure Intrusion Detection System	www.cisco.com

Cyber Cop   www.nai.com

Dragon Sensor   www.intrusion-detection-
                                        system-group.co.uk

Host-Based IDS

Host-based IDS systems reside entirely on a system and monitor possible
intrusions into the system. These can be implemented on Web, database, or
other servers for their specific protection and can be deployed on specific host
systems and report findings to a central console for interpretation and actions
if the program allows. Host-based IDS requires additional management
because each machine must have client software installed in order to function
but must have more control over system functions, such as closing port access
by reconfiguring hosts.allow or hosts.deny files when using TCPWrappers.
Home users would normally use a host-based intrusion detection system to
protect their personal computers while connected to the Internet. Norton Personal Firewall provides a very limited IDS and blocking function using access
control lists. For more information, visit the following sites:

NFR HID   www.nfr.net

Norton Personal Firewall   www.symantec.com

Dragon Squire   www.intrusion-detection-system-group.co.uk

TCPWrappers   ftp.porcupine.org/pub/security

Let's use specific IDS software as an example: the Windows 2000 implementation of Snort.

Data to Collect during Monitoring

Unfortunately, the idea of only collecting header packets or only saving meta-
data does not enable you to verifiably reconstruct the entire activity. (That is
the level of detail needed for evidence against an adversary, should your organization decide legal action is required.) So, we still recommend that you collect everything you can, compress it to offline storage as often as you need, and
then keep it safe.

The people, computing resources, and automated tools it takes to actively
monitor a system, network, or enterprise varies greatly depending on the level
of monitoring you are performing. These days, it can range from little (if any)
extra help needed, all the way to complete outsourcing. The outsourcing of
this activity is referred to as managed security services, and many firms spe-
cialize in this area. We, however, recommend that you take care when considering outsourcing your security and consider any prospective company
carefully. Do they provide trusted, preferably security-vetted personnel?
Remember that the people who manage your security will know all your company's skeletons and hold the keys to the kingdom.

SNORT'S PLACE IN A WINDOWS 2000 ENVIRONMENT

The target audience of this example is middle-of-the-road administrators who might be looking for an easy-to-set up network IDS that will not put a dent in the IT budget. This example will introduce you to Snort.

WHAT IS SNORT?

Snort is an open-sourced, lightweight, *network intrusion detection system* (NIDS). It makes use of an easy-to-learn rules system to detect and log the signatures of possible attacks. It was originally created for the Unix operating systems and has now been ported over to the Windows family of operating systems as well.

The reasons to choose Snort over other NIDS comes from the fact that it is open sourced. It has the following characteristics:

◆ It is a free utility.

◆ Its rules are easy to learn, and it is written in easy-to-understand language.

◆ You can easily detect new exploits as soon as they are announced. You can create rules that apply to any special situation you encounter.

◆ It has an actively supported rules database.

◆ Community support is available through the Internet and sites such as www.snort.org and SiliconDefense.Com, a commercial entity that offers reasonable commercial support for Snort.

Some terms that you will likely see in this paper are as follows:

Sensor.   A sensor is the component of IDS that handles the monitoring of traffic. In the case of Snort, the sensor is the machine that has Snort installed.

Signature.   The sequence or contents of IP packets that are used to identify an attack.

Detect.   An attack detected by a sensor.

NETWORK PLACEMENT

In order to monitor something, you must have access to it based on a promiscuous network interface card that listens to all packets on a single, physical cable. If you want to monitor traffic going to multiple Web servers with one sensor, you will need to place that sensor on a length of cable through which all the packets will travel.

On a simple LAN with no DMZ (see Figure 4.9), there are two optimal places to locate your sensor: between the router and the Internet and between the router and the LAN. The first configuration, denoted with (1), will detect all attacks against the network but will not show you those attacks which actually get through the router and into the LAN. The second configuration, denoted with (2), will show you those attacks which enter the LAN.

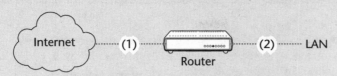

Figure 4.9 A simple LAN.

On a network with a DMZ (and bastion hosts), your sensor can be located in three probable places (see Figure 4.10).

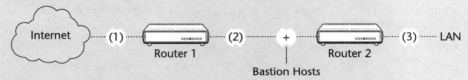

Figure 4.10 A LAN with a DMZ.

The situation shown in Figure 4.10 is more complex. These bastion hosts can offer varying types of services and run different operating systems. If a sensor is placed in location 1, it will detect all attacks against your network.

A sensor placed at location 2 will detect all attacks that make it through your exterior router. If you wish to detect attacks against your bastion hosts, this location is where you will want your sensor to be placed. A sensor at this location will also detect attacks targeted at your LAN, but it will not give you a hint of whether the attack was successful or not.

A sensor placed at location 3 will detect attacks that reach your LAN, but it will not detect attacks targeting your bastion hosts.

You might have decided that sensors at location 1 do not do a lot, and when your router does nothing but route, that situation might be true. If the router at location 1 is a firewall or if it does any sort of packet filtering, that sensor can be compared to a second sensor at location 2 to gauge how well a job the exterior firewall is doing.

Determine your network's layout, what you want to monitor, and where the sensor(s) should be placed. Remember, the sensor will detect all traffic on the physical wire. A standard hub repeats everything from one port to all its other ports. A switch will look for the MAC address of the destination and switch the packet to the proper port.

Most well-designed networks make use of a switch to connect a router to a LAN or bastion hosts. This connection reduces broadcast traffic on the wire. By placing a hub between the router and the switch, you create a node that will enable you to easily move your sensor and accommodate security analysis.

(continued)

SNORT'S PLACE IN A WINDOWS 2000 ENVIRONMENT *(continued)*

MACHINE SELECTION

The only thing worse than no information is wrong information, because it will mislead you and give you a false sense of security. With this fact in mind, you should gauge your network traffic and expectations for NIDS and build a machine accordingly.

A typical machine set up for a low-traffic network can be anywhere from a 300 megahertz (mHz) with 128MB of RAM on up. The one constant you will always want is a fairly large amount of hard drive space and a 100MB network card.

Network traffic varies from site to site and even from segment to segment, so our suggestion is to start on the low end and if you find that packet loss occurs, scale the machine up.

OPERATING SYSTEM INSTALLATION

I have chosen Windows 2000 Professional for my Snort implementations for numerous reasons, namely:

- ◆ Speed of installation and ease of use
- ◆ Fewer reboots due to network configuration changes
- ◆ Support for EFS
- ◆ Ease of IPSec administration
- ◆ Stability
- ◆ Cost versus the benefits mentioned previously (compared to other Windows products)

Think about how you plan on accessing your Snort logs. If you have the public IP addresses to spare, I suggest IPSec and terminal services or some other remote control software. If you are not opposed to manually retrieving the log files or have no public IP addresses to spare, give the Snort machine a private IP (192.168.1.0/24) and dig out a zip drive to which you can copy logs. IPSec will encrypt the packet payload of any communications you have with your Snort sensor, but it will not inhibit the sensors' capability to detect attacks.

Install the standard Win2k package and lock it down like you would a normal bastion host by performing the following steps:

1. Uninstall IIS 5.0.
2. Strengthen your administrator account password.
3. Rename your administrator account.
4. Update to the latest service pack.
5. Apply "Hot Fixes" that deal with malformed packets.
6. Disable the services you will not need (which will be most of them).

SNORT INSTALLATION

The first thing to do (perhaps even before finishing this document) is to visit the Snort Web site at www.Snort.org. Read the *frequently asked questions* (FAQs), and peruse the forums. Get yourself an idea of what you are about to attempt. The "Writing Snort Rules" by Martin Roesch will introduce you to the (very) friendly world of Snort rules.

In the Downloads section of Snort.org, you will find the Win32 binaries of the latest version. I have not tested the MySQL build. Michael Steele of Silicon Defenses has created a document explaining the setup of Snort on Win2k Pro with MySQL. You will need to have a packet capture driver (I recommend Packet2k) installed on your Snort machine (this driver is available in the Tools section of www.SecurityFocus.Net, or an alternate packet capture driver is available at www.netgroup-serv.polito.it/winpcap/install/default.htm).

SNORT SETUP

Now that Snort is on your machine, it is time to get the rule set that will be used to flag attacks. Precanned rule sets will detect known attacks and provide a solid baseline. These are available at www.snort.org.

Copy the rules into a file on your hard drive. Review the switches for Snort, and you will find that you can increase the scope of your logs to not only detect but help you reproduce exploits through the use of -C, -X, and -b. Play around with Snort at first, write a rule that detects all traffic, and notice the output. Modify the logging options until you are comfortable with the amount of output generated.

If you are using Snort to detect short-term threats or script kiddies, then perhaps these logs are all you will need. If you plan on doing a decent job of securing your network, you will want to keep historical records of all your logs. We suggest Snort2HTML to hand-keep logs. This use does not scale well, however, so large outfits might look toward MySQL.

Monitor your Snort machine daily.

A MAINTENANCE TIP (OR TWO)

Your Snort machine will log what will most likely be a high amount of traffic. This action will in turn result in the fragmentation of disk drives. On the other side of the coin, the longer your Snort machine is down for maintenance, the bigger the gap in your security becomes. With this factor in mind, create three partitions when you install Win2k, System (for the OS), Data (for programs), and Swap (for the paging The FAT32 filesystem enables much quicker diskchecks at the cost of file-level security.

This function limits the amount of time the Disk Keeper and Check Disk require for a partition, which will in turn minimize your network's exposure and increase your sensor's longevity and uptime.

Keep up with service packs and hot fixes. Network security is not a one-time installation; you will need to keep tabs on your hardware and upkeep your disk drives. Check Snort to verify minimal packet loss (done with the status report Snort gives you when you stop the program), and update your rule sets.

This example is provided courtesy of Jon Bull.

Computer Forensics

Computer forensics is a science, not an art, in the sense of empirical knowledge built up over time including algorithms to follow for execution. Traditionally, it has been thought of as a science that deals with the application of computer or network knowledge and facts of legal issues and proceedings. For example, forensics would come into play in a situation where an expert witness needed to provide the results of an investigation in a court case or deposition. Today more than ever before, computer forensics has come to mean something more. The term is used to describe the audit review and investigation that takes place when the operations staff is trying (usually desperately) to determine whether an intrusion has occurred and if so, what type of intrusion has taken place.

Because most of the time we are actually referring to the second description, that of responding to an incident whether it is internal or an outside adversary, we do not take the care and the diligence necessary nor do we have the expertise and processes to call it a true forensics activity. That is what you really should do, however, if you ever intend to prosecute an adversary. Therefore, we will discuss what you can do to develop computer or network forensic capability for your own system here. The other forensics addressed (the second type) is covered in Chapter 5, "Domain 4: Risk, Response, and Recovery" under the Response section.

Many approaches can be taken to have computers and networks conform to international standards for forensics analysis. Nevertheless, three tenets must be complied with during a forensic examination:

- Forensically sterile examination media (tools used to conduct the investigation that do not contaminate the object being examined) must be used.
- The examination cannot destroy the integrity of the original media.
- Hard copy and duplicate media as well as reports, court exhibits, and the like must be handled, controlled, marked, and transmitted properly (so that the evidence holds up in court).

The best way we know to accomplish these three tenets each and every time is to pack a "forensics bag" and keep it ready. It should contain everything you might need: evidence stickers, shrink-wrapped forensics analysis software, boxed and sealed blank CDs, floppies, DAT tapes, and at least four of every type of removable media you currently have. You will also need a dedicated printer, extra cartridges, or ink.

The first thing to do in a forensic investigation is to prepare for protecting the potential evidence.

- Take it into custody (take responsibility for it).
- Limit access to the physical area.
- Only those directly involved in the investigation should be near the system while the investigation is proceeding.
- Inspect the physical system.
- Inspect the logical system.

The first thing to understand in a forensics investigation is that the principles are the same regardless of the type of incident that has occurred. While the process that you go through is the same, the details and the actual steps will depend on the investigator and where each piece of evidence leads. It is similar to a treasure hunt. As you discover each piece of data that is applicable, it directs your investigation in a specific direction—and each investigation will have its own unique issues, so you need to be flexible.

For an example of this concept of forensic investigation, see the sidebar "Real-Life Example: Investigating Corruption." This situation was encountered by one of the authors a while ago in the course of her duties as a security officer for a large organization.

This experience and many others occurred before there were formal and standardized processes for investigating computer evidence. So, what do you need to do? Be prepared, develop a checklist, and create your forensics bag. Get some tape, as well. When you are asked to conduct such an investigation, think fast and work slowly. Do not let yourself make quick, rash, or oblique decisions. Get all the facts, then analyze and form an opinion. If your organization needs professional support for forensics, many security consulting firms provide subject matter experts and investigators. For professional resources in this area, review the document on this book's accompanying CD-ROM.

REAL-LIFE EXAMPLE: INVESTIGATING CORRUPTION

Many years ago, I was the organization's system security lead when one day the security detachment (police) asked me to support them in apprehending a potential criminal. What was I going to do, I asked? Well, these poor police guys told me that there were ongoing criminal activities being conducted by Mr. X, using his organization's computer (the computers over which I had security responsibility).

I went to the location of the system. It was a networked PC clone. Here is what I had to consider first:

- Who had been in here touching his stuff?
- Had he booby-trapped the system so that something went crazy when I turned it on?

(continued)

REAL-LIFE EXAMPLE: INVESTIGATING CORRUPTION *(continued)*

Now, to tell the truth, I was not as prepared as we are telling you all to be. I had to think fast and think on my feet. I had these two policemen standing over me, waiting for me to do something magic. I asked the police for evidence tape, and they didn't have any. So, I needed to improvise. I needed to place a sticky something over the I/O ports that were open in the back, over the network connection, and over the floppy drives and take a picture with a clock in the background. I used floppy diskette labels, wrote my name, date, and time on each, and then placed them over the items I mentioned.

I felt that I had to show that we had not spent time putting incriminating data onto his machine. The clock would match with the officer's account of when I arrived. Thank goodness the officers had a Polaroid camera in their car. Then, I turned on the system and logged on (I had admin privileges). I went to the CMOS and reviewed the system date and time. I was writing down each activity I performed on a piece of paper—in order by time. I documented the time on the system and did not peruse the system or spend much time on it at this point. I wanted to make sure it belonged to the person it was supposed to belong to and get as much out as possible. Remember that as you are performing these actions, any activity at all can damage your evidence. I was looking to see whether the owner of the system kept his data files in a single directory. I was lucky—I found most of them in one or two directories. I selected them all and printed the entire contents of the files located in those two directories. Defendants can claim that electronic version of the information is changed at any point before the hearing, so always get it on paper. Then, I used a DOS utility that was resident of the system and printed the directory structure. That fixed the contents of the *hard disk drive* (HDD) with the time. While all that printing was taking place, I did a physical search of the general area to look for diskettes and other peripheral elements that might need to be reviewed. As I located things, I documented a description of it, noting anything of significance. That done, the pictures (always take multiple photos) in hand, I requested the guards to remove the CPU, now under escort by me, and bring it to my office for further examination where I could protect it while I conducted the next phase of the investigation.

The second phase involved using utilities to search the HDD for deleted files, hidden files, and the like. At this time, I have to tell you that in order to perform this action, I had to know what I was looking for. Do not let anyone tell you that they want you to look for and see whether you can see anything unusual. That would make looking in a haystack for a needle easy. At this stage, the worst thing you can do is accidentally destroy the media. You need to make sure (that is why you plan ahead) that precautions are taken during all these steps.

There were many deleted files. I recovered them all and printed them (my office was filled with paper). It took three full days to review all the printed material. I discovered what the authorities were looking for and now had to get back in the system and find it again and this time preserve it. Now, there is newer technology and better processes, but what I did then was open the floppy drive (took the label off) and took another picture. Then, I made copies of the files that had incriminating data onto floppy diskettes as quickly as I could without disturbing the rest of the system. I used new floppies that I had formatted on my own system to prevent the transference of viruses, destructive programs, or other inadvertent writes to/from the original media. If there had been more than data files in the kilobytes range, I would have made a disk copy of the HDD. Usually, you do not perform further investigations on the original media (that must be kept). Once I had safely copied the files in question, I was done with the system and only the analysis remained.

There is a third phase to an investigation. I did not have to go through all of that, but it would be to search and conduct the equivalent of a laboratory examination: review slack space, config files, all executables, all non-standard applications, all space on the HDD, and determine the last time the HDD had disk defrag or cleanup run. I had to do some of these activities to build a case of intentional deletion of incriminating files. The only problem this guy had was that he did not actually run the defrag program correctly, so all the deleted files were not removed from the actual disk.

This story ends with me being called as an expert witness to the federal courthouse in Alexandria, VA. I testified before a grand jury, and the guy is gone. That's forensics.

Sample Questions

1. Which of the following statements is NOT true?

   a. Monitoring is an activity that takes place in real time and views current activity on a network.

   b. Monitoring retains detailed information for later review.

   c. Auditing captures network activity.

   d. Auditing retains information for later review.

2. Relative to information systems security auditing, which of the following is NOT one of the reasons to conduct an audit?

   a. To reconstruct events that might have caused a security breach

   b. To identify a potential breach in security

   c. To reconstruct activities performed during a breach in security

   d. To develop techniques to prevent future breaches

3. Which of the following statements is TRUE?

   a. Most firewall systems do not provide logging functionality.

   b. Application-proxy gateway firewalls provide more comprehensive logging output than stateful inspection packet filter firewalls.

   c. Stateful inspection packet filter firewalls provide more comprehensive logging output than application-proxy gateway firewalls.

   d. Application-proxy gateway firewalls encompass a smaller portion of the OSI model than stateful inspection packet filter firewalls.

4. The mechanism used to synchronize the time reference for installed intrusion detection systems and for logging across the network is:

   a. Network Time Protocol

   b. Synchronous Network Logging Protocol

   c. Time Synchronous Protocol

   d. Network Coordination Protocol

5. One of the rules in a rule set for a boundary router is given as:

RULE	SOURCE ADDRESS	SOURCE PORT	DESTINATION ADDRESS	DESTINATION PORT	ACTION
4	Any	Any	192.168.1.2	SMTP	Allow

Which one of the following items BEST describes the permissions specified by the rule?

a. Prevents external users from directly addressing the firewall system

b. Permits internal users to access external servers

c. Permits inbound connections to the main firewall's SMTP port

d. Instructs the router to pass SMTP traffic to the main firewall, which in turn will forward the message traffic to the respective application proxies

6. Which of the following activities is NOT part of the process for establishing an audit trail?

a. Defining your roadmap

b. Developing your rule set

c. Auditing all violations

d. Not auditing exceptions

7. The following activities are associated with auditing of what type of item?

- Creation, alteration, or dropping of a table
- Creation, alteration, or dropping of an index
- Statements renaming an object
- Performance statistics collection
- Granting and revoking of system type privilege

a. A network server

b. A database server

c. A mail server

d. A Web server

8. Which of the following resources that are impacted by the auditing process poses the most difficulty to management?

a. Auditing systems' hardware

b. Software to implement logging

c. Human resources required for analyzing and interpreting the data

d. Offline storage for preserving the logs for a specified time period

9. Information about which one of the following activities is the LEAST important audit data to collect?

    a. The use of privileged commands

    b. Unsuccessful, unauthorized attempts to access files

    c. Permission modifications

    d. Successful, authorized accessing of files

10. For events that are logged by the auditing process, which of the following data items is the LEAST important to collect?

    a. Date and time of each event

    b. Type of event

    c. Denial of access resulting from excessive logon attempts

    d. Non-system administrator functions

11. The main purpose of monitoring an information system is:

    a. Identifying a potential attack as it is occurring

    b. Reconstructing incidents after they have occurred

    c. Identifying incidents after they have occurred

    d. Preventing the occurrence of incidents

12. Which of the following items is NOT a type of network monitoring?

    a. Network management monitoring

    b. Mouse motion monitoring

    c. Security monitoring

    d. Key stroke monitoring

13. Snort is:

    a. An open-sourced audit system

    b. An open-sourced keystroke monitoring system

    c. A proprietary intrusion detection system

    d. An open-sourced intrusion detection system

14. A type of automated audit tool that provides the auditor with information concerning the network topology and assets is called:

    a. An intrusion detection tool

    b. A monitoring tool

    c. A documentation tool

    d. A discovery tool

15. Automated tools such as SATAN and CYBERCOP perform which one of the following functions?

    a. Vulnerability analysis

    b. Intrusion detection

    c. Data mining

    d. Configuration management

16. Which of the following items is NOT a correct, professional auditing standard?

    a. Due professional care is exercised in all aspects of the information systems auditor's work.

    b. If the information systems audit function is closely related to the area being audited, professional auditing practices must be enforced.

    c. The information systems auditor will provide a report, in appropriate form and content, to the intended recipients upon completion of the audit work.

    d. The responsibility, authority, and accountability of the information systems audit function must be appropriately documented in audit charters or in an engagement letter.

17. A level of diligence that a prudent individual would practice under given circumstances is called:

    a. Best effort

    b. Basic practices

    c. Due care

    d. Least privilege

18. Which of the following statements is TRUE regarding a risk-based audit approach?

    a. The cost to implement controls should be evaluated relative to the potential for loss if no controls are applied.

    b. Residual risk can be eliminated by insurance coverage.

    c. The risk mitigation is independent of management's tolerance for risk.

    d. The means to eliminate risk through controls should be investigated.

19. Risk that is a result of the failure of the auditing process to discover important errors is called:

    a. Controls risk

    b. Preventive risk

    c. Inherent risk

    d. Detection risk

20. A control that is used to identify an area where an error has occurred is called:

    a. Deterrent control

    b. Detective control

    c. Corrective control

    d. Reactive control

21. Which of the following items is MOST important in identifying potential irregularities during the audit process?

    a. Size of the payroll for the organization being audited

    b. Determining whether information systems best practices are used

    c. Existence of a vacation policy that requires employees to take vacation in one or two-week blocks

    d. Identifying the type of gateway used by the organization

22. Control objectives are important in audit engagements because they:

    a. Define audit duration

    b. Define the cost of audit

    c. Identify the main control issues based on management input and risk

    d. Define testing steps

23. Which of the following terms BEST describes "defining the roles and responsibilities of the auditors"?

    a. Audit charter

    b. Audit scope

    c. Audit objectives

    d. Control objectives

24. Which of the following BEST meets the requirements of audit evidence sampling?

    a. A confidence level higher than 90 percent based on repeated polling

    b. Sufficient, reliable, relevant, useful, and supported by appropriate analyses

    c. Should be conducted using the Delphi method

    d. Should be conducted using random sampling

25. What are the key items to consider relative to the reportable findings of an audit?

    a. Audit scope, materiality, and audit charter

    b. Audit objectives, materiality, and management direction

    c. Audit objectives and management direction

    d. Audit objectives only

26. An analysis that ensures that the underlying problem and not the symptoms is addressed is called:

    a. Root cause analysis

    b. Cost benefit analysis

    c. Base problem analysis

    d. Linear causal analysis

27. The definition "determining whether the system is being operated in accordance with accepted industry practices" refers to:

    a. Monitoring

    b. Auditing

    c. Intrusion detection

    d. Vulnerability analysis

28. Which of the following BEST describes the given rule set for a boundary router?

RULE	SOURCE ADDRESS	SOURCE PORT	DESTINATION ADDRESS	DESTINATION PORT	ACTION
4	Any	Any	192.168.1.0	>1023	Allow

    a. Allow external users to connect to the VPN server.

    b. Allow internal servers to connect to external servers.

    c. Allow external servers to send email to the proxy.

    d. Allow return packets from established connections to return to the source systems.

29. Which of the following is NOT one of the processes for establishing an audit trail?

    a. Define your roadmap.

    b. Develop your rule set.

    c. Audit all violations.

    d. Audit all normalizations.

30. Which of the following items is NOT an activity that should be logged on a relational database server?

    a. Creation, alteration, or dropping of a database table

    b. Enabling or disabling of the audit functionality

    c. Any user statement that does not return an error message because the object referenced does not exist

    d. Any user statement that renames a database object

Domain 4: Risk, Response, and Recovery

Goal of Chapter

The goal of this chapter is to present risk management from two perspectives: the system professional's and the organization's. We will discuss the concepts of risk, response, and recovery as three separate topics. This domain is unlike the other domains that we will study. Domain 4 combines three separate topics of significant importance—risk, incident response, and recovery—and places them together intentionally to show their relationship.

Domain Definition

The domain of risk, response, and recovery deals with a significant portion of the SSCP's *common body of knowledge* (CBK). As we learned in Chapter 1, "The Journey toward Information Security: An Overview," one of the goals of security is to have the ability to respond and recover for any incident, intentional or accidental. The three elements of this domain provide that total capability and include:

Risk Management.   This function involves identifying, evaluating (measuring), and controlling risk.

Incident response.   This function describes those activities that are performed when a security-related incident occurs that has the potential for, or has caused, adverse effects to the system or enterprise.

Contingency operations and recovery.   These are those planned activities that enable the critical business functions to continue under less-than-ideal circumstances and return to normal operations.

Risk

In this section, we will discuss what risk is, what you can do with it, how you can measure it, and how you can achieve less of it. Risk has traditionally been seen as the resulting condition of your information system when the collective threats and the collective weaknesses in the system (vulnerabilities) have been analyzed and then mitigated based on the existing safeguards or controls. (Safeguard and control are used synonymously in this chapter). As you will see in this section, risk is defined in several different ways. But in all cases, risk, threat, and vulnerability are distinct and separate properties and are never used synonymously.

What Is Risk?

As we discussed in Chapter 1, to communicate effectively we must use the same lexicon. The authors agree with Peter G. Neuman in his book, *Computer-Related Risks* (Addison Wesley, 1995), when he writes, "There is no standard definition." We have selected three definitions that encompass the overall idea of risk:

1. When we speak of risk, we normally use risk to mean the possibility of suffering harm or loss (danger). In this context, risk is the bad thing that could happen if . . .That definition works for all discussions regarding risk except when we need to perform an analysis of risk. In order to analyze risk we need to have risk represented as the result of specific metrics.

2. Risk: The potential for the realization of unwanted, adverse consequences to human life, health, property, or the environment; estimation of risk is usually based on the expected value of the conditional probability of the event occurring times the consequence of the event given that it has occurred. (This definition is from the *Glossary of Risk Analysis Terms* at www.sra.org.)

3. Risk is a function of the probability of a given threat agent exercising a particular vulnerability and the resulting impact of that adverse event on the organization.

With these three definitions, you can get a good idea of what risk means. But, we cannot have a discussion of risk without discussing and understanding the major elements that must be considered in defining our system or network's risk.

Major System Elements at Risk

The following are simple definitions of the major elements to consider when defining risk.

Assets

Assets are the business resources associated with the system, and there can be tangible and intangible assets. Examples of tangible assets are listed as follows. Intangible assets are resources such as intellectual property or corporate goodwill. The partial or complete loss of an asset might affect the confidentiality, integrity, or availability of the system information or that of the system itself, in addition to having a dollar value associated with that loss.

The following are examples of assets:

- Hardware
  - Servers
  - Mainframes
  - Routers
  - Network cabling
  - Printers
  - Media
  - Backup equipment
- Software
  - Operating systems
  - Major applications
  - Internal developed applications
  - Security software
  - System utilities
  - Test programs
  - Communications software

- Environmental systems
  - Air conditioning
  - Power
  - Water
  - Lighting
  - Building
  - Computer facility
  - Tape and disk library
  - Auxiliary power
  - Auxiliary environmental controls
- Supplies
- Personnel
  - Computer personnel
  - Maintenance personnel
  - Temporary employees and consultants
- Documentation
  - Software
  - Hardware
  - Files
  - Program
  - Applications
  - System
  - SOPs
  - Schedules
  - Audit documents
  - Procedures
  - Emergency plans
  - Vital records
- Information/data
  - Classified
  - Operations
  - Business sensitive

- Planning
- Financial
- Statistical
- Personal
- Logistic
- Other
- Communications
    - Communications equipment
    - Communications lines
    - Communications processors
    - Routers/gateways/multiplexors/switches
    - Telephones
    - Modems
    - Cables

Threats

Any circumstance or event with the potential to harm an information system through unauthorized access, destruction, disclosure, modification of data, and/or denial of service is a threat. To most information system environments, the insider is still by far the single biggest threat. The insider threat might include the following:

- Errors
- Theft
- Misuse
- Abuse
- Sabotage
- Industrial (or government) espionage

Vulnerability

Vulnerability is a weakness in an information system, its system security procedures, internal controls, or implementation that could be exploited by a threat or threat agent.

NOTE Threats and vulnerabilities are normally associated in pairs. When you use the $R = T \times V$ formula, you quickly notice that a vulnerability can exist—but without a threat to exploit it, there is no risk ($0 \times$ anything $= 0$). The same is true when there exists a threat but no vulnerability.

Controls

Controls are operational, technical, or administrative processes or technologies that reduce, mitigate, or transfer risk. Controls are divided into three categories: preventive, detective, and corrective:

Preventive controls.   These inhibit attempts to violate security policy and include controls such as access control enforcement, encryption, and authentication.

Detective controls.   These warn of violations or attempted violations of security policy and include controls such as audit trails, intrusion detection methods, and checksums.

Corrective controls.   These types of controls are put in place to reduce a specific risk. See "Countermeasures."

Safeguards

Safeguards are those controls that provide some amount of protection to an asset. Controls can be operational, technical, or administrative, and multiple-layered controls that utilize all three controls are the best defense against a threat.

Countermeasures

Countermeasures are those controls that are put in place as a result of an analysis of a system's security posture. They can be any action, device, procedure, technique, or other control that reduces the vulnerability of the system. They are the same controls as defined in safeguards but are implemented specifically to reduce an identified and measured risk. Here are some examples of controls:

- Proxy servers
- Providing logical access controls for privacy requirements
- Implementation of the least privilege concept to safeguard corporate intellectual property rights
- Information system security policy (documented)

- Information system security education, awareness, and training
- Contingency planning
- Senior management support and commitment, usually through a vision or mission statement
- A system security staff
- Managing risk through risk identification, analysis, control, and mitigation
- Physical access controls

Exposure

The exposure is the amount or percentage of loss experienced should a threat exploit a vulnerability.

Risk Analysis

An analysis is the process of determining the relationships of threats to vulnerabilities and controls and then (normally through mathematical probability) associating those with potential impacts to system assets. An analysis is an objective process.

Risk Assessment

An assessment takes the analysis as input and makes a determination as to the overall risk. An assessment is a subjective process. The negative impact can be described in terms of loss or degradation of any, or a combination of any, of the following three security objectives: CIA. The following provides a brief description of the consequence (or impact) of its not being met.

Loss of Integrity

Integrity is lost if unauthorized changes are made to the information or system by either intentional or accidental acts. If the loss of system or data integrity is not corrected, continued use of the contaminated system or corrupted data could result in inaccuracy, fraud, or erroneous decisions. Also, violation of integrity might be the first step in a successful attack against system availability or confidentiality. For all these reasons, loss of integrity reduces the assurance of a system.

Loss of Availability

If a critical system is unavailable to its end users, the organization's mission might be affected. Loss of system functionality and operational effectiveness, for example, might result in a loss of productive time—thus impeding the end user's performance of their functions in supporting the organization's mission.

Loss of Confidentiality

System and data confidentiality refers to the protection of information from unauthorized disclosure. The impact of unauthorized disclosure of confidential information can range from jeopardizing the government's national security or a corporation's next product line to the disclosure of personal privacy information (protected by law). Unauthorized, unanticipated, or unintentional disclosure could result in a loss of public confidence, embarrassment, or legal action against the organization.

Threats versus Vulnerabilities

Let's see if we can bring some context to these terms. Threats exist in the world, and they do not typically change over short periods of time—nor do they appear and disappear based on what you are doing with your system.

Vulnerabilities are quite different. Your information system might or might not be vulnerable to any specific threat. Consider this example: The threat of a hurricane exists. We have all seen them, either in person, on TV, or in a movie. Just because the threat of a hurricane exists does not mean you are vulnerable to it. If you live in or nearby an ocean coastline, you are vulnerable. If you live in Kansas City, however, you are not vulnerable. The threat exists, but there is no ability for the threat to take advantage (exploit) any weakness because the threat cannot reach Kansas City. Vulnerabilities are weaknesses in technology or processes or the physical environment that can possibly enable a threat to exploit it—and by exploiting it, either gain something or create a negative impact to your system. The vulnerability might or might not allow complete access to your network; it might only tell the open ports of your firewall. But that information is more than an adversary had previously, so he or she has gained something from your system and will be able to continue progression as long as there are vulnerabilities that can be exploited.

Safeguards reduce a system's vulnerability (exposure) to threats. Many safeguards are mandatory, such as user IDs, passwords, or physical access controls. When a system has undergone a risk analysis or assessment, the risk of that system might be too high. When you wish to specifically reduce a specific vulnerability or exposure, then countermeasures are introduced. They are the same (both controls), but when they are used and why they are used are slightly different. Safeguards are used when you build the system or just because you think it is needed or required. Countermeasures are used as a result of a risk analysis.

Analyzing Risk

So, now that we understand what risk is, we need to understand how it can be assessed. We must identify the risk, analyze (measure) the risk, and then control it. We can do the first two—identify and analyze—by performing a risk analysis. How a risk analysis is performed is determined by the methodology selected. A methodology delineates the processes, procedures, and framework for the outcome of a risk analysis. There are two general methodologies used to analyze risk: quantitative and qualitative (defined as follows):

Quantitative risk analysis.   A quantitative risk analysis results in showing a quantity of some object. Typically, the results (quantity) are addressed in terms of dollars. The processes within this approach are normally mathematical statements of the relation(s) among variables. Also known as risk modeling, quantitative risk analyses are in particular based on probability models that predict the relative frequency of different uncertain outcomes.

Qualitative risk analysis.   A qualitative risk analysis results in a subjective result (quality rating). The results of qualitative analyses are addressed in terms of High, Medium, or Low or on a scale from 0 to 5 (for example).

The following paragraphs describe each of these analyses in detail.

> **NOTE** Although analysis and assessment are often used interchangeably, they do not have the same definition. You perform an analysis, and the results of the analysis enable you to make an assessment.

Quantitative Risk Analysis

The quantitative approach to risk analysis is by far the most formal and the most complex. Quantitative risk analysis deals with probabilities and uncertainty, and many consider it formal risk modeling.

It is much easier to accomplish other types of activities when you have documented costs and controls, as you do in a quantitative analysis. For example, a cost-benefit analysis is much easier to accomplish when needed to justify budgets. The quantitative analysis has several elements that are not present in the qualitative approach, which we describe in the following sections.

Single Loss Expectancy (SLE)

An SLE is the cost (in dollars) that can be lost from the harm to the system or activity by attacks against its assets:

SLE = Asset Value ($) × Exposure Factor

The loss expectancy is the impact should the threat succeed in exploiting the vulnerability.

Annual Loss Expectancy (ALE)

The ALE is derived from the SLE and the *annual rate of occurrence* (ARO). The ALE is the expected yearly dollar value loss from the harm to the system or activity by attacks against its assets:

ALE = SLE × ARO

Return on Investment (ROI)

The ROI provides a method of prioritizing the selection of countermeasures and is determined by calculating the annual cost of countermeasure divided by the ALE:

Annualized cost of countermeasure ($) / ALE

For example, a countermeasure costs $10,000 a year to purchase and maintain (amortized over the life of the asset). The ALE as a result of not having the countermeasure in place was determined to be $15,000. Divide $10,000 by $15,000 to get the ROI. If the ROI is greater than one, the countermeasure should be placed at the high end of the priority list—because you will get the most bang for your buck.

Annual Rate of Occurrence (ARO)

The ARO is written as a probability from 0.0 to 1.0, where 1.0 suggests that an occurrence is guaranteed to happen:

Likelihood of an event taking place × the number of times it could occur in a single year = ARO

Normally, the likelihood (probability) is derived from historical data, such as how often the flood table rises to cause flood damage to your system (or other natural disasters) or how often you are attacked through the Internet. Alternatively, this information can be selected based on empirical knowledge (an educated best guess). The number of times it could occur (the frequency of occurrence) should also be derived based on historical or empirical knowledge.

Exposure Factor (EF)

The *exposure factor* (EF) refers to the harm or loss to the system or activity by presumed successful attacks. The EF is written as either a percentage or a probability. For example, catastrophic and complete loss could be expressed in either of the following two ways:

EF = 100%

EF = 1.0

What if an exposure factor equaled one chance in 100? That EF could be expressed in either of the following two ways:

EF = 0.01

EF = 10%

Qualitative Risk Analysis

A qualitative risk analysis is usually much simpler, certainly less time consuming, and provides higher-level, subjective results than a quantitative risk analysis. The analysis is performed with broad categories of threats and vulnerabilities, subjective impact, and probability of occurrence—resulting in the subjective categorization of each risk.

Automated Risk Assessment

These two methodologies are becoming less distinct due to the wide variety of automated risk tools. While automated tools are a time saver, you are tied to the approach built into the tool you select to use. Table 5.1 provides a listing and description of several automated risk analysis products on the market today. Both manual and automated risk analyses processes have value, and the one you should select is the one that will best represent the expected result of the risk analysis that you require.

Regardless of how effective your risk analysis is, it remains a "snapshot frozen in time" and is only valid for that instant. To make risk analysis more effective, the overall management of the risk must begin.

Table 5.1   Automated Risk Assessment Tools

SRAG	The Department of Justice *Simplified Risk Assessment Guidelines* (SRAG).
FRAP	The *Facilitated Risk Assessment Process* (FRAP).
Delphi	Delphi techniques involve a group of experts independently rating and ranking business risk for a business process or organization and blending the results into a consensus. Each expert in the Delphi group measures and prioritizes the risk for each element or criteria. A facilitator gathers the independent judgments and summarizes them. The summary is fed back to the expert panel along with their independent judgments, giving the opportunity for each expert to compare their judgment against the panel. The process repeats until a consensus is reached.
COBRA	COBRA provides a complete risk-based analysis service, compatible with most recognized methodologies (qualitative and quantitative). It is a questionnaire PC system using 'expert' system principles and an extensive knowledge base. It evaluates the relative importance of all threats and vulnerabilities and generates appropriate recommendations and solutions. In addition, its reports provide a written assessment and relative risk score, or level, for each risk category.
OCTAVE	The *Operationally Critical Threat, Asset, and Vulnerability Evaluation* (OCTAVE) defines the essential components of a comprehensive, systematic, context driven information security risk evaluation. The operational or business units and the IT department work together to address the information security needs of the enterprise (qualitative; high, medium, and low).

What to Do with Risk?

Once we have identified our risk, what can we do with it? We can avoid it, transfer it, ignore it, or accept it.

Total avoidance means that by providing enough protection, you can protect everything. Most sovereign nations used this method to protect their most valuable secrets throughout the majority of the 20th century. As you might recall from the defense department's budgets of the past, protecting national security was very costly. Also, there were still major breaches of security, such as spies, traitors, and hackers. One hundred percent avoidance is not attainable.

An alternative to avoiding risk, however, is to transfer it. Today, many companies can purchase insurance against many losses, sometimes even against computer system based losses—but that is still not the common practice. No sovereign nation or government can buy insurance.

The normally accepted method today, for all, is to accept risk. Acceptance of residual risk (risk remaining after all cost-effective mitigation is performed) is the normal response. From this concept, we have the differentiation in the terms risk and residual risk.

Why Assess Risk?

Risk is all around us and is the product of uncertainty within our lives. We have risk in almost all aspects of our daily living. For example, there is a risk that we will be hit by another automobile while driving or that we will accidentally hit another vehicle. There is the risk that we will not live long enough to pay off our homes and our debts and to leave something for our children. These risks must be evaluated, and appropriate measures (transferred, ignored, avoided, or accepted) must be established. It is the same in the information systems field. It has taken more than 30 years, but the management of risk is now a responsibility of senior management. This situation has occurred as the impact of information technology has increased in the business world.

What Is Risk Management?

Risk management is the process of identifying, measuring, and controlling uncertain events. Most managers today are required to manage their risks, whether they are customer related or information system related. Long gone are the days when organizations could spend resources without thorough justification. Today, managing risk is the number-one issue in information security. Risks are very complex in an information systems environment. There is your system's risk; then there might be the enterprise's risk (multiple systems/networks); and finally, most organizations are connected to business partners or clients, and in that scenario the interconnected systems of different owners have an additional level of risk. Risk is everywhere, and we can identify and measure risk by performing a risk analysis. We control risk through the application of safeguards and countermeasures (controls), which reduce risk to a tolerable level for the organization. Risk is managed by continually reviewing and taking responsible actions based on the risk.

An Effective Risk-Assessment Methodology

The risk-assessment methodology presented in this section is taken directly from the U.S. *National Institute of Standards and Technology* (NIST). We want to thank that organization for enabling us to share a viable, current risk-assessment methodology with our readers. We highly recommend this method of risk assessment; it is one of the best we have seen in a very long time.

Risk assessment is the first process in the risk management methodology. Organizations use risk assessment to determine the extent of the potential threat and the risk associated with an IT system throughout its *software development life cycle* (SDLC).

Risk is a function of the likelihood of a given threat agent (or threat source) exploiting a particular vulnerability and the resulting impact of that adverse event on the organization, R. This information is typically displayed as follows:

Risk = Threat times Vulnerability, or R = T × V

To determine the likelihood of a future adverse event, threats to an IT system must be analyzed in conjunction with the potential vulnerabilities and the controls in place for the IT system. Impact refers to the magnitude of harm that a threat acting on a vulnerability could cause. The level of impact is governed by the potential mission impacts, which in turn produces a relative value for the IT assets and resources affected (for example, the criticality and sensitivity of the IT system components and data). The NIST risk assessment methodology encompasses nine primary steps, which are outlined in the following list, depicted in Figure 5.1, and described in detail in the following paragraphs:

1. Gather information about system characteristics.
2. Identify threats.
3. Identify vulnerabilities.
4. Analyze the controls that have been implemented.
5. Determine the likelihood that a potential vulnerability might be implemented.
6. Analyze the impact of someone acting upon a vulnerability.
7. Determine the level of risk to the IT system.
8. Recommend controls that could mitigate or eliminate the identified risks.
9. Document the results in an official report or briefing.

Step 1: System Characterization

In assessing risks for an IT system, the first step is to define the scope of the effort. In this step, the boundaries of the IT system are identified along with the resources and the information that constitute the system. Characterizing an IT system establishes the scope of the risk assessment effort, delineates the operational authorization (or accreditation) boundaries, and provides information (for example, hardware, software, system connectivity, and responsible division or support personnel) essential to defining the risk.

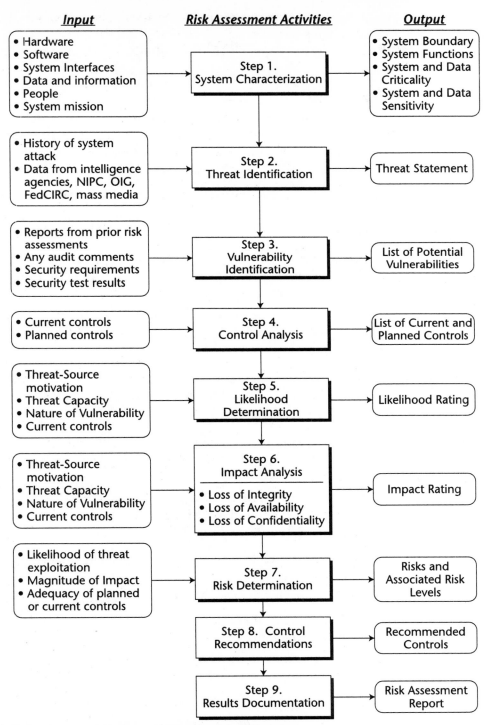

Figure 5.1   A risk assessment methodology flowchart.

The methodology described here can be applied to assessments of single or multiple, interrelated systems. In the latter case, it is important that the domain of interest and all interfaces and dependencies be well defined prior to applying the methodology.

System-Related Information

Identifying risk for an IT system requires a keen understanding of the system's processing environment. The person(s) who conducts the risk assessment must therefore first collect system-related information, which is usually classified as follows:

- Hardware and software system interfaces (for example, internal and external connectivity)
- Data and information
- Persons who support and use the IT system
- System mission (for example, the processes performed by the IT system that support the organization)
- System and data criticality (for example, the system's value or importance to an organization)
- System and data sensitivity

Additional information related to the operational environment of the IT system and its data includes, but is not limited to, the following:

- The functional requirements of the IT system
- Users of the system (for example, system users who provide technical support to the IT system and application users who use the IT system to perform business functions)
- System security policies governing the IT system (organizational policies, federal requirements, laws, and industry practices)
- System security architecture
- The level of protection required to maintain system and data integrity, confidentiality, and availability
- Current network topology (for example, a network diagram)
- Information storage protection that safeguards system and data confidentiality, availability, and integrity
- Flow of information pertaining to the IT system (for example, system interfaces, system input, and an output flowchart)

- Technical controls used in the IT system (for example, built-in or add-on security products that support identification and authentication, discretionary or mandatory access control, audit, residual information protection, and encryption methods)

- Management controls pertaining to the IT system (for example, rules of behavior and security planning)

- Operational controls used for operation of the IT system (for example, personnel security, backup, contingency, and resumption and recovery operations; system maintenance; offsite storage; user account establishment and deletion procedures; and controls for the segregation of user functions, such as privileged user access versus standard user access)

- Physical security environment of the IT system (for example, facility security and data center policies)

- Environmental security implemented for the IT system processing environment (for example, controls for humidity, water, power, pollution, temperature, and chemicals)

For a system in the initiation or design phase, system information can be derived from the design or requirements document. For an IT system under development, it is necessary to define key security rules and attributes planned for the future IT system. System design documents and the system security plan can provide useful information about the security of an IT system that is in development.

For an operational IT system, data is collected about the IT system in its production environment, including data concerning system configuration, connectivity, and documented and undocumented procedures and practices. Therefore, the system description can be based on the security provided by the underlying infrastructure or on future security plans for the IT system.

Information-Gathering Techniques

Any or a combination of the following techniques can be used in gathering information relevant to the IT system within its operational boundary:

Questionnaire.   To collect relevant information, risk assessment personnel can develop a questionnaire concerning the management and operational controls planned for or used in the IT system. This questionnaire should be distributed to the applicable technical and non-technical management personnel who are designing or supporting the IT system. The questionnaire could also be used during on-site visits and interviews.

On-site interviews.   Interviews with IT system support and management personnel can enable risk assessment personnel to collect useful information about the IT system (for example, how the system is operated and managed). On-site visits also enable risk assessment personnel to observe and gather information about the physical, environmental, and operational security of the IT system. For systems still in the design phase, the on-site visit would be a face-to-face data gathering exercise and could provide the opportunity to evaluate the physical environment in which the IT system will operate.

Document review. Policy documents (for example, legislative documentation and directives), system documentation (for example, the system user guide, system administrative manual, the system design and requirement document, and the acquisition document), and security-related documentation (for example, the previous audit report, risk assessment report, system test results, system security plan, and security policies) can provide good information about the security controls used by and planned for the IT system. An organization's mission impact analysis or asset criticality assessment provides information regarding system and data criticality and sensitivity.

Use of automated scanning tools. Proactive technical methods can be used to collect system information efficiently. For example, a network mapping tool can identify the services that run on a large group of hosts and provide a quick way of building individual profiles of the target IT systems.

Information gathering can be conducted throughout the risk assessment process, from Step 1 (system characterization) through Step 9 (results documentation).

Output from Step 1

The following results should be outputted upon successful completion of Step 1:

- Characterization of the IT system assessed
- A good picture of the IT system environment
- Delineation of system boundary

Step 2: Threat Identification

A threat is the potential for a particular threat source to successfully exercise a particular vulnerability. A vulnerability is a weakness that can be accidentally triggered or intentionally exploited. A threat source does not present a risk when there is no vulnerability that can be exercised. In determining the likelihood of a threat (Step 5), one must consider threat sources, potential vulnerabilities (Step 3), and existing controls (Step 4).

> **THREAT**
>
> The potential for a threat source to exercise (accidentally trigger or intentionally exploit) a specific vulnerability

Threat Source Identification

The goal of this step is to identify the potential threat sources and compile a threat statement listing potential threat sources that are applicable to the IT system being evaluated.

> **NOTE** During the initial phase, a risk assessment could be used to develop the initial system security plan.

A threat source is defined as any circumstance or event with the potential to cause harm to an IT system. The common threat sources can be natural, human, or environmental.

In assessing threat sources, it is important to consider all potential threat sources that could cause harm to an IT system and its processing environment. For example, although the threat statement for an IT system located on a hill might not include natural flooding because of the low likelihood of such an event occurring, environmental threats such as a bursting pipe can quickly flood a computer room and cause damage to an organization's IT assets and resources. Humans can be threat sources through intentional acts, such as deliberate attacks by malicious persons or disgruntled employees, or unintentional acts, such as negligence and errors. A deliberate attack can be either (1) a malicious attempt to gain unauthorized access to an IT system (for example, via password guessing) in order to compromise system and data integrity, availability, or confidentiality or (2) a benign, but nonetheless purposeful, attempt to circumvent system security. One example of the latter type of deliberate attack is a programmer writing a Trojan horse program to bypass system security in order for the (Trojan) attack to succeed.

> **THREAT SOURCE**
>
> Either (1) intent and method targeted at the intentional exploitation of a vulnerability or (2) a situation and method that might accidentally trigger a vulnerability

COMMON THREAT SOURCES

Natural Threats.   Floods, earthquakes, tornadoes, landslides, avalanches, electrical storms, and other such events

Human Threats.   Events that are either enabled by or caused by human beings, such as unintentional acts (inadvertent data entry or operational mistake) or deliberate actions (network based attacks, malicious software upload, or unauthorized access to confidential information).

Environmental Threats.   Long-term power failure, pollution, chemicals, liquid leakage.

Motivation and Threat Actions

Motivation and the resources for carrying out an attack make humans potentially dangerous threat sources. Table 5.2 presents an overview of many of today's common human threats, their possible motivations, and the methods or threat actions by which they might carry out an attack. This information will be useful to organizations studying their human threat environments and customizing their human threat statements. In addition, reviews of the history of system break-ins; security violation reports; incident reports; and interviews with the system administrators, help desk personnel, and user community during information gathering will help identify human threat sources that have the potential to harm an IT system and its data that might be a concern where vulnerability exists.

Table 5.2   Human Threats: Threat Source, Motivation, and Threat Actions

THREAT SOURCE	MOTIVATION	THREAT ACTIONS
Hacker, cracker	Challenge	Hacking
	Ego	Social engineering
	Rebellion	System intrusion, break-ins
		Unauthorized system access
Computer criminal	Destruction of information	Illegal information disclosure
	Monetary gain	Unauthorized data alteration
		Computer crime (for example, cyber stalking)

Table 5.2 *(continued)*

THREAT SOURCE	MOTIVATION	THREAT ACTIONS
		Fraudulent act (in other words, replay, impersonation, and interception)
		Information bribery
		Spoofing
		System intrusion
Terrorist	Blackmail	Destruction
	Exploitation	Bomb/terrorism
	Revenge	Information warfare
		System attack (for example, distributed denial of service)
		System penetration
		System tampering
Industrial espionage (companies, foreign governments, and other government interests)	Competitive advantage	
Economic espionage	Economic exploitation	Information theft
		Intrusion on personal privacy
		Social engineering
		System penetration
		Unauthorized system access (access to classified, proprietary and/or technology-related information)
Insiders (poorly trained, disgruntled, malicious, negligent, dishonest, or terminated employees)	Curiosity	Assault on an employee
	Ego	Assault on an employee
	Intelligence	Blackmail

(continued)

Table 5.2   *(continued)*

THREAT SOURCE	MOTIVATION	THREAT ACTIONS
	Monetary gain	Browsing of proprietary information
	Revenge	Computer abuse
	Unintentional errors and omissions (for example, data entry error or programming error)	Fraud and theft
		Information bribery
		Input of falsified, corrupted data
		Interception
		Malicious code (for example, virus, logic bomb, or Trojan horse)
		Sale of personal information
		System bugs
		System intrusion
		System sabotage
		Unauthorized system access

An estimate of the motivation, resources, and capabilities that might be required to carry out a successful attack should be developed after the potential threat sources have been identified in order to determine the likelihood of a threat acting on a system vulnerability, as described in Step 5 (see *Step 5: Likelihood Determination*).

The threat statement, or the list of potential threat sources, should be tailored to the individual organization and processing environment (for example, end-user computing habits). In general, information about natural threats (for example, floods, earthquakes, and storms) should be readily available. Known threats have been identified by many government and private-sector organizations. Intrusion detection tools also are becoming more prevalent, and government and industry organizations continually collect data on security events—thereby improving their ability to realistically assess threats. Sources of information include, but are not limited to, the following:

- Intelligence agencies (for example, the Federal Bureau of Investigation's National Infrastructure Protection Center at www.nipc.gov)
- National Oceanographic and Atmospheric Association (NOAA) historical data (www.noaa.gov)
- Federal Emergency Management Agency (FEMA) at www.fema.gov
- Federal Computer Incident Response Center (FedCIRC) at www.fedcirc.gov
- Mass media, particularly Web-based resources such as:

    www.SecurityFocus.com

    www.SecurityWatch.com

    www.SecurityPortal.com

    www.SANS.org

Output from Step 2

The following result should be output upon successful completion of Step 1:

- A threat statement containing a list of threat sources that could exploit system vulnerabilities

Step 3: Vulnerability Identification

The analysis of the threat to an IT system must include an analysis of the vulnerabilities associated with the system environment. The goal of this step is to develop a list of system vulnerabilities (flaws or weaknesses) that could be exploited by the potential threat sources.

Table 5.3 presents examples of vulnerability/threat pairs. This list is not all-inclusive and is by no means meant to be representative of the quantity that you might discover associated with your system.

VULNERABILITY

A flaw or weakness in system security procedures, design, implementation, or internal controls that could be exercised (accidentally triggered or intentionally exploited) and result in a security breach or a violation of the system's security policy.

Table 5.3 Vulnerability/Threat Pairs

VULNERABILITY	THREAT SOURCE	THREAT ACTION
Terminated employees' system identifiers (ID) are not removed from the system.	Terminated employees	Dialing into the company's network and accessing company proprietary data
Company firewall enables inbound Telnet, and guest ID is enabled on XYZ server.	Unauthorized users (for example, hackers, terminated employees, computer criminals, and terrorists)	Using Telnet to XYZ server and browsing system files with the guest ID
The vendor has identified flaws in the security design of the system; however, new patches have not been applied to the system.	Unauthorized users (for example, hackers, disgruntled employees, computer criminals, or terrorists)	Obtaining unauthorized access to sensitive system files based on known system vulnerabilities
Data center uses water sprinklers to suppress fire; tarpaulins to protect hardware and equipment from water damage are not in place.	Fire, negligent persons	Water sprinklers being turned on in the data center

Recommended methods for identifying system vulnerabilities are through the use of vulnerability sources, the performance of system security testing, and the development of a security requirements checklist.

Note that the types of vulnerabilities that will exist, and the methodology needed to determine whether the vulnerabilities are present, will usually vary depending on the nature of the IT system and its life cycle phase:

- If the IT system has not yet been designed, the search for vulnerabilities should focus on the organization's security policies, planned security procedures, and system requirement definitions and the vendors' or developers' security product analyses (for example, white papers).

- If the IT system is being implemented, the identification of vulnerabilities should be expanded to include more specific information, such as the planned security features described in the security design documentation and the result of system security test and evaluation.

- If the IT system is operational, the process of identifying vulnerabilities should include an analysis of the IT system security features and the security controls, technical and procedural, used to protect the system.

Vulnerability Sources

The technical and non-technical vulnerabilities associated with an IT system's processing environment can be identified via the information-gathering techniques described in Step 1. A review of other industry sources (for example, vendor Web pages that identify system bugs and flaws) will be useful in preparing for the interviews and in developing effective questionnaires to identify vulnerabilities that might be applicable to specific IT systems (for example, a specific version of a certain operating system). The Internet is another source of information about known system vulnerabilities posted by vendors, along with hot fixes, service packs, patches, and other remedial measures that might be applied to eliminate or mitigate vulnerabilities. Documented vulnerability sources that should be considered in a thorough vulnerability analysis include, but are not limited to, the following:

- Previous risk assessment documentation of the IT system
- The IT system's audit reports, system anomaly reports, security review reports, and system test and evaluation reports
- Vulnerability lists, such as the NIST I-CAT vulnerability database (http://icat.nist.gov)
- Security advisories, such as FedCIRC and the Department of Energy's Computer Incident Advisory Capability (CIAC) bulletins
- Vendor advisories
- Commercial computer incident/emergency response teams and post lists (for example, SecurityFocus.com forum postings)
- Information Assurance Vulnerability Alerts (IAVA) and bulletins for military systems
- System software security analyses

System Security Testing

Proactive methods—employing system testing—can be used to identify system vulnerabilities efficiently and can be done on a recurring basis—the frequency of which depends on the criticality of the IT system and available resources (for example, allocated funds, available technology, and persons with the expertise to conduct the test). Test methods include:

- Automated vulnerability scanning tool
- Security test and evaluation (ST&E)
- Penetration testing

The automated vulnerability scanning tool is typically used to scan a group of hosts or a network for known vulnerable services (for example, the system enables anonymous *File Transfer Protocol* [FTP], sendmail relaying). We should note, however, that some of the potential vulnerabilities identified by the automated scanning tool might not represent real vulnerabilities in the context of the system environment. For example, some of these scanning tools rate potential vulnerabilities without considering the site's environment and requirements. Some of the vulnerabilities flagged by the automated scanning software might actually not be vulnerable for a particular site but might be configured that way because their environment requires it. Thus, this test method might produce false positives.

ST&E is another technique that can be used in identifying IT system vulnerabilities during the risk assessment process. It includes the development and execution of a test plan (for example, test script, test procedures, and expected test results). The purpose of system security testing is to test the effectiveness of the security controls of an IT system as they have been applied in an operational environment. The objective is to ensure that the applied controls meet the approved security specification for the software and hardware and implement the organization's security policy or meet industry standards.

Penetration testing can be used to complement the review of security controls and ensure that external facing facets of the IT system are secure. Penetration testing, when employed in the risk assessment process, can be used to assess an IT system's ability to withstand intentional attempts to circumvent system security. Its objective is to test the IT system from the viewpoint of a threat source and to identify potential failures in the IT system protection schemes.

The results of these types of security testing will help identify a system's vulnerabilities.

Development of Security Requirements Checklist

During this step, the risk assessment personnel determine whether the security requirements stipulated for the IT system, and collected during system characterization, are being met by existing or planned security controls. Typically, the system security requirements can be presented in table form, with each requirement accompanied by an explanation of how the system's design or implementation does or does not satisfy that security control requirement.

A security requirements checklist contains the basic security standards that can be used to systematically evaluate and identify the vulnerabilities of the assets (personnel, hardware, software, information), manual procedures, processes, and information transfers associated with a given IT system in the following security areas:

- Management
- Operational
- Technical

Table 5.4 lists security criteria suggested for use in identifying an IT system's vulnerabilities in each security area.

Table 5.4   Security Criteria

SECURITY AREA	SECURITY CRITERIA
Management Security	Assignment of responsibilities
	Continuity of support
	Incident response capability
	Periodic review of security controls
	Personnel clearance and background investigations
	Risk assessment
	Security and technical training
	Separation of duties
	System authorization and reauthorization
	System or application security plan
Operational Security	Control of airborne contaminants (for example, smoke, dust, chemicals)
	Controls to ensure the quality of the electrical power supply
	Data media access and disposal
	External data distribution and labeling
	Facility protection (for example, computer room, data center, office)
	Humidity control
	Temperature control
	Workstations, laptops, and standalone personal computers
Technical Security	Communications (for example, dial-in, system interconnection, routers)
	Cryptography
	Discretionary access control
	Identification and authentication
	Intrusion detection
	Object reuse
	System audit

The outcome of this process is the security requirements checklist. Sources that can be used in compiling such a checklist include, but are not limited to, the following government regulatory and security directives and sources applicable to the IT system processing environment: Computer Security Act of 1987 Federal Information Processing Standards Publications (www.firstgov.gov):

- OMB Circular A-130, November 2000 (www.omb.gov)
- Privacy Act of 1974 (www.omb.gov)
- System security plan of the IT system assessed
- The organization's security policies, guidelines, and standards
- Industry practices

The control objectives are abstracted directly from long-standing requirements found in statute, policy, and guidance on security and privacy.

The results of the checklist (or questionnaire) can be used as input for an evaluation of compliance and noncompliance. This process identifies system, process, and procedural weaknesses that represent potential vulnerabilities.

Output from Step 3

The following result should be outputted upon successful completion of Step 3:

- A list of the system vulnerabilities that could be exercised by the potential threat sources

Step 4: Control Analysis

The goal of this step is to analyze the controls that have been implemented or are planned for implementation by the organization to minimize or eliminate the likelihood (or probability) of a threat's acting on a system's vulnerability.

> **NOTE** Because the risk assessment report is not an audit report, some sites might prefer to address the identified vulnerabilities as observations instead of findings in the risk assessment report.

To derive an overall likelihood rating that indicates the probability that a potential vulnerability might be exercised within the construct of the associated threat environment (see *Step 5: Likelihood Determination*), the implementation of current or planned controls must be considered. For example, a vulnerability (e.g., a system or procedural weakness) is not likely to be exercised or the likelihood is low if there is a low level of threat source interest or capability or if there are effective security controls that can eliminate—or reduce the magnitude of—harm.

The following paragraphs discuss control methods, control categories, and the control analysis technique.

Control Methods

Security controls encompass the use of technical and non-technical methods. Technical controls are safeguards that are incorporated into computer hardware, software, or firmware (for example, access control mechanisms, identification and authentication mechanisms, encryption methods, and intrusion detection software). Non-technical controls are management and operational controls, such as security policies, operational procedures, and personnel, physical, and environmental security.

Control Categories

The control categories for both technical and non-technical control methods can be further classified as either preventive or detective. These two subcategories are explained as follows:

Preventive controls. These inhibit attempts to violate security policy and include controls such as access control enforcement, encryption, and authentication.

Detective controls. These warn of violations or attempted violations of security policy and include controls such as audit trails, intrusion detection methods, and checksums.

The implementation of such controls during the risk mitigation process is the direct result of the identification of deficiencies in current or planned controls during the risk assessment process (for example, controls are not in place or controls are not properly implemented).

Control Analysis Technique

As discussed in Step 3, development of a security requirements checklist or the use of an available checklist will be helpful in analyzing controls in an efficient and systematic manner. The security requirements checklist can be used to validate security noncompliance as well as compliance. Therefore, it is essential to update such checklists to reflect changes in an organization's control environment (for example, changes in security policies, methods, and requirements) to ensure the validity of the checklist.

Output from Step 4

The following result should be output upon successful completion of Step 4:

- List of current or planned controls used for the IT system to mitigate the likelihood of a vulnerability being exercised and reduce the impact of such an adverse event

Step 5: Likelihood Determination

To derive an overall likelihood rating that indicates the probability that a potential vulnerability might be exercised within the construct of the associated threat environment; the following governing factors must be considered:

- Threat source motivation and capability
- Nature of the vulnerability
- Existence and effectiveness of current controls

The likelihood that a potential vulnerability could be exercised by a given threat-source can be qualitatively described as high, medium, or low. The selection of High, Moderate or Low, even if this is a qualitative analysis, should be based on as much evidence as possible. See *Step 3: Vulnerability-Threat Pairs*.

Table 5.5 describes these three likelihood levels.

Output from Step 5

The following result should be output upon successful completion of Step 5:

- Likelihood rating (High, Medium, Low)

Step 6: Impact Analysis

The next major step in measuring level of risk is to determine the adverse impact resulting from a successful threat source acting on a vulnerability. Before beginning the impact analysis, it is necessary to complete the system characterization, Step 1, to have the following necessary information:

- System mission (for example., the processes performed by the IT system)
- System and data criticality (for example, the system's value or importance to an organization)

Table 5.5   Likelihood Definitions

LIKELIHOOD LEVEL	LIKELIHOOD DEFINITION
High	The threat source is highly motivated and sufficiently capable, and controls to prevent the vulnerability from being exercised are ineffective.
Medium	The threat source is motivated and capable, but controls are in place that might impede successful exercise of the vulnerability.
Low	The threat source lacks motivation or capability, or controls are in place to prevent, or at least significantly impede, the vulnerability from being exercised.

System and Data Sensitivity

The information about system and data sensitivity can be obtained from existing organizational documentation, such as the mission impact analysis report or asset criticality assessment report. A mission impact analysis (also known as business impact analysis [BIA] for some organizations) prioritizes the impact levels associated with the compromise of an organization's information assets based on a qualitative or quantitative assessment of the sensitivity and criticality of those assets. An asset criticality assessment identifies and prioritizes the sensitive and critical organization information assets (for example, hardware, software, systems, services, and related technology assets) that support the organization's critical missions.

If this documentation does not exist or such assessments for the organization's IT assets have not been performed, the system and data sensitivity can be determined based on the level of protection required to maintain the system and data's availability, integrity, and confidentiality. Regardless of the method used to determine how sensitive an IT system and its data are, the system and information owners are the ones responsible for determining the impact level for their own system and information. Consequently, in analyzing impact, the appropriate approach is to interview the system and information owner(s).

Therefore, the adverse impact of a security event can be described in terms of loss or degradation of any, or a combination of any, of the following three security goals: integrity, availability, and confidentiality. The following list provides a brief description of each security goal and the consequence (or impact) of its not being met:

Loss of integrity.   System and data integrity refers to the requirement that information be protected from improper modification. Integrity is lost if unauthorized changes are made to the data or IT system by either intentional or accidental acts. If the loss of system or data integrity is not corrected, continued use of the contaminated system or corrupted data could result in inaccuracy, fraud, or erroneous decisions. Also, violation of integrity might be the first step in a successful attack against system availability or confidentiality. For all these reasons, loss of integrity reduces the assurance of an IT system.

Loss of availability.   If a mission-critical IT system is unavailable to its end users, the organization's mission might be affected. Loss of system functionality and operational effectiveness, for example, might result in loss of productive time, thus impeding the end users performance of their functions in supporting the organization's mission.

Loss of confidentiality.   System and data confidentiality refers to the protection of information from unauthorized disclosure. The impact of unauthorized disclosure of confidential information can range from the jeopardizing of national security to the disclosure of Privacy Act data.

Unauthorized, unanticipated, or unintentional disclosure could result in loss of public confidence, embarrassment, or legal action against the organization.

Some tangible impacts can be measured quantitatively in lost revenue, the cost of repairing the system, or the level of effort required to correct problems caused by a successful threat action. Other impacts (for example, loss of public confidence, loss of credibility, damage to an organization's interest) cannot be measured in specific units but can be qualified or described in terms of high, medium, and low impacts. Because of the generic nature of this discussion, this guide designates and describes only the qualitative categories (high, medium, and low) impact (see Table 5.6).

Quantitative versus Qualitative Assessment

In conducting the impact analysis, consideration should be given to the advantages and disadvantages of quantitative versus qualitative assessments (see the section *Analyzing Risk*, earlier in this chapter). The main advantage of the qualitative impact analysis is that it prioritizes the risks and identifies areas for immediate improvement in addressing the vulnerabilities. The disadvantage of the qualitative analysis is that it does not provide specific quantifiable measurements of the magnitude of the impacts, therefore making a cost-benefit analysis of any recommended controls difficult.

The major advantage of a quantitative impact analysis is that it provides a measurement of the impacts' magnitude, which can be used in the cost-benefit analysis of recommended controls. The disadvantage is that, depending on the numerical ranges used to express the measurement, the meaning of the quantitative impact analysis might be unclear, requiring the result to be interpreted in a qualitative manner. Additional factors often must be considered to determine the magnitude of impact. These might include, but are not limited to, the following factors:

- An estimation of the frequency of the threat-source acting on the vulnerability over a specified time period (for example, 1 year)
- An approximate cost for each occurrence of the threat-source acting on the vulnerability
- A weighted factor based on a subjective analysis of the relative impact of a specific threat-source acting on a specific vulnerability

Output from Step 6

The following result should be output upon successful completion of Step 6:

- Magnitude of impact (high, medium, or low)

Table 5.6   Magnitude of Impact Definitions

MAGNITUDE OF IMPACT	IMPACT DEFINITION
High	Exercise of the vulnerability (1) might result in the highly costly loss of major tangible assets or resources; (2) might significantly violate, harm, or impede an organization's mission, reputation, or interest; or (3) might result in death or serious injury.
Medium	Exercise of the vulnerability (1) might result in the costly loss of tangible assets or resources; (2) might violate, harm, or impede an organization's mission, reputation, or interest; or (3) might result in human injury.
Low	Exercise of the vulnerability (1) might result in the loss of some tangible assets or resources or (2) might noticeably affect an organization's mission, reputation, or interest.

Step 7: Risk Determination

The purpose of this step is to assess the level of risk to the IT system. The determination of risk for a particular threat/vulnerability pair can be expressed as a function of the following factors:

- The likelihood of a given threat-source attempting to act on a given vulnerability
- The magnitude of the impact should a threat-source successfully act on the vulnerability
- The adequacy of planned or existing security controls for reducing or eliminating risk

To measure risk, a risk scale and a risk-level matrix must be developed. The following sections present a standard risk-level matrix and the resulting risk levels.

Risk-Level Matrix

You can find the final determination of mission risk by multiplying the ratings assigned for threat likelihood (for example, probability) by the threat impact (or loss). Table 5.7 shows how the overall risk ratings might be determined based on inputs from the threat likelihood and threat impact categories. The following matrix measures 3x3 and shows threat likelihood (High, Medium, and Low) and threat impact (High, Medium, and Low). Depending on the site's requirements and the granularity of risk assessment desired, some sites might use a 4x4 or a 5x5 matrix. The latter can include Very Low/Very High threat likelihoods and Very Low/Very High threat impacts to generate a Very Low/Very High risk level. A Very High risk level might require possible system shutdown or stopping of all IT system integration and testing efforts.

The sample matrix in Table 5.7 also shows how the overall risk levels of High, Medium, and Low are derived. The determination of these risk levels or ratings might be subjective. The rationale for this justification can be explained in terms of the probability assigned for each threat likelihood level and a value assigned for each impact level. Here is an example:

- The probability assigned for each threat likelihood level is 1.0 for High, 0.5 for Medium, and 0.1 for Low.

- The value assigned for each impact level is 100 for High, 50 for Medium, and 10 for Low.

Description of Risk Level

Table 5.8 describes the risk levels shown in the previous matrix. This risk scale, with its ratings of High, Medium, and Low, represents the degree or level of risk to which an IT system, facility, or procedure might be exposed if a given vulnerability were exercised. The risk scale also presents actions that senior management, the mission owners, must take for each risk level.

Output from Step 7

The following result should be outputted upon successful completion of Step 7:

- Risk level (High, Medium, Low)

Table 5.7 Risk-Level Matrix

THREAT LIKELIHOOD		IMPACT	
Low (10)		Medium (50)	High (100)
High (1.0)	Low 10 X 1.0 = 10	Medium 50 X 1.0 = 50	High 100 X 1.0 = 100
Medium (0.5)	Low 10 X 0.5 = 5	Medium 50 X 0.5 = 25	Medium 100 X 0.5 = 50
Low (0.1)	Low 10 X 0.1 = 1	Low 50 X 0.1 = 5	Low 100 X 0.1 = 10

Risk Scale: High (51 to 100); Medium (11 to 50); Low (1 to 10)

Table 5.8 Risk Scale and Necessary Actions

RISK LEVEL	DESCRIPTION AND NECESSARY ACTIONS
High	If an observation or finding is evaluated as a high risk, there is a strong need for corrective measures. An existing system might continue to operate, but a corrective action plan must be put in place as soon as possible.
Medium	If an observation is rated as medium risk, corrective actions are needed and a plan must be developed to incorporate these actions within a reasonable period.
Low	If an observation is described as low risk, the system's DAA must determine whether corrective actions are still required or decide to accept the risk.

NOTE If the level indicated on certain items is so low as to be deemed "negligible" or not significant (for example, if its value is less than 1 on a risk scale of 1 to 100), you might wish to hold these ratings aside in a separate category in lieu of forwarding them to management for action. This course of action will enable you to make sure that the risk-level information is not overlooked when the next periodic risk assessment is conducted. This method of categorization also establishes a complete record of all risks identified in the analysis. These risks might move to a new risk level on a reassessment, perhaps because of a change in threat likelihood and/or impact. Thus, it is critical that their identification not be lost in the exercise.

Step 8: Control Recommendations

During this step of the process, controls that could mitigate or eliminate the identified risks, as appropriate to the organization's operations, are provided. The goal of the recommended controls is to reduce the level of risk to the IT system and its data to an acceptable level. The following factors should be considered in recommending controls and alternative solutions to minimize or eliminate identified risks:

- Effectiveness of recommended options (for example, system compatibility)
- Legislation and regulation
- Organizational policy
- Operational impact
- Safety and reliability

The control recommendations are the results of the risk assessment process and provide input to the risk mitigation process, during which the recommended procedural and technical security controls are evaluated, prioritized, and implemented.

> **NOTE** Not all possible recommended controls can be implemented to reduce loss. To determine which ones are required and appropriate for a specific organization, a cost-benefit analysis should be conducted for the proposed recommended controls to demonstrate whether the costs of implementing the controls can be justified by the reduction in the level of risk. In addition, the operational impact (for example, effect on system performance) and feasibility (for example, technical requirements and user acceptance) of introducing the recommended option should be evaluated carefully during the risk mitigation process.

Output from Step 8

The following result should be outputted upon successful completion of Step 8:

- Recommendation of control(s) and alternative solutions to mitigate risk

Step 9: Results Documentation

Once the risk assessment has been completed (threat sources and vulnerabilities identified, risk analyzed, and recommended controls provided), the results should be documented in an official report or briefing.

A risk assessment report (see Figure 5.2) is a management report that helps senior management—the mission owners—make decisions on policy, procedural, budget, and system operational and management changes. Unlike an audit or investigation report, which looks for wrongdoings, a risk assessment report should not be presented in an accusatory manner but as a systematic and analytical approach to assessing risk so that senior management will understand the risks and allocate resources to reduce and correct potential losses. For this reason, some people prefer to address the threat/vulnerability pairs as observations instead of findings in the risk assessment report.

Output from Step 9

The following result should be outputted upon successful completion of Step 9:

- Risk assessment report that describes the threats and vulnerabilities, measures the risk, and provides recommendations for control implementation.

EXECUTIVE SUMMARY

I. Introduction

- *Purpose*
- *Scope of this risk assessment*

Describe the system components, elements, users, field site locations (if any), and any other details about the system to be considered in the assessment.

II. Risk Assessment Approach

Briefly describe the approach used to conduct the risk assessment, such as.
- *The participants (e.g., risk assessment team members)*
- *The technique used to gather information (e.g., the use of tools, questionnaires)*
- *The development and description of risk scale (e.g., a 3 × 3, 4 × 4 , or 5 × 5 risk-level matrix)*

III. System Characterization

Characterize the system, including hardware (server, router, switch), software (e.g., application, operating system, protocol), system interfaces (e.g., communication link), data, and users. Provide connectivity diagram or system input and output flowchart to delineate the scope of this risk assessment effort.

IV. Threat Statement

Compile and list the potential threat-sources and associated threat actions applicable to the system assessed.

V. Risk Assessment Results

List the observations (vulnerability/threat pairs). Each observation must include:

- *Observation number and brief description of observation (e.g., Observation 1: User system passwords can be guessed or cracked)*
- *A discussion of the threat-source and vulnerability pair*
- *Identification of existing mitigating security controls*
- *Likelihood discussion and evaluation (e.g., High, Medium, or Low likelihood)*
- *Impact analysis discussion and evaluation (e.g., High, Medium, or Low impact)*
- *Risk rating based on the risk-level matrix (e.g., High, Medium, or Low risk level)*
- *Recommended controls or alternative options for reducing the risk.*

VI. Summary

Total the number of observations. Summarize the observations, the associated risk levels, the recommendations, and any comments in a table format to facilitate the implementation of recommended controls during the risk mitigation process.

Figure 5.2 A sample risk assessment report.

Response

Although management has a responsibility for ensuring the development of sound approaches when responding to incidents, the SSCP can take the lead in this area by developing responses for predetermined scenarios and by being prepared to act when a response is needed.

What Is a Response?

As we discussed in Chapter 1, "The Journey toward Information Security: An Overview," in order to communicate effectively we must use the same lexicon. The term response refers to *incident response*, which describes those activities that are performed when a security-related incident occurs that has the potential for, or has caused, adverse effects to the system or enterprise. Without a pre-developed response plan, there is no chance to determine whether an attack is widespread or focused on a specific system. The incident response capability must have the capability to act on incidents and with procedures in place, rather than reacting to incidents.

Is your situation an incident or an emergency? Traditionally, when we discuss incident response, we are discussing the computer emergency response capability or team (CERC or CERT). When this term came into existence after the Morris Worm Internet attack in 1988, everyone used the same term: CERT. Carnegie Mellon University (CMU) set up the CERT/CC in November 1988, and all was going well until the military services decided they had to have one, too. So, there was the AFCERT and the ACERT. The only problem was the U.S. Navy, however. The Navy did not have emergencies—it only had incidents—and that was the justification used to establish a Navy CIRT. The concept of CERT has grown and evolved since then and now includes many forensic activities as well as contingency operations (see Figure 5.3). For the rest of this section, we will use the term *incident* as the larger collection of all incidents including emergencies.

In addition to tremendous growth in the scope of incident response, the following international organizations have sprung up to provide critical tools and support capabilities to the security practitioner:

- On the international level (for multi-country incidents), there is the International Consortium of Computer Incident and Security Teams: FIRST (www.first.org).

- We worked with the Australian Federal Police and their computer crime staff a long time ago. Together, we set a trap and caught and prosecuted Rock*, a cracker in the early 1990s: AUSCERT at www.aucert.org.au.

- In Japan, try www.jpcert.or.jp.
- In Germany, try www.bsi.bund.de.
- In Poland, there is www.cert.pl.
- In Argentina, contact the Argentinian CERT at www.arcert.gov.ar.
- In Canada, you have www.acert.ca.

In the United States, there are several levels of organizations:

- At the national level, for private companies and government use there is:
  - CERT/CC at www.CERT.org
  - U.S. *National Infrastructure Protection Center* (NIPC) at www.nipc.gov
- For the federal government, civilian, and military, if you think it has national security implications, the civilian agencies or the military can contact the *National Security Incident Response Capability* (NSIRC) that the NSA hosts.
- For U.S. civilian agencies, if they do not have their own internal agency, they can visit www.FEDCIRC.gov.
- The U.S. Department of Energy's Computer Incident Advisory Capability
- *NASA Automated Systems Incident Response Capability* (NASIR) at www.nasirc.nasa.gov/nasa
- For the Department of Defense or Joint Commands, visit www.cert.mil.
  - Army CERT: www.fiwc.navy.mil
  - Navy NAVCIRT: www.infosec.nosc.mil
  - Air Force CERT: afcert.csap.af.mil

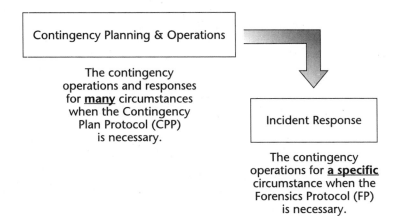

Figure 5.3   Relationship of incident response to contingency planning and forensics.

There are many types of incidents that you will respond to as a part of your work. We have categorized some of them in Table 5.9.

NOTE In most cases, the type of response is not driven by the type of incident but by the potential impact or risk to the system's assets.

Table 5.9 Sources and Examples of Incidents

GENERAL SOURCE OF INCIDENTS		EXAMPLES
Unintentional	Human related	Operations Error causing system crash
		User downloads and executes virus code
		Human error
	Non-human related	Lightning strike causing power failure then a system crash
		Failure of roof during a rainstorm
		Equipment failure
Intentional	Human related	Sabotage
		Trojan horse or other malicious code
		Hacker
		Insider or disgruntled employee
		Misuse
		Unauthorized access
		Unauthorized privileges
	Non-human	Bomb
		Terrorist Act
Either Intentional or Unintentional	Unknown	Explosions
		Viral infections
		Fires
		Denial of Service (DoS)
		Unauthorized use of services

Incident Response Steps

Currently, there is no single, worldwide-accepted practice for incident response. The approach we present here has been used within several organizations and over time has proven to be a successful approach. To emphasize the need for an incident response capability, the statistics from CC/CERT's Web site show that the number of incidents have risen drastically—from 3,734 in 1998 to 52,658 in 2001. Already, there have been 73,359 incidents reported for the first through third quarters of 2002.

How Do You Plan?

There is empirical evidence that strongly suggests that money spent on planning before an incident occurs is the best-spent money. Here is where the correlation between contingency planning, forensics, incident response, and even administration merge. By developing or assisting in the development of detailed contingency plans and having adequate security administration, you will have more than 75 percent of the incident response process already documented. When you have plans, you are able to act and not react. When you have a plan and follow that plan during an incident the results have far fewer mistakes. We discussed administration in Chapter 3, "Domain 2: Administration," and we will discuss contingency planning later in this chapter—but we will deal with certain aspects of both topics here. Let's discuss the incident response planning process.

The first part of the planning process is to determine the incidents for which you will prepare. The easy answer is "everything." The realistic answer, however, is that even if you think you have covered everything, something will eventually happen for which you have not prepared. For that reason, your planning should be incremental in nature. Tackle the incidents with the biggest potential negative impact first. Then, you should continue to develop your plan as you have time and other resources. To help you decide what incidents should have procedures and processes developed, we have listed some common incidents in Table 5.10. These should, depending on your specific environment, have contingency/response plans at a minimum.

These incidents can occur alone or in combinations. The level of detail for procedures and processes will vary, depending on the criticality of your system as well as the practicality of documenting everything.

Table 5.10   How Incidents Align to System/Network Impact

IMPACT TO SYSTEM/NETWORK	INCIDENTS
Destruction	A/C
	Power
	Fire
	Lightening/tornadoes/hurricanes/floods
	Other environmental problems
	Virus or malware
	Misuse/abuse of system or services by insider/disgruntled employee
	Bomb or other sabotage
	Hardware failures
	S/W failures
Disclosure	Perimeter devices failure
	Active intrusion
	Virus or malware
	Misuse/abuse of system or services by insider/disgruntled employee
	Evacuations
	Hardware failures
	S/W failures
Modification	Data corruption or loss
	Virus or malware
	Misuse/abuse of system or services by insider/disgruntled employee
	S/W failures
Denial of service	Environment failures (see above)
	Communications failure
	Reduced or no network services
	ISP not available
	Virus or malware
	Active intrusion

Table 5.10   *(continued)*

IMPACT TO SYSTEM/NETWORK	INCIDENTS
	Misuse/abuse of system or services by insider/disgruntled employee
	Bomb or other sabotage
	Evacuations
	Hardware failures
	S/W failures

As part of your administration duties, you have documented *standard operating procedures* (SOPs) that are step-by-step procedures for conducting most functions associated with your system. These are the basis of your system operations. You cannot build contingency plans for abnormal operations without having the normal operations documented; at least, you should not. If you have SOPs, that is good. If you do not, you need to get them in place. The following are the SOPs that should be developed initially:

- Security administration
- Public access servers
- Reporting procedures
- Systems administration
- Operations log
- Backup procedures
- Training procedures

Your organization should insist on it. Not having SOPs is a significant vulnerability, because only the system administrators know how to accomplish critical tasks: it is called key personnel dependency.

NOTE Without SOPs, your organization is vulnerable.

So, you have documented procedures for critical tasks associated with your system. What is the state of your contingency plan? Refer to the later section, *Recovery* to build adequate plans for contingency operations. If you already have detailed contingency plans and SOPS, you are closing in on incident response. As shown in Figure 5.4, you need to instill a continuous improvement process over the incident response activities. You can improve each and every time you have to respond.

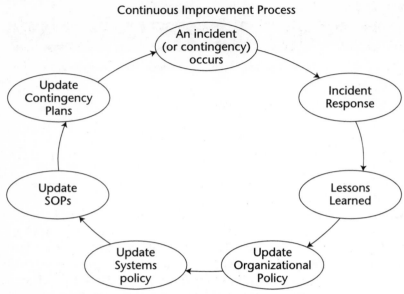

Figure 5.4 The lifecycle of an incident response capability.

NOTE The difference in contingency planning and incident response planning is the FOCUS of the actions, not the actions themselves.

Contingency plans are exercised (implemented, activated, and used) when an abnormal activity or event takes place. An incident is just one example of when a contingency plan would be activated. All incidents are examples of events that should be covered by contingency plans, but there are contingency plans for events or activities that are not categorized as incidents. The difference is whether there is a *potential for a security breach*. Use the flowchart in Figure 5.5 to assist you with analyzing the situation.

If there is no potential for a security breach, then the contingency plan is exercised along with the contingency protocol. When there is a potential for a security breach, it is an incident; the contingency plan is exercised and the incident response protocol is followed. If there is a real threat of a security breach, then the forensics protocol is simultaneously followed. That process is complicated, so here is an example.

Still using Figure 5.5 as a basis, let's say that a firewall goes down. The following is the process you would go through to determine which protocol to use:

SCENARIO 1

1. What is the situation? After inspection, it is determined that the firewalls power supply got fried.

2. What could the implications be as a result? There could be an opportunity for unauthorized access to the system and the disclosure of sensitive information to the outside world.

3. What is the actual change in our vulnerability? The firewalls that are in use, fail-safe (closing all ports).

4. What could have caused this situation? There could be intentional sabotage, or it could have been an environmental issue such as a storm.

5. What did cause this situation? After discussing with the staff in the room, the agent that caused the failure was a lightening strike during the current storm. Therefore, there is no concern of that lightening being wielded by an adversary; there is no potential for the disclosure of sensitive information nor unauthorized access.

This time, we change the scenario a bit.

SCENARIO 2

1. What is the situation? (Apparent misuse of privileges by a user.)

2. What could the implications be as a result? There could be an opportunity for disclosure of sensitive information; the user could cause DoS, destruction, or modification of data.

3. What is the actual change in our vulnerability? We are very vulnerable to a user who has significant privileges.

4. What could have caused this situation? There could be a hacker masquerading as a user, or it could be a disgruntled employee, an insider attack, or simply misuse.

5. What caused this situation? After a quick analysis, the user is not logged in from a normal location, nor does he *ever* log in late at night. At this point, with this much information the situation becomes an incident because there is the potential that a security breach is occurring or has occurred.

The potential for security breach directs that the forensics protocol be followed. Therefore, there is no concern of that lightning being wielded by an adversary, and there is no potential for the disclosure of sensitive information nor unauthorized access.

If the second scenario had occurred but the user was typically on at night and normally accessed the system from the present location, it would still be an incident because the potential existed that the user was out to cause some damage just by misusing privileges.

The identification and analysis of the potential incident is absolutely critical. Figure 5.5 formalizes the two scenarios we just explored.

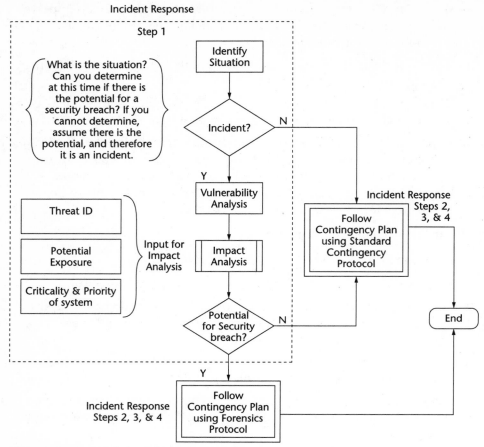

Figure 5.5 Determining which protocol to use.

The following are the planning activities we must document:

1. Develop SOPs. We discuss SOPs earlier in this section and include the following procedures for incident response:

   Identify.   You cannot act on a situation if you do not know that it exists. In addition to audit tools, intrusion detection systems and network monitoring are great assets for identifying incidents early. Accurate verification of an incident is vital and therefore should involve the expertise of the security staff.

   Contain.   The purpose is to limit the scope and magnitude of an incident and to keep the incident from becoming a larger problem.

   Eradicate.   Depending on the nature of the incident, eradicating the cause might involve:

- Purging malicious code from all systems and media
- Completely restoring applications and data from the most recent unaffected backup
- Complete rebuild of servers (new operating system and services)
- Assisting law enforcement with the collection of evidence and apprehension of the hacker

Recover.   Actions to recover from security breaches and correct system failures should be carefully and formally controlled. The procedures should ensure that only clearly identified and authorized staff are allowed access to live systems and data, that all actions taken are documented in detail, that the integrity of business systems and controls is confirmed with minimal delay, that actions are reported to management, and that the incident/emergency is reviewed for lessons learned.

2. Develop Contingency Plans. See *Recovery: The Third Part of Contingency Planning*.

3. Develop protocols:

CP.   See the section on contingency planning to develop the procedures for contingency activities. The primary focus of contingency protocol is to get the critical business functions up and running as soon as possible. This protocol is unacceptable when an analysis must be accomplished or when a potential security breach has occurred.

FP.   See the section on forensics to develop procedures for the collection of audit trails and similar evidence—the communication and documentation of the process. Maintain a provable chain of custody. Logs should be maintained to track suspicious events, the name of the system, the time, and other details related to the observations. Even though these might not seem pertinent at the time, these details might prove to be quite beneficial in fixing the problem and supporting possible lawsuits. The forensics protocol is based on documenting for evidence and not, as the contingency plan protocol does, on the resumption of critical processes as soon as possible.

4. Develop a process for ID and analysis of the situation. See Figure 5.5.

5. Develop a notification process; that is, develop escalation procedures for notifying:

- Local staff
- Senior management
- Your *Internet service provider* (ISP)

- Local law enforcement
- Incident response centers

6. Develop roles, responsibilities, and authorities for contingency/ incident response operations. It is our experience that you must have the authority to act when an incident is occurring. Typically, that authority is greater than during normal operations. For example, you must have the authority (or access to the authority) to shut down the operational systems, disconnect the ISP, shut down all network connections to the outside, and so on.

7. Create a hard copy secondary repository (three-ring binder) of all plans and procedures. The idea of having everything online is terrific until your systems are compromised. Just assume that you will not have access to your online data. Fall back to the hard copy.

Recovery

Although management has the responsibility for ensuring the development of sound approaches to recover from incidents, the SSCP should take the lead in this area by developing responses for predetermined scenarios. The entire contingency planning process excludes the possibility that personnel safety or life is in jeopardy. It deals with the systems, networks, information, and other system-related assets. Under any circumstance that places life or safety at risk, your primary concern should be for yourself and your staff—following normal fire/safety evacuation procedures when possible.

What Is Contingency Planning?

We have discussed types of contingency plans in the previous section regarding incident response. Contingency planning normally consists of three separate activities: emergency operations, also known as contingency operations; backup plans and procedures, so everyone knows the location and dates of backups; and restoration or recovery plans. Out of that initial three-part contingency planning process, several specific types of contingency plans have evolved—each with a slightly different focus and used in various situations. For example:

Contingency Plans (CP).   The documented, organized plan for emergency response, backup operations, and recovery maintained by an activity as part of its security program that will ensure the availability of critical resources and facilitates the continuity of operations in an emergency situation.

Disaster Recovery Plans **(DRPs).**   The plans and procedures that have been developed to recover from a disaster that has made the system operations impossible.

Continuity of Operations Plans **(COOP).**   The plans and procedures documented to ensure continued critical operations during any period where normal operations are impossible.

Business Continuity Plans **(BCP).**   The plans and procedures developed that identify and prioritize the critical business functions that must be preserved; the procedures for continued operations of those critical business functions during any disruption (other than a disaster) to normal operations.

Two definitions appear to be almost identical, and another appears to be a subset of the others. Why is that? Recall our discussion in Chapter 1 regarding the lexicon. Contingency planning has come to the system security discipline from the mega-computer centers, where they had total responsibility for protecting the information and for providing access to it. The COOPs have arrived from the military while DRPs and BCPs have come to us from the business environment. Because we are learning information system security, we will focus on contingency planning.

A standard CP contains the plan and procedures for three elements: (1) emergency response, (2) backup operations, and (3) recovery. A CP is normally associated with the security plans of the system or enterprise and plays a supporting role in system security. While a CP can be quite complicated, its validity is unquestionable because it draws its information on the criticality of the information from the system risk analysis. The risk analysis provides direction regarding critical business functions, system characteristics, and configuration. If, on the other hand, the risk analysis identifies no critical business functions and/or data, then a CP can be as simple as a one-page document that tells the reader to write with pen and paper. Let's review the three parts of the CP, one at a time.

Emergency Response

This response is also known as contingency operations, because not all contingencies are deemed emergencies. There are generally two types of contingency operations: (1) actions based on an immediate (and temporary) situation and (2) actions taken based on the foreknowledge that the incident might *not* be short term. The contingencies can range from a hard drive crash to a disaster. The impact can be to just the communications lines to the power, or it can affect the facility, the building, the community, or the general area. A CP provides processes and procedures to keep the critical functions running under any of those contingencies. When the impact is significant, such as a disaster, the CP provides the processes and procedures for recovering from a disaster in the near term and then final restoration.

The way a contingency plan provides processes for contingency operations is through the use of scenarios. As shown in the following scenario by predetermining many contingencies, we are able to document the steps we go through in that situation. This action minimizes the chances for a mistake and maximizes the availability of critical business functions.

SCENARIO: MAJOR APPLICATION OR OPERATING SYSTEM (SOFTWARE) FAILURE

RISK LEVEL:
Low

ASSETS REQUIRED:
The *Systems Administrator* (SA) is required to support this scenario. SAs need to troubleshoot and repair application and/or system failure and reinitialize system and reconnect networks upon the restoration of functionality.

LOCAL IMPACT:
Possible loss of a mission-critical application or system

REMOTE IMPACT:
Possible loss of connectivity to regional and national offices

CONTINGENCY PLAN:
In the event of a major s/w failure:

1. Transition all critical users to an alternate system.

2. Restore the system from its most current backup.

3. If that fails, restore the system from the protected original source (CDs, tape, and so on).

4. Restore data files if required.

MITIGATION:
The system has been rigorously tested.
The northeast regional office is set up as our alternate site.
On-site backups exist.
Off-site backups exist.
The original s/w is located with off-site backups.

RESTORE NORMAL OPERATIONS:
Test the system to ensure that it is operational and functioning correctly.
Redirect any users who were affected back to our site.

SCENARIO: VIRUS ACTIVITY

RISK LEVEL:
Medium

ASSETS REQUIRED:
System administrator is needed to repair any damage done by the virus and prevent further attacks

LOCAL IMPACT:
A possible loss of network functions until the source of the virus is discovered and eradicated

REMOTE IMPACT:
Possible spread of virus to/from remote locations

CONTINGENCY PLAN:
In the event of a virus infection:

1. Investigate the spread of the virus.
2. Isolate known infected system(s).
3. Allow users of non-infected systems to continue to work.

    If you cannot get control over the virus within 30 minutes and before it spreads significantly, then you must:

1. Disconnect the LAN from the WAN until the virus is under control.
2. Notify the department head of issue.
3. The SA will disconnect all users from the LAN.
4. Follow local SOPs to detect and remove virus-infected files.
5. Restore files from the backup tape if necessary to remove the virus.

MITIGATION:
Virus-checking software is installed on all workstations and servers. The virus definition files are constantly updated.
   Backups are done for all mission-critical systems data to ensure survivability.

RESTORE NORMAL OPERATIONS:
Ensure that all systems and the LAN are operational and virus free.
Notify users of system availability.

Backup Operations

This part of the CP is absolutely vital to ensure that the plan works when needed. Backup operations include many functions, some of which we list here:

- What to back up, how often to back it up, and how long to keep backups
- Whether to use offsite storage and who is authorized to transport backups to offsite locations

- When backups should be placed onsite and when they should be placed offsite

- How to inventory and retrieve a backup

- What storage media should be used for short-term and long-term backups?

The way a contingency plan provides for backup operations is by having the plan that holds the answers to those functions. So, when a situation exists that requires contingency operations, the backup plan will tell you where your information is stored, how old it is, and the media on which it is written.

SCENARIO: CORRUPT INPUT DATA

RISK/LEVEL:
Low

ASSETS REQUIRED:
The network team might be required to determine whether network corruption occurred. The LAN administrator might be required to redirect users to a mirror site. The SA will be required to restore system functions and connectivity.

LOCAL IMPACT:
A temporary loss of critical business functions

REMOTE IMPACT:
A possible spread of corrupt data to/from other sites

CONTINGENCY PLAN:
In the event that something should happen:

1. Transfer inoperable functions to the northeast regional office.

2. Troubleshoot to determine the cause. Refer to local *standard operating procedures* (SOPs).

3. Restore system data from the backup tapes. Refer to the local SOPs.

MITIGATION:

1. Nightly backups are stored on-site.

2. Weekly backups are stored off-site.

3. Restore normal operations.

4. Verify that the system is operational and functioning correctly.

5. Redirect any users who were sent to the northeast regional office.

6. Notify users.

Restoration and Recovery

There are three recovery options:

- Recovery at the primary operating site (home)
- Recovery to an alternate site for critical functions
- Restoration of the full system after a catastrophic loss (disaster)

The process of restoring services is time-consuming and costly, except when recovering from the smallest of events.

The CP plan's restoration section should contain the steps necessary to operate at alternate sites and return to normal operations at the primary site, including equipment lists, software lists, furniture, racks, power requirements, and the like. If you are in private industry, work with the insurance company to determine what information they will need, and then build your plan based on that information. Determine timeframes for replacement and whether rental equipment is reimbursable. If you are in civil service, identify the replacement costs for all IT-related assets because there is no insurance in the federal government, and locate other agencies that might use the same technology and that would support you in the event of a localized event.

There are three types of alternate sites for operations: a hot site, a warm site, and a cold site, and these facilities are normally contracted through subscription services. The type of site you would choose, if any, for a contingency site should be based on your risk assessment. If your system/network/data is critical enough to warrant having an offsite facility at all, then which type of site is a decision that you need to assess. The following are some of the questions to ask to determine which type of site you need: What is your business need for the most critical data? Is it less than one hour, one to four hours, four to eight hours, the next day, two days, three days, five days, or greater than five days? If the answer is more than three days, you do not need any alternative facility. If it is less than one hour, you need the whole hot site configuration. The other types of sites fit in between, depending on your environment.

Hot site. The hot site is a physical location where you can walk in with your data and start processing your critical business functions. A hot site contains the power, *heating, ventilation, and air conditioning* (HVAC), connectivity, the servers, workstations, and peripheral devices that support your critical applications and even your software. It is set aside exclusively for your organization.

It might even contain a mirror of your data. The major advantage of a hot site is that you show up and start processing. The major drawback is the price of such a site. It ends up costing as much as the normal operational facility, so you pay double just in case.

Warm site.   A warm site is much better than a cold site: It is a computer facility. It has the power, HVAC, connectivity, and servers that should be compatible. You must get the workstations (perhaps), software, data, and personnel to the site and set it all up in order to begin processing. The advantage to this type of alternate site is that it is not all that expensive. The major drawback is that the site is not preconfigured and it will take time to set up.

Cold site.   The cold site is a facility that has power and HVAC. It does not have communications or computer equipment. In the event that you had to set up an alternate site for processing, the cold site is not a real option. Many large companies have a cold site that they share across the organization, and it is the least-expensive solution for alternative site locations. If you had internal resources for running cables, a warehouse full of servers and network devices, and a large IT budget, then it might be a cost-effective alternative.

CP Testing

A CP must be tested, because testing provides an opportunity to identify weaknesses in the plan and to ensure that the plan works. Testing also verifies that the CP meets the organization's needs and requirements, and the CP test must identify a leader. This person will direct the activities of the exercise by defining any tests and the actual CP operations when required. Each time the CP test is performed, it should be divided into the following six phases:

Preparedness.   Preparedness refers to what needs to be done prior to an event. This phase should cover reviewing the contingency plans and updating them to make certain they cover what is needed, such as points of contact information. In addition, if the test to be conducted is going to involve company personnel, clear testing is needed with physical security staff and human resources prior to doing activities such as fire drills or other evacuation activities that could result in harm to a non-participant in the drill.

Occurrence.   Occurrence refers to steps to take when the event occurs. The step-by-step process should include what to do, who will do what, where it should be done, and where everything is located must be documented and followed.

Activation.   Activation means the steps required to begin recovery. Typically, the leader calls for recovery to begin once he or she has quickly assessed the actions taken to move from normal operations to contingency operations.

Ongoing.   Ongoing activities continue recovery and maintain operations at an alternate site.

Restitution.   Restitution refers to activities that are required to restore/ rebuild service or communications to the primary operating site. These activities should be documented in as much detail as possible, including *points of contact* (POCs) for external services (the building owners, the electric company, your computer vendors, and so on). If the real event you were responding to was major, such as a nature disaster or a terrorist attack of your building, you will not have that information. Remember that you will need lots of details about your system, your data, your communications, and so on if you are to rebuild.

Closeout.   Closeout refers to activities required prior to declaring that recovery is complete. In addition to this last phase, the closeout, the leader typically has a debriefing to the contingency players a day or two after the test. There, he or she will go over what went well and what did not go so well. That way, the preparedness can begin again, and next time will be better.

CP testing can be performed regularly without tremendous cost by using various forms of testing. There are five types of testing:

- Checklist test
- Table top (structured walkthrough) test
- Simulation test
- Parallel test
- Full-interruption test

We discuss each of these in more detail in the following paragraphs.

Checklist Test

During a checklist test, copies of the CP are distributed to each participant. The plan is reviewed to ensure that all procedures and critical areas are addressed. It is also reviewed to ensure that POCs are accurate and that their contact information is current. This type of test should be performed at least annually. While it is the least complex and takes the least amount of effort and resources, it is still a good way to address the adequacy of your contingency plan.

Table Top (Structured Walkthrough) Test

In a table top test situation, usually some of the CP participants meet in a large conference room and go through the entire plan step by step. This run-through enables a group to uncover potential issues that might not come up except in a real contingency operation scenario. The CP leader determines the scenario for the test and assigns responsibility to participants for varying portions of the CP test (just as in a real CP operation). The scenario might be as simple as the system is down. This type of test is more detailed than the checklist because each step is considered in light of the actual scenario. For example, in one table top test we have recognized that we needed someone from the finance staff to be part of the CP team because they are the only staff members who have purchasing authority. We would have been unable to execute the real contingency plan had we not discovered this omission during testing.

Simulation Test

A simulation test is almost as real as it gets. All the participants, business members, technical, and support—as defined in the CP—are assigned their CP roles. They might go through all the exact steps they would in the event of a real contingency operation and take their queue and their assignments from the CP leader. The leader might designate a specific time, such as 10:45 A.M., for the start of the test. At 10:45 A.M., he or she declares that the external network has been shut down by the phone company; emergency line repairs will take 16 hours. The CP leader might then declare the potential impact of the event. Our payload goes up on the NASA shuttle tomorrow morning at 8 A.M., and we will not be able to monitor or manipulate it as was intended. That is the event that is being simulated. In addition to the event being simulated, the alternate site (if there is one) is also simulated. The CP leader should designate a room separate from their normal operations area that will be considered the alternate site location. Then, the participants, business, tech, and support get the resources they are responsible for, and they go to their assigned location. If they are responsible for others, they have to locate those people and deliver them to the predetermined location. This action is a very good teaching tool, because things happen; people forget things; they do not have transportation; grab the wrong backup; and so on. The goal of this test is to ensure that all participants are able to fulfill their responsibilities and nothing crucial has been overlooked. This type of test, because it is more extensive than the previous two, should not be done often. Once a year is adequate for most organizations, but again it really depends on the criticality of your information/system/network.

Parallel Test

A parallel test is a complete live test of contingency operations without taking the operational system down. Normally, this test is complete—exercising a contingency that requires evacuation of the primary operational site, relocation to the alternate site; setting up and processing successfully from the alternate site; and reconstituting operations back at the primary site without losing data. The primary objective of this test is to make certain that the alternative site's systems, software, and our data can and does function as we intend under a contingency operation. All designated staff actually move to the alternate site and start working at the alternate site. This type of test is very complex, costly, and is only second in exhaustiveness to the full interruption test. This test does *not* shut down the primary operations. If something is discovered that prevents alternative site critical operations, the business will not suffer the consequences because the live system and the test system are running in parallel.

Full-Interruption Test

A full interruption test is a complete live test of contingency operations. The CP team acts as if an event has occurred that has activated the contingency plan. This form of test is used mainly to determine whether the team is adequately trained and whether the plan will really work when needed. The time when the CP must be executed is not the time to find out that the CP team is not responsive or that a plan does not work. This test is a very expensive one: all operations cease and contingency operations take over, people must be transported, alternate sites must be engaged, and so on. Normally, only business-critical operations are reinitiated at the alternate site. Once the test is successfully processing at the alternate site, the CP team must reconstitute the operations back at the primary site without losing data.

There are ways to engage in most of these test types without activating the entire CP team or the entire contingency plan. The following are partial tests that can be accomplished. By running partial tests throughout the year, the CP staff maintains their skills:

Loss of communications site (data).   This scenario can be performed in a checklist or table top test format with minimal resources and costs. This test can be performed by the technical staff.

Loss of all audio/data communications.   This scenario can be performed in a checklist or table top test format with minimal resources and costs. You can perform this test with technical staff, as well.

Loss of business functions.   This scenario can be performed in a checklist or table top test format with minimal resources and costs. This test should be done at least twice a year as company core business functions change in this economic environment. It would be devastating to have the incorrect critical functions identified for your company.

Loss of physical facility.   This scenario can be performed in a checklist or table top test format with minimal resources and costs. In this scenario, having facilities staff and physical security support would be beneficial in discovering any pitfalls in the existing plan.

Contingency plan testing is an excellent way to get the staff trained on the contingency operations.

NOTE If you run a contingency plan test for the loss of all communications, do *not* rely on cell phones as a viable alternative for contacting critical personnel. Based on our personal experience of September 11, 2001, when a real disaster occurred at the Pentagon and in New York, cell phone signals were not available and people could not reach their points of contact.

Sample Questions

1. Which choice gives the BEST description of risk reduction?

   a. Altering elements of the enterprise in response to a risk analysis

   b. Removing all risk to the enterprise at any cost

   c. Assigning any costs associated with risk to a third party

   d. Assuming all costs associated with the risk internally

2. Which choice is an example of a incident due to a human event, rather than a non-human incident?

   a. Sabotage

   b. Financial collapse

   c. Structure collapse

   d. Utility failure

3. Place the following backup processing alternatives in order from the least-expensive solution to the most expensive:

   a. Warm site

   b. Hot site

   c. Cold site

   d. Mutual aid agreement

4. Which group represents the MOST likely source of an asset loss through inappropriate computer use?

   a. Crackers

   b. Employees

   c. Hackers

   d. Flood

5. Which statement about risk is not accurate?

   a. Risk is identified and measured by performing a risk analysis.

   b. Risk is controlled through the application of safeguards and countermeasures.

   c. Risk is managed by periodically reviewing and taking responsible actions based on the risk.

   d. Risk can be completely eliminated through risk management.

6. Which statement most accurately describes contingency operations and recovery?

    a. The function of identifying, evaluating (measuring), and controlling risk

    b. Activities that are performed when a security-related incident occurs

    c. Planned activities that enable the critical business functions to return to normal operations

    d. Transferring risk to a third-party insurance carrier

7. Which choice is NOT a commonly accepted definition for a disaster?

    a. An occurrence that is outside the normal computing function

    b. An occurrence or imminent threat to the entity of widespread or severe damage, injury, loss of life, or loss of property

    c. An emergency that is beyond the normal response resources of the entity

    d. A suddenly occurring event that has a long-term negative impact on social life

8. Which choice MOST accurately describes a threat?

    a. Any weakness in an information system

    b. Protective controls

    c. Multi-layered controls

    d. Potential for a source to exploit a specific vulnerability

9. What is considered the major disadvantage to employing a "hot" site for disaster recovery?

    a. Exclusivity is assured for processing at the site.

    b. Annual testing is required to maintain the site.

    c. The site is immediately available for recovery.

    d. Maintaining the site is expensive.

10. Which choice MOST accurately describes a safeguard?

    a. Potential for a source to exploit a specific vulnerability

    b. Controls in place that provide some amount of protection for the asset

    c. Weakness in internal controls that could be exploited by a threat or threat agent

    d. A control designed to counteract an asset

11. Which choice is NOT an accurate statement about an organization's incident-handling response capability?

    a. It should be used to provide the ability to respond quickly and effectively to an incident.

    b. It should be used to prevent future damage from incidents.

    c. It should be used to detect and punish senior-level executive wrong-doing.

    d. It should be used to contain and repair damage done from incidents.

12. Which choice is NOT a role or responsibility of the person designated to manage the contingency planning process?

    a. Providing direction to senior management

    b. Providing stress-reduction programs to employees after an event

    c. Ensuring the identification of all critical business functions

    d. Integrating the planning process across business units

13. Which choice MOST accurately describes a countermeasure?

    a. An event with the potential to harm an information system through unauthorized access

    b. Controls implemented as a direct result of a security analysis

    c. The *Annualized Rate of Occurrence* (ARO) multiplied by the *Single Loss Exposure* (SRO); ARO × SLE

    d. A company resource that could be lost due to an incident

14. Which disaster recovery/emergency management plan testing type is considered the most cost-effective and efficient way to identify areas of overlap in the plan before conducting more demanding training exercises?

    a. Full-scale exercise

    b. Walk-through drill

    c. Table-top exercise test

    d. Evacuation drill

15. Which choice MOST closely depicts the difference between qualitative and quantitative risk analysis?

    a. A quantitative RA does not use the hard costs of losses, and a qualitative RA does.

    b. A quantitative RA makes a cost-benefit analysis simpler.

    c. A quantitative RA results in a subjective (High, Medium, or Low) result.

    d. A quantitative RA cannot be automated.

16. Which choice is an incorrect description of a control?

    a. Detective controls discover attacks and trigger preventative or corrective controls.

    b. Controls are the countermeasures for vulnerabilities.

    c. Corrective controls reduce the effect of an attack.

    d. Corrective controls reduce the likelihood of a deliberate attack.

17. What is the main advantage of using a qualitative impact analysis over a quantitative analysis?

    a. Identifies areas for immediate improvement.

    b. Provides a rationale for finding effective security controls.

    c. Makes a cost-benefit analysis simpler.

    d. Provides specific measurements of the impacts' magnitude.

18. Which choice is NOT a common information-gathering technique when performing a risk analysis?

    a. Distributing a questionnaire

    b. Employing automated risk assessment tools

    c. Interviewing terminated employees

    d. Reviewing existing policy documents

19. Put the following general steps in a qualitative risk analysis in order:

    a. The team prepares its findings and presents them to management.

    b. A scenario is written to address each identified threat.

    c. Business unit managers review the scenario for a reality check.

    d. The team works through each scenario by using a threat, asset, and safeguard.

20. Which choice is usually the number one-used criterion to determine the classification of an information object?

    a. Useful life

    b. Value

    c. Age

    d. Personal association

21. What is the prime objective of risk management?

    a. Reduce the risk to a tolerable level.

    b. Reduce all risk regardless of cost.

    c. Transfer any risk to external third parties.

    d. Prosecute any employees that are violating published security policies.

22. Which choice best describes a business asset?

    a. Events or situations that could cause a financial or operational impact to the organization

    b. Protection devices or procedures in place that reduce the effects of threats

    c. Competitive advantage, credibility, or goodwill

    d. Personnel compensation and retirement programs

23. Which choice is the MOST accurate description of a "cold" site?

    a. A backup processing facility with adequate electrical wiring and air conditioning but no hardware or software installed

    b. A backup processing facility with most hardware and software installed, which can be operational within a matter of days

    c. A backup processing facility with all hardware and software installed and 100 percent compatible with the original site: operational within hours

    d. A mobile trailer with portable generators and air conditioning

24. Which question is NOT accurate regarding the process of risk assessment?

    a. The likelihood of a threat must be determined as an element of the risk assessment.

    b. The level of impact of a threat must be determined as an element of the risk assessment.

    c. Risk assessment is the final result of the risk management methodology.

    d. Risk assessment is the first process in the risk management methodology.

25. Which statement is NOT correct about safeguard selection in the risk analysis process?

    a. Maintenance costs need to be included in determining the total cost of the safeguard.

    b. The most commonly considered criteria is the cost effectiveness of the safeguard.

    c. The best possible safeguard should always be implemented regardless of cost.

    d. Many elements need to be considered in determining the total cost of the safeguard.

26. Which choice most accurately reflects the goals of risk mitigation?

    a. Analyzing the effects of a business disruption and preparing the company's response

    b. Analyzing and removing all vulnerabilities and threats to security within the organization

    c. Defining the acceptable level of risk that the organization can tolerate and assigning any costs associated with loss or disruption to a third party, such as an insurance carrier.

    d. Defining the acceptable level of risk that the organization can tolerate and reducing risk to that level.

27. Which choice represents an application or system demonstrating a need for a high level of availability protection and control?

    a. The application contains proprietary business information and other financial information, which if disclosed to unauthorized sources, could cause unfair advantage for vendors, contractors, or individuals and could result in financial loss or adverse legal action to user organizations.

    b. Unavailability of the system could result in inability to meet payroll obligations and could cause work stoppage and failure of user organizations to meet critical mission requirements. The system requires 24-hour access.

    c. The mission of this system is to produce local weather forecast information that is made available to the news media forecasters and the general public at all times. None of the information requires protection against disclosure.

    d. Destruction of the information would require significant expenditures of time and effort to replace. Although corrupted information would present an inconvenience to the staff, most information, and all vital information, is backed up by either paper documentation or on disk.

28. Put the five disaster recovery testing types in their proper order, from the most extensive to the least.

    a. Full-interruption

    b. Checklist

    c. Structured walk-through

    d. Parallel

    e. Simulation

29. Which type of backup subscription service listed would require the longest recovery time?

    a. A hot site

    b. A mobile or rolling backup service

    c. A warm site

    d. A cold site

30. Which of the following would best describe a "hot" backup site?

    a. A computer facility with electrical power and HVAC but with no applications or recent data installed on the workstations or servers prior to the event

    b. A computer facility available with electrical power and HVAC and some file/print servers, although the applications are not installed or configured and all of the needed workstations might not be on site or ready to begin processing

    c. A computer facility with no electrical power or HVAC

    d. A computer facility with electrical power and HVAC, all needed applications installed and configured on the file/print servers and enough workstations present to begin processing

CHAPTER 6

Domain 5: Cryptography

The science of cryptology includes two major branches: cryptography and cryptanalysis. Cryptography is the ancient science of designing cipher systems (secret writing) and is also known as encryption. Encryption was first developed in antiquity to hide the meaning of messages written on papyrus, stone, or cloth. Cryptanalysis is the branch of study dedicated to the process (sometimes referred to as an art) of deducing the plain-text message without knowing the secret key or the algorithm (breaking the encryption).

This question comes up repeatedly: How much about cryptology do system security practitioners need to know to do their jobs? We do not have a specific answer, but we do know the following:

- You need to understand what cryptography can do to help you provide security to your system or enterprise.

- You need to understand which encryption techniques are better used under specific conditions.

- You should understand the differences in approaches used.

Our Goals

For each of the seven domains, our goal is to provide you with three things:

1. Enough information about the domain so that you will be prepared to sit for the SSCP examination.

2. An understanding of how the overall system or enterprise security objectives, CIA, are carried through to the services and mechanisms within this domain.

3. An understanding of how the services and mechanisms of this domain provide security—through one or more of the protection, detection, and reaction aspects of system security.

We do not believe you need to be taught the basics of each security service and/or security mechanism. You know your job as a systems administrator or network administrator. What we do intend to do is to provide you with the connections and concepts that bring those isolated technical and administrative processes that you perform into the bigger picture: system security practice.

Domain Definition

According to (ISC)², "The cryptography area addresses the principles, means, and methods used to disguise information to ensure its integrity, confidentiality, authenticity, and non-repudiation."

We (the authors) have had certain ramifications from spending our adult lives in protecting national security systems from adversaries. One of the ramifications we never considered, however, was how our professional lives would impact our children's lives. Here is a case in point: One child's favorite movie of all time (since she was nine years old) is "Sneakers" (Universal Studios; 1992). In that movie, the day had arrived when a brilliant but slightly off-balanced cryptographer developed the ultimate code-breaking machine. This machine actually deciphered every cipher ever built or (conceivably) that would ever be developed. The world, if this machine was used by criminals or nations, would be an extremely scary place—and the power of such a machine would be like the ultimate weapon. On the other hand, if it were released to the world at large, it would instantly create a world where there were "no more secrets."

That was fiction. For now there are still plenty of secrets to keep (and therefore, the need for cryptography). Cryptography has supported our need for maintaining secrecy for a very long time.

Definitions of Cryptographic Terms

For this chapter to work, we need to define these terms up front for easy reference. Many if not most of the terminology used in cryptology and COMSEC (communications security) are either unique to the field or have a separate definition that applies to this field only. See Figure 6.1.

Algorithm. A formally defined set of rules for solving a (typically mathematical) problem. There are many commonly known algorithms:

- Rijndael. This algorithm is the basis for the United States' new encryption standard, the *Advanced Encryption Standard* (AES). See the document on the accompanying CD for a detailed discussion of the new standard.
- Skipjack. This algorithm is used in the clipper chip. Skipjack is a secret algorithm developed by the *National Security Agency* (NSA) to support the efforts of law enforcement. See the section later in this chapter on the clipper chip for more detail.
- RC2, 4,5&6. *Rivest's Cipher* (RC) 2, 4, 5, and 6 are ciphers developed as improvements over DES. See the section on RSA for more detail.
- CAST-128. CAST uses a variable key length from 40 bits to 128 bits. *Pretty Good Privacy* (PGP) implements CAST-128, and it is considered a strong algorithm.

Cipher. An algorithm for encryption and decryption and replaces a piece of information (an element in plain text) with another object with the intent to conceal meaning. Typically, the replacement rule is governed by the secret key. There are two types of ciphers: block ciphers and stream ciphers.

- **Block cipher.** A symmetric encryption algorithm in which a block of plain-text bits (typically 64) is transformed as a whole into a cipher-text block of the same length. Block ciphers are traditionally considered more resistant to cryptanalysis than stream ciphers, mainly due to the properties of confusion and diffusion.
- **Stream cipher.** A symmetric encryption algorithm in which cipher-text output is produced bit by bit or byte by byte from a stream of plain-text input.

Ciphertext. A message that is rendered unreadable to hide its contents

Cryptanalysis. The process (sometimes referred to as an art) of deducing the plain-text message without knowing the secret key or the algorithm

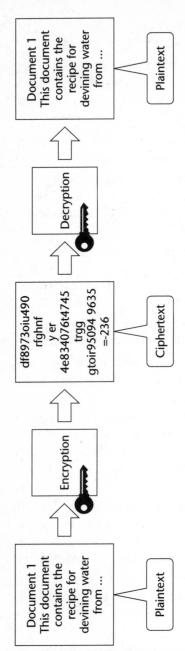

Figure 6.1 An illustration of encryption.

Cryptography. Cryptography is the science of designing cipher systems.

Cryptology. The overarching term that encompasses cryptography (cryptanalysis)

Deciphering. The process of transforming ciphertext into its plain text; it means the same thing as decryption.

Digital certificate. An attachment to a message that uniquely identifies the contents and the sender. Information contained in the certificate includes a public key, a version number, the issuer's name, a serial number, the individual's (or end entity's) name, public key, validity period for use, and optionally other attributes or privileges. An end entity can be either a person or a component, such as a computer or application.

Digital signatures. Digital signatures are used in the same fashion as personal signatures in everyday life: They are authentication mechanisms. By encrypting a small amount of data using the sender's private key and attaching it to the message, both the source and the integrity of the message are validated. A digital signature algorithm must ensure that the following conditions are met:

- The receiver must be able to validate the sender's signature.

- The signature must not be forgeable.

- The sender of a signed message must not be able to deny it (non-repudiation).

Enciphering. The process of transforming plain text into ciphertext. It means the same thing as encryption.

Key (crypto-variable). Secret information that is used for encryption and decryption.

One-time pad. A method of encryption where a randomly generated list of numbers is created and the message is encrypted by using this "pad." A one-time pad was originally known as the Vernam Cipher. Because there is no mathematical or statistical relationship between the pad and the message, the one-time pad is considered the most secure form of encryption. It is not used often, though, because both the sender and receiver need to have a copy of the pad and provide protection for the key (pad).

Message digest. See *Secure hash function.*

Plaintext. A human-readable message that is not encrypted

RC2, RC4, and RC5. Ronald Rivest—the same person who co-invented RSA—also developed RC2, RC4, and RC5. According to RSA's Web site, www.RSAsecurity.com, "RC stands for Ron's Code or Rivest's Cipher." These are all encryption algorithms built for RSA Security. See the "Common Cryptographic Systems" section in this chapter.

- RC2 is a stream cipher that was built to be faster than and a replacement for DES.

- RC4 is a stream cipher used for file encryption in commercial products and in SSL.

- RC5 is a block cipher—a symmetric-key algorithm with perhaps the most flexibility of all algorithms in use today. It provides a variable block size, a variable key length, and a variable number of rounds.

Secure hash function.   Hashing is a mathematical method of creating a small message block that can be used to verify the integrity of a message. The secure hash is known as a message digest, a hash, or a cryptographic checksum. There are various implementations of secure hashing algorithms, such as *Secure Hash Algorithm 1* (SHA-1), *Message Digest 4* (MD4), and *Message Digest 5* (MD5). The algorithm is applied by the sender against an unencrypted message, and a hash is returned (usually much smaller than the original message). The sender encrypts the message and sends it along with the hash. Once the message is deciphered, the hashing algorithm is performed on the unencrypted message. The secure hash is sent with the message, and the hash performed on the decrypted message is compared. If the hash output is the same in both instances, then the integrity of the unencrypted message is verified. A secure hash can be thought of as a unique identifier for a message. Much like a biometric reading, where your voice or your retina can identify you, so can the secure hash—it identifies the message. Secure hashes are sometimes referred to as one-way functions because they cannot be reverse-engineered. The one-way function refers to a mathematical function that is easily computed, but to reverse the computation to arrive at the original equation is infeasible. You can undermine this process by using a trap door.

Trap door.   In the cryptographic world, a trap provides a secret (code or other entry capability) that enables the one-way hash to be broken.

Watermark.   A watermark is the process of hiding information inside another medium to provide protection for the owner or manufacturer (see Figure 6.2). With watermarks, the owners could prove the identity of the real owner. Quality writing paper manufacturers used watermarks, and today's music, art, and movie production firms are using watermarks to protect their copyrights.

Steganography.   Steganography is the art of hiding the existence of a message in a different medium. (See the section entitled *Steganography* for more information.)

A watermark doesn't show without special equipment, or searching diligently for it. Can you find it on this sample page?

Isaac Consulting Group Inc 2002

Figure 6.2 Example of a watermark.

The History of Cryptology: An Overview

The original goal of cryptography was secrecy. With the content of a message encrypted (or hidden), only the intended recipient would be able to read it. As you can see in Table 6.1, many different ways of hiding messages have been developed throughout history, and their numbers have been limited only by the imagination of humans. As computers have evolved in the 20th and 21st centuries, cryptanalysts and cryptologists have been able to use computers to both develop more sophisticated methods of hiding information and break more complex algorithms.

Table 6.1 A Sample of Cryptologic Events in History

510 BC	50 BC	1404-1472	1518	1585	1790
Sparta Military used scroll to send messages	Caesar Shift Cipher	Leon Battista Alberti develops the "cipher wheel" using the first polyaphabetic substitution cipher	The monk, Trithemium published 1st book on Cryptology, "The six books of Polygrapheai." Trithemium describes the "tableu recta"	Vigenère Square developed. Looks just like the "tableu recta"	Jefferson Wheel Cipher

(continued)

Table 6.1 *(continued)*

1844-1865	1918-1929	1930-1934	1935-1938	1939-1948
Telegraph U.S. Civil War uses route ciphers (with codebooks) to encrypt & decrypt messages over telegraph lines	Gilbert Vernam develops Vernam Cipher Freidman connects cryptography & Mathematics Yardley ran the MI-8's Black Chamber	Rotor Machines first built (Enigma and Purple are rotor machines) Poland breaks German machine, Enigma (Rotor based) U.S. SIS starts studying Rotor Machine ciphers	Germans change Enigma by adding more rotors Japanese change (updated) their encryption machine, to one known as RED (Rotor machine) Several computers built to assist in breaking Enigma Code Alan Turing breaks German U boat Enigma U.S. can read all RED cryptosystem	Japanese change to a machine known as PURPLE (rotor machine) PURPLE machine code broken by Rowlett/Friedman team at SIS First general purpose computer, ENIAC, built

Caesar Shift Cipher (Mono-Alphabetic Substitution)

One of the earliest known users of effective cryptography was Gaius Julius Caesar. He—or, more than likely, one of his staff members—devised a simple cipher to be used for all privileged communications (particularly war or battlefield communications).

The Caesar cipher simply shifted the alphabet a predetermined number of positions. In a two-shift cipher, the letter "A" would be "C" and "C" would be "E." You could have a four-shift cipher (shown as follows) or a six-shift cipher (moving over six positions) or any other number. If Caesar used English, the shift cipher would work as shown in Figure 6.3.

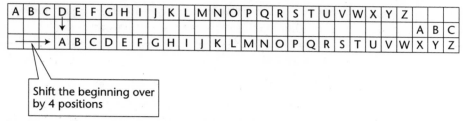

Shift the beginning over
by 4 positions

Figure 6.3 Sample of a four-shift Caesar shift cipher.

Using the shift cipher in Figure 6.3, if Julius Caesar wanted to send a message to his general that his reinforcements were close by, he might have written, "Troops one day south." Using the Caesar shift cipher, that message would be enciphered to read, "QOLRMP LKB AXV PLRQE."

Leon Batista Alberti (1404-1472) was the first to provide a key for cryptographic messages. He is sometimes referred to as the father of western cryptography. Before the mid-15th century, you only needed to determine the algorithm that was used to encrypt the message. As shown in Figure 6.4, now for the first time a key (something in addition to the algorithm) had to be determined in order to decipher the code.

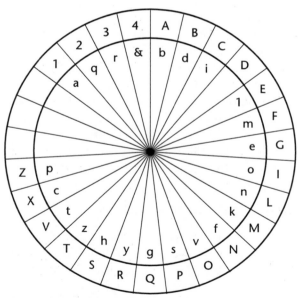

Figure 6.4 The Alberti wheel cipher.

Alberti's wheel was really the first implementation of the polyalphabetic cipher. The outside set of numbers is the plain text, and the inside numbers are the ciphertext that corresponds. How it differs from the monoalphabetic cipher is that there is no direct relationship between the two parts of the wheel. The inner wheel spins freely:

1. To work this cipher, select a message that you wish to send: "Danger is near."

2. Now, pick a key letter that both the sender and the receiver know. We will use 'a.' So, to send the total package (the key and the message), you will do the following.

3. Set the inner wheel to line up the "a" with a chosen starting position, such as "R." Write this letter as your first character in the encrypted message.

4. Now, simply write down the outer wheel letters that correspond to the rest of the message (inner wheel letters). You get "Ritrvxapzrxta."

5. In order to decrypt this message, you simply do the reverse. You know the key, and the text is encrypted, so set the inner wheel "a" to the "R" of the outer wheel. Then, you can decrypt the rest of the message one letter at a time.

While encrypting a message, the code could be changed by the sender entering another upper-case letter to be used as the alignment code (that both the sender and receiver know, such as 'a').

In 1518, a Benedictine monk named Johannes Trithemius wrote *Polygraphiae* (Figure 6.5), which was the first published treatise on cryptography. This treatise was six volumes in length and covered the state of the art in cryptology at that time. After the Renaissance, much of this type of endeavor was not appreciated, and much was lost. As a matter of fact, when the United States seriously took up cryptology at the beginning of the 20th century, many of those individuals had to rely on books such as the *Polygraphiae* for knowledge.

Vigenère Square (Polyalphabetic Substitution)

Blaise de Vigenère developed this very early polyalphabetic cipher, shown in Figure 6.6. The Vigenère square, as it is known, was developed in 1586 and was broken in the middle of the 19th century. This encryption technique was one of the methods used during the U.S. Civil War, although the cipher is rumored to have been broken before the war began.

Figure 6.5 One of the remaining original copies of the *Polygraphiae*.
Courtesy of the National Cryptologic Museum

To use the Vigenère square (see Figure 6.6), select a key (a letter going down the outside column) and then substitute the message letters for the corresponding letter on the "key" row. For example, if the message you need to encrypt is "You are known," follow these steps:

1. Select a key.

   We'll select "h."

2. Go down the key column to the "h" position.

3. Now, use that row of letters for substituting your message.

   Y becomes F.

   O becomes V.

   U becomes B.

   Repeat this process until you have the complete message: FVB HYL RUVDU.

4. To decrypt this message, follow the opposite process.

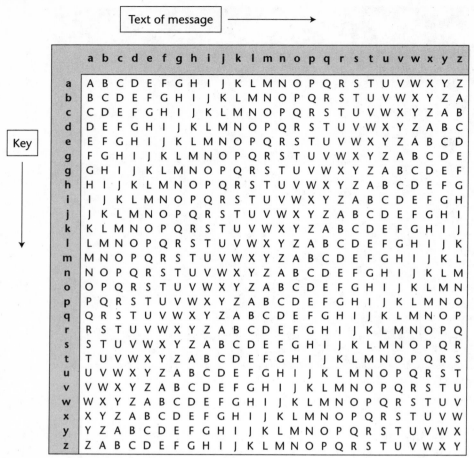

Figure 6.6   The Vigenère Square.

Thomas Jefferson (1743-1826), a U.S. statesman, architect, farmer, inventor, and the third President of the United States, designed a polyalphabetic wheel cipher. (See Figure 6.7.) It is not known if it was ever used; however, some believe that Jefferson used one during his time in France as a diplomat.

Vernam Cipher

In 1918, Gilbert Vernam discovered that the Vigenère cipher was vulnerable to cryptanalysis due to the frequency of the plain-text distribution having a relationship to the frequency of the ciphertext distribution. Vernam knew that all forms of encryption that use a key smaller then the message must be used multiple times during the process of enciphering. Once a key is used more than once, a repetition or decipherable pattern might be able to be discerned by cryptanalysis. The message might be deciphered completely or partially without knowing the secret key.

Figure 6.7 A model of Thomas Jefferson's wheel cipher.
Courtesy of the National Cryptologic Museum

So, Vernam suggested that using a random key of the same length as the message would work to reduce the possibility of breaking a cipher. A cipher-text built on that type of key would not be vulnerable to cryptanalysis. This task was performed but used a running tape that did eventually repeat but not within a message, unless it was extremely long. Joseph Mauborgne improved the cipher some time later by ensuring that no repetition existed. When used as intended, the one-time-pad is still the only unbreakable cipher in the world.

If not used properly, however, it is as vulnerable as any other cipher. For example, the Soviet intelligence branch once reused one-time pads several years after they had originally been distributed to their field agents in Britain. The British intelligence service (the cryptanalysts) noticed some patterns in the coded messages. They began searching through archival files for comparisons of all encrypted communications intercepts and found the previously used ones. Based on the ability of the cryptanalysts, various secret communications were compromised.

In the 1920s, Herbert O. Yardley (1889-1958) headed the highly secret U.S. organization of MI-8 (Military Intelligence, Section 8). Nicknamed the "Black Chamber," this organization's purpose was to develop, study, and break the diplomatic codes of other countries. According to the National Cryptologic Museum, the U.S. Secretary of State, Charles Evans Hughes—in order to improve his negotiating position during the Washington Naval Conference of 1921-1922—used the decrypted information provided by Yardley. He was extremely successful. While he seemed to be outmaneuvering the Japanese for a more favorable agreement on naval capital ships, he was actually being told their negotiating position before he went into the bargaining sessions each day.

This time period was before computational power was behind breaking codes. Yardley and his staff recognized that what humans code, other humans can decode. In most cases, true randomness does not exist. People fall into patterns of behavior as well as using patterns in their codes.

The MI-8 was closed down in 1929. Yardley, who had been the head of MI-8, decided to write about the activities of now non-existent organizations and their secret inner workings (see Figure 6.8). When Yardley published *The American Black Chamber*, the American age of cryptology was born.

Yardley's book was one of the very few available on the science of cryptology, but other work in cryptology was underway. Recently, stories of how cryptography has shaped the United States have emerged that were previously unknown except to a few.

Figure 6.8 Yardley leaves his mark.
Courtesy of the National Cryptologic Museum

Rotor Machines

The rotor-based cipher machines were used extensively in the first half of the 20th century by every major nation and many private companies. These machines, which look somewhat like old typewriters (see Figure 6.9), took keyed entry (just as a typewriter does). A rotor machine has a set of independently rotating cylinders, and many machines had three or four rotors. Each rotor (if English language-based) had 26 input positions and 26 output positions (the implementation of a monoalphabetic cipher). But this setup is only half of the rotor machines' process. When an electrical signal is sent by a specific key, the other cylinders (2-X) rotate at different speeds. This part of the process is called a transposition cipher. Using this figure as an example, if we input "hi" after a two-cylinder rotor machine has processed it, the "hi" becomes "yo" (that was not intentional, but we are not redrawing this graphic).

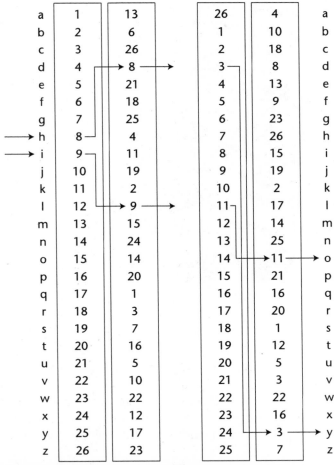

Figure 6.9   The conceptual diagram of a Rotor machine.

Figure 6.10 The Enigma machine.

Courtesy of the National Cryptologic Museum

The Enigma machine (like the one shown in Figure 6.10) is an example of a rotor-based cipher machine. The Enigma machine was used by the German Nazis before and during World War II to encrypt messages. The Nazis were so sure of its strength that they never considered that it could, or would, be broken—but Poland first broke the code in the 1930s. The Germans responded by changing the machine (adding more rotors), and when the Poles had no luck

A BIT MORE OF HISTORY

The SIS changed its name several times until it settled on the *National Security Agency* (NSA) after WWII.

breaking the new cipher, they gave it to the British. A few years later during World War II, the British (Allen Turing and associates) broke the German U-boat Enigma cipher in 1939-1940.

During this same time period of World War II, the Japanese used a version of the rotor machines. The Japanese version, known as the Red, and then the more advanced Purple machine, was supposed to be a physical combination of complete rotor machines electronically wired together. So, instead of seeing one machine, with the "Purple" there were two side by side. The Japanese "Purple" machine cipher was broken by the Rowlett and Friedman team at the Army's *Signals Intelligence Service* (SIS).

No complete Purple machine was ever captured. Figure 6.11 shows a fragment of one that was found in the courtyard of the Japanese embassy in Berlin after the city fell in 1945. It is on display at the National Cryptologic Museum.

Figure 6.11 A fragment of a Japanese Purple machine.
Courtesy of the National Cryptologic Museum

Code Talkers

The code talkers were Native Americans who, during World War II, used their language to hide the true meaning of the radio communications and effectively helped the allies to win the war. The code talkers were assigned to radio positions in the U.S. Army, the U.S. Navy, and the U.S. Marine Corps. The Navajo code talkers, for example, took part in the battles of Guadalcanal, Tarawa, Peleliu, and Iwo Jima. At Iwo Jima, Major Howard Connor, Fifth Marine Division signal officer, declared, "Were it not for the Navajos, the Marines would never have taken Iwo Jima." In fact, the Navajo code talkers took part in every assault that the U.S. Marines conducted in the Pacific from 1942 to 1945. While they used their language as a form of encryption to communicate mission plans, their locations, the locations of their enemies, and other critical information, the Axis countries listened on with perplexity and perhaps anxiety. The Native American code was never broken. This story, along with many others, has surfaced in the past 12 years (most recently in the film "Windtalkers" (MGM; 2002)) to show us the importance that cryptography has had in the United States and in global history.

DES

In 1975, the U.S. government standardized the *Digital Encryption Standard* (DES). Until that point, there was no single encryption algorithm approved or even a de facto standard. DES is a symmetric cryptography system based on a 56-bit key. Today, we recognize the potential vulnerability of such a short key; however, it was not broken publicly until 1998, when a group funded by the *Electronic Frontier Foundation* (EFF) did so in approximately 56 hours. We have a detailed discussion on DES in the section "Common Cryptographic Systems."

Public Key Cryptography

Whitfield Diffie and Martin Hellman are credited as the pioneers of public key cryptography. In 1976, they published the first paper describing a public key cryptographic system. Using the algorithm developed by Ralph C. Merkle and Martin E. Hellman, known as the Merkle-Hellman algorithm, they (all three) patented the first public key cryptographic system: the Knapsack algorithm. While all public key cryptographic systems owe their beginnings to Diffie-Hellman, the Knapsack algorithm was later found insecure.

Clipper Chip

The clipper chip is a hardware implementation of an encryption approach: the *Escrowed Encryption Standard* (EES). It was based on a technology called the

Very Large-Scale Integration (VLSI) circuit built by NSA. It was a huge national-level effort on the part of the U.S. government in the 1990s, and the intent was to provide law enforcement access to ciphertext messages. The algorithm on which the clipper chip is based is called SkipJack. SkipJack is a symmetric (secret) block cipher that provides for key escrowing by third parties. The idea was to have the escrow key stored and protected at NIST and the Department of Treasury. The escrowed key is known as a *law enforcement access field* (LEAF). When law enforcement received a court order to place a wiretap on a suspect, the law enforcement staff would contact NIST or the Treasury (the Treasury because the U.S. Secret Service is owned by them) to receive the LEAF. With the LEAF, they could decrypt messages from that one suspect.

This information has to be placed in context with the times. The exponential speed with which technology was embraced by the developed world, and especially the United States, was extraordinary. Law enforcement and the law itself could not keep pace. The criminal element of our society figured out very quickly how it could use the new technologies to keep from being caught by the law. Just think about what our law enforcement officials were facing: criminals had cell phones and computers and used major networks such as the Internet. But they also used encryption for their phone communications and encryption for their stored files on their systems, and they used encryption during the transmission of email and online activities. There was *no* ability for law enforcement to legally eavesdrop on conversions (because it was garbled), nor did it help to capture their electronic activity (with a court order) because that was also encrypted.

But, regardless of the times, many citizens and businesses—most without criminal intent—use encryption for privacy, and the idea of the government having the ability to access their information was too fearful. So, when the U.S. government started to make serious advances with the clipper chip, advertising the development of a standard national encryption algorithm that the government could decipher—enough disapproval by the citizenry finally forced the effort to close down (or at least get placed on a slow track).

Security and Cryptography

For the objectives of security (CIA), cryptography provides a significant amount of protection. (See Figure 6.12.) Many people today believe that security begins and ends with encryption, however. Cryptology as it exists today supports the tenets of both confidentiality and integrity. Advanced cryptography can provide confidentiality, data integrity, non-repudiation, and authenticity but not availability. We discuss each of these in the following paragraphs.

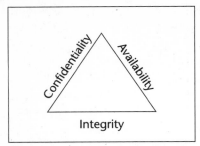

Figure 6.12   Objectives of security.

Confidentiality

Confidentiality (or privacy, if you prefer) was the original justification for encryption. As you discovered in reading the material on the history of cryptology, mankind has had reasons to keep information secret almost as long as we have existed. Confidentiality, as an objective of security, is implemented through making the message unreadable to all—except to the intended recipient, of course. Encryption can be used to provide confidentiality for information stored on a piece of paper, for electronic information stored on a computer, for a message being hand-carried across town, or information being electronically transmitted to the space shuttle in outer space. Encryption is arguably the very best method for providing confidentiality.

As an example, Debra received an encrypted message from Mike. She decrypted it, and the contents contained the message, "Let's go out for pizza." Debra and Mike can have complete confidence that no one else has seen the message. But, there is no way for Debra to verify that it was actually Mike who sent the message. The code (or key) could have been broken (compromised), and this message could have been sent by someone pretending to be Mike. What should she do? It would be very embarrassing if he had not sent the message and she reacted to it thinking that he had sent it. What if he changed his mind after he sent it and pretended that he did not send it?

Integrity

Integrity is the security objective that deals with the problem of not being able to verify that the information received is the very same information that was sent. In most fields, integrity is the number one security objective. Think of integrity as "I don't care if anyone else sees it as long as no one else can change it." It was not until the 1970s that researchers discovered that encryption techniques can also be used for providing integrity. Today, we have several ways in which encryption provides different types of integrity. For example, there are digital signatures that provide the same degree of authenticity as a handwritten signature and digital certificates that are used to transmit a public key; in addition, other information can be used to verify that the certificate (and therefore the key that was transmitted within it) was created by a trusted entity.

So, let's go back to our example. A couple of hours later, Debra received a second encrypted message from Mike. She decrypts it, and the message says, "Are you available tomorrow?" She notices that the message carries a digital signature this time. She knows that he sent it; he cannot deny it. She picks up the phone and makes the date.

As you can see from the previous paragraph, encryption misses the security tenet of availability. There is much more to security than encryption. On the other hand, you cannot have decent security today without encryption.

Encryption Techniques

William Stallings, in the second edition of *Cryptography and Network Security* (Prentice Hall, 2002), points out that all cryptographic systems (encryption) can be divided based on their use, their approach to plain-text processing, and a number of keys. We (the authors) believe that is a great way to think of cryptographic systems. By dividing cryptographic systems into discrete divisions, we can more easily represent the concepts, their similarities, and their differences. This feature is especially important if you are learning new material. We have taken that idea and fully developed it in our discussions here. See Table 6.2.

Table 6.2 The Division of Cryptographic Systems

How encryption is used	Substitution (Permutations of either or both)
	Transposition (Permutations of either or both)
How the plaintext is processed	Block cipher
	Stream cipher
Number of keys	Symmetric keys: Same key, secret key
	Asymmetric keys: Different keys, one private and one public. Uses a key-pair.

How Encryption Is Used

Earlier in this chapter, we went through some of the highlights from the history of cryptology. Throughout those pages, there are two fundamental approaches to encrypting information: substitution and transposition.

Substitution ciphers are the oldest known forms of encryption and have been used since antiquity to keep secret the meaning of messages. In a substitution approach, the characters remain in their original state but the value is changed. A simple algorithm was developed to "shift" each character in a message a predetermined number of times (within the alphabet space). This predetermined number (the number to shift over) is the key portion of the encryption and had to be known by both parties involved in the message transfer.

If the letter A were to be encrypted and the key was 3, then the letter would be replaced with D. D is three letters down in the alphabet, laid out in a linear fashion. The alphabet is assumed to be linear, and once the shifting passes the end of the alphabet, it wraps back to the beginning. So, the letter Y would be replaced with B by traversing three steps: Z, A, and B. There are only 26 different ways of encrypting each letter, which makes this form very insecure. The strength of this encryption lay in the fact that no one knew the algorithm.

This form of encryption was used by Gaius Julius Caesar and is known today as the Caesar Shift Cipher (see the section "History of Cryptography: An Overview"). The Caesar shift cipher is a monoalphabetic substitution cipher, which means that it uses a single alphabet during the encryption. Once the adversaries deduced that the letters were simply being shifted, there was no reason to find the key. The encryption could be broken via a brute force attack. Brute force involves trying every possible value of the key. This attack was trivial because it involved taking a part of a message and simply shifting the characters 1 through 26 until a readable message appeared. This type of encryption can also be broken through the use of frequency analysis.

Polyalphabetic substitution is performed through the use of multiple alphabets. Blaise de Vigenère was the first to invent this type of cipher. The Vigenère Square (see Figure 6.6) was much more sophisticated in its approach to encryption. As an example, the Vigenère Square prevented the cryptanalysis based on normal frequency distribution of letters in words because the same letter in the alphabet could be encrypted multiple ways during the message. The Vigenère Square was eventually broken through the discovery of periods or repetition in encrypted messages.

Transposition ciphers involve shifting the place of the character but retaining the value. Essentially, the characters of a message are jumbled in order to hide their meaning. A very simple transposition cipher known as *fence post* can be easily performed without the use of computers (see Figure 6.13). Suppose that the message to be encrypted was "Meet me behind the school." Alternating letters of the message would be placed on different lines, and the message would then be enciphered by writing down the message from left to right on each line.

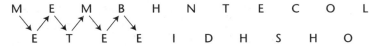

Figure 6.13   A simple transposition cipher.

After being written down in this form, the message can be enciphered left to right in the first row and then the second as follows: "MEMBHNTECOL ETEEIDHSHO." In order to decipher the message, the process would simply be reversed.

Modern encryption approaches still use derivations of the substitution and transposition ciphers.

How the Plaintext Is Processed

Text can be processed (enciphered and encrypted) by using one of two ciphers: block or stream. Block ciphers take a block of data, typically 64 bits long, and encrypt the entire block. Stream ciphers encrypt one bit or one byte at a time.

Stream ciphers have a one-to-one relationship between the plain text and the ciphertext. If there are 15 bytes in the message you wish to send, there will be 15 bytes in your ciphertext. The advantage of stream ciphers is their speed, because there is little operational overhead associated with stream ciphers. An example of a stream cipher used in the computing environment today is *Secure Socket Layer* (SSL), which uses the RC4 encryption algorithm. Stream ciphers should be considered for only one-time use because they are vulnerable to cryptanalysis attacks. With SSL (RC4), Netscape—the developer—created a new key stream for each connection made. With this type of implementation, the stream cipher is very much like a one-time pad.

Block ciphers are more complex in their encryption approach, selecting various-sized blocks of data and performing encryption activities on each block. There are three properties associated with block ciphers that create this complexity and therefore its strength against cryptanalysis:

Padding.   Because block ciphers work in blocks of (normally) 64 bits, the message will be padded to fill the final bits of the block. This feature adds a layer of difficulty, however, because the message's true length cannot be determined.

Confusion.   The property that disassociates the statistical relationship of the plain text to the key in order to prevent or minimize cryptanalysis based on statistics.

Diffusion.   The property that disassociates the plain text quantity of bits or bytes of words from the quantity of ciphertext.

Because there is no direct association between the ciphertext (as in the stream cipher) and the plaintext, there is less vulnerability to brute-force attacks. Block ciphers have more overhead, but they are the primary approach used in almost all communications today. The keys can be reused, unlike stream ciphers (see Figure 6.14). The plain-text message is, "The dog is brown." The stream cipher of that message contains the same number of characters; the block cipher does not. Blocks ciphers include DES, Triple DES, and AES (see the following section, "Common Cryptographic Systems").

DES is an example of a block cipher. It uses blocks of 64 bits and a 56-bit key. It was the standard for more than 25 years for encryption (and has been broken on numerous occasions). Triple DES seemed poised to take its place as the NIST set about to evaluate and name a successor to DES in 1999. On October 2, 2000, however, NIST selected AES as the new standard for data encryption. The AES algorithm is capable of using cryptographic keys of 128, 192, and 256 bits. The AES algorithm, Rijndael (pronounced Rhine-doll), was developed by Vincent Rijmen and Joan Daemen. See the section titled "Common Cryptographic Systems" for a detailed discussion. The AES standard for encryption became effective on May 26, 2002 and appears in the document on the CD-ROM accompanying this book.

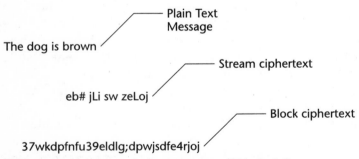

Figure 6.14   A text example of stream and block ciphers.

Number of Keys

There are two approaches to keys in cryptology: one shared key and separate keys that work as a pair. In order to understand how encryption really works and the differences in approaches, you need to understand the concept of keys. Keys play a central role in all cryptosystems. A key is the secret piece of information used to encrypt and decrypt a message, and the key can be a physical object, a password, or some other secret that cannot be easily guessed. There are secret keys in both symmetric and asymmetric encryption, and there are public keys only in asymmetric encryption.

When the same shared secret key is used for both the encrypting and the decrypting, as shown in Figure 6.15, it is referred to as a symmetric key system.

For the symmetric key system to function, both the sender and receiver must have the same key. This key, because it is the single key required to encrypt and decrypt, must be protected at all times—including during the exchange of the key between the people (or systems) that wish to communicate. Therein lies the biggest problem with symmetric cryptosystems: key management.

Key management for symmetric cryptosystems is complex and difficult. For example, if you wish to communicate (in secret) to 100 other people, there would have to be 100 copies of the key and they would all have to be secretly delivered and protected so that there could be no interception of the key. Then, when you wanted to update or change your key, all the other copies of the key would have to be destroyed and new copies sent out again. That process might not sound too complex, but our example involves only one user who has one small group with which to communicate. Imagine a company with international offices, 100,000 employees, 23,000 business partners, and a secret key for each possible combination of communicators.

Asymmetric cryptosystems were designed to improve on the shortcomings of the symmetric systems. An asymmetric system contains a key pair—a private key that never needs to be sent anywhere and a public key that can be sent everywhere. The private key is used to generate a public key. As shown in Figure 6.16, the public key is available to everyone. This asymmetric cryptosystem is referred to most often as public key cryptography. (For more about public key cryptography, see *What Is a Public Key Infrastructure (PKI)*).

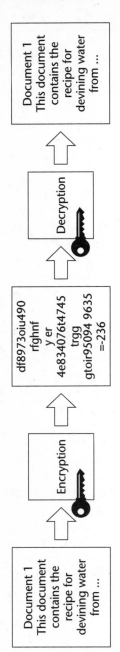

Figure 6.15 Representation of symmetric (same-key) cryptography.

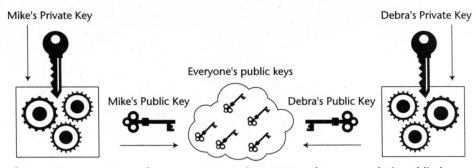

Figure 6.16 Everyone who uses asymmetric cryptography creates their public keys and makes them available.

How messages are encrypted and decrypted is shown in Figure 6.17. Let's say that Debra wants to send a message to Mike. She gets a copy of his public key. She uses her private key and his public key to encrypt the message.

To see how this process works, let's look at Figure 6.18:

1. The sender, Debra, has a message that needs to be sent to the receiver, Mike.

2. Debra locates Mike's public key.

3. Debra encrypts the message by using Mike's public key and her private key.

4. The encrypted message is transmitted to Mike.

5. Mike sees that the message is from Debra, so he gets Debra's public key.

6. Mike uses Debra's public key and his private key to decrypt the message.

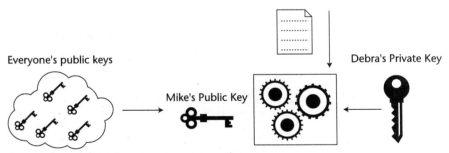

Figure 6.17 Encrypting by using a public-key system.

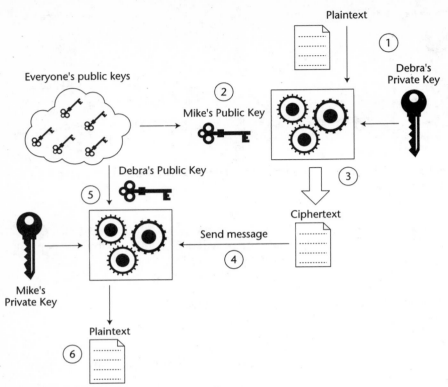

Figure 6.18 The public key cryptography process.

The primary obstacle associated with symmetric systems is key management. It is very difficult to keep secret keys secret for any length of time. The management also includes a mechanism for providing new keys to all parties at certain regular intervals and for revoking compromised keys, with no easy way to notify everyone. Those very issues have been addressed with the development of asymmetric systems. While there have been many advances in the past 30 years, there is still room for many more.

Common Cryptographic Systems

What are the algorithms based on today? All cryptographic systems (symmetric and asymmetric) are built based on mathematical principles that are directly derived from the substitution and transposition of years gone by. Where the true advances have come are in the development of algorithms based on extremely difficult mathematics (infeasible until the supercomputer era). Some complex mathematical functions have two properties that are relied on to develop strong algorithms for cryptosystems today: 1) some mathematical calculations are extremely time-consuming to perform, even when considering the use of computers, and 2) some mathematical functions are very difficult (impossible) to inverse. Prime number factorization and logarithmic functions are two examples.

Data Encryption Standard (DES)

The *Data Encryption Standard* (DES) is one of the most famous forms of symmetric key encryption because it has been the accepted standard form of encryption for the United States since its acceptance in 1977. Horst Feistal originally built an encryption algorithm, Lucifer, in 1972. The patent was filed on behalf of his employer, IBM, and IBM submitted Lucifer to NIST in 1974 as a result of a request for proposals. The NIST was trying to identify a non-military encryption algorithm for use in the U.S. government. Lucifer was forwarded to NSA, where the original algorithm was modified along with the key length (from 128 bits in Lucifer to 56 bits). After NSA finished its review, the algorithm was named the Digital Encryption Standard and was approved by NIST for government use (with its 56-bit key) in 1977. Because of the key length, DES requires at most 2^{56} tries to guaranteed success (breaking the key). The NIST recertified DES in 1982, 1987, and again in 1993. In 1987, NSA proposed an upgrade to DES by using the advanced VLSI chip, but this proposal did not happen. The DES encryption algorithm has begun to show its weaknesses due to the computing power in existence today. DES has a vulnerability to brute-force attacks and man-in-the-middle attacks because of the relatively small key size (56 bits). In 1998, DES was broken. In 1999, NIST decided not to recertify DES and began looking for a new algorithm. A new one has been found: the *Advanced Encryption Standard* (AES); see *Advanced Encryption Standard* (AES).

Triple DES

There are two implementations of Triple DES: two-key Triple DES and three-key Triple DES. Several Internet-based applications, such as PGP and S/MIME, use the three-key Triple DES. All versions of Triple DES work as follows: The plain text is encrypted by using key 1, then it is encrypted with key 2, and finally it is encrypted with key 3 and transmitted (see Figure 6.19).

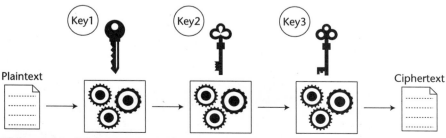

Figure 6.19   Triple DES encryption.

The recipient receives the encrypted message and uses key 3, then key 2, and finally key 1 to decrypt the message (see Figure 6.20). If this example is a two-key Triple DES, then key 3 is actually key 1 used again.

The algorithm for Triple DES was a lengthy process and slowed the overall performance. DES and Triple DES have four modes of operation, and these are important to know because they are used for different applications:

Electronic codebook **(ECB).** ECB is the simplest mode. It takes each 64-bit block and encrypts it with the same 56-bit key and is used primarily for transmitting small amounts of data, such as a DES key.

Cipher Block Chaining **(CBC).** The ECB is very simple and not very secure for large quantities of data (more than 64 bits). CBC takes the process of ECB and adds the XOR or the previous cipherblock so effectively that the deciphering cannot take place without knowing the previous block's content as well as the initial key. According to Stallings, CBC can support both confidentiality and authenticity.

Cipher Feedback Mode **(CFM).** In this mode, DES performs as a stream cipher by encrypting bits or bytes instead of blocks.

Output Feedback Mode **(OFM).** OFM also turns the DES block cipher into a stream cipher. OFM is used for key generation as well as stream encryption.

RSA

In 1978, Ron Rivest, Adi Shamir, and Leonard Adelman published a paper on public-key cryptography that implemented Diffie-Hellman's conceptual ideas regarding the ability to have confidentiality without sharing a secret key. The RSA (the first letter of each creator's last name) scheme has withstood the test of time and remains a sound public key cryptosystem. RSA is a block cipher and is accepted globally today and implemented widely. Its strength lies in its longer keys (RSA uses 512- or 1024-bit keys). RSA's strength comes from its use of factoring extremely large prime numbers (see the discussion at the beginning of this section). RSA is used for encryption, digital signatures, and key exchange.

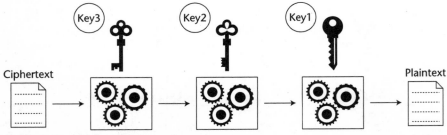

Figure 6.20 Triple DES decryption.

Elliptic Curve Cryptography (ECC)

Elliptic curve cryptography (ECC) is a new approach to public key cryptography. The tremendous computational power available today makes ciphers that were infeasible because of their difficult computation a decade or two ago reasonable today. This power for alternative complex ciphers is placing pressure on DES, RSA, and others to significantly increase the bit length of their blocks in order to remain secure. ECC can provide the same level of security with a much smaller overhead due to the use of modular exponentiation of discrete logarithmic functions.

Advanced Encryption Standard (AES)

Advanced Encryption Standard (AES) is the subject of one of the documents on this book's accompanying CD-ROM, where we have the new NIST standard. The AES is based on the Rijndael algorithm and is a symmetric cryptosystem (one secret, shared key). The Rijndael algorithm has compactness of code, simplicity of design, and a resistance to all currently known types of attacks. AES has three options of key length that can be chosen: 128, 192, or 256 bits.

IDEA

IDEA is another example of a symmetric block cipher widely used today. It uses a 128-bit key to encrypt 64-bit blocks. IDEA is compact in its implementation and is therefore very easy to implement in hardware, such as the VLSI. The underlying algorithm for IDEA is CAST-128, developed by Carlise Adams and Stafford Tavares at NORTEL. PGP implements the IDEA cipher and has been placed in the public domain for individual development and use.

Kerberos

Kerberos (also known as Cerberos) is an authentication system, but we felt that it should be addressed within this chapter. Kerberos is really much more than an authentication system; it is a security system that provides authentication, secure channels, integrity, confidentiality, access control, authorization, and nonrepudiation. This security system does just about everything you would ever want, except once again—as with cryptography in general—there is no mechanism for availability. Kerberos works much like another authentication system: Public Key Infrastructure (PKI). (For more information, see *What Is a Public Key Infrastructure (PKI)?*).

Cryptography in Networks

As our understanding of the implications of a truly global Internet becomes mature, the research into ways to provide adequate security for data traversing the Internet and internal networks has received wide support. We address a few of the significant security enhancements that have come from the field of cryptography.

Internet Protocol Security (IPSec)

The *Internet Protocol Security* (IPSec) is the name given to the group of standards that provides security to the actual IP packets at the network layer of the TCP/IP protocol stack. IPSec uses two protocols: *authentication header* (AH) and the *encapsulating security payload* (ESP), which we describe in the following paragraphs.

Authentication Header (AH)

AH supports access control, data origin authentication, connectionless integrity, and the rejection of replay attacks. AH does not provide confidentiality to the actual data, so the data is still visible as it traverses the network.

Encapsulating Security Payload (ESP)

ESP provides support for confidentiality, access control, limited traffic flow confidentiality, and the rejection of replay attacks. The ESP provides encryption to the actual data in the IP packet.

Secure Socket Layer (SSL)

The SSL is the Internet protocol that provides authentication and encryption during a session. SSL works at the transport layer of the TCP/IP protocol stack and completes a "secret handshake" (both sides knowing the secret handshake) between the server and the client. This secret handshake is maintained during the entire session and provides authentication and confidentiality (privacy). It was developed by Netscape in 1994 to provide security for their Internet client-server activities.

Secure HyperText Transport Protocol (S-HTTP)

Secure HyperText Transport Protocol (S-HTTP) is a security-enhanced version of HTTP. S-HTTP provides end-to-end protection (a secure pipe) between servers and their clients. S-HTTP provides authentication, confidentiality, nonrepudiation, and integrity and uses the NIST *Digital Signature Standard* (DSS), x.509 certificates, and is under consideration as a standard by the *Internet Engineering Task Force* (IETF).

Cryptography for Email

As with networks in general, the cryptographic community has responded with amazing products—some free, some for a fee, and some within a short span of time.

Secure Multipurpose Internet Mail Extensions (s/MIME)

Secure Multipurpose Internet Mail Extensions (s/MIME) is a security-enhanced version of MIME (the Internet email format standard). S/MIME, originally developed by RSA, uses encryption and digital signatures to provide security for email.

Pretty Good Privacy (PGP)

Phil Zimmerman developed PGP and gave it away for free. PGP was one of the first public key implementations for general users on the Internet and provides encryption, public key management, and digital signatures. It was practically an overnight success. PGP gave the users of internetworked systems the ability to protect their own personal emails and files.

Privacy Enhanced Mail (PEM)

Privacy Enhanced Mail (PEM) is an IETF-developed security protocol for email on the Internet. PEM is a standard that can be implemented on any email system; it provides confidentiality, authentication, and nonrepudiation.

Cryptography for E-Commerce

For e-commerce, security has been one of the biggest inhibitors. Standards and framework activities such as SET, described as follows, are changing the way we do business as companies and as individuals.

Secure Electronic Transaction (SET)

Secure Electronic Transaction (SET) is an e-commerce-driven protocol framework that provides confidentiality and integrity for online transactions. Originally, in 1997 MasterCard and Visa started the SET protocol. SET calls for the following features:

- Confidentiality of data
- Integrity of data
- Authorization
- Interoperability

For confidentiality, SET calls for DES encryption. For integrity, the RSA algorithm is used for digital signature. For authorization, both the cardholder and merchants used X.509 certificates. For interoperability, the standards are open for other manufacturers.

Transaction Layer Security (TLS)

This protocol, TLS, is the successor to SSL3.0. This de facto standard protocol provides confidentiality, integrity, and authentication to applications. TLS is located in the transaction layer of the TCP/IP protocol stack.

What Is a Public Key Infrastructure (PKI)?

When we look for formal definitions and come across more than four different ones, we have a tendency to fall back on what we know to be stable and consistent. The *Committee on National Security Systems'* (CNSS) INFOSEC glossary (2001) defines PKI as the "framework established to issue, maintain, and revoke public key certificates accommodating a variety of security technologies, including software." So, to put this concept in layperson terms, a PKI is the policies, procedures, and technology required to manage and maintain the system that has come about as a result of the integration of public-key encryption's key pairs with cryptographic digital signatures and the digital certificates validating the keys. This infrastructure is still new and evolving; however, due to the complex nature of the implementations and its costliness, the standard implementer seems to be a reasonably large organization with considerably high activity over public networks.

WHY DO WE NEED AN ENTIRE INFRASTRUCTURE TO SUPPORT PKI?

It is quite simple: It is not simple. Key management is the hardest part of any cryptographic system.

The focus for a PKI is on preserving the validity and integrity of the certificate. The certificate is a mechanism that validates your public key. The common components in a PKI are as follows:

Certificate Authority **(CA).**   The third party (usually) who is trusted to authenticate the public key by issuing a digital certificate. The CA issues and revokes certificates.

Registration Authority **(RA).**   The entity that manages the certificate life cycle, including repositories (x.500 or LDAP) and the certificate revocation list. In many implementations, the RA is internal to the CA.

Clients.   The certificate holders who are issued certificates and who use them.

Key management.   This term refers to recovery, storage, destruction, and generation.

The steps a sender goes through (the PKI process) to get and use a certificate are listed as follows:

1. Mike places a request for a certificate to the CA.
2. The RA gets a public key from Mike or generates a key pair.
3. The policy authority authenticates Mike (many times accomplished through email address or Social Security number).
4. The certificate manufacturer generates the asymmetric certificate key pair.
5. The certificate issuer sends the certificate to Mike and to a repository.
6. Now, Mike sends Debra a message signed with his certificate and then encrypted with his private key.
7. Debra receives an encrypted message from Mike.
8. Debra locates Mike's public key and decrypts the message. It is signed with a certificate.
9. Debra goes to the CA and requests a status of Mike's certificate.
10. The CA checks with the repository that includes a *certificate revocation list* (CRL).
11. The CA reports to Debra that Mike's certificate is valid.
12. Debra now has confidence that the message she received from Mike actually came from Mike, and Mike cannot deny that he signed and sent it.

A PKI or a Kerberos implementation can, as you can see in Table 6.3, fulfill many of the same services needed in an organization. As with many other security services we have discussed in this book, you need to use your roadmap and implement mechanisms based on your needs.

Table 6.3 A Comparison of PKI with Kerberos

PKI	KERBEROS
CA	KDC (Key distribution center)
	TGS (ticket granting service)
	AS (Authentication Service)
PK certificate (long time months or years)	Ticket (short time hours or days)
Private key-public key pair	Session Key
Trust is in the issuing authority (CA)	Trust is in the issuing authority (KDC)

NOTE Kerberos is a system based on symmetric key cryptography and not on public key cryptography.

Steganography

Steganography is the art of hiding the existence of a message. In Greek, it means "covered writing." This technique involves hiding a message within another message or in a form where it cannot be recognized. Originally, this task could be accomplished by hiding messages in elaborate drawings by using stylized lettering. Simple techniques, such as microdot, have been developed today, however. For example, a secret message could be created in a text file and saved. Then, a second (innocuous) message is created as the decoy. At some point in the decoy message where a period is required, the sender will embed the secret message and shrink the size until it resembles a period. A casual glance by an unintended reader would not be able to discern that the period was hiding a message because it was so small. Many other forms of steganography exist that are more advanced and involve the use of computers to find or create "spaces" or "gaps" in files to hide messages. Messages can be hidden in forms such as picture files. By this means, a person could electronically hide a message in an image file and send the image to the recipient. The sender and receiver would be the only ones that know that a message is hidden or who would know how to extract the message from the file.

There are many commercial and free programs available that enable a computer user to create and read standard file formats and extract hidden information. The information could be hidden in data, audio, a picture, or any other file format. Common use today includes the hiding of information in picture files, which is accomplished by modifying bit(s) used to display pixels that create the display of the picture. Some loss of quality is incurred by using this method, and data bleed can occur and become evident in displayed pictures as vertical lines or color inconsistencies. The benefit of steganography is in the covert channel used to transmit the data (hidden in a normal transmission), rather than sending an encrypted message that is assumed to contain a secret message.

Watermarks

Watermarking is a form of steganography and is used by commercial (mainly) entities that want to ensure copyright laws are enforceable. This process is done by embedding information into the product (software, DVD, CD, picture file, and so on) that identifies the owner and provides copyright protection. It was originally developed to mark the paper products produced by a manu-facturer. Each manufacturer embedded their own mark (logo) into the background of the paper to identify themselves, and this mark could be seen when held up to the light. Commercial photographic prints all contain some form of imprinted (usually visible) logo or identification of the copyright owner. Newer data watermarking schemes use various methods to ensure that the owner of a work is identified and that this information cannot be removed from the work. Each new protection mechanism established by commercial product developers is met with a barrage of inquisitive people attempting to crack the mechanism and allow the removal of the watermark, copyright, or copy protection.

Cryptanalysis

Cryptanalysis is the process (sometimes referred to as an art) of deducing the plain-text message without knowing the secret key or the algorithm. When assessing the strength of a cipher, the term work factor is often used to describe the level of cryptanalysis that must be applied to render the cryptographic system broken. A cryptographic system can be broken with one of three approaches: known plain text, ciphertext only, or chosen plain text (we discuss these three in the following paragraphs).

Known Plain-Text Approach

A known plain-text approach is when some amount of plain-text information and its encrypted ciphertext is provided to the cryptanalyst. Under this scenario, the cryptanalyst can use the relationship of the plain text to the cipher-text to hopefully determine the key and then decrypt the entire message. An example of this approach is the Rosetta Stone.

The Rosetta Stone is the famous piece of black basalt that was found in early 1799 in Egypt. Up to that time, many people had tried to understand the hieroglyphs that were drawn over so much of the Egypt of antiquity. Some had surmised that hieroglyphs could be interpreted by the association of ideas to pictures; then others said that hieroglyphics were not even a language. There was no ability in the world to understand this ancient language. Then, a young French military man found this stone (it was 3'9" long by 2'4.5" wide and 11" thick) that contained three rows of writing. The top row was hieroglyphs, and the second and third were ancient writing. Scholars recognized two of the three bands as writings of Demontic script and Ancient Greek. With the second and third bands partially recognizable (the condition of the block and the size of the sample), over the next 25 years the hieroglyphics were interpreted for the first time since the days when they were drawn on temple walls. The Rosetta Stone provided the means to decrypt previously unreadable hieroglyphs.

Ciphertext-Only Approach

This approach is the most difficult of all methods of attacking an encrypted message. The approach used when the crytopanalyst has the entire ciphertext and knows the method used for encryption and decryption is normally started with a brute-force attack. The cryptanalyst might try to collect other messages to compare or watch and wait for a mistake to be made. As some information about the message becomes known, such as the language in which it is written or its automated representation, such as ASCII or bits (0,1), the cryptanalyst has more with which to work. This approach works much easier with stream ciphers because the one-to-one relationship is also an added piece of information.

Chosen Plain-Text Approach

When the cryptanalyst has the method of encryption and decryption, a method is determined to get the sender of encrypted message—a message that is known to the cryptanalyst. When that known message is encrypted, it provides enough additional data to allow the breaking of the key. An example of this approach, from Thomas Barr's *Invitation to Cryptography* (Prentice Hall; 2002), took place during the WWII battle for Midway Island. The Allies had determined (through cryptanalysis) that the Japanese were going to attack, but the Japanese used a code word for the location: AF. The Allies knew of a few possible locations that could be the target, and they could not figure out how to determine which location they were speaking of. Midway was one of the possible locations. So, the Navy came up with an idea. From Midway, Navy personnel sent a message to the fleet in plain text about the water distillation plant being broken and there being little fresh water available. The communication transmission was intercepted by the Japanese (of course), and when the

Japanese message was intercepted by the U.S. fleet and decrypted, it contained the message, "AF is low on water." So, they were able to ascertain the location of the attack, Midway, and prepare for battle.

Cryptography and the Federal Government

If you are a U.S. federal worker, you have heard the terms Type 1 encryption and Type 2 encryption used in the U.S. federal government for decades:

Type 1 product.   Type 1 refers to that classified or controlled cryptographic item or product that uses a classified national security agency algorithm. Type 1 products are approved by the federal government for securely encrypting classified and sensitive U.S. government information.

Type 2 product.   Type 2 refers to that cryptographic product that is unclassified (as compared to Type 1, which is classified) and is endorsed by the *National Security Agency* (NSA) for use in the protection of national security systems, as defined in Title 40 U.S.C. Section 1452.

Type 3 Algorithm.   This algorithm is cryptographic and registered with the NIST and is published as a *Federal Information Processing Standard* (FIPS) for use in protecting unclassified sensitive information or commercial information.

Type 4 Algorithm.   This algorithm is a cryptographic algorithm registered with NIST but *not* published as an FIPS.

Sample Questions

1. A strong hash function, H, and its output message digest, MD, have which of the following characteristics relative to a message, M, and another message, Ml?

   a. H(M) = MD, where M is of fixed length and MD is of fixed length

   b. H(M) = MD, where M is of variable length and MD is of fixed length

   c. H(M) = H(M1)

   d. H(M) = MD where M is of variable length and MD is of variable length

2. The *Secure Hash Algorithm* (SHA) is specified in the:

   a. Data Encryption Standard

   b. Digital Signature Standard

   c. Digital Encryption Standard

   d. Advanced Encryption Standard

3. What are MD4 and MD5?

   a. Symmetric encryption algorithms

   b. Asymmetric encryption algorithms

   c. Hashing algorithms

   d. Digital certificates

4. What is the block length of the Rijndael cipher?

   a. 64 bits

   b. 128 bits

   c. Variable

   d. 256 bits

5. What is the key length of the Rijndael block cipher?

   a. 56 or 64 bits

   b. 512 bits

   c. 128, 192, or 256 bits

   d. 512 or 1024 bits

6. The hashing algorithm in the *Digital Signature Standard* (DSS) generates a message digest of:

   a. 120 bits

   b. 160 bits

   c. 56 bits

   d. 130 bit

7. The *Wireless Application Protocol* (WAP) analog of SSL in the TCP/IP protocol is:

   a. *Wireless Transport Layer Security Protocol* (WTLS)

   b. *Wireless Session Protocol* (WSP)

   c. *Wireless Transaction Protocol* (WTP)

   d. *Wireless Application Environment* (WAE)

8. Components of an IPSec *Security Association* (SA) are:

   a. Sockets security parameter and destination IP address

   b. *Authentication Header* (AH) and source IP address

   c. Security parameter index and destination address

   d. *Security Parameter Index* (SPI), *Authentication Header* (AH) or the *Encapsulation Security Payload* (ESP), and the destination IP address

9. Key clustering is:

   a. The identification of weak keys in symmetric key algorithms

   b. When two different keys encrypt a plain-text message into the same ciphertext

   c. When one key encrypts a plain-text message into different cipher-texts when the key is applied at different times

   d. When one key in a keyed hash function generates different message digests when applied at different times

10. The following table describes what cryptographic function?

INPUTS	OUTPUT
0 0	0
0 1	1
1 0	1
1 1	0

    a. Hash

    b. Keyed hash

    c. *Exclusive OR* (XOR)

    d. OR

11. In a block cipher, diffusion:

    a. Conceals the connection between the ciphertext and plain text

    b. Spreads the influence of a plain-text character over many ciphertext characters

    c. Is usually implemented by non-linear S boxes

    d. Cannot be accomplished

12. The hard, one-way function that characterizes the elliptic curve algorithm is:

    a. Finding the prime factors of very large numbers

    b. The discrete logarithm problem

    c. RSA

    d. The knapsack problem

13. What does the *Secure Sockets Layer* (SSL)/*Transaction Security Layer* (TSL) do?

    a. Implements confidentiality, authentication, and integrity above the transport layer

    b. Implements confidentiality, authentication, and integrity below the transport layer

    c. Implements only confidentiality above the transport layer

    d. Implements only confidentiality below the transport layer

14. The Skipjack algorithm is used in:

    a. PGP

    b. The Clipper Chip

    c. DSS

    d. AES

15. In most security protocols that support authentication, integrity, and confidentiality,

    a. AES is used to create digital signatures.

    b. Private-key cryptography is used to create digital signatures.

    c. DES is used to create digital signatures.

    d. Public-key cryptography is used to create digital signatures.

16. Which of the following is an example of a symmetric key algorithm?

    a. Rijndael

    b. RSA

    c. Diffie-Hellman

    d. Knapsack

17. A polyalphabetic cipher is also known as a:

    a. One-time pad

    b. Vigenère cipher

    c. Steganography

    d. Vernam cipher

18. Which of the following is NOT a characteristic of a symmetric key algorithm?

    a. Secure distribution of the secret key is a problem.

    b. Most algorithms are available for public scrutiny.

    c. Work factor is a function of the key size.

    d. Is slower than asymmetric key encryption.

19. Which of the following is an example of an asymmetric key algorithm?

    a. IDEA

    b. DES

    c. 3 DES

    d. Elliptic curve

20. Microdots, invisible ink, and hiding information in digital images is called:

    a. Hybrid cryptography

    b. Diffusion

    c. Steganography

    d. Confusion

21. The classic Caesar cipher is a:

    a. Polyalphabetic cipher

    b. Monoalphabetic cipher

    c. Transposition cipher

    d. Code group

22. The modes of DES do NOT include:

    a. Electronic Code Book

    b. Cipher Block Chaining

    c. Variable Block Feedback

    d. Output Feedback

23. The Rijndael Algorithm is also known as the:

    a. *Advanced Encryption Standard* (AES)

    b. *Data Encryption Standard* (DES)

    c. *Digital Signature Algorithm* (DSA)

    d. IDEA algorithm

24. Which of the following is true?

    a. The work factor of triple DES is the same as for double DES.

    b. The work factor of single DES is the same as for triple DES.

    c. The work factor of double DES is the same as for single DES.

    d. No successful attacks have been reported against double DES.

25. In public-key cryptography,

    a. Only the private key can encrypt and only the public key can decrypt.

    b. Only the public key can encrypt and only the private key can decrypt.

    c. The public key is used to encrypt and decrypt.

    d. If the public key encrypts, then only the private key can decrypt.

26. Which of the following characteristics does a one-time pad have if used properly?

    a. It can be used more than once.

    b. The key does not have to be random.

    c. It is unbreakable.

    d. The key has to be of greater length than the message to be encrypted.

27. The Clipper Chip is described by which of the following:

    a. The National Security Standard

    b. The Escrowed Encryption Standard

    c. Fair Public-Key Cryptosystem

    d. Advanced Encryption Standard

28. In a digitally signed message transmission using a hash function,

    a. The message digest is encrypted in the private key of the sender.

    b. The message digest is encrypted in the public key of the sender.

    c. The message is encrypted in the private key of the sender.

    d. The message is encrypted in the public key of the sender.

29. A ciphertext attack where the selection of the portions of ciphertext for the attempted decryption is based on the results of previous attempts is known as:

    a. Known plain text

    b. Chosen ciphertext

    c. Chosen plain text

    d. Adaptive chosen ciphertext

30. A trap door is which of the following?

    a. A mechanism, usually in multilevel security systems, that limits the flow of classified information to one direction

    b. A mechanism in a database system that restricts access to certain information within the database

    c. A method of sending a secret key

    d. A secret mechanism that enables the implementation of the reverse function in a one-way function

CHAPTER

7

Domain 6: Data Communications

Communications—whether voice, imagery, or data—is blending together at an unparalleled rate. This domain must somehow cover everything in one chapter. We focus on networks and how data, imagery, or voice is moved from one system to another. Data can be in transit, in storage, or in processing. First to be examined is how data is transmitted; then we examine how security is implemented on the network. This domain grows and expands almost weekly, so we advise you to read as much as you can—and as often as you can—to stay abreast of current developments.

Our Goals

For each of the seven domains, our goal is to provide you with three things:

1. Enough information about the domain so that you will be prepared to sit for the SSCP examination.

2. An understanding of how the overall system or enterprise security objectives, CIA, are carried through to the services and mechanisms within this domain.

3. An understanding of how the services and mechanisms of this domain provide security through one or more of the protection, detection, and reaction aspects of system security.

We do not believe you need to be taught the basics of each security service and/or security mechanism. You know your job as a system administrator or network administrator. What we intend to do is provide you with the connections and concepts that bring those isolated technical and administrative processes that you perform into the bigger picture: system security practice.

Domain Definition

According to (ISC)^2, "The data communications area encompasses the structures, transmission methods, transport formats and security measures used to provide integrity, availability, authentication and confidentiality for data transmitted over private and public communications paths."

Data Communication Fundamentals

The distinct difference between telecommunications and data communications has blurred as technology has taken over so much of our lives. For this chapter and for this domain, we need to refocus on the subset of telecommunications known as data communications. Computers connected via networks push, pull, collect, and manipulate data, and these functions are the purest form of data communications. But, before we examine how data is transmitted, we need to determine what data is. Data are the element of information, where data is the plural of datum (this term is not in general use).

Data communications takes place at every level of an information system. The *central processing unit* (CPU) sends messages to the various parts of the system, including input-output devices; applications send requests for support to various drivers; and the communications path carries these requests if the component is not local to the CPU. Data communications are constantly occurring. As we move outside the single CPU system, those requests from inside the system are joined by user requests, other system requests, other component requests, and of course, the responses. These types of data communications, external to the system, are normally carried by networks.

A network is the interconnection of two or more computers in such a way that there is communication (data flow) between the computers. If we look at the previous paragraph, different subsystems within a computer were sending requests and responses; those same subsystems can place requests (and send responses) to and from the other computers on the network. So, effectively, by networking the computers you have enhanced their capacity to perform certain activities. In fact, by sharing resources and processing capability, this method is exactly how distributed microprocessor-based systems today have 10 times or even 100 times the power of the large mainframes of the 1970s.

Physical Aspects of Data Communications

Now that we have a sense of what data is and that it is transmitted from one subsystem to another and from one system to another, we need to address the physical aspects of the data and how it is transmitted.

Data is turned into one of two types of signals: digital signals or analog signals. Digital signals are discrete (present or not present), and analog signals are continuously varying (see Figures 7.1 and 7.2).

Analog Signals

Analog signals (see Figure 7.1) are the oldest form of data communications. They are created by varying the frequency, phase, or amplitude of a signal. The old telephone system was an analog system; your voice was converted to an analog signal flowing over *plain old telephone system* (POTS) analog lines. As the voice changes during a conversation, the frequency, pitch, and many other factors change to convey the words to the recipient. Analog signals can be used to transmit data from one system to another across the telephone lines, but because the data is represented internally to the computer as digital, it must be converted to analog so that the transmission can be understood and then converted back at the other end. That is what modems do very well. Modems, called so because they modulate-demodulate, are still used regularly where analog transmission lines are used.

Analog signals can also be used to perform computer functions such as addition. A signal could be generated that has the values represented by a waveform that grow by a measurable number (1) each time a unit of data is to be added. Two numbers could be represented by waveforms of differing heights, and these waveforms could be combined to produce a waveform that can be read to represent the addition of the two numbers.

Analog signal

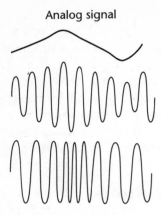

Figure 7.1 Analog signal representation.

Digital Signals

Digital signals are represented best by the on/off circuit or gate. When power (an electrical current) is applied (turned on), there is a signal. As soon as power is removed (turned off), the signal is gone. It is easiest to think of a light switch. If you add a timing mechanism, like the internal clock of a system, you can read the digital representation at each clock tick (as shown in Figure 7.2). At clock tick one, a 10-volt signal is present (On). The "1" represents this condition. At the subsequent clock ticks, the remainder of the data is represented: On, Off, On, Off, and On (10101).

Digital signal

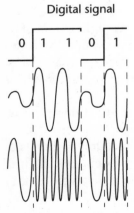

Figure 7.2 Digital signal representation.

Conducted Media

Data is transmitted from its source to its destination through one of two types of media: conducted or radiated. Conducted media physically conducts, or carries, the signal as it traverses the circuit. Conducted media are physical media over which the data travels. The three principal means are wire, cable, and fiber (see Figure 7.3). Wire conductors include CAT3 and CAT5 twisted pairs (copper wire), coaxial cable, and fiber-optic cable. Wires enable the transmission of electrons, and these electron transmissions can be modified to represent the specific data to be communicated. Two cans on a copper wire represent a simple form of analog communications. One voice causes the wire to vibrate, and this vibration is transferred to the can at the other end and results in a voice. Data communications over copper wire are easier to control, and this technique has been widely used in analog and digital communications. Wires are covered so that contact with another metal does not affect transmissions. Copper wires can be run through walls and floors to connect devices, and they can be folded in half and still retain all desired properties of transmission. The most common copper wire form is twisted pair and is generally used for telephone communications. Copper cable is also used in some gigabit Ethernet implementations.

Copper Wire

Copper wire twisted pairs come in both *unshielded twisted pair* (UTP) and *shielded twisted pair* (STP) versions. Category 5 cable is normally used for data or network communications when the speed requirements are not more than 100Mbps. See Table 7.1.

Figure 7.3   Examples of copper wire, fiber-optic cable, and coaxial cable.

Table 7.1 Twisted Pair Examples

COMMONLY USED TWISTED PAIRS	PRIMARILY USED FOR:
Category 3 UTP/STP	For use mainly in older, slower networks; provides up to 10Mbps speed
Category 4 UTP/STP	For use with Token Ring networks; provides speeds up to 16Mbps
Category 5 UTP/STP	For use with LANs of any variety; provides speeds up to 100Mbps (1,000,000 bps)
Category 7 UTP/STP	For use with high-speed networks; provides speeds up to 1Gbps (1,000,000,000 bps)

Coaxial Cable

Coaxial cable consists of a wire surrounded by a metal sleeve that reduces radio interference. Coaxial cable comes in two types: normal digital coaxial (a 5ohm cable) and high-speed digital and/or multimedia coaxial (a 75ohm cable). This second type of cable is generally used in television transmissions because of the high bandwidth. It is increasingly being used for network home users who already have cable TV installed. The cable TV companies have installed equipment that enables TV (mainly analog) and data signals to travel the coaxial cable together. Coaxial can carry narrow band (base band) transmissions or broadband transmissions.

Fiber Optics

Fiber optics enables the communication of data by using light pulses to represent a form of digital data (On or Off). The fiber, which carries the data, is usually encased so that light cannot exit the fiber pipe and also provides protection for the delicate fiber running within. The fiber is made of a glass that is pliable to some extent, yet retains the desired properties of clarity and strength. These properties enable the cable to be laid through floors and walls. Fiber can be bent to go around corners without affecting the light transmission (unless the fiber is broken by bending too much). These fibers can be affected by heat, pressure, and bending but are relatively easy to install and use and will last indefinitely. Fiber transmits light pulses at 186,000 miles per second (the speed of light) and is the highest data transfer rate of all media.

Radiated Media

Data can also be transmitted from its source to its destination through radiated media, which does not use conductors. The signals radiate through the air between the transmitter and receiver. Radiated media-based systems include pagers, cellular and cordless telephony, and some packet radio systems. Radio waves, microwaves, infrared light, and lasers are the most popular methods of wireless communication. Each method uses a different portion of the electromagnetic spectrum and has its own strengths and weaknesses. Laser has the longest length of possible transmission but cannot travel through solid objects. A small portion of the electromagnetic spectrum from 4×10^{14} through 7×10^{14} Hz in frequency is the frequency of the radiation that determines the color of light that we are seeing. Radiated differs from conductive transmission in that no physical connection exists between the source and destination. The energy signal travels through space instead of down a wire.

Figure 7.4 shows the regions of the electromagnetic spectrum in increasing frequencies and energy and decreasing wavelengths.

Most networks using radiated media (cellular, infrared, etc.) are particularly vulnerable to eavesdropping. In addition, many wireless-based LANs are being surreptitiously used as points of entry to their network or to the Internet by unauthorized users through the process of war-chalking. War-chalking is the shorthand method used to document the location of a free access point for a wireless device. These chalk marks are often located on the side of a building or on the ground.

Radio Waves

Radio waves have been used in communications since Marconi discovered how to harness this force. Data communication using newer technology has evolved to allow transmission via radio waves, and they encompass the entire spectrum from 10KHz to 1GHz.

Microwave

Microwave transmissions can range up to 45 Mbps. The bandwidth of a microwave channel can be subdivided into numerous subchannels that can be shared by voice and data. Microwaves transmit between the 1 GHz to 500GHz frequency.

Satellites

Satellites in geosynchronous orbit (22,300 miles above the earth at the equator) remain over the same point on the planet's surface. Satellites are used to relay point-to-point communications that travel by line of sight between two points that are not within sight of each other.

Microwave data transmissions are beamed to a satellite, and the satellite then relays the transmission to another spot on the Earth. Microwaves have a higher communications capacity, but there is some lag time between sending, relaying, and retransmitting communications.

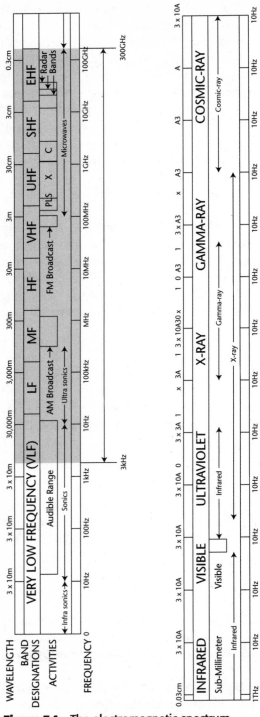

Figure 7.4 The electromagnetic spectrum.

Infrared

Infrared light is an alternative to using radio waves for data communications at short distances. Infrared provides increased security (it can only be intercepted via line-of-sight) and better performance (no interference by radio or microwaves). It uses the spectrum between 500 GHz and 1 *terahertz* (THz). Infrared remote control units have existed for years (your TV remote control operates in the infrared spectrum).

There are four types of infrared transmissions:

Line of sight. The line-of-sight implementation is the standard way of using an infrared LAN. A line-of-sight refers to the receiving and sending devices having a clear direct path for transmission.

Reflective. In a reflective network, the signals reflected off the walls or ceilings are passed to the waiting device.

Broadband optical telepoint. Broadband optical telepoint networks are the fastest of the four. This technology is capable of transmitting high-quality multimedia such as voice, data, and graphics.

Scatter. A scatter infrared network only works in an area of no more than 100 feet with a slow signal transmission. Scatter infrared bounces off walls and ceilings, eventually hitting the receiving device. It is good for use within a small space.

As we discussed, there are two types of transmission media: conducted media and radiated media (see Table 7.2).

Table 7.2 Physical Characteristics of Transmission Media

CONDUCTED	RADIATED
Electrical conductors	Radio frequency
■ Wire	■ Broadcast
■ Coaxial	■ Microwave
	■ Satellite
Light conductors	Light frequency
■ Fiber optics	■ Infrared
	■ Laser

Transmission Approaches

There are three approaches to transmitting signals: unicast, broadcast, and multicast. Each is used for specific purposes:

Unicast.   A transmission that travels directly from the sender to the (only) receiver and is the normal communication method used with the World Wide Web. For example, you enter the destination address to a Web site that you wish to visit. You press Enter, and the Web site responds with Web pages to your computer (alone).

Broadcast.   A transmission sent to all computers on a network. A data transmission is sent to a special destination (broadcast) address. All computers listening for transmissions to the broadcast address receive this broadcast. For example, a radio broadcast is sent to anyone who wants to listen to the channel (or broadcast address). A SPAM email is often sent based on a broadcast address.

Multicast.   Members of a group (users) who have expressed interest (subscribed) in the data. Only those subscribing to this group will receive these data transmissions. Data communications bandwidth is reduced by sending transmissions over paths only once, instead of once per receiver. Internet multicast addresses range from 224.0.0.0 through 239.255.255.255. An example is teleconferencing and video conferencing direct communications only to subscribed members.

Bandwidth

Bandwidth represents the signal capacity of the medium—the size of the pipe through which data flows (see Figure 7.5). Digital data transmissions are usually represented by bits or bytes per second, and analog transmissions are usually represented by cycles per second. Most data paths are set to a fixed bandwidth, but technology enables the distribution of bandwidth over a single medium. If a digital data bandwidth is rated at 1200 *bits per second* (bps), this bandwidth could be split into smaller slices to create 300 bps and 900 bps slices that fit a 1200 bps pipe.

Broadband versus Narrowband

Currently, two types of bandwidth are used for transporting the data transmission: broadband and narrow band (base band). You can readily see their similarities and differences by studying Figure 7.5.

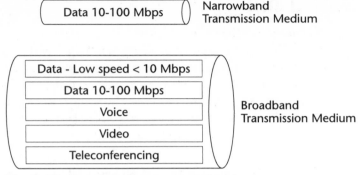

Figure 7.5 Broadband versus narrowband.

Spread Spectrum

Spread spectrum uses multiple frequencies over which to send a message. This method of transmission reduces the chances for interference (no single interference activity will destroy the entire message). Spread spectrum also improves the reliability of the network and somewhat increases the security of the message (you cannot easily eavesdrop over multiple frequencies). There are two types of spread-spectrum systems: direct sequence and frequency-hopping implementations.

Frequency-hopping implementation. The frequencies divide into hops; hence the name *frequency hopping*. The hopping sequence does several things. The blocks of data are transmitted on different frequencies, and the receiver gets the signals and puts the block in the right order.

Direct sequence implementation. Direct sequence codes a message by digitizing it and uses a multi-pattern to represent each original bit in the message. This method tends to use bandwidth inefficiently, but transmissions are suitable for bandwidth sharing because they offer an improved signal-to-noise ratio compared with narrow-band transmissions.

Networks

Under this discussion of networks, we will cover six types: LANS, MANS, WANS, intranets, the Internet, and extranets. When we discuss networks, we need to discuss two aspects: the physical topology (how the connections are actually connecting the computers) and the logical topology (how data travels across the media).

Local Area Networks (LANs)

A *local area network* (LAN) is a network that is geographically small. Normally, a LAN is no larger than a single building or even contained within a few floors of a building. It can be as small as two workstations and one peripheral device, such as a printer. For our discussions, as we continue, we will assume a LAN that has several workstations, a file server, and network devices. A network card connects a computer to a LAN. *Network interface cards* (NICs) provide this interface and are available in various formats and speeds.

Two types of LANs exist:

Wired.   Coaxial, Ethernet, fast Ethernet, and gigabit Ethernet all use copper wire as their conduit for carrying signals from one place to another. Other wired LAN types include fiber optics, which use light transmissions to represent data in transit over the network.

Wireless.   These non-wire LANS are gaining in popularity, but they do present additional security concerns. Security protocols have been developed to make these more secure, but insecure implementations have been occurring since their inception.

Wired LANs are the original networks. These operate in relatively small areas, such as a home, office, or building. Generally, systems connected to a LAN are directly connected without the use of routers; however, as the size of our LANs has grown, routers and gateways serve several purposes. They can be used to minimize traffic on segments of a LAN (when the LAN is large) by filtering traffic that does not need to pass through and also to provide a measure of security by segmenting sections of the LAN (the traffic) from each other.

Wide Area Networks (WANs)

Wide area networks (WANs) are not just big LANs. A major difference is distance: WANs cover large geographical areas while LANs are normally confined to a group of offices or a building. WANs typically connect computing facilities, providing the user with access to multiple mainframes located in different cities, for example. WANs are normally very high-speed networks to make up for the distance. Fiber is used whenever possible (or gigabit Ethernet) to provide for the faster speed and the broader capability. Because of their differences, WANs can more easily provide for multicasting such as audio, video, and data over one network.

Metropolitan Area Networks (MANs)

Metropolitan area networks (MANs) do not seem to have taken on an identity as individually unique as WANs and LANs. MANs operate in a distinct area defined by high-speed communications lines and equipment and typically cover a metropolitan area.

Intranets

An intranet is a privately owned network based on Internet technology and protocols that an organization uses for its own internal purposes. An intranet is normally closed to outsiders, but external access can be provided to authorized persons via dialup or *virtual private network* (VPN). This approach to networking provides for additional security because the data is not being transmitted across the public switched network or any provider-based wiring. It is all owned, managed, and protected by your organization.

The Internet

The Internet is the global interconnection of LANs, MANs, and WANs. The Internet project started in 1969 with several research organizations and universities. Originally called the ARPANET, its purpose was to connect research organizations that supported the Defense Department. In the early 1990s, it became the Internet because it was growing with private users—many of whom had started using it during their university days. Commercial use of the Internet began in earnest by the mid-1990s as consumers learned to use the Internet and corporations figured out how to make it profitable. By 1989, there were more than 100 sites actively participating in this network. Today, the Internet is worldwide—in every country in the world—and growing more rapidly than anyone could have believed. In fact, by 2002 it was estimated that nearly 160 *million* hosts were on the Internet (see Figure 7.6).

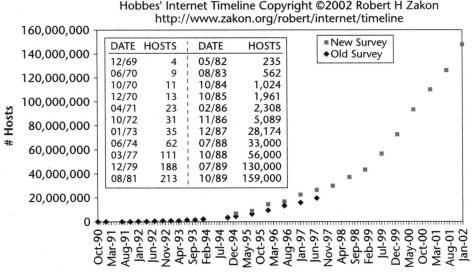

Figure 7.6 Number of hosts on the Internet.

The *World Wide Web* (WWW) is the method used to access information contained on resources located throughout the Internet. The Web uses various protocols to provide access to information ranging from audio, data to video, and more. Figure 7.7 shows the more than 38 *million* Web sites that existed at the beginning of this year. The Web has changed the way many people in the world work and play. With the Internet and the Web, many security issues of military or government concern in years past are every family's and individual's concern.

Extranets

An extranet is a private network that uses the Internet protocol and the public telecommunication system to securely share a part of a business's information. By establishing authentication and identification (through some I&A mechanism), members of the wider community (not just the internal staff) can access the information, post orders, request assistance, and so on without doing so in a public forum. Typically, a VPN or secure Web site is used to implement this technology.

Specific communities of interest have realized the added value of communicating with members by using the Internet as a means. Web portals have been established, and many *business-to-business* (B2B) and *business-to-employee* (B2E) enterprises are using the concepts of the extranet.

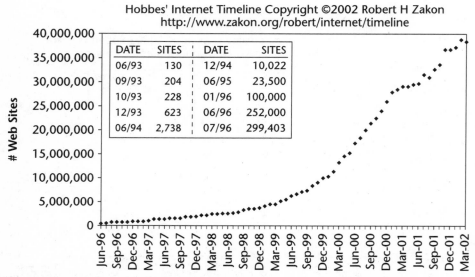

Figure 7.7 Number of Web sites as of March 2002 reached 38,118,962.

Virtual Private Networks (VPNs)*

If a business needs to conduct secure communications between several different locations, a private network can be constructed by leasing or installing private communication lines. A less expensive and more flexible alternative is installing a *virtual private network* (VPN) that uses the Internet as the transport medium and employs security measures to ensure that the communications are indeed private. Although the VPN's traffic crosses the Internet, VPN protection prevents most unauthorized users from reading and/or modifying the traffic. Of course, if a compromise occurs at either end of the VPN, the data is not secure. In particular, spyware or viruses on the computer can sniff passwords and thereby circumvent the VPN security, putting the organization at risk. This reason is why it is imperative for telecommuters to protect their computers.

VPN Security

VPNs can provide some or all of the following types of protection:

Connectionless integrity.   A guarantee that the message received is the exact one that was sent and that no tampering has occurred. Connectionless means that messages are sent from the sender to the receiver, but no attempt is made to ensure that they are received in order or that any (or all) were in fact received. Integrity is provided through the use of a *message authentication code* (MAC) and a symmetric secret key. Two MACs that are commonly used for this purpose are HMACSHA1 and HMACMD5.

Data origin authentication.   A guarantee that the message actually was sent by the apparent originator of the message and not by another user masquerading as the supposed message originator.

Confidentiality or privacy.   A guarantee that even if the message is "read" by an eavesdropper, the contents are not understandable except to the authorized recipient. Confidentiality is provided through the use of an encryption algorithm and a symmetric secret key. Triple DES is a widely used encryption algorithm; NIST's newly defined *Advanced Encryption Algorithm* (AES) is beginning to replace triple DES.

Traffic analysis protection.   An assurance that an eavesdropper cannot determine who is communicating with whom or determine the frequency and volume of communications between specific entities.

Access protection.   Control over which network resources can be accessed by telecommuters and what types of network traffic can be initiated by or exchanged with telecommuters.

*This section appears courtesy of NIST. Used by permission.

Which of these protections are actually supplied by a particular VPN implementation depends on the configuration, access policies, and setup of the VPN.

VPN Modes of Operation

There are two basic modes in which VPNs can function for telecommuting: host-to-host or host-to-gateway. Host-to-host mode enables the telecommuter to conduct protected communications with one or more other hosts. In this case, each host would have to be equipped with a VPN client that can interoperate with the VPN clients on the other hosts. The more common scenario (host to gateway) involves a firewall or gateway (which we will refer to as a security gateway) that is VPN-enabled; it functions as a gatekeeper for the business network that the telecommuter wants to access. In this case, the telecommuter's host needs a VPN client that is compatible with the security gateway's VPN implementation. The telecommuter can then conduct protected communications with the hosts that reside on the network (protected by the security gateway). A gateway-to-gateway VPN is also possible, but this setup would not be appropriate for a telecommuter because it is employed between two or more office networks (for example, headquarters and regional offices). Today's cable modems and cable/DSL routers generally enable the traversal of VPN data (often referred to as VPN or IPSec passthrough mode), but they do not provide VPN capabilities and protections themselves.

Peer Authentication

Before a telecommuter can conduct VPN secured communications, each party involved in the communication must verify its identity with the other party. This action provides not only security for the data being transferred but non-repudiation of the participants' identification as well. The most common methods of peer authentication are as follows.

Public Key Certificate

As described earlier, public keys can be freely shared without needing a secure channel of communications. This situation means, however, that we need some method of verifying that a given public key belongs to whomever is claiming it. A public key certificate can be used for this type of verification, and a security gateway will generally possess its own public key certificate. A telecommuter will also have a certificate issued by an authority recognized by the security gateway. When a user attempts to make a connection to the VPN through the security gateway, the gateway will present the user (in reality, the VPN software on the user's computer) with its certificate that will be checked to ensure that the gateway is correct (to avoid spoofing attacks). Next, the security gateway will require a certificate from the user (again the VPN software on the user's computer generally performs this step) to ensure that the user has authorized access. Once the user is authorized, the VPN connection will be initiated. This function is a very secure method of authentication.

One-Time Password

A one-time password is changed after each use; it is useful when the password is not adequately protected from compromise during login (for example, the password is transmitted over an insecure network). Under this approach, each user is given a password generator that looks much like a pocket calculator or a software program that can generate the passwords. The user enters a *personal identification number* (PIN) to activate the password generator, and the password generator creates a random password (or number sequence) using a procedure that is duplicated at the central system. The user will then enter the generated password in the VPN software on his or her machine that will in turn forward it to the security gateway. If the passwords generated by the user and the security gateway match, the user is authorized to use the VPN. If the password is intercepted, an intruder could not use it for later access because it is valid only for this session.

Password

A password is a protected or private character string used to authenticate and identify. Generally, a password is encrypted during transmission for protection. When authenticating to a security gateway, the user enters a password. The VPN client then generates an encrypted hash of the password and sends it to the gateway. The security gateway then compares the hash to the one it has on file for the user. If the two match, the user is authenticated and connected to the VPN.

Policy Configuration

The fortunate telecommuter will obtain a VPN client that has been preconfigured to satisfy the employer's security policies. If that is not the case, the VPN client will need to be configured with security protections that satisfy the employer's security requirements.

Many VPN clients will enable VPN-secured traffic to be either encrypted or integrity protected without requiring both types of protection. For a truly secure VPN, both encryption and integrity protection should be applied. Without encryption, unauthorized parties can read the traffic. Without integrity protection, encrypted traffic is susceptible to attacks that can result in unauthorized modification of the message. Some of the policy-related choices are as follows:

Encryption algorithm.   Triple DES (Data Encryption Standard) is the encryption algorithm that is most commonly used today. NIST's AES (Advanced Encryption Standard) has been approved and will most likely replace triple DES as the default VPN encryption algorithm. Many VPN clients are configured with DES as the default encryption algorithm; AES or triple DES are preferable to DES, because traffic using DES for encryption could be decrypted (although only with sophisticated hardware and software) by parties other than the intended recipient.

MAC (message authentication code) algorithm.   The MAC algorithm provides integrity to the VPN traffic. HMAC SHA1 is the national standard message authentication algorithm. HMAC MD5 is also usable for today's VPNs.

Selective or total protection.   Most VPN clients will enable either some or all of the traffic to be protected. By implementing total protection, encryption and integrity will be applied to all VPN traffic.

VPN Operation

The following steps are necessary to create a VPN:

1. Install the VPN client.
2. Obtain the required public-key certificates, password(s), and/or onetime password generator. If all protected communications will be handled by the gateway, no other peer credentials are required. If the telecommuter will be conducting peer-to-peer VPN communications, however, credentials valid for those peers will be required as well. They can be obtained beforehand or exchanged in the course of the VPN negotiations. If the latter method will be used, it is important to ensure that the VPN client can dynamically request and process these credentials.
3. Configure the VPN client.
4. Put the VPN client into "operational" mode.
5. Perform a trial run. A number of VPN clients have a "test" button that will perform this function. It is important to ensure that after a VPN client is installed and configured, both outbound and inbound communications can still take place successfully. It is also a good idea to try to send and receive some unauthorized traffic to ensure that unprotected communications are unsuccessful.

A VPN serves as an encrypted "tunnel" between two organizations (or hosts) that makes it possible for secured communication to occur over public networks. This tunnel enables a variety of different types of traffic, rather than a single, encrypted connection such as an e-commerce credit card transaction using a Web server. To ensure correct operation, the VPN must be carefully configured on both the organization's central office systems and the telecommuter's remote system. Users should also be educated on VPN operation, because current implementations are not as simple or "transparent" as some other security applications. Organizations considering a VPN should thus proceed with caution, first ensuring that security goals cannot be achieved with less-complex mechanisms. If a VPN is used, the organization's system administrators should be responsible for correctly configuring the VPN and for providing telecommuters with properly configured software for their offsite systems.

Physical Topologies

There are three predominant physical topologies for networking, and these topologies can be used for small home office networks, corporations, and even large organizations. The topology refers to the physical construction of the infrastructure of the network. Three popular choices are star, bus, and ring.

Star Topology

A star network (see Figure 7.8) consists of a central hub, or node, to which all devices are connected directly. Many wireless LANs are built based on the star topology. This approach becomes cumbersome and difficult to manage when many components are used, however, and typically no more than 10 to 15 devices hang on a star network.

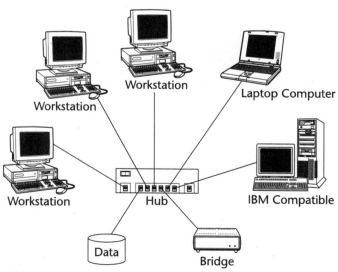

Figure 7.8 Star topology.

Bus Topology

On a bus network (see Figure 7.9), each component broadcasts across the bus, listens to all traffic, and picks up that which is directed to that component. Many LANs are implemented with a bus backbone running through the building or floors. Then, as components need to be added to it, they only have to be attached to the closest point of the bus. The speed of the backbone is often higher than the speed of the component to the bus. As this topology is usually implemented, *Carrier Sense Multiple Access* (CSMA) or Ethernet is used in a bus topology, but tokens can also be used. In a CSMA implementation, all components listen to all packets that are "broadcast" and rejected by all except the intended recipient. Collision detection is implemented so that when a collision is detected, the transmitter waits a specified amount of time before trying again. Ethernet is known today as CMSA/CD and is defined in the IEEE 802.3 standard.

Ring Topology

A ring topology (see Figure 7.10) has all the devices connected in a circle. Many fiber-optic networks are implemented by using this topology. In a ring topology, the data flows in one direction around the ring. Normally, tokens control network access. The device with a token can use the network, and a device without a token must wait until one is freed up by the device using the network. This arrangement ensures that no collisions occur on the network. Problems exist when tokens are lost and must be regenerated to re-enable network communications. FDDI generally uses dual rings, each having their own token with data flowing in opposite directions.

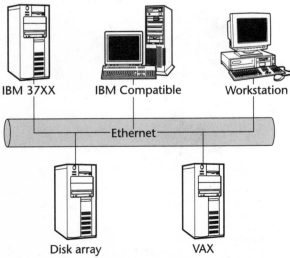

Figure 7.9 Bus topology.

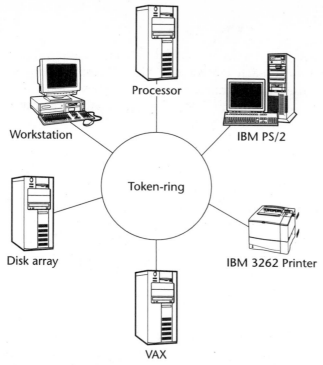

Figure 7.10 Ring topology.

Logical Topologies

Logical topologies are concerned with how data travels across the physical media. Each unique topology requires a method of communicating over the physical circuits making up the network infrastructure. All stations within a network must be able to send and receive data to be effective; connectivity alone does not ensure proper communications. Logical topologies are typically placed in two categories: bus and ring.

Bus

Ethernet is a logical bus network topology that can be implemented as a bus or star physical topology. Ethernet uses CSMA/CD to implement this logical topology and allow communications over the network.

Ring

Token ring is a logical topology that is physically configured as a star topology. Communications over the network are accomplished by using a token that is passed throughout the ring, with each workstation regenerating the token. The owner of the token has the right to transmit, and all other stations must wait until the owner frees the token for reuse. This function enables the physical network to function as a communications media.

Standards

Several standards bodies are associated with information systems and system security, namely the *International Standards Organization* (ISO), the *American National Standards Institute* (ANSI), and the *Institute of Electrical and Electronic Engineers* (IEEE). We discuss these organizations and contributions in the following paragraphs.

IEEE Standards

The IEEE is a professional society in the United States. Among its responsibilities is setting many of the LAN standards. The IEEE Standards Project 802, as it was called, was started in the late 1970s. Its primary task was to establish standards for implementing LANs. At that time, there were more than 40 separate implementations. Several of the standards the IEEE has developed are listed as follows.

802.X Standards

- 802.3 is the LAN architecture to run on Ethernet. This standard was initially written in 1985, and standard Ethernet runs at 10 Mbps.
- 802.5 is the LAN architecture to run on the Token Ring network.
- 802.6 describes Ethernet MANs.
- 802.8 deals with fiber-optic implementations of Ethernet.
- 802.9 deals with integrated voice and data networks.
- 802.11 is the LAN architecture to run on a wireless network.

Ethernet

Standard Ethernet networks are implemented by using twisted-pair copper wires at 10 Mbps (10BaseT).

Fast Ethernet

Fast Ethernet is Ethernet at 100Mbps, typically over Category 5 twisted pair. Most NIC cards today are at least 10/100 Mbps to support the continually increasing transmission speeds required by users. In 1995, 100Mbps became the Ethernet standard transmission speed (100Base standards).

Gigabit Ethernet

A gigabit Ethernet is an Ethernet running 1 Gbps, 1000 Mbps, or 1,000,000 bps. This speed can be achieved using a specially shielded copper 150-Ohm cable that can only extend 25 meters. More typical implementations include the use of existing Category 5 UTP cabling or fiber-optic cables extending up to 5 km (1000Base standards).

NOTE All Ethernet systems transmit by using CSMA/CD.

The main difference of the various types of Ethernet is the speed, which is derived from a change in the physical media carrying the signals. See Table 7.3.

International Organization for Standardization (ISO)

The ISO produces international standards on many subjects, one of which is information technology. The ISO's work is not limited to any particular branch; it covers all technical fields except electrical and electronic engineering standards. These are the responsibility of the *International Electrotechnical Commission* (IEC). Information technology standardization is carried out by a joint ISO/IEC technical committee (JTC 1), whose Web site is at www.jtc1.org.

Table 7.3 Relationship of Media to IEEE Standards

COMMONLY USED NAME	MEDIA	BANDWIDTH	IEEE DESIGNATION
10Base2	Coaxial/Thinnet	10Mbps	802.3
10BaseT	Cat5 UTP	10Mbps	802.3
10Base5	Coaxial/Thicknet	10 Mbps	802.3
100BaseT	Cat5 UTP	100Mbps	802.3u
Fast Ethernet	Cat5 UTP	100Mbps	802.3u
Gigabit Ethernet (1000Base)	Cat5 or Fiber-optic	1,000,000 bps/ 1000Mbps	802.3z and 802.3ab

American National Standards Institute (ANSI)

ANSI is an organization that administers and coordinates the voluntary standardization and conformity assessment system for the United States and is based in Washington, D.C. ANSI is the U.S. representative to the ISO.

International Telecommunication Union (ITU)

ITU is an international radio and telecommunications recommendation organization headquartered in Geneva, Switzerland. The ITU develops recommendations (standards) for use in the telecommunications field. They also publish telecommunication technology, regulatory, and standards information. Their Web site is located at www.itu.int. The ITU is comprised of three sectors:

ITU-R.   Radio Communication Sector.

ITU-T.   Telecommunication Standardization Sector; in 1993, it replaced the former *International Telegraph and Telephone Consultative Committee* (CCITT) that originated in 1865.

ITU-D.   Telecommunications Development Sector.

Protocols

Protocol refers to the suite of conventions and rules for use within a single layer of the network model.

The X Protocols

ITU-T develops recommended international communications standards including the Group (fax), V. (modem), and X. (networking) protocol standards and many others. The X.protocol standard includes those found at www .itu.int/rec. The following are some of the X. recommendations.

X.400

X.400 was developed as a universal standard for the envelope used in email. The proper name for X.400 is "Message handling services: Message handling system and service overview." It is used in the presentation layer for email, and the X.400 series pertains to message handling.

X.500

"Information technology—Open Systems Interconnection—The Directory: Overview of concepts, models, and services" is X.500. It recommends a standard to link together email systems by using a standard addressing format and is used in the presentation layer for directory services.

X.509

X.509 is part of the X.500 series that is used in the presentation layer for digital certificates used in the directory service.

X.25

X.25 is the specification for the interface for data terminal and data circuit termination equipment in a packet-switched network interface between *Data Terminal Equipment* (DTE) and *Data Circuit-terminating Equipment* (DCE) for terminals operating in the packet mode and connected to public data networks by dedicated circuit. It is used in the first three layers: physical, data link, and network.

Transmission Control Protocol/Internet Protocol (TCP/IP)

In the 1970s, Vinton Cerf and Robert Kahn proposed a set of protocols that would allow the interconnection of many networks that spanned vendors and operating systems. The U.S. government realized the importance of such an effort and funded several projects. The TCP/IP suite, as it is normally called, has become the de facto Internet work protocol suite—even overshadowing the ISO's OSI. The TCP/IP network model contains only four layers while the OSI model contains seven (see *OSI Seven-Layer Model*).

User Datagram Protocol (UDP)

With the TCP/IP suite, the upper layer can use either TCP or UDP to transport data. UDP is used when a packet can be directed toward a specific port at the destination.

NetBEUI

The native Windows NT networking protocol is known as NetBEUI.

Wireless Access Protocol (WAP)

This protocol is specifically designed to provide wireless devices with limited memory capacities with the ability to communicate over limited bandwidth circuits. The *Wireless Transport Layer Security* (WTLS) protocol defines the security layer of *Wireless Access Protocol* (WAP).

Remote Access Protocols

RAS and RADIUS are the two primary types of remote access protocols, which are explained in the paragraphs that follow.

Remote Access Services (RAS)

RAS is a feature built into Windows NT that enables users to log into an NT-based LAN by using a modem, an X.25 connection, or a WAN link. RAS works with several major network protocols, including TCP/IP, IPX, and NetBEUI. To use RAS from a remote node, you need a RAS client program, which is built into most versions of Windows, or any PPP client software. For example, most remote control programs work with RAS.

RAS is dedicated to handling users that are not on a LAN but who need remote access to it. The remote access server enables users to gain access to files and print services on the LAN from a remote location. For example, a user who dials into a network from home by using an analog modem or an ISDN connection will dial into a remote access server. Once the user is authenticated, he or she can access shared drives and printers as if he or she were physically connected to the office LAN.

Remote Authentication Dial-In User Service (RADIUS)

The *Remote Authentication Dial-In User Service* (RADIUS) is an authentication and accounting system used by many *Internet Service Providers* (ISPs). When you dial in to the ISP, you must enter your username and password. This information is passed to a RADIUS server, which checks that the information is correct and then authorizes access to the ISP system. Though not an official standard, the RADIUS specification is maintained by a working group of the IETF.

Internet Protocol Security (IPSec)

IPSec is the most widely used secure network protocol, and it provides VPN capabilities at the *Internet Protocol* (IP) layer of communications. In other words, all types of Internet traffic can be IPsec protected independently of the specific applications that conduct the communications. The applications do not need to be aware of the protection and do not need to be altered in any way to enable it. IPSec incorporates a key management protocol, the *Internet Key Exchange* (IKE), which is used to negotiate the secret keys that protect VPN communications as well as the level and type of security protections that will characterize the VPN.

Secure Sockets Layer (SSL) or Transport Layer Security (TLS)

Originally developed by Netscape and known as SSL, the TLS protocol was subsequently adopted, renamed, and slightly modified by the IETF. It is a session-oriented protocol that provides security at the transport layer—a higher layer in the TCP/IP protocol stack than IP. It can more easily provide individual user-level access protection than the current IPsec; however, applications must be modified specifically to use TLS, and each individual session must establish its own TLS protection. In addition, TLS can protect only applications that run over TCP. TLS is currently widely used to protect Web browser traffic. The WTLS protocol is used on wireless devices to provide transport-level security.

Layer 2 Tunneling Protocol (L2TP)

L2TP is an extension of the *Point-to-Point Protocol* (PPP) and was developed to augment the security features available with the *Point-to-Point Tunneling Protocol* (PPTP). L2TP enables a dial-up user to connect to an IP network and authenticate the user's identity through the use of an authentication protocol such as *Remote Authentication Dial-In User Service* (RADIUS). It then creates a PPP tunnel, encapsulating the phone link in an IP packet and enabling the non-IP phone traffic to act like any other Internet traffic. For users who dial into a local *Internet Service Provider* (ISP) that is not co-located with the network gateway, L2TP creates an extended tunnel that includes the PPP tunnel and the ISP-to-gateway leg—extending from the dial-up user to the network entry point. This function enables the user to authenticate his or her identity directly to the network; however, L2TP does not include any mechanism for encryption or authentication of its traffic.

Several protection schemes have been suggested, providing protection of L2TP traffic by IPSec and resulting in a secure VPN. These schemes sacrifice some IPSec access control capabilities, however. L2TP is also used by some IPSec VPNs to supplement nonstandard areas within IPSec, such as the exchange of policy or configuration information between a telecommuter and a security gateway.

Point-to-Point Tunneling Protocol (PPTP)

PPTP is a predecessor to L2TP that shares L2TP's major goals. A version of PPTP, with proprietary Microsoft extensions, is found in most Microsoft Windows operating systems. Thus, it is an attractive and widely accessible vehicle for the creation of VPNs. The underlying security of Microsoft's original PPTP implementation and the improved L2TP version has been questioned, however.

Some VPN clients use proprietary technologies. A single VPN client often enables the user to choose between a proprietary VPN scheme and a standardized scheme. Proprietary schemes restrict the user to a particular vendor's VPN products and should be avoided wherever possible. Standardized schemes also benefit from security analysis and testing performed by a wider community of users and analysts.

Models for Network Communication

The following sections discuss the primary models for network communication.

OSI Seven-Layer Model

The reference model for *Open Systems Interconnection* (OSI) is a standard reference model for communication in a network and is an *International Standards Organization* (ISO) development standard. The OSI model exists mainly to simplify the process of understanding how computer systems communicate in a network environment (see Table 7.4). The model has seven layers:

- Layer 1: Physical Layer
- Layer 2: Data Link Layer
- Layer 3: Network Layer
- Layer 4: Transport Layer
- Layer 5. Session Layer
- Layer 6: Presentation Layer
- Layer 7: Application Layer

We will discuss each of these layers in the paragraphs that follow.

Physical Layer

Layer 1 represents the actual physical communication between hardware. It specifies the electrical connections between the transmission media and the system. For example, it describes how many and which pins will carry specific signals and even the shape and size of the connectors. Finally, it determines the speed at which the data will flow and in which direction (or both).

Table 7.4 The OSI Model Mapped to Functions of the Network

OSI LAYER	WHAT IT REPRESENTS	MAIN ACTIVITY
Layer 7	Application	Email, Web browsers, FTP
Layer 6	Presentation	Protocol conversions, cryptographic translations
Layer 5	Session	Session management
Layer 4	Transport	Reliability, integrity, TCP
The three lower layers (1-3):		
Layer 3	Network	IP
Layer 2	Data Link	PPP, SLIP
Layer 1	Physical	Network Interface Card, twisted pairs, coaxial, fiber

Data Link Layer

The data link layer determines the physical path of communication to the next node. *Logical Link Control* (LLC) and *Media Access Control* (MAC) take place at this layer and are defined in IEEE 802.3 standards. The data link layer defines the format of the data frame (packet), which includes a checksum, the source and destination address, and the data. Error detection is also done at this layer by using a checksum.

Network Layer

Layer 3 determines the route that the actual packets take to reach their destination. Layer 3 addresses are known as the *Internet Protocol* (IP) addresses. IP is responsible for routing (directing datagrams from one network to another). The IP identifies each host through a 32-bit IP address—for example, 128.45.29.10. The first three positions (bytes) of the address identify the network, and the remaining bytes identify the host on that network.

Transport Layer

Layer 4 generates the address of an end user and makes certain that the blocks of data or packets have been received, that no duplication exists, and that none have been lost. Two transport protocols, the *Transmission Control Protocol* (TCP) and the *User Datagram Protocol* (UDP), are used at this layer.

Session Layer

Layer 5 is where two computers establish, synchronize, maintain, and end a single session. Authentication takes place at this level, along with activities such as data transfer. There are three modes for the session layer: simplex, half duplex, and full duplex.

Presentation Layer

The sixth layer, the presentation layer, is responsible for formatting data exchange. This layer is where character sets are converted, data are encrypted, and usually where encryption takes place. Converting is the primary function, such as ASCII and EBCDIC translations taking place as well as the translation/conversion for many other formats such as MPEG, TIFF, GIF, and JPEG.

Application Layer

Layer 7 of the OSI model provides the protocols needed for users to use the network for whatever they need (X.400 protocols for email and x.500 if directory services are required). The application layer also performs management activities if the user is working with distributed databases.

Security Services and Mechanisms

The OSI has defined the following six security services in its reference model:

- Authentication
- Data confidentiality
- Access control
- Non-repudiation
- Logging and monitoring
- Data integrity

In addition to the six security services, the OSI model describes eight security mechanisms:

- Encipherment
- Digital signature
- Access control
- Data integrity
- Authentication

- Traffic padding
- Routing control
- Notarization

TCP/IP Network Model

Although the OSI model is widely used and often cited as the standard, the TCP/IP protocol has been used by most Unix workstation vendors. TCP/IP is designed around a simple four-layer scheme and does omit some features found under the OSI model. It also combines the features of some adjacent OSI layers and splits other layers. The four network layers defined by the TCP/IP model are as follows:

Layer 1 (Link).   This layer defines the network hardware and device drivers.

Layer 2 (Network).   This layer is used for basic communication, addressing, and routing. TCP/IP uses IP and ICMP protocols at the network layer.

Layer 3 (Transport).   This layer handles communication among programs on a network. TCP and UDP protocols also fall within this layer.

Layer 4 (Application).   End-user applications reside at this layer. Commonly used applications include NFS, DNS, arp, rlogin, talk, FTP, ntp, and traceroute.

Network Testing Techniques

Techniques for providing security are covered throughout the book. In this chapter, we discuss the importance of testing your network. One of the most effective activities you can perform is to continuously validate, through active testing, your network's security posture. The following section is provided courtesy of NIST.

Reasons for Testing a System

The primary reason for testing a system is to identify potential vulnerabilities and subsequently repair them. The number of reported vulnerabilities is growing daily; for example, the number of new information system vulnerabilities reported to the Bugtraq database has more that quintupled since the start of 1998—from an average of 20 to more than 100 per month. In addition, the Computer Security Institute and the FBI's joint survey of 643 computer security practitioners in U.S. corporations, government agencies, financial institutions, medical institutions, and universities found that 90 percent of survey respondents detected cyber attacks in the past year, with 273 organizations reporting $265,589,940 in financial losses.

Typically, vulnerabilities are used repeatedly by hackers to exploit weaknesses that organizations have not corrected. A report in a SANS Security Alert, dated May 2000, provides a discussion of this issue. A small number of flaws in software programs are responsible for the vast majority of successful Internet attacks. A few software vulnerabilities account for the majority of successful attacks because attackers do not like to do extra work. They exploit the best-known flaws with the most effective and widely available attack tools. They also count on organizations not fixing the problems.

In a study involving federal agencies, security software vendors, security consulting firms, and incident response teams, a consensus was reached in developing a top-20 list of critical Internet security vulnerabilities. SANS Security Alert lists these vulnerabilities and outlines recommendations and suggestions for overcoming these weaknesses. In this environment, security testing becomes critical to all organizations that are interested in protecting their networks.

Testing is a fundamental security activity that can be conducted to achieve a secure operating environment while fulfilling an organization's security requirements. Testing enables an organization to accurately assess its system's security posture. Also, testing, using the techniques recommended in this report enables an organization to view its network the same way an attacker would—thus providing additional insight and advantage.

Security Testing and the System Development Life Cycle

Evaluating system security can and should be conducted at different stages of system development. Security evaluation activities include, but are not limited to, risk assessment, *certification and accreditation* (C&A), system audits, and security testing at appropriate periods during a system's life cycle. These activities are geared toward ensuring that the system is being developed and operated in accordance with an organization's security policy. This section discusses how security testing, as a security evaluation activity, fits into the system development life cycle.

Typically, testing is conducted after the system has been developed, installed, and integrated during implementation and operational steps. Figure 7.11 illustrates the system development life cycle along with suggested activities to be conducted during the steps. During the implementation step, *security testing and evaluation* (ST&E) should be conducted on particular parts of the system and on the entire system as a whole. Penetration testing is also recommended at this stage to ensure that the existing system configuration is secure prior to full implementation. These activities should be repeated periodically (for example, at a minimum every three years for ST&E) or whenever a major change is made to the system. For systems that are exposed to constant threat (for example, Web servers) or that protect critical information (for example, firewalls), testing should be conducted more frequently (in other words, quarterly).

Once a system is operational, it is important to ascertain its operational status; that is, whether a system is operated according to its current security requirements. This examination includes both the actions of people who operate or use the system and the functioning of technical controls. Various types of tests can be conducted to gain an assessment of the operational status of the system (see Step 4 in Figure 7.11). The types of tests selected and the frequency in which they are conducted depends on the importance of the system and the resources available for testing.

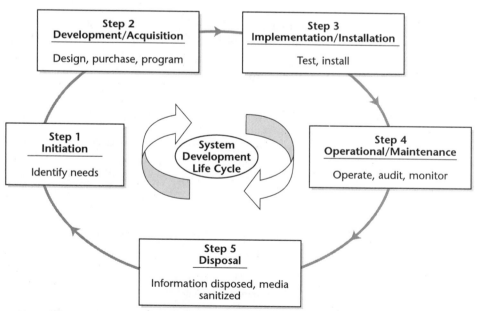

Figure 7.11   Security testing and the system development life cycle.

Documentation

Security testing provides insight into other system development life cycle activities. Security testing results should be documented and made available for staff involved in other IT and security-related areas. Specifically, security testing results can be used in the following ways:

- As a reference point for corrective action
- Defining mitigation activities to address identified vulnerabilities
- As a benchmark for tracing an organization's progress
- To assess the implementation status of system security requirements
- To conduct cost/benefit analysis
- To enhance other lifecycle activities, such as risk assessments, C&A, and performance improvement efforts

Security Management Staff

Because security testing provides input into and can be a part of multiple system development life cycle phases, a number of IT and system security staff might be interested in its execution and result. This section provides a list of those roles and identifies their responsibilities related to security testing. These roles might vary with the organization, however, and not all organizations will have the identical roles described here.

Senior IT Management/Chief Information Officer (CIO)

The senior IT management/CIO ensures that the organization's security posture is adequate. The senior IT management provides direction and advisory services for the protection of information systems for the entire organization. The senior IT management/CIO is responsible for the following activities that are associated with security testing:

- Coordinating the development and maintenance of the organization's information security policies, standards, and procedures
- Ensuring the establishment of, and compliance with, consistent security evaluation processes for departments throughout the organization
- Participating in developing processes for decision making and the prioritization of systems for security testing

Information Systems Security Program Managers

The information systems security program managers oversee the implementation of and compliance with the standards, rules, and regulations specified in the organization's security policy. The ISSMs are responsible for the following activities associated with security testing:

- Developing and implementing standard operating procedures (security policy)
- Complying with security policies, standards, and requirements
- Ensure that critical systems are identified and scheduled for periodic testing according to the security policy requirements of each respective system

Information Systems Security Officers

Information Systems Security Officers (ISSOs) are responsible for overseeing all aspects of information security within a specific organizational entity. They ensure that the organization's information security practices comply with organizational and departmental policies, standards, and procedures. ISSOs are responsible for the following activities associated with security testing:

- Developing security standards and procedures for their area of responsibility
- Cooperating in the development and implementation of security tools and mechanisms
- Maintaining configuration profiles of all systems controlled by the organization, including but not limited to, mainframes, distributed systems, microcomputers, and dial access ports
- Maintain operational integrity of systems by conducting tests and ensuring that designated IT professionals are conducting scheduled testing on critical systems

System and Network Administrators

System and network administrators must *daily* address the security requirements of the specific system(s) for which they are responsible. Security issues and solutions can originate from either outside (for example, security patches and fixes from the vendor or computer security incident response teams) or within the organization (for example, the security office). The administrators are responsible for the following activities associated with security testing:

- Monitoring system integrity, protection levels, and security-related events
- Following up with detected security anomalies associated with their information system resources
- Conducting security tests as required

Managers and Owners

Managers and owners of a system oversee the overall compliance of their assets with their defined/identified security requirements. They are also responsible for ensuring that test results and recommendations are adopted as appropriate.

Types of Security Testing

The following section describes each testing technique and provides additional information on the strengths and weakness of each. This information is also summarized in Tables 7.5 and 7.6. Some testing techniques are predominantly human initiated and conducted. Other tests are highly automated and require less human involvement. Regardless of the type of testing, staff that set up and conduct security testing should have significant security and networking knowledge, including significant expertise in one or more of the following areas: network security, firewalls, intrusion detection systems, operating systems, programming, and networking protocols (such as TCP/IP and Microsoft NetBIOS).

The following types of testing are described in this section:

- Network mapping
- Vulnerability scanning
- Penetration testing
- Security testing and evaluation
- Password cracking
- Log review
- Integrity checkers
- Virus detection
- War dialing

Often, several of these testing techniques are used in conjunction to gain a more comprehensive assessment of the overall network security posture. For example penetration testing almost always includes network mapping and vulnerability scanning to identify vulnerable hosts and services that might be targeted for later penetration. None of these tests by themselves will provide a complete picture of the network or its security posture. Table 7.5 at the end of this section summarizes the strengths and weaknesses of each test.

Network Mapping (Discovery)

Network mapping involves using a port scanner to identify all active hosts connected to an organization's network, network services operating on those hosts (for example, *file transfer protocol* [FTP] and *hypertext transport protocol* [HTTP]), and the specific application running the identified service (for example, *Internet Information Server* [IIS] and Apache for the HTTP service). The result of the scan is a comprehensive list of all active hosts and services operating in the address space scanned by the port-scanning tool. The name *network map* is a misnomer, however, because the port scanner sees the network as flat address space and does not typically provide any meaningful graphical representation of the scanned network.

Network scanners, such as Nmap, first identify active hosts in the address range specified by the user using *Transport Control Protocol/Internet Protocol* (TCP/IP), *Internet Control Message Protocol* (ICMP), ECHO, and ICMP ECHO_REPLY packets. Once active hosts have been identified, they are scanned for open TCP and *User Datagram Protocol* (UDP) ports that will then identify the network services operating on that host. A number of scanners support different scanning methods that have different strengths and weaknesses usually explained in the scanner documentation. For example, certain scans are better suited for scans through firewalls, and others are better suited for scans internal to the firewall.

All basic port scanners will identify active hosts and open ports, but some scanners provide additional information on the scanned hosts. The information gathered during this open port scan will often identify the target operating system. This process is called operating system fingerprinting. For example, if a host has TCP port 135 and 139 open, it is most likely a Windows NT or 2000 host. Other items such as the TCP packet sequence number generation, and responses to ICMP packets also provide a clue to identifying the operating system. Operating system fingerprinting is not foolproof. Firewalls that filter (block) certain ports and types of traffic and system administrators can configure their systems to respond in nonstandard ways in order to camouflage the true operating system.

In addition, some scanners will assist in identifying the application running on a particular port. For example, if a scanner identifies that TCP port 80 is open on a host, it most likely means that the host is running a Web (HTTP) server. Identifying which Web server product is installed, however, can be critical for identifying vulnerabilities. For example, the vulnerabilities for Microsoft's IIS server are very different from those associated with Apache Web server. One way to identify the application is by listening on the port to capture the banner information that is transmitted by the server when a client (a Web browser in this example) connects. Banner information is generally not visible to the end user (at least, in the case of Web servers/browsers); however, it is transmitted and can provide a wealth of information (including the application type, application version, and even operating system type and version). Again, this method is not foolproof because a security-conscious administrator can alter the transmitted banners. The process of capturing banner information is sometimes called *banner grabbing*.

A major limitation of using port scanners is that while they identify active hosts, services, applications, and operating systems, they do *not* identify vulnerabilities. The determination of vulnerability must be made by human interpretation. Identifying vulnerabilities requires interpretation of the mapping and scanning results, and from these results, a qualified individual can ascertain what services are vulnerable. Although the scanning itself is highly automated, the interpretation is not.

Organizations should conduct network mapping to do the following:

- Check for unauthorized hosts connected to the organization's network
- Identify vulnerable services
- Identify deviations from the allowed services defined in the organization's security policy
- Prepare for penetration testing

Although network mapping is mostly an automated activity, it requires a relatively high level of human expertise to interpret the results. It can also disrupt network operations by consuming bandwidth and slowing network response times. Network mapping provides a means for an organization to maintain control of its IP address space, however, and to ensure that its hosts are configured to run only approved network services. Network mapping should be conducted quarterly to discover unauthorized hosts and to verify that only approved services are run on the network. To minimize disruptions to operations, scanning software should be carefully selected. Network mapping can also be conducted after hours to ensure minimal impact to operations.

Network mapping results should be documented, and identified deficiencies should be corrected. The following corrective actions might be necessary as a result of network mapping:

- Disconnect unauthorized hosts.

- Disable or remove unnecessary and vulnerable services.

- Modify vulnerable hosts to restrict access to vulnerable services to a limited number of required hosts (for example, host level firewall or TCP wrappers).

- Modify enterprise firewalls to restrict outside access to known vulnerable services.

Vulnerability Scanning

Vulnerability scanners are commonly used in many organizations—they take the concept of a port scanner to the next level. The vulnerability scanner identifies not just hosts and open ports but any associated vulnerabilities automatically, instead of relying on human interpretation of the results. Most vulnerability scanners also attempt to provide information on mitigating discovered vulnerabilities.

Vulnerability scanners provide system and network administrators with proactive tools that can be used to identify vulnerabilities before an adversary. A vulnerability scanner is a relatively fast and easy way to quantify an organization's exposure to surface vulnerabilities.

Vulnerability scanners attempt to identify vulnerabilities in the hosts scanned and can help identify out-of-date software versions, vulnerabilities, applicable patches or system upgrades, and validate compliance with or deviations from the organization's security policy. To accomplish this task, vulnerability scanners identify operating systems and major software applications running on hosts and match them with known vulnerabilities. They also employ large databases of vulnerabilities to identify vulnerabilities associated with commonly used operating systems and applications.

The scanner will often provide significant information and guidance on mitigating discovered vulnerabilities for each discovered vulnerability. In addition, vulnerability scanners can automatically make corrections and fix certain discovered vulnerabilities (assuming that the operator of the vulnerability scanners has .root or administrator access to the vulnerable host).

Vulnerability scanners have some significant weaknesses, however. Generally, they only identify surface vulnerabilities and are unable to address the overall risk level of a scanned network. Although the scan process itself is highly automated, vulnerability scanners can have a high false-positive error rate (reporting vulnerabilities when none exist). In other words, an individual with expertise in networking and operating system, security, and administration must interpret the results.

Because vulnerability scanners require more information than port scanners to reliably identify the vulnerabilities on a host, vulnerability scanners tend to generate significantly more network traffic than port scanners. This situation might have a negative impact on the hosts or network being scanned or network segments through which scanning traffic is traversing. Many vulnerability scanners also include tests for *denial of service* (DoS) attacks that, in the hands of an inexperienced user, can have a considerable negative impact on scanned hosts.

Another significant limitation of vulnerability scanners is that they rely on constant updating of the vulnerability database in order to recognize the latest vulnerabilities. Before running any scanner, be sure to install the latest updates to its vulnerability database. Some vulnerability scanner databases are updated more regularly than others (frequency of updates should be a major consideration when choosing a vulnerability scanner).

Vulnerability scanners are better at detecting well-known vulnerabilities at the expense of more esoteric ones, primarily because it is impossible for any one product to incorporate all known vulnerabilities in a timely manner. It is also due to the desire of the manufacturers to keep the speed of their scanners high (more vulnerabilities detected requires more tests, which slows the overall scanning process).

Vulnerability scanners provide the following capabilities:

- Identifying active hosts on a network
- Identifying active and vulnerable services (ports) on hosts
- Identifying application and banner grabbing
- Identifying operating systems
- Identifying vulnerabilities associated with discovered operating systems and applications
- Testing compliance with host application usage/security policies
- Establishing a foundation for penetration testing

Vulnerability scanners can be of two types: network scanners and host scanners. Network scanners are used primarily for mapping an organization's network and identifying open ports. In most cases, these scanners are not limited by the operating system of targeted systems. The scanners can be installed on a single system on the network and can quickly locate and test numerous hosts. Host scanners have to be installed on each host to be tested and are used primarily to identify specific host operating system and application misconfigurations and vulnerabilities. Host scanners have high-detection granularity and usually require not only host (local) access but also a root or administrative account. Some host scanners offer the capability to repair any misconfigurations.

Organizations should conduct vulnerability scanning to validate that operating systems and major applications are up to date on security patches and software version. Vulnerability scanning is a reasonably labor-intensive activity that requires a high degree of human involvement with interpreting the results. It might also be disruptive to network operations by taking up bandwidth and slowing response times; however, vulnerability scanning is extremely important for ensuring that vulnerabilities are mitigated as soon as possible before they are discovered and exploited by adversaries. Vulnerability scanning should be conducted at least quarterly. Highly critical systems such as firewalls, public Web servers, and other perimeter points of entry should be scanned at least bimonthly.

Vulnerability scanning results should be documented, and discovered deficiencies should be corrected. The following corrective actions might be necessary as a result of vulnerability scanning:

- Upgrade or patch vulnerable systems to mitigate identified vulnerabilities as appropriate.

- Deploy mitigating measures (technical or procedural) if the system cannot be immediately patched (for example, an application system upgrade will make the application running on top of the operating system inoperable) in order to minimize the probability of this system being compromised.

- Tighten configuration management program and procedures to ensure that systems are upgraded routinely.

- Assign a staff member to monitor vulnerability alerts and mailing lists, examine their applicability to the organization's environment, and initiate appropriate system changes.

- Modify the organization's security policies, architecture, or other documentation to ensure that security practices include timely system updates and upgrades.

Penetration Testing

Penetration testing is security testing in which evaluators attempt to circumvent the security features of a system based on their understanding of the system's design and implementation. The purpose of penetration testing is to identify methods of gaining access to a system by using common tools and techniques developed by hackers. This testing is highly recommended for complex or critical systems (for example, most organization's networks).

Penetration testing can be an invaluable technique to any organization's information security program; however, it is a very labor-intensive activity and requires great expertise to minimize the risk to targeted systems. At a minimum, it might slow the organization's networks response time due to network mapping and vulnerability scanning. Furthermore, the possibility exists that systems might be damaged in the course of penetration testing and might be rendered inoperable. Although this risk is mitigated by the use of experienced penetration testers, it can never be fully eliminated.

Because penetration testing is designed to simulate an attack and use tools and techniques that might be restricted by law, federal regulations, and organizational policy, it is imperative to get written permission for conducting penetration testing prior to starting. This written permission, often called the rules of engagement, should include the following:

- Specific IP addresses/ranges to be tested
- Any restricted hosts (that is, hosts, systems, and subnets not to be tested)
- A list of acceptable testing techniques (for example, social engineering and DoS) and tools (for example, password crackers and network sniffers)
- Times when scanning is to be conducted (for example, during business hours and after business hours)
- IP addresses of the machines from which penetration testing will be conducted so that administrators can differentiate the legitimate penetration testing attacks from actual hacker attacks
- Points of contact for both the penetration testing team, the targeted systems, and networks
- Measures to prevent law enforcement being called with false alarms
- The handling of information collected by a penetration testing team

Generally, appropriate individuals should receive a warning before the testing begins to avoid law enforcement officials from being inappropriately called. Penetration testing can be overt or covert. These two types of penetration testing are commonly referred to as blue teaming and red teaming. Blue teaming involves performing a penetration test with the knowledge and consent of the organization's IT staff. Red teaming involves performing a penetration test without the knowledge of the organization's IT staff but with full knowledge and permission of upper management. Some organizations designate a trusted third party for the red teaming exercises to ensure that an organization does not take measures associated with the real attack without verifying that an attack is indeed underway (that is, the activity that they are seeing does not originate from an exercise). The trusted third party provides an agent for the testers, the management, and the IT and security staff that mediates the activities and facilitates communications. This type of test is useful for testing not only network security but also the IT staff's response to perceived security incidents and their knowledge and implementation of the organization's security policy. Red teaming can be conducted with or without warning.

Of the two types of penetration tests, blue teaming tends to be the least expensive and most used. Red teaming, because of it stealth requirements, requires more time and expense. To be stealthy, a penetration testing team acting as a red team will have to slow its scans and other actions to move below the ability of the target organization's IDS and firewall to detect their actions. Red teaming, however, provides a better indication of everyday security of the target organization because system administrators will not be on heightened awareness.

A penetration test can be designed to simulate an inside and/or an outside attack. If both internal and external testing is to be performed, the external testing usually occurs first. With external penetration testing, firewalls usually limit the amount and types of traffic that are allowed into the internal network from external sources. Depending on what protocols are allowed through, initial attacks are generally focused on commonly used and allowed application protocols such as FTP or HTTP. With the external testing, the barriers between the internal and external networks are what can increase the time, difficulty, and cost of performing an external test.

To simulate an actual external attack, the testers are not provided with any real information about the target environment other than targeted IP address/ ranges. They must covertly collect information before the attack and gather information on the target from public Web pages, newsgroups, and the like. They then use port scanners and vulnerability scanners to identify targeted hosts. Because they are most likely going through a firewall, the amount of information is far less than they would get if operating internally. After identifying hosts on the network that can be reached from the outside, they attempt to compromise one. If successful, they then leverage this access to compromise others hosts that are not generally accessible from outside. For this reason, penetration testing is an iterative process that leverages minimal access to eventually gain full access.

An internal penetration test is similar to an external except that the testers are now on the internal network (in other words, behind the firewall) and are granted some level of access to the network (generally as a user but sometimes at a higher level). The penetration testers will then try to gain a greater level of access to the network through privilege escalation. The testers are provided with information about a network as somebody with their provided privileges would have. This person is generally a standard employee, although it can also be anything up to and including a system or network administrator depending on the goals of the test.

Penetration testing consists of four phases (see Figure 7.12).

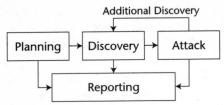

Figure 7.12 Four-stage penetration testing methodology.

In the planning phase, rules are identified, management approval is finalized, and the testing goals are set. The planning phase sets the groundwork for a successful penetration test (no actual testing occurs in the planning phase).

The discovery phase starts the actual testing. Network mapping (port scanning) is used to identify potential targets. In addition to port scanning, other techniques are commonly used to gather information on the targeted network:

- *Domain Name System* (DNS) interrogation
- InterNIC (whois) queries
- Searching target organization's Web server(s) for information
- Searching the organization's Lightweight Directory Access Protocol (LDAP) servers for information
- Packet capture (generally only during internal tests)
- NetBIOS enumeration (generally only during internal tests)
- Network Information System (NIS) (generally only during internal tests)
- Banner grabbing

The second part of the discovery phase is vulnerability analysis. During this phase, services, applications, and operating systems of scanned hosts are compared against vulnerability databases (for vulnerability scanners, this process is automatic). Generally, human testers use their own database or public databases to identify vulnerabilities manually. This manual process is better for identifying new or obscure vulnerabilities but is much slower than an automated scanner.

Executing an attack is at the heart of any penetration test. This point is where previously identified potential vulnerabilities are verified by attempting to exploit them. If an attack is successful, the vulnerability is verified and safeguards are identified to mitigate the associated security exposure. Frequently, exploits that are executed during attack execution do not grant the maximum level of access that an attacker can gain. Instead, they might result in the testing team learning more about the targeted network and its potential vulnerabilities, or they might induce a change in the state of the security of the targeted network. In either situation, additional analysis and testing is required to determine the true level of risk for the network (represented in the feedback loop in Figure 7.13 between the attack and discovery phase of a penetration test).

Where vulnerability scanners only check that a vulnerability might exist, the attack phase of a penetration test exploits vulnerability—confirming its existence. Most vulnerabilities exploited by penetration testing and malicious attackers fall into the following categories:

Kernel flaws. Kernel code is the core of an operating system. The kernel code enforces the overall security model for the system, and any security flaw that occurs in the kernel puts the entire system in danger.

Buffer overflows. A buffer overflow occurs when programs do not adequately check input for appropriate length and is usually a result of poor programming practice. When this situation occurs, arbitrary code can be introduced into the system and executed with the privileges of the running program. This code often can be run as root on Unix systems and SYSTEM (administrator equivalent) on Windows systems.

Symbolic links. A symbolic link or symlink is a file that points to another file. Often, there are programs that will change the permissions of a file. If these programs run with privileged permissions, a user could strategically create symlinks to trick these programs into modifying or listing critical system files.

File descriptor attacks. File descriptors are nonnegative integers that the system uses to keep track of files, rather than using specific filenames. Certain file descriptors have implied uses. When a privileged program assigns an inappropriate file descriptor, it exposes that file to compromise.

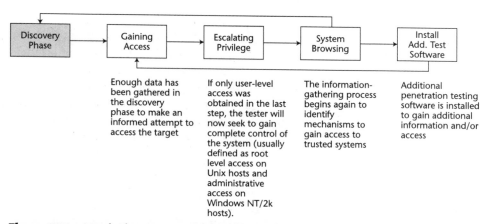

Figure 7.13 Attack phase steps with loopback to the discovery phase.

Race conditions.   Race conditions can occur when a program or process has entered into a privileged mode but before the program or process has given up its privileged mode. A user can time an attack to take advantage of this program or process while it is still in the privileged mode. If an attacker successfully manages to compromise the program or process during its privileged state, then the attacker has won the race. Common race conditions include signal handling and core file manipulation.

File and directory permissions.   File and directory permissions control which users and processes have access to what files and directories. Appropriate permissions are critical to the security of any system. Poor permissions could allow any number of attacks, including the reading or writing of password files or adding allowable hosts to connect in the rhost file.

Trojans.   Trojan programs can be custom built or could include programs such as BackOrifice, NetBus, and SubSeven. Kernel root kits could also be employed once access is obtained that enables a back door into the system at any time.

Social engineering.   Social engineering is the technique of using persuasion and/or deception to gain access to, or information about, information systems. It is typically implemented through human conversation or other interaction. The usual medium of choice is telephone but can also be email or even face-to-face contact. Social engineering generally follows two standard approaches. In the first approach, the penetration tester poses as a user who is experiencing difficulty and calls the organization's help desk in order to gain information about the target network or host, to obtain a login ID and credentials, or to have a password reset. The second approach is to pose as the help desk and call a user in order to get the user to provide his or her user id(s) and password(s). This technique can be extremely effective.

The reporting phase occurs simultaneously with the other three phases of the penetration test (see Figure 7.13). In the planning phase, rules of engagement, test plans, and written permission are developed. In the discovery and attack phase, written logs are usually kept and periodic reports are made to system administrators and/or management as appropriate. Generally, at the end of the test there is an overall testing report that describes the identified vulnerabilities, provides a risk rating, and gives guidance on the mitigation of the discovered weaknesses.

Conducting penetration testing is extremely important for determining how vulnerable an organization's network is and the level of damage that can occur if compromised. Due to the high cost and potential impact of penetration testing, performing it annually might be sufficient. The results of penetration testing should be taken very seriously, and discovered vulnerabilities should be mitigated. As soon as possible, the results should be presented to management. Corrective measures can range from closing discovered and exploited vulnerabilities to modifying an organization's security policies and procedures to improve security practices to conducting security awareness training for personnel to ensure that they understand the implications of poor system configurations and poor security practices. Organizations should consider conducting less labor-intensive testing activities on a regular basis to ensure that they are in compliance with their security policies and maintain the required security posture. If an organization performs other tests (for example, network mapping and vulnerability scanning) regularly between the penetration testing exercises and corrects discovered deficiencies, it will be well prepared for the next penetration testing exercise and for a real attack.

Security Testing and Evaluation

Security Test and Evaluation (ST&E) is an examination or analysis of the protective measures that are placed on an information system once it is fully integrated and operational. The objectives of the ST&E are:

- To uncover design, implementation, and operations flaws that could allow the violation of security policy
- To determine the adequacy of security mechanisms, assurances, and other properties to enforce the security policy
- To assess the degree of consistency between the system documentation and its implementation

The scope of an ST&E plan typically addresses computer security, communications security, emanations security, physical security, personnel security, administrative security, and operations security. Computer security is comprised of the measures and controls that protect the system against DoS and unauthorized disclosure, modification, or destruction of the system's data. Computer security can be tested through configuration and operational testing to validate that system security mechanisms have been implemented and are working properly. Configuration testing is performed by comparing the installed configuration against the approved configuration found in the security requirements, security concept of operations, or another similar document. Operational testing provides an assessment of the systems security mechanisms in an operational environment to determine whether the mechanisms are enforcing the site's security policy. Operational testing is performed through the execution of predefined tests, and these tests establish a baseline for configuration management and system testing.

Communication security comprises the measures and controls taken to prevent unauthorized access through telecommunications. Testing is performed to ensure that communications links are protected to a level commensurate with the sensitivity level of the data being transferred. Additionally, communication testing should determine that the system connection does not introduce new vulnerabilities to the network.

Emanations security analyzes unintentional data-related or intelligence-bearing signals that, if intercepted and analyzed, disclose the information transmission received, handled, or otherwise processed by any information processing equipment. Emanations security testing is performed through interception and analysis of electronic signals emitted from the system. Proper emanation security protects the site from electronic eavesdropping.

The physical security portion of the ST&E is performed to determine whether the physical environment where the system resides is adequate for the protection and operation of the system. This part of testing is performed through analysis of the security features of the facility, its adequacy to the protection of the system, and of power and environmental systems to ensure that a proper operating environment can be maintained.

Personnel security is the process whereby trustworthiness and suitability of personnel is verified. For the ST&E, this includes ensuring that access to the equipment is limited to only those personnel who require access.

Administrative security comprises the management constraints and supplemental controls established to provide an acceptable level of protection for data. Administrative security is also known as procedural security. Testing for the administrative section of the ST&E should include analysis of the design and adoption of day-to-day procedures for the operation of the system. This part of the test should also determine the adequacy of the site's contingency plan.

Operations security is an analytical process by which potential adversaries are denied information about capabilities and intentions by identifying, controlling, and protecting evidence of the planning and execution of sensitive activities and operations. Operations security in the ST&E is performed through the analysis of the systems ability to limit access to this information. The benefit derived from operations security testing is that it verifies that information is not being provided to adversaries that would help them to circumvent network security.

Password Cracking

Password cracking programs can be used to identify weak passwords. Password cracking verifies that users are employing sufficiently strong passwords. Passwords are generally stored and transmitted in an encrypted form called a hash. When a user logs on to a computer/system and enters a password, a hash is generated and compared to a stored hash. If entered and stored hashes match, the user is authenticated.

During a penetration test or a real attack, password cracking uses captured password hashes. Passwords hashes can be intercepted when they are transmitted across the network (using a network sniffer), or they can be retrieved from the targeted system. The latter generally requires administrative or .root access on the target system.

Once the hashes are obtained, an automated password cracker rapidly generates hashes until a match is found. The fastest method for generating hashes is a dictionary attack that uses all words in a dictionary or text file. There are many dictionaries available on the Internet that cover most major and minor languages, names, favorite television shows, and so on. So, any dictionary word—no matter how obscure—is weak.

Another method of cracking is called a hybrid attack, which builds on the dictionary method by adding numeric and symbolic characters to dictionary words. Depending on the password cracker being used, this type of attack will try a number of variations. It will try common substitutes of characters and numbers for letters (for example, p@ssword and h4ckme). Some will also try adding characters and numbers to the beginning and end of dictionary words (for example, password99 and password$%).

The most powerful password cracking method is called the brute-force method. Although brute force can take a long time, it usually takes far less time than most password policies specify for password changing. Consequently, passwords found during brute-force attacks are still too weak. Brute force randomly generates passwords and their associated hashes; however, because there are so many possibilities, it can take months to crack a password. Theoretically, all passwords are crackable from a brute-force attack if given enough time and processing power. Penetration testers and hackers often have multiple machines across which they can spread the task of cracking passwords, which can greatly shorten the length of time required to crack strong passwords. A strong password is one that is long (greater than 10 characters at least) and complex (contains both upper- and lower-case letters, characters, and numbers). See the CD-ROM accompanying this book for an example of how to use the Windows password cracker L0pht Crack.

Password crackers should be run on the system on a monthly basis or even continuously to ensure correct password composition throughout an organization. The following actions can be taken if an unacceptably high number of passwords can be cracked:

- If the cracked passwords were selected according to policy, the policy should be modified to reduce the percentage of crackable passwords. If such policy modification would lead to users writing down their passwords because they are difficult to memorize, an organization should consider replacing password authentication with another form of authentication.

■ If cracked passwords were not selected according to policy, the users should be educated on possible impacts of weak password selections. If such violations by the same users are persistent, the management might consider a disciplinary action against those users. Many server platforms also enable the system administrator to set minimum password length and complexity.

Reviewing Logs

Various system logs can be used to identify deviations from the organization's security policy, including firewall logs, IDS logs, server logs, and any other logs that are collecting audit data on system and network. While not traditionally considered a "testing" activity, log review and analysis can provide a dynamic picture of ongoing system activities that can be compared with the intent and content of the security policy. Essentially, audit logs can be used to validate that the system is operating according to policy.

For example, if an IDS sensor is placed behind the firewall (within the enclave), its logs can be used to examine the service requests and communications that are allowed into the network by the firewall. If this sensor registers unauthorized activities beyond the firewall, it indicates that the firewall is no longer configured securely.

A free IDS sensor with ample support is Snort. Snort is a lightweight network intrusion detection system capable of performing real-time traffic analysis and packet logging on IP networks. It can perform protocol analysis, content searching/matching, and can be used to detect a variety of attacks and probes, such as buffer overflows, stealth port scans, CGI attacks, SMB probes, and OS fingerprinting attempts. Snort uses a flexible rules language to describe traffic that it should collect or pass as well as a detection engine that uses a modular plugin architecture. Snort has a real-time alerting capability as well, incorporating alerting mechanisms for syslog, a user-specified file, a UNIX socket, or WinPopup messages to Windows clients using Samba's smbclient. Snort has three primary uses: a straight packet sniffer like tcpdump, a packet logger (useful for network traffic debugging and so on), or as a full-blown network intrusion detection system.

Manual audit log review is extremely cumbersome and time consuming. Automated audit tools provide a means to significantly reduce the required review time and will print reports (predefined and customized) that would summarize the log contents to a set of specific activities. It is critical that any filters applied to the logs filter out what is unwanted and pass everything else. If you filter only on what is wanted, then any exception events will also be filtered.

Log reviews should be conducted at least weekly regardless of how the results are used. For the specific purpose of testing implementation of required security configurations, a monthly frequency might be sufficient with the exception of on demand reviews resulting from major system upgrades that require validation. The following actions can be taken if a system is not configured according to policies:

- Reconfigure the system as required to reduce the chance of compromise.
- Or, change firewall policy to limit access to the vulnerable system or service.
- Change firewall policy to limit accesses from the IP subnet that is the source of compromise.

Checking File Integrity

A file integrity checker computes and stores a checksum for every guarded file and establishes a database of file checksums. It provides a tool for the system administrator to recognize changes to files, particularly unauthorized changes. Stored checksums should be recomputed regularly to test the current value against the stored value to identify any file modifications. A file integrity checker capability is usually included with any commercial host-based intrusion detection system.

While an integrity checker is a useful tool that does not require a high degree of human interaction, it needs to be used carefully to ensure that it is effective. A file integrity checker requires a system that is known as secure to create the first reference database. Otherwise, cryptographic hashes of a compromised system can be created and therefore create a false sense of security for the tester. The reference database should be stored offline so that an attacker cannot compromise the system and hide his or her tracks by modifying the database. A file integrity checker can also generate false-positive alarms. Each file update and system patch implementation changes the file and will therefore require an update of the checksum database. Therefore, keeping the database up-to-date might be difficult. Even if the integrity checker is run only once (when the system is first installed), however, it can still be a useful activity for determining which files have been modified in case of a suspected compromise. Finally, attackers have demonstrated the ability to modify a file in ways the commonly used 32-bit *Cyclic Redundancy Check* (CRC) checksum could not detect. Therefore, stronger checksums are recommended to ensure the integrity of data that is stored in the checksum database.

Integrity checkers should be run daily on a selection of system files that would be affected by a compromise. Integrity checkers should also be used when a compromise is suspected for determining the extent of possible damage.

If an integrity checker detects unauthorized system file modifications, the possibility of a security incident should be considered and investigated according to the organization's incident response and reporting policy and procedures.

Using Virus Detectors

A computer virus is a string of code that attaches itself to another computer program or document. Once it is attached, it replicates itself by using some of the resources of the co-opted program or document to replicate and attach itself to other host programs and documents. Malicious code is not limited to viruses; there are several types of malicious code that are generally detected by antivirus software even though the code is not strictly speaking a virus. The other categories of malicious code include worms, Trojans, and malicious mobile code.

The impact of a virus, Trojan, worm, or malicious mobile code can be as harmless as a popup message on a computer screen or as destructive as deleting all the files on a hard drive. With any malicious code, there is also the risk of exposing or destroying sensitive or confidential information.

There are two primary types of antivirus programs available: those that are installed on the network infrastructure and those that are installed on end-user machines. Each has advantages and disadvantages, but both used in conjunction are generally required for the highest level of security.

The virus detector installed on the network infrastructure is server based and is usually installed on mail servers and on or in conjunction with firewalls at the network border of an organization. The advantage of the server-based virus detection programs is that they can detect viruses before they enter the network or before a user downloads his or her email. The other advantage of server-based virus detection is that all virus detectors require frequent updating to remain effective. This task is much easier to accomplish on the server-based programs due to their limited number relative to client hosts. Unfortunately, server-based programs can have a negative effect on performance of a network.

The other type of virus detection software is installed on end-user machines. This software detects malicious code in emails, floppies, hard disks, documents, and the like—but only for the local host. It also sometimes detects malicious code from Web sites. This type of virus detection program has less impact on network performance but generally relies on end users to update their signatures, which is not always reliable. Also, end-user virus protection cannot protect the network from all virus threats.

No matter what type of virus detection program is being used, it cannot offer its full protection unless it has an up-to-date virus identification database (sometimes called virus signatures) that enable it to recognize all viruses. If the virus detection program is not up to date, it usually will not detect a new virus.

To detect viruses, antivirus software compares file contents with the known computer virus signatures, identifies infected files, and repairs them if possible or deletes them if not. More sophisticated programs also look for virus-like activity in an attempt to identify new or mutated viruses that would not be recognized by the current virus detection database. While not perfect, this system can provide an additional layer of protection with the cost of some false positives.

Viruses and other malicious code, such as worms and Trojans, can be enormously destructive to a computer system and to information that is relied upon for the success of an organization. The most important aspect of virus detection software is frequent regular updates of virus definition files and on-demand updates when a major virus is known to be spreading throughout the Internet. The more often the database is updated, the more viruses the antivirus software will be equipped to detect. If these preliminary steps are taken, the chances of a major virus infection are minimized. Virus definition files should be updated at least bimonthly and whenever a major outbreak of a new virus occurs.

War Dialing

In a well-configured network, one of the vulnerable areas often overlooked is the presence of unauthorized modems. These unauthorized modems provide a means to bypass most or all of the security measures in place to stop unauthorized users from accessing a network that enables hackers and network administrators to dial large blocks of phone numbers in search of available modems. This process is called war dialing. A computer with four modems can dial 10,000 numbers in a matter of days. Certain war dialers will even attempt some limited automatic hacking when a modem is discovered. All will provide a report on the discovered numbers with modems.

War dialing should be conducted at least annually and performed after hours to limit the potential disruption to employees and to the organization's phone system (it of course has to be balanced with the danger that modems might be turned off after hours and therefore will not be detected). It should include all numbers that belong to an organization, except those that could be impacted negatively by receiving a large number of calls (for example, 24-hour operation centers and emergency numbers). Most war dialing software enables the tester to exempt particular numbers from the calling list.

If any unauthorized modems are identified, they should be investigated and removed if appropriate. Generally, the *Private Branch Exchange* (PBX) administrator should be able to identify the user to whom the number was assigned. If removal is not possible, the PBX should be configured to block inbound calls to the modem. If inbound calls are required, ensure that a strong authentication method is in place.

Although attacks via the Internet get much publicity, many successful attacks are launched through unauthorized modems. The increase in laptops has exacerbated this problem, because most have a modem. A single compromise via an authorized modem could give an attacker direct access to a network—and because it avoids perimeter security, it is more likely to go undetected.

Summary Comparisons of Network Testing Techniques

Table 7.5 provides a comparison of the testing techniques discussed previously.

Table 7.5   A Comparison of Testing Procedures

TYPE OF TEST	STRENGTHS	WEAKNESSES
Network Mapping	Fast Efficiently scans a large number of hosts (approximately 30 seconds per host) Many excellent freeware tools available Highly automated (for scanning component) Low cost	Does not directly identify known vulnerabilities Generally used as a prelude to penetration testing not as final test Requires significant expertise to interpret results
Vulnerability Scanning	Fairly fast Efficiently scans a large number of hosts (approximately 2 minutes per host) Some freeware tools available Highly automated (for scanning) Identifies known vulnerabilities Often provides advice on mitigating discovered vulnerabilities High cost (commercial scanners) to low (freeware scanners) Easy to run on a regular basis	High false positive rate Generates large amount of network traffic Not stealthy (e.g., easily detected by IDS, firewall and even end users) Can be dangerous in the hands of a novice (particularly DoS attacks) Often misses latest vulnerabilities Identifies only surface vulnerabilities

TYPE OF TEST	STRENGTHS	WEAKNESSES
Penetration Testing	Tests network using the methodologies and tools that hackers employ	Requires great expertise
		Very labor intensive
	Verifies vulnerabilities	Slow, target hosts may take hours/days to crack
	Goes beyond surface vulnerabilities and demonstrates how these vulnerabilities can be exploited iteratively to gain greater access	Due to time required not all hosts on medium or large sized networks will be tested individually
	Demonstrates that vulnerabilities are not purely theoretical	Dangerous when conducted by inexperienced testers
	Can provide the realism and evidence needed to address security issues	Certain tools and techniques may be banned or controlled by agency regulations (e.g., network sniffers, password crackers, etc.)
	Social engineering allows for testing of procedures and the human element network security	
		Expensive
		Can be organizationally disruptive
		Legal complications (get written permission to conduct and make sure all necessary personnel are notified)
Security Testing and Evaluation	Not as invasive or risky as some other tests	Does not verify vulnerabilities
	Includes policy and procedures	Generally does not identify newly discovered vulnerabilities
	Generally requires less expertise than vulnerability scanning or penetration testing	
		Labor intensive
	Addresses physical security	Expensive

(continued)

Table 7.5 *(continued)*

TYPE OF TEST	STRENGTHS	WEAKNESSES
Password Cracking	Quickly identifies weak passwords Provides clear demonstration of password strength or weakness Easily implemented Low cost	Potential for abuse Certain organizations restrict use Needs full processing power of a powerful computer
Log Reviews	Provides excellent information Only data source that provides historical information	Cumbersome to review Automated tools not perfect can filter out important information
File Integrity Checkers	Reliable method of determining whether a host has been compromised Highly automated Low cost	Does not detect any compromise prior to installation Checksums need to be updated when system is updated
Virus Detectors	Excellent at preventing and removing viruses Low/Medium cost	Require constant updates to be effective Server based versions may have significant impact on performance Some false positive issues Ability to react to new, fast replicating viruses is often limited
War Dialing	Effective way to identify unauthorized modems	Legal and regulatory issues especially if using public switched network Slow

Table 7.6 describes a general schedule and list of evaluation factors for testing categories. Category 1 systems are those sensitive systems that provide security for the organization or that provide other important functions. These systems would include:

- Firewalls, routers, and perimeter defense systems such as for intrusion detection
- Public access systems such as Web and email servers
- DNS and directory servers
- Other internal systems that would likely be intruder targets

Category 2 systems are generally all other systems—that is, those systems that have firewalls and other protections but that still must be tested periodically.

Prioritizing Security Testing

Security testing should be conducted during implementation, operational, and maintenance phases of the system life cycle. The type of test selected and the frequency with which it is conducted is relative to the life cycle phase in which the system is in, the cost of the selected type of test for each system, and the impact on operations if identified vulnerabilities specific to each system are exploited. These multidimensional values can be evaluated and applied effectively by breaking down testing requirements into two phases: minimum required testing and comprehensive security testing.

Minimum versus Comprehensive Testing

Minimum required testing refers to those tests that should be conducted as a bare minimum. It is imperative that even organizations with limited resources for security testing perform an appropriate level of security testing to ensure security. Minimum required testing should be conducted for systems both during the implementation and operational phases of the life cycle. The minimum testing activities differ in these phases, however. Minimum testing in the implementation phase involves conducting a *security test and evaluation* (ST&E), while in the operations and maintenance phase it involves conducting most of the testing techniques.

Comprehensive testing refers to conducting *all* tests regularly. Comprehensive testing can be costly and time consuming. Some organizations might not have the resources to conduct this in-depth security testing. As in minimum required testing, the comprehensive testing activities differ during the phases. Comprehensive testing during the implementation phase involves conducting ST&E and penetration testing, while in the operational and maintenance phase it involves conducting all tests with a scheduled frequency.

Table 7.6 Summarized Evaluation Factors

TEST TYPE	CATEGORY 1 FREQUENCY	CATEGORY 2 FREQUENCY	COMPLEXITY	LEVEL OF EFFORT	RISK	BENEFIT
Network Mapping	Quarterly	Annually	Medium	Medium	Medium	Enumerates the network structure and determines the set of active hosts, and associated software
						Identifies unauthorized hosts connected to a network
						Identifies open ports
						Identifies unauthorized services
Vulnerability Scanning	Quarterly or bimonthly	Annually	High	High	Medium	Enumerates the network structure and determines the set of active hosts, and associated software
						Identifies a target set of computers to focus vulnerability analysis
						Identifies potential vulnerabilities on the target set
						Validates that operating systems and major applications are up to date with security patches and software versions

TEST TYPE	CATEGORY 1 FREQUENCY	CATEGORY 2 FREQUENCY	COMPLEXITY	LEVEL OF EFFORT	RISK	BENEFIT
Penetration Testing	Annually	Annually	High	High	High	Determines how vulnerable an organization's network is to penetration and the level of damage that can be incurred
						Tests IT staff's response to perceived security incidents and their knowledge of and implementation of the organization's security policy and system's security requirements
ST&E	At least every 3 years or when significant changes occur	At least every 3 years	High	High	High	Uncovers design, implementation, and operational flaws that could allow the violation of security policy
						Determines the adequacy of security mechanisms, assurances, and other properties to enforce the security policy
						Assesses the degree of consistency between system documentation and implementation

(continued)

Table 7.6 *(continued)*

TEST TYPE	CATEGORY 1 FREQUENCY	CATEGORY 2 FREQUENCY	COMPLEXITY	LEVEL OF EFFORT	RISK	BENEFIT
Password Cracking	Monthly	Yearly	Low	Low	Low	Verifies that the policy is effective in producing passwords that are more or less difficult to break Verifies that users select passwords that are compliant with the organization's security policy
Log Reviews	Weekly	Weekly	Medium	Medium	Low	Validates that the system is operating according to policies
Integrity Checkers	Monthly and in case of suspected incident	Monthly	Low	Low	Low	Detects unauthorized file modifications
Virus Detectors	Weekly or as required	Weekly or as required	Low	Low	Low	Detects and deletes viruses before successful installation on the system
War Dialing	Annually	Annually	Low	Low	Medium	Detects unauthorized modems and prevents unauthorized access to a protected network

Prioritization Process

The goal of security testing is to maximize the benefit to the organization as a whole. Deciding on the types and frequency of testing during the operational and maintenance phase (both for minimum and comprehensive testing) involves a prioritization process based on an analysis of the impact and benefit to the overall organization's systems. While deciding what to test for during the implementation phase involves a single system, the same decision during the operational and maintenance phase is more complicated. To maximize the value of testing, the prioritization process should consider the interconnectivity of systems. The CIO or a senior IT manager should be involved in the prioritization process to ensure that organizational perspective is incorporated. This section describes the prioritization process that can be used. The prioritization process can be done in a series of five steps, namely:

1. Identify and rank system sensitivity and criticality.
2. Conduct an impact analysis.
3. Determine the cost of performing each test type per system.
4. Identify benefits of each test type per system.
5. Prioritize systems for testing.

We will discuss each of these steps in detail in the paragraphs that follow.

Step 1: Identifying and Ranking System Sensitivity and Criticality

The organization's systems have to be identified and ranked for testing priority. Usually, these are the systems required by an organization to maintain business operation and to achieve its missions. The following rankings for sensitivity also can be used to assist in ranking systems:

High   The organization cannot effectively perform part of its mission without the system or the information it processes and stores; costs to perform the mission would be greatly increased.

Medium   Operational effectiveness is seriously degraded but the mission can be completed through workarounds at moderately increased costs.

Low   The system and its information are not mission related. (Note that the reason for existence of such systems might be called into question.)

Step 2: Conducting Impact Analysis

Impact analysis considers the extent of damage that a system would sustain if identified vulnerabilities are exploited and then evaluates the level of impact

of the sustained damage on the organization's operations. Impact is determined based on the value of information that the system processes and stores
and on the criticality of the system to the organization's mission. NIST Special
Publication 800-30, Risk Management Guide, goes into greater detail on
conducting impact analysis; readers are encouraged to read this publication.
Impact can be expressed in qualitative terms expressed as follows:

High   Successful exploitation could result in unavailability, modifica-
            tion, disclosure, or destruction of valued data or other system
            assets or loss of system services for an unacceptable period,
            resulting in degradation of mission impact or possible injury
            to persons.

Medium   Successful exploitation could result in discernible but recover-
            able unavailability, modification, disclosure, or destruction of
            data or other system assets or loss of system services, resulting
            in transitory mission impact and no injury to persons.

Low   Any unavailability, modification, disclosure, or destruction of
            data or degradation of system services is detected easily and
            corrected without causing a significant mission impact.

Impact analysis should also determine, to the extent possible, the cost of
possible damage caused by an incident and the cost of bringing the system
back to operational status.

Step 3: Determining Cost of Performing Each Test Type per System

When system ranking is determined, the cost of conducting each test should
be ascertained. The cost depends on a number of factors:

- Size of the system to be tested: *Local Area Network* (LAN), *Wide Area
  Network* (WAN), single database, or major application.

- Complexity of the system to be tested: testing a network of a large
  organization with a heterogeneous operating system environment will
  be more costly.

- Level of human interaction required for each test.

- Whether it is possible and appropriate to select a sample for conducting
  the tests and the size of the sample (while it might not make sense to
  conduct network mapping on a sample of network hosts, selecting
  sample hosts for penetration testing is entirely possible).

- For each system, the costs of conducting each type of test should be
  quantified.

Step 4: Identifying the Benefits of Each Test Type per System

To ensure that the cost of testing does not exceed its value to the organization, the benefits of conducting the tests should be identified and qualified or quantified as much as possible. While the overall benefit of testing is in identifying vulnerabilities before an attacker exploits them, it involves multiple dimensions. The following are examples of factors that should be considered in identifying the benefits of testing:

- Value of gained knowledge about systems and networks that was absent prior to testing; improved knowledge facilitates better organizational control of its assets

- Significantly decreased probability of successful intrusion or business disruption by testing and correcting discovered deficiencies; an organization reduces the number of vulnerabilities that can be exploited

Step 5: Prioritizing Systems for Testing

The results of Steps 1 to 4 should be evaluated and ranked to prioritize the identified systems for security testing. This analysis should yield a list of systems, in a descending order, by system criticality, impact, and benefit. The list will include required resources (costs) for conducting each type of test for each system under consideration. The starting point for determining minimum required resources should be minimum testing for critical systems. The resources, available for security testing, should then be identified and compared with required resources. If the gap between required and available resources does not cover minimum testing for critical systems, as defined in the list of prioritized systems, additional resources should be sought to conduct minimum security testing. Cost of testing as calculated will provide quantitative evidence of why more resources are required. After the funding is identified for the most critical systems, the lower priority items might be tested with less frequency and in descending order. The result of this final step is a prioritized list of critical systems that will be tested with associated testing techniques and frequency.

Sample Questions

1. Which statement about the difference between analog and digital signals is correct?

   a. Analog signals cannot be used for data communications.

   b. A digital signal produces an infinite waveform.

   c. An analog signal produces a sawtooth waveform.

   d. An analog signal can be varied by amplification.

2. Which answer is NOT true about the difference between TCP and UDP?

   a. UDP is considered a connectionless protocol, and TCP is connection-oriented.

   b. TCP is considered a connectionless protocol, and UDP is connection-oriented.

   c. TCP acknowledges the receipt of packets, and UDP does not.

   d. UDP is sometimes referred to as an unreliable protocol.

3. Which choice is correct about the difference between conducted versus radiated transmission media?

   a. Microwave is a conducted transmission media.

   b. Infrared is a radiated transmission media.

   c. Fiber-optic cable uses a radiated transmission media.

   d. UTP uses a radiated transmission media.

4. Which choice describes the range for Internet multicast addresses?

   a. 0.0.0.0. through 255.255.255.255

   b. 127.0.0.1 through 127.255.255.255

   c. 192.168.0.0 through 192.168.255.255

   d. 224.0.0.0 through 239.255.255.255

5. Which UTP cable category is rated for 1Gbps?

   a. Category 4

   b. Category 6

   c. Category 5

   d. Category 7

6. Which choice BEST describes UTP cable?

   a. UTP consists of a hollow outer cylindrical conductor surrounding a single, inner conductor.

   b. UTP requires a fixed spacing between connections.

   c. UTP consists of two insulated wires wrapped around each other in a regular spiral pattern.

   d. UTP carries signals as light waves.

7. To what does 10Base-2 refer?

   a. 10 Mbps thinnet coax cabling rated to 185 meters maximum length

   b. 10 Mbps thicknet coax cabling rated to 500 meters maximum length

   c. 10 Mbps baseband optical fiber

   d. 100 Mbps unshielded twisted pair cabling

8. FDDI uses what type of network topology?

   a. Ring

   b. Bus

   c. Switched

   d. Star

9. Which choice is NOT an element of IPSec?

   a. *Encapsulating Security Payload* (ESP)

   b. *Authentication Header* (AH)

   c. *Security Association* (SA)

   d. *Point Tunneling Protocol* (PPTP)

10. Which IEEE protocol defines wireless transmission in data rates up to 54 Mbps but is expected to be backward-compatible with existing 802.11b-based networks?

    a. IEEE 802.11g

    b. IEEE 802.11b

    c. IEEE 802.11a

    d. IEEE 802.15

11. Which LAN transmission method describes a packet sent from a single source to a single destination?

    a. Unicast

    b. Multicast

    c. Broadcast

    d. Anycast

12. Which choice BEST describes a property of UDP?

    a. Creates seven distinct layers

    b. Wraps data from one layer around a data packet from an adjoining layer

    c. Provides "best-effort" delivery of a data packet

    d. Makes the network transmission deterministic

13. Which choice employs a dedicated, point-to-point technology?

    a. Frame Relay

    b. SMDS

    c. T1

    d. X.25

14. Which TCP/IP protocol operates at the Transport layer?

    a. FTP

    b. IP

    c. TCP

    d. NFS

15. Which is a property of fiber-optic cabling?

    a. Employs copper wire in the single, inner conductor

    b. Transmits at slower speeds than copper cable

    c. Harder to tap than copper cabling

    d. Consists of two insulated wires wrapped around each other

16. Which choice about L2TP is NOT true?

    a. L2TP is a predecessor to PPTP.

    b. PPTP is a predecessor to L2TP.

    c. L2TP does not include any mechanism for encryption or authentication of its traffic.

    d. L2TP is used by some IPSec VPNs.

17. Which process is an OSI Data Link layer function?

    a. Internetwork packet routing

    b. LAN bridging

    c. SMTP gateway services

    d. Signal regeneration and repeating

18. The protocol of the *Wireless Application Protocol* (WAP), which performs functions similar to SSL in the TCP/IP protocol, is called the:

    a. *Wireless Session Protocol* (WSP)

    b. *Wireless Application Environment* (WAE)

    c. *Wireless Transport Layer Security Protocol* (WTLS)

    d. *Wireless Transaction Protocol* (WTP)

19. Which of the following is considered a property of Ethernet networks?

    a. These networks were originally designed to serve large, bandwidth-consuming applications.

    b. Workstations cannot transmit until they receive a token.

    c. All end stations are attached to a MSAU.

    d. These networks were originally designed to serve sporadic and only occasionally heavy traffic.

20. Which IEEE standard defines wireless networking in the 2.4GHz band with speeds of up to 11 Mbps?

    a. 802.5

    b. 802.11a

    c. 802.3

    d. 802.11b

21. Which choice most accurately describes S/MIME?

    a. It gives a user remote access to a command prompt across a secure, encrypted session.

    b. It uses two protocols: the Authentication Header and the Encapsulating Security Payload.

    c. It is a widely used standard of securing email at the Application level.

    d. It enables an application to have authenticated, encrypted communications across a network.

22. Which choice defines an interface to the first commercially successful, connection-oriented packet-switching network?

    a. X.25

    b. Frame Relay

    c. SMDS

    d. ATM

23. Which standard defines copper cable as its physical media?

    a. 1000BaseLX

    b. 1000BaseSX

    c. 1000BaseCX

    d. 100BaseFX

24. Which protocol is a management protocol for IP networks?

    a. ICMP

    b. RARP

    c. TFTP

    d. ARP

25. Which IEEE protocol specifies an Ethernet bus topology using CSMA/CD?

    a. IEEE 802.5

    b. IEEE 802.3

    c. IEEE 802.11

    d. IEEE 802.1D

26. Which type of cabling is referred to as "ThickNet"?

    a. 10Base2

    b. 10Base5

    c. Twinax

    d. UTP Cat5

27. Which choice is a Presentation layer specification for digital certificates?

    a. X.500

    b. X.509

    c. X.25

    d. X.400

28. What could be a problem with Token Ring-type network topology?

    a. Lost tokens must be regenerated to re-enable network communications.

    b. Cabling termination errors can crash the entire network.

    c. A cable break can stop all communications.

    d. The network nodes are connected to a central LAN device.

29. Which statement about VPNs is incorrect?

    a. L2TP is used by some IPSec VPNs.

    b. Proprietary schemes restrict the user to a particular vendor's VPN products.

    c. Some VPN clients use proprietary technologies.

    d. Proprietary schemes benefit from testing by a wider community of users.

30. Which choice is NOT a type of security testing?

    a. Penetration testing

    b. War gaming

    c. Vulnerability scanning

    d. Network mapping

CHAPTER 8

Domain 7: Malicious Code

Malicious code (or malware, as it is known in some groups) is an ever-increasing threat to information systems. Normally, for a threat to impact a system, there is a known vulnerability that the threat exploits (takes advantage of). Malicious code relies not on "true vulnerabilities" but on the functionality and complexity of modern systems and the human element to get the job done. Significant research has been accomplished and recommendations have been developed for this area of system security.

All of this information about malicious code comes from the National Security Agency's Information Assurance Technology Framework. This work is unpublished but available to the public. Unless you are comfortable with government-speak, however, government documents can be quite wordy. We have tried to synopsize, synthesize, and reorganize the information to bring it to you in a format that will enable you to study.

What we continue to strive for is simple: giving you the tools that you need to do your job to provide security to the information systems you are responsible for protecting. Given that, you do not need to know the signature of current viruses; you need to know how to prevent them if at all possible (and when it is not possible, to quickly find them and eradicate them before they do harm). We hope that we have hit the mark regarding malicious code. But just as important as understanding what to do with malware is the ability to continue to stay current with continuously changing threats. Through our work as security professionals, we have occasion to use the resources listed at the end of this book and thought that you might want access to these resources as well. These URLs link to places that offer current information and provide a support environment for you to continue your studies.

Malicious code protection typically is provided at two places in the architecture: at the gateway and at workstations that access information services. Malicious code can infiltrate and destroy data through network connections if allowed beyond the gateway or through individual user workstations. Today, the majority of individual users keep all data files on networks or shared-file systems instead of on diskettes. Therefore, the continual application of protection of network connections at the gateway is essential. Malicious code usually enters existing networks through the gateway by means of security loopholes or email attachments. Its intent is to cripple the network and individual workstations. Malicious code can also attack the network through protocols; typically, *File Transfer Protocol* (FTP), *Hypertext Transport Protocol* (HTTP), and *Simple Mail Transfer Protocol* (SMTP) (email). The individual user workstation is then subsequently infected. In Figure 8.1, a simplified network is illustrated with several workstations connected to a single gateway and through that to the Internet.

Although a single user can bring an infected disk to work, infecting his or her workstation and eventually the entire network, the majority of infections by malicious code result from file sharing across different protocols. Malicious codes attacking individual user workstations are primarily macro viruses and other less potentially destructive viruses. These viruses typically enter systems through email attachments; however, as the IATF shows in the 2002 framework, their primary intent is not destruction. When viruses cause mass disruption in services, this limits propagation (a bad thing for a virus).

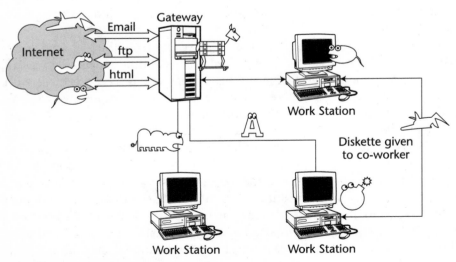

Figure 8.1 A simple network example.

Our Goals

For each of the seven domains, our goal is to provide you with three things:

1. Enough information about the domain so that you will be prepared to sit for the SSCP examination.

2. An understanding of how the overall system or enterprise security objectives, CIA, are carried through to the services and mechanisms within this domain.

3. An understanding of how the services and mechanisms of this domain provide security through one or more of the protection, detection, and reaction aspects of system security.

We do not believe you need to be taught the basics of each security service and/or security mechanism. You know your job as a system administrator or network administrator. What we intend to do is provide you with the connections and concepts that bring those isolated technical and administrative processes that you perform into the bigger picture: system security practice.

Domain Definition (Subject Overview)

According to (ISC)², "The malicious code area encompasses the principles, means and methods used by programs, applications and code segments to infect, abuse or otherwise impact the proper operation of an information processing system or network."

What Is Malicious Code?

Malicious code is the name used for any program (for example, an application or an applet) that adds, deletes, or modifies a system's legitimate software baseline for the purpose of causing disruption, harm, or to circumvent or subvert the existing system's function. Malicious code has been a problem as long as there have been programmers. We normally think of malicious code as being built intentionally, but many software developers have inadvertently developed an application that did the unexpected. This situation is especially true when the development takes place with C or C++ type languages that fail to meet some basic principles of language—namely, their ability to write outside the boundary (buffer overrun), which is a serious security threat that has been associated with many vulnerabilities.

Sheer numbers explain why the world is so susceptible and so vulnerable to malicious code. The most recent statistics from the Internet Software Consortium (www.isc.org) identified 162,128,493 hosts interconnected through the Internet in July 2002. For a security practitioner, malicious code has reached epidemic proportions and should be at the top of your list of threats to your system. The numbers of systems, combined with the age at which people become users and the users' level of sophistication, all mean that there are more systems to attack, more attacks, and greater risks from malicious code than at any time in the past. In addition to providing more avenues for attack, the complexity of our systems now makes it easier to hide or mask malicious code in the billions of lines of code necessary to run the systems of the world. Software vendors like Microsoft, IBM, or Oracle, which spend millions on software development and testing, cannot always create benign programs even when an elaborate installation program is used.

The stereotyping of malicious code writers, or any other adversary in the field of information system security, is a tactical error on the part of security staff. There are as many reasons to develop malware (short for malicious software) as there are developers of it. Those reasons range from curiosity, a desire to pursue a risky activity, or a disgruntled employee all the way to rogue state-sponsored information warfare. Your time is much better spent not trying to figure out why but in spending the time to have a prevention, detection, and reaction capability ready when it does hit you. Almost inevitably, it will.

Those who develop or use malicious code are commonly known as hackers, but this term is a misnomer, and we want to straighten it out. So, we went to the original "online hacker jargon file." This document has been around since the 1980s and is a continuously updated source of information regarding jargon. It can prove to be a valuable asset to the security practitioner when trying to understand "geek-speak," either written or coded. There are more than just definitions here; there is a rich history of the terminology. Learn, grow, and use the language correctly. The following discussion regarding hackers, crackers, and phreaks are extracted from "The OnLine Hacker Jargon File," version 4.3.3, 20, September 2002.

Hackers. [originally, someone who makes furniture with an axe] 1. A person who enjoys exploring the details of programmable systems and how to stretch their capabilities, as opposed to most users, who prefer to learn only the minimum necessary. 2. One who programs enthusiastically (even obsessively) or who enjoys programming rather than just theorizing about programming. 3. A person capable of appreciating hack value. 4. A person who is good at programming quickly. 5. An expert at a particular program, or one who frequently does work using it or on it; as in `a Unix hacker'. (Definitions 1 through 5 are correlated, and people who fit them congregate.) 6. An expert or enthusiast of any kind. One might be an astronomy hacker, for example. 7. One who enjoys the intellectual challenge of creatively overcoming or circumventing limitations. 8. [deprecated]

A malicious meddler who tries to discover sensitive information by poking around. Hence `password hacker', `network hacker'. The correct term for this sense is **cracker***.*

The term hacker also tends to connote membership in the global community defined by the net (see the network. For discussion of some of the basics of this culture, see the How To Become A Hacker FAQ. It also implies that the person described is seen to subscribe to some version of the hacker ethic (see hacker ethic).

It is better to be described as a hacker by others than to describe oneself that way. Hackers consider themselves something of an elite (a meritocracy based on ability), though one to which new members are gladly welcome. There is thus a certain ego satisfaction to be had in identifying yourself as a hacker (but if you claim to be one and are not, you'll quickly be labeled **bogus***).*

This term seems to have been first adopted as a badge in the 1960s by the hacker culture surrounding TMRC and the MIT AI Lab. We have a report that it was used in a sense close to this entry's by teenage radio hams and electronics tinkerers in the mid-1950s.

Crackers. One who breaks security on a system. Coined ~1985 by hackers in defense against journalistic misuse of hacker. An earlier attempt to establish `worm' in this sense around 1981-82 on Usenet was largely a failure.

Use of both these neologisms reflects a strong revulsion against the theft and vandalism perpetrated by cracking rings. The neologism "cracker" in this sense may have been influenced not so much by the term "safe-cracker" as by the non-jargon term "cracker," which in Middle English meant an obnoxious person (e.g., "What cracker is this same that deafs our ears / With this abundance of superfluous breath?" - Shakespeare's King John, Act II, Scene I) and in modern colloquial American English survives as a barely gentler synonym for "white trash".

While it is expected that any real hacker will have done some playful cracking and knows many of the basic techniques, anyone past larval stage is expected to have outgrown the desire to do so except for immediate, benign, practical reasons (for example, if it's necessary to get around some security in order to get some work done).

Thus, there is far less overlap between hackerdom and crackerdom than the mundane reader misled by sensationalistic journalism might expect. Crackers tend to gather in small, tight-knit, very secretive groups that have little overlap with the huge, open poly-culture this lexicon describes; though crackers often like to describe themselves as hackers, most true hackers consider them a separate and lower form of life. (Jargon File 4.3.3)

Phreaks. The art and science of cracking the phone network (so as, for example, to make free long-distance calls). 2. By extension, security-cracking in any other context (especially, but not exclusively, on communications networks) (see cracking).

At one time phreaking was a semi-respectable activity among hackers; there was a gentleman's agreement that phreaking as an intellectual game and a form of *exploration was OK, but serious theft of services was taboo. There was significant crossover between the hacker community and the hard-core phone phreaks who ran semi-underground networks of their own through such media as the legendary "TAP Newsletter". This ethos began to break down in the mid-1980s as wider dissemination of the techniques put them in the hands of less responsible phreaks. Around the same time, changes in the phone network made old-style technical ingenuity less effective as a way of hacking it, so phreaking came to depend more on overtly criminal acts such as stealing phone-card numbers. The crimes and punishments of gangs like the `414 group' turned that game very ugly. A few old-time hackers still phreak casually just to keep their hand in, but most these days have hardly even heard of `blue boxes' or any of the other paraphernalia of the great phreaks of yore.*

Types and Characteristics of Malicious Code*

Many people misuse the word *virus*, assuming that it means anything that infects their computer and causes damage. The correct term is really *malicious code*. A virus is only one example of malicious code.

Viruses

There are several classes of viruses, ranging from innocuous to catastrophic. An understanding of each class is crucial to understanding the evolutionary process of an infiltrating virus. Innocuous viruses reside in unobtrusive areas of the system and cause no noticeable disruption. These viruses infect diskettes and other media that come into contact with the system but intend no damage. Humorous viruses cause aggravating events to occur, humorous messages to appear, or graphic images to be displayed. Although irritating, these viruses intend no damage and are commonly used for jokes. Potentially, the most disruptive and difficult to detect are the data-altering viruses that alter system data. The viruses modify data file numeric information in spreadsheets, database systems, and other applications, such as changing all occurrences of the number 3 to the number 8. Catastrophic viruses erase critical system files and immediately cause widespread destruction. The viruses scramble key information tables and/or remove all information on all disks, including shared and network drives. The *operating system* (OS) is software that controls all inputs and outputs to the system and manages the execution of programs. A virus can infect the OS in two ways: by completely replacing one or more OS programs or by attaching itself to existing OS programs and altering functionality. Once a virus has altered or changed OS functionality, it can control many OS processes that are running. To avoid detection, the virus usually creates several hidden files

*The remainder of this material is courtesy of the NSA's IATF.

within the OS source code or in "unusable" sectors. Because infections in the OS are difficult to detect, they have deadly consequences on systems relying on the OS for basic functions.

Virus Lifecycle

The lifecycle of a virus consists of two phases:

Phase 1: Replication.   This phase could last a few weeks to several years. In this phase, viruses typically remain hidden and do not interfere with normal system functions. Viruses also actively seek out new hosts to infect, such as attaching themselves to other software programs or infiltrating the OS. A virus that is attached to an executable program executes its instructions before passing control to the program (see Figure 8.2). These viruses are hard to detect because they only infect a small number of programs on a disk, and the user does not suspect their existence.

Phase 2: Activation.   During this phase, the beginning of gradual or sudden destruction of the system occurs. Typically, the decision to activate is based on a mathematical formula with criteria such as date, time, number of infected files, and others. The possible damage at this stage could include destroyed data, software or hardware conflicts, space consumption, and abnormal behavior.

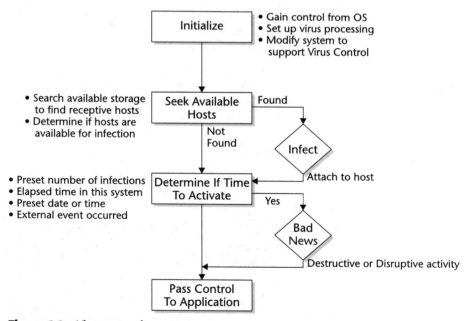

Figure 8.2   Virus execution.

LAN users, administrators, and individual workstation/personal computer users should scan for viruses because of the unrealized potential for harm. Numerous viruses make major computing disasters inevitable. Extraordinary damage caused by these viruses can result in loss of man hours, the disruption of normal activities, and wasted monetary resources. Therefore, the unrealized potential for harm is the main reason why malicious code scanning and prevention are extremely important.

Macro Viruses

The 1995 advent of macro programming for applications like Microsoft Word and Excel automated repetitive keystroke functions but also created an effective new way for viruses to spread. Word and Excel data files had previously been data-only files, like text-only email messages—unable to harbor viruses because they did not include executable code.

Virus writers soon discovered that these applications' macros could also be used to create viruses. At the same time, the sharing of documents and spreadsheet files via email became increasingly commonplace between users both within and between companies, creating the most effective virus carrier ever. Among the factors contributing to the dominance of macro viruses is the *Visual BASIC for Applications* (VBA) programming language, which makes it as easy for virus writers to create time-robbing macro viruses as it does for users to create legitimate time-saving macro commands.

Once the macro-infected file is accessed, it replaces one of the Word or Excel standard macros with an infected version that can then infect all documents with which it comes into contact. Macro viruses usually disable the macro menu selection, making users unable to see what macros are executing.

Today, macro viruses like "I Love You" are the most prevalent computer viruses in the wild—accounting for the vast majority of virus encounters in corporations. Today's widespread sharing of macro-enabled files, primarily through email attachments, is rapidly increasing along with the associated macro virus threat.

Table 8.1 describes the current impact of several macro viruses compared to an older virus and the associated costs to corporations.

Table 8.1 Comparison of Macro Viruses

VIRUS	YEAR	TYPE	TIME TO BECOME PREVALENT	ESTIMATED DAMAGES
Jerusalem, Cascade, Form	1990	Executable file, boot sector	3 Years	$50 million for all viruses over 5 years
Concept	1995	Word macro	4 months	$60 million

VIRUS	YEAR	TYPE	TIME TO BECOME PREVALENT	ESTIMATED DAMAGES
Melissa	1999	Email enabled Word macro	4 days	$93 million to $385 million
I Love You	2000	Email enabled Visual Basic script/word macro	5 hours	$700 million

Macro Viruses

Application programs on a system provide users with significant functionality. A macro virus can easily infect many types of applications such as Microsoft Word and Excel. To infect the system, these macro viruses attach themselves to the application initialization sequence. When an application is executed, the virus' instructions execute before control is given to the application. These macro viruses move from system to system through email file sharing, demonstrations, data sharing, and disk sharing. Viruses that infect application programs are the most common and can lie dormant for a long time before activating. Meanwhile, the virus replicates itself, infecting more and more of the system.

Polymorphic Viruses

Polymorphic viruses alter their appearance after each infection. Such viruses are usually difficult to detect because they hide themselves from antivirus software. Polymorphic viruses alter their encryption algorithm with each new infection. Some polymorphic viruses can assume over two billion different guises. This means that to be effective against a polymorphic virus, antivirus software products must perform heuristic analysis, as opposed to spectral analysis that can find simpler viruses.

There are three main components of a polymorphic virus:

- A scrambled virus body
- A decryption routine
- A mutation engine

In a polymorphic virus, the mutation engine and virus body are both encrypted. When a user runs a program infected with a polymorphic virus, the decryption routine first gains control of the computer, then decrypts both the virus body and the mutation engine. Next, the decryption routine transfers control of the computer to the virus, which locates a new program to infect. At this point, the virus makes a copy of itself and the mutation engine in *random access memory* (RAM). The virus then invokes the mutation engine, which randomly generates a new decryption routine capable of decrypting the virus yet bearing little or no resemblance to any prior decryption routine. Next, the virus encrypts the new copy of the virus body and mutation engine. Finally, the virus appends the new decryption routine, along with the newly encrypted virus and mutation engine, onto a new program. As a result, not only is the virus body encrypted, but also the virus decryption routine varies from infection to infection. This confuses a virus scanner searching for the telltale sequence of bytes that identifies a specific decryption routine. Therefore, with no fixed signature to scan for, and no fixed decryption routine, no two infections look alike.

A good way to contain a polymorphic virus is to set up false data directories or repositories to fool the attacker into thinking that he or she has reached exploitable data. This function can significantly reduce the risk of being attacked. The polymorphic virus executes in these false data directories, and is fooled into believing it has infected the entire system. In reality, the directories are either deleted or nonexistent, and the virus is thus unable to infect the system.

Stealth Viruses

Stealth viruses attempt to hide their presence from both the OS and the antivirus software. Some simple techniques include hiding the change in date and time as well as hiding the increase in file size. Stealth viruses sometimes encrypt themselves to make detection even harder. Stealth viruses also enter systems through simple download procedures. Unsuspecting users can do little against this type of infection except download files only from trusted sources.

Multipartite Virus

Multipartite viruses are also known as companion viruses. This type of virus is a combination of two or more virus attacks, which can spread as either virus.

Attack Scripts

Attack scripts are offensive code that crackers called "script kiddies" download malicious code from the Internet and run it against any number of targets. This act is also intentional. The most common attack seen is the buffer overflow.

Viruses and Email

Today's office worker receives an average of more than 40 email messages each day. Many of these messages have Microsoft Word or Excel data files attached that might carry macro viruses (see the section on macro viruses for detail discussion). Because plain-text data cannot carry the executable program code viruses need to copy and spread themselves, the text messages of email are, by themselves, unable to spread viruses. The virus danger from email stems from attachments containing active executable program files with extensions such as: CLASS, OCX, EXE, COM, and DLL—and from macro-enabled data files. These attachments do not even need to be opened, as many mail clients automatically display all attachments. To prevent attachments from automatically being displayed, simply configure the mail client to prompt the user. Another safeguard is to identify file extensions prior to opening attachments so the infection of many computer systems might be prevented. These attachments could contain malicious code that could be masquerading as another file type.

Virus Creation

Viruses can be created by using various techniques. But generally speaking, they can be classified as simple or complex:

Simple.   Simple viruses do not attempt to hide themselves and are easy to write. Users with little computer knowledge can use Internet programs to create these viruses. Since thousands of sites contain virus source code, users can easily download and use existing viruses to infect systems. Users with slightly more computer knowledge might even alter existing virus source code or combine several viruses to create a new undetectable virus capable of compromising systems.

Complex.   Complex viruses require more source code than simple viruses, which is used to conceal them from systems. Knowledge of assembly language is required to manipulate interrupts so these viruses can remain hidden. While hiding, complex viruses replicate, and will destroy data later. A complex virus is divided into three parts: the replicator, the concealer, and the bomb. The replicator part controls spreading the virus to other files, the concealer keeps the virus from being detected, and the bomb executes when the activation conditions of the virus are satisfied. After these parts are created and put together, the virus creator can infect systems with a virus that current antivirus software cannot detect.

Virus Hoaxes

The Internet is constantly being flooded with information about malicious code. However, interspersed among real virus notices are computer virus hoaxes. Virus hoaxes are false reports about nonexistent viruses, often claiming to do impossible things. While these hoaxes do not infect systems, they are still time consuming and costly to handle. Corporations usually spend much more time handling virus hoaxes than handling real virus incidents. The most prevalent virus hoax today is the "Good Times Hoax" that claims to put your computer's *central processing unit* (CPU) in an "nth-complexity infinite binary loop that can severely damage the processor." In this case, there is no such thing as an nth-complexity infinite binary loop. Virus hoaxes are estimated to cost more than genuine virus incidents. No antivirus product will detect hoaxes because they are not viruses, and many panic when they receive a hoax virus warning and assume the worst—making the situation much worse.

Worms

Worms are constructed to infiltrate legitimate data processing programs and alter or destroy the data. Although worms do not replicate themselves as viruses do, the resulting damage caused by a worm attack can be just as serious as a virus, especially if not discovered in time. However, once the worm invasion is discovered, recovery is much easier because there is only a single copy of the worm program to destroy, as the replicating ability of the virus is absent. A worm can infect the OS in two ways: by completely replacing one or more OS programs or by attaching itself to existing OS programs and altering functionality. Once a worm has altered or changed OS functionality, it can control many OS processes that are running. To avoid detection, the worm usually creates several hidden files within the OS source code or in "unusable" sectors. Since infections in the OS are difficult to detect, they have deadly consequences on systems relying on the OS for basic functions.

A prevalent worm, "Ska," is a Windows email and newsgroup worm. An email attachment disguised as Happy99.exe will display fireworks when executed the first time. After execution, every email and newsgroup posting sent from the machine will cause a second message to be sent. Because people receive Happy99.exe from someone they know, people tend to trust this attachment and run it. Then the worm causes damage by altering functionality of the WSOCK32 *dynamic library link* (DLL) file. Now, the worm can actively attack other users on the network by placing itself on the same newsgroups or same email addresses to which the user was posting or mailing.

Trojan Horses

A Trojan horse is an apparently harmless program or executable file. Trojan horses can also be carried via Internet traffic such as FTP downloads or downloadable applets from Web sites, and are often in the form of an email message that contains malicious code. Once a Trojan horse gets into a computer or network, it can unleash a virus or other malicious code, take control of the computer infrastructure, and compromise data or inflict other damage. The Melissa virus that struck in 1999 is a good example of a harmful Trojan horse. Attached to a harmless-looking email message, the virus accessed Microsoft Outlook, replicated itself, and sent itself to many other users listed in the recipient's email address book. The resulting email-sending flurry caused many Microsoft Exchange servers to shut down while users' mailboxes flooded with bogus messages. The Trojan horse cannot only compromise enterprise computers and networks by rapidly infecting entire networks, but also can invite unauthorized access to applications that results in downtime and costs to business potentially reaching into the millions of dollars.

Trojan Horses

Trojan horses are another threat to computer systems. Trojan horses can be in the guise of anything a user might find desirable, such as a free game, mp3 song, or other application. They are typically downloaded via HTTP or FTP. Once these programs are executed, a virus, worm, or other type of malicious code hidden in the Trojan horse program is released to attack the individual user workstation and subsequently a network.

Logic Bombs

Logic bombs are programs added to an already existing application. Most are added to the beginning of the application they are infecting, so they are run every time that application is run. When the infected program is run, the logic bomb is run first and usually checks the condition to see if it is time to run the bomb. If not, control is passed back to the main application and the logic bomb silently waits (see Figure 8.3). When the right time does come, the rest of the logic bomb's code is executed. At that time, the hard disk might be formatted, a disk erased, memory corrupted, or anything else. There are numerous ways to trigger logic bombs: counter triggers, time triggers, replication triggers (activate after a set number of virus reproductions), disk space triggers, and video mode triggers (activate when video is in a set mode or changes from set modes). There are also *Basic Input Output System* (BIOS) *read-only memory* (ROM) triggers (activate when a set version of BIOS is active), keyboard triggers, antivirus triggers (activate when a virus detects variables declared by virus-protection software, such as "SCAN_STRING"), and processor triggers (activate if a program is run on a particular processor).

Logic bombs cannot replicate themselves and therefore cannot infect other programs. If the program that is infected is given to someone else and the right conditions are met on that computer, however, it will go off.

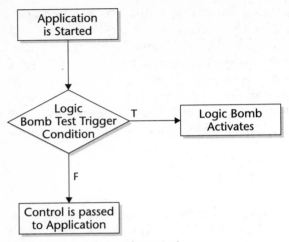

Figure 8.3   Logic bomb execution.

After a logic bomb has been activated, it can maliciously attack a system in the following ways:

- Halt machine
- Make garbled noise
- Alter video display
- Destroy data on disk
- Exploit hardware defects
- Cause disk failure
- Slow down or disable OS
- Cause monitor failures by writing illegal values to control ports of video cards
- Cause keyboard failure
- Corrupt disks
- Release more logic bombs and/or viruses (indirect attacks)

These attacks make logic bombs an extremely destructive type of malicious code.

Malicious Code Protection

The objective in this section is to clarify the importance of protection from destructive malicious code. Information is provided regarding malicious code protection techniques and how malicious code infiltrates a system. Detection and recovery tactics are described as well as different types of malicious code scanners used to protect systems.

Malicious code protection enables authorized *local area network* (LAN) users, administrators, and individual workstation/personal computer users to safely conduct daily functions in a secure manner. Logic bombs contain all types of malicious code and activate when certain conditions are met. Viruses, worms, and logic bombs can also be concealed within source code disguised as innocent programs like graphic displays and games. These apparently innocent programs are called Trojan horses. The quantity of new malicious code introduced into the computing environment has increased exponentially. This situation has occurred for several reasons. Computer users have become increasingly proficient and sophisticated, and software applications have become increasingly complex. Some brands of software are now widely used, thus their bugs and security loopholes are often known to intelligent users capable of writing destructive code. With the widespread use of personal computers that lack effective malicious code protection mechanisms, it is relatively easy for knowledgeable users to author malicious software and dupe unsuspecting users into copying or downloading it. In addition, since virus information and source code is readily available through the Internet and other sources, creating viruses has become a relatively simple task.

Malicious Code Detection System Requirements

The following list presents representative malicious code detection system requirements from a customer's perspective of needs. The malicious code detection system needs to:

- Allow access to all services available on the *wide area networks* (WAN) using any of the existing and emerging networking technologies and applications.
- Be able to locate the source and type of an infection, be able to react to such intrusions, and be able to fully reconstitute the system following damage caused by intrusions.
- Have minimal operational effect on the user.
- Have minimal operational effect on performance of the associated components.
- Have appropriate documentation for its use and upgradability and contain all currently available references and resources.
- Allow automatic malicious code prevention programs to run in the background.
- Allow a disaster recovery plan to recover data if necessary.
- Provide adequate scanning tools to be able to contain an identified virus by isolating affected systems and media.

- Have appropriate means to trace all incoming and outgoing data, including email, FTP transactions, and Web information.

- Be able to, in the event that the Internet is unavailable for any reason, still have access to virus updates from the manufacturer or vendor of the antivirus product.

- Monitor usage as required by the administrator.

- Scan for malicious software at the enclave boundary and at individual workstations.

- Log and analyze source-routed and other packets; react to or restrict malicious code attacks.

- Allow a rapid disconnect from the network in the event of a detected malicious code attack.

Configuration Management Requirements

The following have been identified as representative configuration and/or management requirements for malicious code detection systems:

- Be updated with regard to relevant security issues (malicious code detection, system vulnerability) so that maximum protection is provided.

- Be capable of preventing worm programs from infecting networks by allowing the administrator to disable the network mail facility from transferring executable files.

- Be configured by the administrator to filter all incoming data, including email, FTP transactions, and Web information for all types of malicious code.

- Allow the administrator to automatically create policy for network usage that details what sort of computing activity will and will not be tolerated.

- Allow regular backups of all system data by the administrator.

- Provide adequate controls such as strong user authentication and access control mechanisms on network connections for the administrator.

- Be capable of setting additional passwords or authentication for select files and accounts accessed from network ports.

- Be capable of placing restrictions on types of commands used on networks and in select files.

- Deny access to system manager accounts from network ports if possible.

- Monitor usage of the network during odd hours if possible and create a log of all activity for the system administrator.

- Provide no more than one administrator account (that is, not give other users administrator privileges).

Potential Attack Mechanisms

Malicious code can attack LAN users, administrators, and individual workstation/personal computer users in numerous ways, such as modifying data in transit, replaying (inserting previously collected data), exploiting the capabilities of mobile code, exploiting data execution, inserting and exploiting malicious code, exploiting protocols or infrastructure bugs, and modifying malicious software during production and/or distribution.

Network Attacks

With the number of networks increasing exponentially, potential threats to these networks are numerous and devastating. The most common attack is to deny service by generating large volumes of *Transmission Control Protocol/ Internet Protocol* (TCP/IP) traffic. The target site is rendered "unavailable" to the rest of the Internet community. The next level of *denial-of-service* (DOS) attacks is the distributed DOS-attack where several machines on the target site are exploited. Distributed DOS attacks are the most effective and insidious because they generate more traffic from other sources, making it much harder to identify the attacker's source, and subsequently more difficult to resolve. An example of a distributed DOS attack was the attack by "coolio" in February 2000, which caused the crash of numerous Web sites in the United States, including eBay, CNN, Yahoo!, and E*Trade. This attack involved sending *Internet Control Message Protocol* (ICMP) echo request datagrams (ping packets) to the broadcast address of networks using a faked or "spoofed" IP address of the host to be attacked. The IP host responds to these ICMP echo requests on either the nominal address or the broadcast address of its interfaces. When the broadcast address of a network was pinged, all active hosts on that network responded, and for any one request, there were many replies. This amplification makes distributed DOS attacks very powerful and causes large networks to crash.

Trapdoors

Trapdoors provide easy access for system administrators and authorized personnel to a system or a system's resources. Individuals can usually gain this access without a password. When these trapdoors are exploited, however, threats to a computer system are created. Authorized or unauthorized users with knowledge of trapdoors, can plant various types of malicious code into sensitive areas of a system. Therefore, the first layer of defense, prevention of malicious code, is bypassed, and the system must rely on detection and removal mechanisms to rid the system of the newly introduced malicious code.

Insider Attacks

Traditionally, insiders are a primary threat to computer systems. Insiders have legitimate access to the system and usually have specific goals and objectives. They can affect availability of system resources by overloading processing or storage capacity, or by causing the system to crash. Insiders can plant Trojan horses in sensitive data files, which attack the integrity of the entire system. Insiders can also exploit bugs in the OS by planting logic bombs or by causing systems to crash. All of these attacks by insiders are difficult to prevent, as legitimate access is essential to all users for crucial daily functions.

Connection/Password Sniffing

Other threats to the integrity of a system include connection and password "sniffing." A "sniffer" is malicious software or hardware that monitors all network traffic, unlike a standard network station that only monitors network traffic sent explicitly to it. Software sniffers can be a real threat to a network because they are "invisible" and easily fit on all workstations and servers. The specific threat presented by sniffers is their ability to catch all network traffic, including passwords or other sensitive information sent in plain text. An added threat to network security is that detecting sniffers on other machines is extremely difficult.

Mobile Code

Mobile code is an exciting jump forward in distributed processing capability. But with the newer technologies comes a significant opportunity for malicious code to enter systems. Mobile code is software that is transmitted across a network from a remote system or location to a local system and is then executed on that local system, often without explicit action on the part of the user. The local system can be a PC, workstation or smart device (such as a PDA, mobile phone, Internet appliance, and so on). Examples of mobile code include ActiveX, Java applets, browser-based scripts, and HTML email. Mobile code is also known as downloadable code or active content.

Malicious Mobile Code

Security practitioner should implement a system of controls that provide an ability to categorize and control the use of mobile code in order to minimize the risk associated with this form of malicious code. Once the categories are established, set rules for allowing and disallowing mobile code based on those rules. The rules should be developed considering the type or organization you have, their needs regarding receiving mobile code, and so on. In Table 8.2 we offer a sample categorization of mobile code used by several organizations.

Table 8.2 Category 1 Mobile Code

CATEGORY	DISCUSSION	EXAMPLES	RULES
Category 1	Category 1 mobile code exhibits a broad functionality, allowing unmediated access to workstation, host and remote system services and resources. This category has few or no counter-measures that can be applied to the known vulnerabilities. When this code is executed, it typically requires full access to all system resources or doesn't execute at all.	ActiveX Windows Scripting Host (when used to execute mobile code) Unix Shell Scripts (when used as mobile code) DOS Batch Scripts (when used as mobile code)	To the extent possible, all systems capable of executing mobile code shall be configured to disable the execution of Category 1 mobile code obtained from outside the protection layers of the organization.
Category 2	Category 2 mobile code technologies have full functionality, allowing mediated or controlled access to workstation, host, and remote system services and resources. Category 2 mobile code technologies may have known security vulnerabilities but also have known fine-grained, periodic, or continuous countermeasures or safeguards.	Java applets and other Java mobile code Visual Basic for Applications (VBA) LotusScript PerfectScript Postscript	Category 2 might be used if the mobile code is obtained from a trusted source over an assured channel (such as through a VPN or with encryption). In addition, Category 2 mobile code, whether or not obtained from a trusted source over an assured channel, might be used if it executes in a constrained environment without access to

(continued)

Table 8.2 *(continued)*

CATEGORY	DISCUSSION	EXAMPLES	RULES
Category 2 (continued)	While Category 2 mobile code technologies can pose a moderate threat to information systems.		local system and network resources (file system, Windows registry, network connections other than to its originating host).
			Where possible, web browsers and other mobile code enabled products shall be configured to prompt the user prior to the execution of Category 2 mobile code. Where feasible, protections against malicious Category 2 mobile code technologies shall be employed at end user systems and at enclave boundaries.
Category 3	Category 3 mobile code technologies support limited functionality, with no capability for unmediated access to workstation, host, and remote system services and resources. Category 3 mobile code might have a history of known vulnerabilities, but also support fine-grained, periodic, or continuous security safeguards. Category 3 mobile code technologies pose a limited risk to systems.	Javascript (include Jscript and ECMAScript variants) VBScript *Portable Document Format* (PDF)	Shockwave/Flash Category 3 mobile code technologies might be used in information systems.

Potential Countermeasures

This section is subdivided into several types of countermeasures that can be applied to prevent and/or remove malicious code: malicious code scanning products, electronic security (access constraint countermeasures), trapdoor access constraints, network security, connection and password sniffing countermeasures, and physical security. Last, we present an overall approach for countering malicious code.

Malicious Code Scanning Products

Malicious code scanning products are used to prevent and/or remove most types of malicious code, including viruses, worms, logic bombs, and Trojan horses, from a system. The use of malicious code scanning products with current virus definitions is crucial in preventing and/or detecting attacks by all types of malicious code. The damage done to files as a result of a malicious code attack might be restored from backups. But make certain you go back far enough to have a backup that is malicious code free.

Electronic Security

Electronic security typically refers to access constraint mechanisms used to prevent malicious code from being introduced into a system, intentionally or unintentionally, by authorized or unauthorized users. Unintentional system infiltration is the primary reason to implement access constraint mechanisms. If a set number of attempts to input a password correctly is exceeded, the system administrator must be contacted immediately. The system or system administrator should ensure that users change their passwords frequently and should not allow the use of dictionary words. This prevents easy decryption of passwords. Checksums can also be used; however, they only pertain to some strains of viruses. All of these electronic security measures protect against employees' intentionally or inadvertently deploying malicious code into a system or network.

The following are additional access constraint countermeasure requirements:

Provide data separation.   For data that is allowed access to the protected network workstation, steps should be taken to constrain the portion of the system that can be affected in case of a malicious code attack.

Employ application-level access control.   Access restrictions might also be implemented within a workstation or at various points within a LAN to provide additional layers and granularity of protection against authorized and unauthorized malicious code attacks.

Trapdoor Access/Distribution

To protect against unauthorized use of trapdoors to introduce malicious code, reliable companies should be used when considering software and hardware purchases. When inputting data, you should only use reliable inputting individuals and use monitoring devices to monitor them. Reliable system administrators should remove passwords immediately after an employee leaves a company. All of these prevention techniques are crucial to prevent malicious code from infiltrating systems through trapdoors.

Network Security

A boundary protection mechanism at the gateway must be used within a network. There are also several ways to protect a network against distributed DoS attacks by malicious code. An administrator can secure hosts on the network by replacing rlogin and rexec commands with ssh or other encrypted commands. IP spoofing should be prevented to keep hosts from pretending to be others and TCPwrappers should be used to limit connections to authorized sources. Do not allow ICMP to broadcast outside the network and multicast addresses entering from outside the network. These few preventive methods will help prevent distributed DoS attacks.

Connection and Password Sniffing Countermeasures

Although sniffing of Internet traffic is difficult to stop, there are several ways to defend a system and make sniffing difficult. First, use an encryption mechanism (for example, *Secure Sockets Layer* [SSL]) to allow encryption of message transmissions across Internet protocols whenever possible. Also, encrypt email through the use of *Pretty Good Privacy* (PGP) and *Secure Multi-Purpose Internet Mail Extensions* (S/MIME). When email is sent encrypted, to read email it must be unencrypted. If mail programs allow attachments to automatically run, malicious code can still infect a system. The malicious code will be encrypted with the rest of the message and activate when you read the decrypted message. Also, implement ssh or other encrypted commands instead of insecure remote login. To stop password sniffers, use secure remote access and smart cards to keep passwords private. To protect a LAN from sniffing, replace a hub with a switch, which is extremely effective in practice. Although sniffers can still access the LAN, it becomes more difficult for them to do so. It is important to note that the use of encryption can render virus detection programs unusable if the transmission is encrypted when it is processed by the virus detector.

Physical Security

To be physically secure against potential infections by malicious code, the system must be protected from physical attack. It is necessary to use a monitoring system to authenticate users to restrict physical access. Once access is granted, users' actions must be monitored.

An Overall Approach to Counter Malicious Code

So, what do you do to keep the oldies but goodies away, including the most recent versions? There are many reputable sources available today providing recommendations on the prevention of viruses and other malware. We have tried to synthesize the best and provide that to you. At the end of the book is a listing of authoritative sources for receiving information and support on malware attacks:

- Purchase, apply, and consistently administer virus software.
- Update the data files for the virus software every week if possible.
- Block incoming ports on the firewalls that are not essential for your business.
- Block email attachments that are executables.
- Restrict users from bringing floppies, home computers from outside.
- Discourage the downloading of software (even for PDAs) from the Internet.
- E-visit reputable sources on the Web.
- Ensure that users get security training and are taught not to send junk emails and e-chain letters.

Detection Mechanism

The detection mechanism enables users to detect the presence of malicious code, respond to its presence, and recover data or system files if possible.

Detect

The objectives for detection are to discover attacks at or inside the protected boundary as well as to facilitate tracking and prosecuting of adversaries. Malicious code detection involves the continual probing of internal networks for the existence of services or applications infected by malicious code. This might be done routinely to assist in the selection of additional appropriate countermeasures, to determine the effectiveness of implemented countermeasures, or to detect all types of malicious code. The following are typical security capability requirements associated with malicious code detection and system probing.

- Provide centralized operation.
- Provide automated reports.
- Recommend corrective action.
- Archive significant security events.
- Display and record status in real time.

Respond

To respond to the presence of detected malicious code within a system or network, malicious code scanning must be performed. The following are typical security capability (countermeasure) requirements:

- Detect the occurrence of infection and locate malicious software; for example, a virus found in local memory.
- Perform scanning automatically; for example, run continual malicious code scans throughout the day on systems.
- Implement scanning at the network gateway and at network components, such as the desktop.
- Identify specific malicious code; for example, macro virus.
- Remove malicious code from all infected systems so that it cannot infect further; for example, boot from uninfected write-protected boot diskette, then remove the malicious code from the system.
- Correct all effects of malicious code and restore system to original state; for example, check all diskettes with files that might have been in disk drives during virus residency; reload files as appropriate.
- Reload program backups in cases where malicious code cannot be completely identified or where removal is not possible.
- Perform manually initiated scanning regularly; for example, scan for malicious code after any Internet downloads.

Recover

To recover data from the infection of malicious code, first concentrate on the specific area infected. The recovery process will take longer if malicious code has been in the system for a longer time. The number of computers that have been infected is also important as it affects time and resources for recovery. There are four stages in the infection process, and each stage requires a different amount of time and resources for recovery.

Stage 1: Local Memory Infection.   If malicious code is caught in the first few hours before an appropriate host is found and replication begins, the following straightforward approach can be applied:

- Power down.
- Cold reboot with a clean, write-protected diskette.
- Run a utility program to check the hard disk and remove any infected files.
- Locate and destroy the source containing the malicious code.

Stage 2: Local Disk Storage Infection.   If an infection goes undetected, malicious code will infect an increasing number of programs and data files over time. In this case, the removal process becomes more complicated and several things could happen. If data and program files have been destroyed, it is possible that a complete reformat of the infected media will be required for recovery. File backups can also be dangerous due to the risk of reinfection during the restoration process. Total data loss might occur.

Stage 3: Shared File System Infection.   The risk of malicious code infecting the network attached to a computer is very high. If the infection is widespread, it is possible that a reformat of the entire medium will be required for recovery. Many things could happen during the recovery process. Again, file backups can be dangerous due to the risk of reinfection during the restoration process. One complication is numerous computers attached to the infected network will also be infected. The malicious code must be removed simultaneously from all workstations as well as the network. Another complication is that other users might have saved the malicious code unknowingly onto a floppy disk that might infect the entire network later.

Stage 4: System-Wide Removable Media Infection.   An infected computer will infect many of the physical disks it contacts. This is an extremely difficult situation to deal with for numerous reasons. Malicious code infects all types of removable media, such as floppy diskettes, removable hard disks, reel and cartridge tapes, and so on. Once an infected disk has successfully infected a network computer, the number of infected disks drastically increases. A complication with all the infected disks is the possibility of reinfection after malicious code has been discovered and removed. Although scanning devices would have been updated since the original infection and would catch many possible reinfections, new malicious code, like the polymorphic virus that changes itself after each infection, could still compromise the network. Malicious code could also reach client sites and computers.

Administrative Countermeasures

Administrative concerns regarding infection by malicious code include training, policy, and coping with fears about malicious code and computers. It is crucial for administrators to minimize stress due to computer viruses while not blaming employees.

Administrators can combat fears about malicious code and computers in many ways. The staff should be educated and motivated with regard to malicious code protection, detection, and recovery. A review of computer security with a risk analysis of exposure to infection and likely consequences should be conducted. A corporate policy with information about malicious code should be distributed to all staff. In addition, special briefing sessions should be held for all staff involved with computing functions. Administrators need to institute prevention programs that incorporate safe computing practices that should be posted at all terminals. Regular training sessions on safe computing should be scheduled. Administrators should also have a disaster recovery plan that is practiced on worst-case scenarios. Twenty-four-hour emergency phone numbers should be displayed. Employees should also be cautioned to avoid overreaction. Deploy robust backup facilities to minimize consequential damage.

System Backup

There are two main strategies to follow when performing a system backup: workstation strategy and network strategy. In either case, planning and testing should occur to make certain the strategies function as designed.

Workstation Strategy

The best backup strategy for workstations is to back up often. If the workstation is running the Windows OS, there are some simple backup tools already provided. Several utilities and programs are also available from other companies to assist users in performing backups. The following features can make backup chores more bearable: incremental backup, unattended scheduling, and easy, simple restoration. Incremental backup saves changes made since the most recent full or incremental backup. This backup is important because users who do not want to wait to back up a system can use incremental backup as a substitute for a lengthy full backup. Scheduling uses software automation to execute backup chores without the need for personal interaction. Although a backup medium must be selected and in place, the user does not need to be present for the actual backup. Zip drives and small tape drives are also cost-effective solutions used to back up workstation data.

Network Strategy

The best backup strategy for networks is an approach that combines several features to save time and effort, and still assure complete backups. Execute full backups often. Since backups take up network, server, and/or workstation resources, it is best to run full backups when nobody is working. In addition, open files are skipped during backup and do not get backed up at all until some future time when the file is closed and not being used. Having few to no users holding files open will ensure the greatest backup saturation possible. Full backups are most efficiently executed in the evenings. Store the full backup tape off site. On each of the remaining workdays of the week, using a separate tape for each day, run an incremental backup and store it off site, too. The last full backup of the month should be permanently moved off site and held for archival purposes. Therefore, if a network is attacked by malicious code, these backup techniques will ensure data integrity and allow all systems to be recovered.

Types of Malicious Code Detection Products

Most computer malicious code scanners use pattern-matching algorithms that can scan for many different signatures at the same time. Malicious code detection technologies have to include scanning capabilities that detect known and unknown worms and Trojan horses. Most antivirus products search hard disks for viruses, detect and remove any that are found, and include an auto-update feature that enables the program to download profiles of new viruses so that it will have the profiles necessary for scanning. The virus-like signatures these programs recognize are quite short: typically 16 to 30 bytes out of the several thousand that make up a complete virus. It is more efficient to recognize a small fragment than to verify the presence of an entire virus, and a single signature might be common to many different viruses.

Updates

Maintaining an effective defense against virus and hostile code threats involves far more than the ability to produce perfect detection rates at a given point in time. With an average of nearly 300 new viruses discovered each month, the actual detection rate of AV software can decline rapidly if not kept current. This AV protection should be updated regularly. As new viruses are discovered, corresponding cures are developed to update protections. These updates should not be ignored. AV systems should do these updates automatically, reliably, and through a centrally controlled management framework. To stay current, these scanning programs must be updated when new viral strains are found and antiviral codes are written. Most computer-virus scanners use pattern-matching algorithms that can scan for many different signatures at the same time. This is why enterprise-class AV solutions must be able to offer timely and efficient upgrades and updates across all client and server platforms.

Often, in large enterprise environments, a typical acquisition and deployment strategy is to deploy one brand of AV software at end-user workstations and a different vendor's product on the email, file, and application server environments. This function broadens the spectrum of coverage because in any given instance, one vendor is typically ahead of another in releasing the latest round of virus signature discoveries.

Pre-Infection Prevention Products

Pre-infection prevention products are used as the first level of defense against malicious code. Before the code actually attacks a system, prevention products should be applied. Email filtering products are available that do not allow executable programs or certain file types to be transferred. Also, options in browsers that limit the use of and/or disable Java and ActiveX plug-ins should be implemented. Simply changing browser options enables the user to see hidden files and file extension names and could prevent opening an infected file masquerading as a normal text file. These essential pre-infection prevention products are the first level of defense against malicious code attacks.

Infection Prevention Products

Infection prevention products are used to stop the replication processes and prevent malicious code from initially infecting the system. These types of products, protecting against all types of malicious code, reside in memory all the time while monitoring system activity. When an illegal access of a program or the boot sector occurs, the system is halted and the user is prompted to remove the particular type of malicious code. These products act like filters that prevent malicious code from infecting file systems (see Figure 8.4).

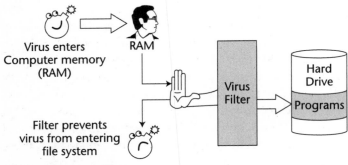

Figure 8.4 Virus filter.

Short-Term Infection Detection Products

Short-term infection detection products detect an infection very soon after the infection has occurred. Generally, the specific infected area of the system is small and immediately identified. These products also detect all types of malicious code and work on the principle that all types of malicious code leave traces. Short-term infection detection products can be implemented through vaccination programs and the snapshot technique.

Vaccination Programs

Vaccination programs modify application programs to allow for a self-test mechanism within each program. If the sequence of that program is altered, a virus is assumed and a message is displayed. The drawbacks to this implementation include the fact that the boot segment is very hard to vaccinate, and the malicious code might gain control before the vaccination program can warn the user. The majority of short-term infection detection products use vaccination because it is easier to implement.

Snapshot Technique

The snapshot technique has been shown to be the most effective means of detection. Upon installation, a log of all critical information is made. During routine system inspections (snapshots) the user is prompted for appropriate action, if any traces of malicious code are found. Typically, these system inspections occur when the system changes: disk insertion, connection to different Web sites, and so on. This technique is difficult to implement in short-term infection detection products and is not widely used; however, when the snapshot technique is used in combination with a vaccination program, you achieve an effective level of protection against malicious code.

Long-Term Infection Detection Products

Long-term infection detection products identify specific malicious code on a system that has already been infected for some time. They usually remove the malicious code and return the system to its prior functionality. These products seek a particular virus and remove all instances of it. Two different techniques are used by long-term infection detection products: spectral analysis and heuristic analysis.

Spectral Analysis

Using spectral analysis, long-term infection detection products search for patterns from code trails that malicious code leaves. To discover this automatically generated code, all data is examined and recorded. When a pattern or subset of it appears, a counter is incremented. This counter is used to determine how often a pattern occurs. Using these patterns and the quantity of their occurrence, these products then judge the possible existence of malicious code and remove all instances of it. These products search for irregularities in code and recognize them as particular instances of malicious code.

Heuristic Analysis

Using heuristic analysis, long-term infection detection products analyze code to figure out the capability of malicious code. The underlying principle that governs heuristic analysis is that new malicious code must be identified before it can be detected and subsequently removed. This technique is much less scientific, as educated guesses are created. Because they are guesses, heuristic analysis does not guarantee optimal or even feasible results; however, it is impossible to scientifically analyze each part of all source code. Not only is this effort unproductive, it is terribly inefficient. Typically, good, educated guesses are all that is needed to correctly identify malicious code in source code. These long-term infection detection products then remove all instances of the detected malicious code.

DOS file viruses typically append themselves on the end of .EXE files. DOS file viruses can also append themselves to the beginning or end of .COM files (see Figure 8.5). Other infection techniques are also possible but less common.

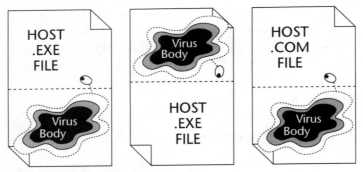

Figure 8.5 DOS file infection.

Interoperability Concerns

The different types of products mentioned above must be used together to create effective protection against all types of malicious code. Many layers of defense must be in place for a system to deal effectively with malicious code. If each type of product is implemented in a system, four different levels of defense are created. Before malicious code can attack a system, it must first get to the system through the pre-infection prevention products. If it gets that far, the second layer of defense, prevention products will attempt to stop the malicious code from replicating. If that is not successful, then the detection products will try to locate and remove the infection before it reaches the majority of the system. If the malicious code reaches the entire system, identification products can apply two different techniques to remove the infection. Each of these levels of defense is essential to the prevention of infection and the protection of a system.

Today, commercial software packages combine all the above levels of defense and provide malicious code protection services. With new computer systems connecting to the Internet daily, security problems will also grow at an exponential rate. Unless a well-defined security policy is in place, information technology managers will continue to lose the battle against computer viruses. Despite the fact that antivirus applications are essential for the detection of known viruses, no mail filter or malicious code scanner can defend against a new mail worm attack. The recent "I Love You" virus was caught quickly and still did a wealth of damage. It seems to only be a matter of time before someone figures out how to send email viruses or worms that infect systems without opening attachments. While the current state of software is not sophisticated enough to stop brand new viruses from entering systems, antivirus application makers are producing software that can prevent the damaging, data-altering effects of the malicious code.

Products Offering Protection at the Workstation

A workstation can be protected from malicious code attacks in many ways. The implementation of pre-infection prevention, infection prevention, infection detection, and infection identification products provide four separate levels of defense and are essential in protecting a workstation. Although this is the best way to protect a workstation, other techniques can be applied. New malicious code protection products introduce a "sandbox" technology allowing users the option to run programs such as Java and ActiveX in quarantined sub-directories of systems. If malicious code is detected in a quarantined program, the system simply removes the associated files, protecting the rest of the system. Another protection mechanism is to allow continual virus definition updates that are transparent to the user. Implementing these updates at boot time or periodically (one hour, two hours, and so on) drastically reduces the chance a system will be infected with newly discovered malicious code. In the past six months alone, more than 4,000 new viruses have been discovered. Without current virus definition updates, a system is left vulnerable to the devastating effects from malicious code.

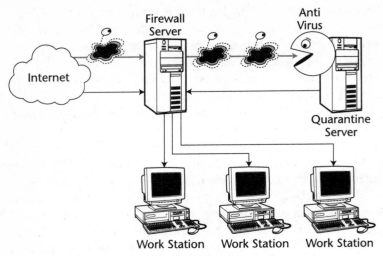

Figure 8.6 Intelligent Scanning Architecture (ISA).

Products Offering Protection at the Network Gateway

When protecting a network, a number of issues must be considered. A common technique used in protecting networks is to use a firewall with Intelligent Scanning Architecture (ISA) or other architecture that provides this capability (see Figure 8.6). In this technique, if a user attempts to retrieve an infected program via FTP, HTTP, or SMTP, it is stopped at the quarantine server before it reaches the individual workstations. The firewall will only direct suspicious traffic to the antivirus scanner on the quarantine server. This technique scales well since LAN administrators can add multiple firewall or gateway scanners to manage network traffic for improved performance. In addition, users cannot bypass this architecture, and LAN administrators do not need to configure clients at their workstations.

Other useful scanning techniques for a network include continuous, automated malicious code scanning using numerous scripts. Simple commands can be executed and numerous computers in a network can be scanned for possible infections. Other scripts can be used to search for possible security holes through which future malicious code could attack the network. Only after fixing these security holes can a network withstand many attacks from malicious code.

Criteria for Selecting Protection Products

When selecting antivirus products, two important guidelines must be followed. The "best" product might not be good enough by itself. In addition, since data security products operate in different ways, one product might be more useful than another in different situations. When selecting a particular malicious code protection product, its installation must be considered. Is the program shipped on *compact disc* (CD) or on 1.44MB disks? Does the installation itself operate smoothly? There should be no questions without answers when properly installing a product. This product should be easy to use, providing clear and uncluttered menu systems as well as meaningful screen messages.

Help systems are essential, as users need current information regarding all types of malicious code. The trend is to provide on-line help; however, manuals should also be provided with the product. The malicious code protection product should be compatible with all hardware and software and should not create conflicts. The company that produces the product should be stable and able to provide necessary local technical support for all questions and problems. The product should be fully documented, that is, all messages and error codes should be deciphered and full installation guides and how-to manuals should be provided. The computers to run this software must meet the hardware and software requirements specified by the manufacturer. The malicious code protection software should function properly and perform its duties without failing. Rating each of these categories will allow a company to choose the best malicious code protection product for its needs.

Example Cases

Case 1: Macro Virus Attack

Problem

Within a network environment, macro virus attacks are increasing exponentially. In Figure 8.7, a macro virus has infected an enclave via an email attachment sent by an outsider. This email attachment is a text document that enables macros. The email recipient has emailed this document to his coworkers and saved it to diskette to view at home. A macro virus initiates when the document is opened and macros are enabled. As soon as the document is opened, the macro virus infects standard macros in the word processing program. After altering functionality of these standard macros, this virus replicates and infects many of the documents with which it comes into contact.

Solution

There are many ways to prevent, detect, respond to, and restore from macro virus attacks. The first level of defense is prevention so the macro virus does not reach the system. In a network environment, the first contact with the macro virus will be at the gateway. If the network is configured properly and using ISA (Protection at the Network Gateway) the macro virus should be stopped at the quarantine server. It is crucial to have current virus definition updates in the malicious code detection software on the quarantine server.

These updates should occur continually, and should be transparent to the user. Implementing these updates at boot time, or periodically (hourly) drastically reduces the chance a system will be infected by a newly discovered macro virus. So, these updates prevent new macro viruses from infecting the entire network. If the macro virus is not stopped at the gateway, individual workstations should detect the presence of the macro virus and remove it. At the next layer of defense, the individual user workstation will scan all incoming email attachments for the presence of malicious code. If the malicious code detection software discovers the macro virus, the file is simply deleted and the system and network are preserved. If virus updates are automatic, virus definitions for the quarantine server and the individual workstation should be the same at the time of original system infiltration. In this case, the detection software at the workstation will probably detect the macro virus. If virus updates are not automatic, the individual user workstation will probably not detect the presence of the macro virus. This is because most users do not update their virus definitions as quickly as the system administrator of the quarantine server does. If this new macro virus has infected many workstations during a time frame of several days, however, the possibility of vendors discovering this macro virus and updating their virus definitions increases. Once this macro virus is detected by an individual workstation, the system administrator should automatically be notified.

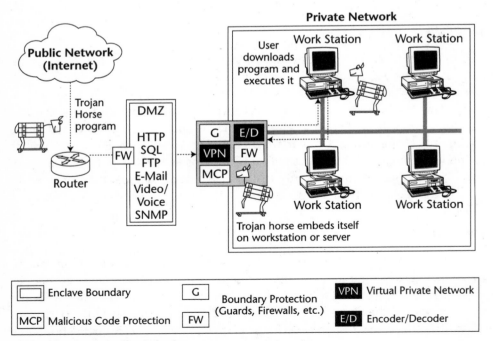

Figure 8.7 Macro-virus infection.

If the macro virus does infect the network by infecting workstations, the virus must be detected and removed. Typically, new macro viruses are detected when a user notices abnormal computer behavior and that abnormality is investigated. Another way to detect viruses is through automatic virus scanning with virus software definition updates. Once the presence of the macro virus is detected, it is essential to update all virus definition updates in all copies of malicious code protection software throughout the network. Then, several methods can be applied to remove all instances of the macro virus. If the infection has occurred recently (within a few hours), you should use short-term infection detection products. Using the snapshot technique, or vaccination programs, all instances of the macro virus are detected and then removed. If the infection is not recent, long-term infection detection products should be used. Using spectral and/or heuristic analysis, all instances of the macro virus are detected and then removed.

If the macro-virus has fully infected network workstations, however, the macro virus removal will then allow for the data recovery process to begin. By practicing simple system backup procedures, applications and data can be restored from tape backups with minimal data loss. After updating malicious code definitions for all malicious code protection software, the reconstituted network is then ready to proceed with daily functions. Any damage caused by the macro virus is removed and the system is restored to its prior functionality.

If the unsuspecting user places the macro virus on his or her home computer via diskette, many problems can occur. Not only can the home computer become infected, but the network could also be reinfected. After modifying the infected file at home, the user can bring the file back to the office and infect his individual workstation. However, since the virus definitions should have been updated, the malicious code protection at the workstation should identify the virus and remove it. The user should then scan the home computer and remove all infections on that computer as well.

Case 2: Polymorphic Virus Attack

Problem

Polymorphic viruses represent the upper echelon of computer viruses. Today's polymorphic viruses are very difficult to detect using conventional antivirus search engines because they possess the capability to mutate themselves and conceal their digital identity as they spread. The unique ability of this form of virus to change its signature to avoid detection makes it virtually undetectable, and therefore potentially disastrous in nature.

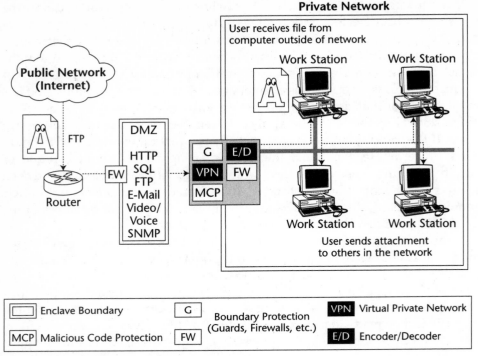

Figure 8.8 Polymorphic virus infection.

Polymorphic viruses infect enclaves in much the same way as macro viruses. In Figure 8.8, a polymorphic virus enters a system through FTP, as an unsuspecting user retrieves a single file from a computer outside the network. The user then sends this file via an email attachment to other coworkers throughout the network.

Once that file is accessed by any user, the polymorphic virus begins its programming and begins to replicate by emailing itself to the entire address book on its newfound host. It continuously changes its digital signature to escape the detection capabilities if any antivirus application is resident.

Solution

Polymorphic viruses increasingly represent serious threats to computer networks. Prevention, detection, containment, and recovery from potentially lethal polymorphic computer viruses should be an important task of every user, network administrator, and senior management officer. Establishment of an adhered to antivirus computer policy is a must for all those requiring any degree of protection for their systems against polymorphic virus attacks.

To successfully prevent polymorphic viruses from entering into a computer system, potential vulnerabilities must be identified and eliminated. Attackers often look to exploit the most obvious vulnerability of a computer network. Inadequate security mechanisms allow unauthorized users entry into computer systems, potentially allowing data to be compromised, replaced, or destroyed. Determent of attackers can be accomplished by having a predetermined computer protection plan in place. Also, contingency plans will enable the containment of and eventual recovery from a polymorphic virus attack. Another technique for preventing polymorphic virus attacks is to set up false data directories or repositories to fool the attacker (see the section in this chapter titled *Polymorphic Viruses*). Preparation for any incident of an attack and knowledge of how a given attack might occur is all part of the strategic virus protection plan that should be implemented prior to operation of a computer network.

Detection of polymorphic viruses becomes exponentially easier when the polymorphic virus signature is cataloged in an antivirus definition table and updated regularly to all systems gateways. This can happen in one of two ways. A user can notice altered functionality on a workstation, and after technicians investigate the problem, the polymorphic virus is finally discovered. Then, technicians inform vendors who update the virus definitions for others. A user can also remove the polymorphic virus after vendors have updated their virus definitions by downloading the newest virus definitions and scanning the entire system. Establishment of an updating policy not only for system gateways, but also for individual computer workstations, greatly increases the likelihood of preventing a polymorphic virus from entering and replicating itself on a given network.

Recovery methodologies are integral to the overall readiness of an antivirus prevention plan. Even the best-prepared plans sometimes fail. Having written procedures in place to recover from a catastrophic event could mean the difference between a company surviving or going out of business. Recovery consists of virus-free tape backups of recent data, providing an environment free from all viruses, and restoring the network to pre-virus infection operation. There are inexpensive software applications that unobtrusively track disk activity in such a way that they can return a system to precisely the way it was prior to a computer virus incident. Backing up data or implementation of a mirroring solution is essential to having a ready alternative source of providing information to users on a moment's notice. Unless uniformly adopted throughout the entire organization, a plan will have little chance of ever becoming successful. Dedicated personnel responsible for predetermined actions in anticipated situations are crucial for the protection of computer systems.

Case 3: Trojan Horse Attack

Problem

There exists a growing threat from another type of malicious software, the Trojan horse. In Figure 8.9, a Trojan horse has been embedded into an existing network. A user downloaded a program that he thought was useful; however, after executing it, he realized it was not exactly what he needed. So, he deleted the file from his computer. This unsuspecting user did not realize that the program downloaded was a Trojan horse that embedded itself into the network as a sniffer program after it was executed. Although this event occurred several weeks ago, there have been no problems in the network until now, when employees are noticing forged emails being sent to various clients.

Solution

Eradication of a Trojan horse encompasses many of the same procedures taken to eradicate macro and polymorphic viruses (see "Case 1: Macro Virus Attack" and "Case 2: Polymorphic Virus Attack"). The Trojan horse can contain a virus inside of the apparently harmless program. However, in this case, something

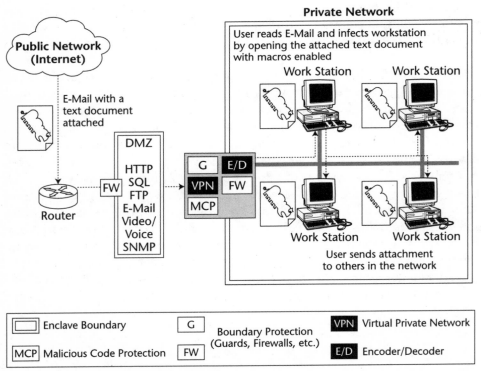

Figure 8.9 Trojan horse infection.

else must be done to rid the network of the sniffer program hidden inside the Trojan horse. There is no one solution to prevent, detect, or remove sniffers. Because sniffer programs are extremely difficult to detect, the first level of defense against them is to make sniffing difficult. The network should use a switch instead of a hub to prevent sniffing of internal user passwords. By using an encryption mechanism for message transmissions and email transactions, sniffing of important data such as passwords can be prevented. The use of ssh or other encrypted commands can help keep passwords private. Another precaution against password sniffing is the use of one-time passwords. It does an attacker no good to sniff a password that is only valid during a very short time period.

In this case, the presence of sniffers is suspected since numerous forged emails have occurred. By applying the above measures of encryption and secure commands, sniffers can be rendered ineffective as passwords become much harder to decipher. It is also a good practice to change passwords often, or have the system administrator force users to change their passwords periodically to decrease the chance sniffer program users have time to decrypt encrypted passwords.

Also, we cannot stress enough how important it is to establish a complete and comprehensive malicious code protection backup system. If sniffer program users gain unauthorized access to the network, user applications and data files could be deleted. The only countermeasure in this case is to change all passwords and restore the system to prior functionality from full system backups. When systems are restored, however, the sniffer must not be restored also.

Sample Questions

1. Which one of the following characteristics is NOT associated with a computer virus?

   a. Malicious code that infects files and can infect the boot sector

   b. A program that replicates itself without the approval of the user

   c. Malicious code that attaches to a host program and propagates when the infected program is executed

   d. Malicious code that is hidden in a program that has a useful function or apparently useful function

2. A malicious computer program that is activated when a particular state of the computer occurs, such as a particular date and time, is called a:

   a. Polymorphic virus

   b. Logic bomb

   c. Retro virus

   d. Keyed virus

3. Code that can be downloaded from a network and executed on a local computer is known as:

   a. A virtual machine

   b. A dynamic machine

   c. Mobile code

   d. Pointer code

4. Which one of the following is NOT a characteristic of a worm virus?

   a. Can remain on an infected computer indefinitely

   b. Requires operating systems that support the execution of downloaded programs

   c. Creates multiple replicas of itself on the infected computer until memory is used up and the infected computer crashes

   d. Requires a means to transmit itself to other networked computers

5. A virus that conceals the modifications that it makes to a computer's files is called a:

   a. Hidden virus

   b. Proxy virus

    c. Stealth virus

    d. Multipartite virus

6. An individual that creates or uses programs to break into telephone systems to be able to access other computers is called a:

    a. Hacker

    b. Phreaker

    c. Cracker

    d. Social engineer

7. Which of the following statements regarding malicious code is NOT true?

    a. Worms and viruses replicate themselves.

    b. Trojan horses and viruses replicate themselves.

    c. Trojan horses and viruses are associated with other programs.

    d. A worm does not need another program to serve as a host.

8. Malicious code that is set to execute when a user, A, logs on 110 times is a:

    a. Stealth virus

    b. Polymorphic virus

    c. Worm

    d. Logic bomb

9. An attack script is which one of the following?

    a. A step-by-step procedure that a cracker follows to initiate attacks on networks

    b. Malicious code that can be downloaded from different sites on the Internet and used to mount an attack on computing resources

    c. A rehearsed social engineering ploy to gain access to passwords

    d. The product of applying a keyed hash function to a sensitive message

10. Which one of the following procedures is NOT recommended for detecting malicious code and preventing malicious code attacks?

    a. Deploying virus scanning software

    b. Education of employees

    c. Downloading of software from the Internet

    d. Disable ports that are not required for the organization's business

11. An excellent approach to defending against malicious code is an access control layered defense. Which one of the following is NOT a component of this type of defense?

    a. Making backups of "clean" files

    b. Restricting who can physically gain entry to areas containing computing resources

    c. Controlling who has the ability to read, write, and copy files

    d. Restricting the use of specific computing resources to those who require those resources to perform their assigned job functions

12. A virus that is associated with loading of the operating system into memory on startup is called a:

    a. Boot sector virus

    b. Companion virus

    c. Macro virus

    d. Source code virus

13. Which one of the following items best describes the accuracy of the following statement: "Only executable programs can contain viruses, therefore files that are not executable are not a concern relative to malicious code"?

    a. True

    b. True with one exception

    c. False

    d. False with one exception

14. Two general categories of stealth virus capabilities are:

    a. Write stealth and copy stealth

    b. Read stealth and write stealth

    c. Size stealth and write stealth

    d. Size stealth and read stealth

15. Which one of the following is NOT a reason that peer-to-peer networks are more vulnerable to file-resident virus attacks than network servers?

    a. Because every workstation on a peer-to-peer network can function both as a client and a server, the network is more resistant to file-resident virus attacks.

    b. Viruses can be transmitted from one workstation to another on a peer-to-peer network.

   c. Because every workstation on a peer-to-peer network can function both as a client and a server, the network is less resistant to file-resident virus attacks.

   d. Peer-to-peer network security is usually weaker than what exists on a network server.

16. Which choice BEST describes a simple virus, as opposed to a complex virus?

   a. Users who have little computer knowledge can use Internet programs to create simple viruses.

   b. Simple viruses attempt to conceal themselves from systems.

   c. A simple virus is divided into three parts: the replicator, the concealer, and the bomb.

   d. Knowledge of assembly language is required to manipulate interrupts so that simple viruses can remain hidden.

17. Which choice is NOT a common part of a complex virus?

   a. Replicator

   b. Macro

   c. Bomb

   d. Concealer

18. Which choice is NOT a step in the polymorphic virus infection process?

   a. The decryption routine first gains control of the computer and decrypts both the virus body and the mutation engine.

   b. The decryption routine transfers control of the computer to the virus, which locates a new program to infect.

   c. The virus makes a copy of itself and the mutation engine in RAM.

   d. The virus creates a network backdoor to enable unauthorized entry at a later date.

19. Which choice is an incorrect statement about pre-infection prevention?

   a. Pre-infection prevention products are used as the first level of defense against malicious code.

   b. Email filtering products that do not enable executable programs or certain file types to be transferred.

   c. Options in browsers that limit the use of and/or disable Java and ActiveX plug-ins.

   d. Pre-infection prevention products are much less scientific than post-infection products because they use educated guesses.

20. Which choice is NOT true about virus vaccination programs?

    a. The majority of short-term infection detection products use vaccination because it is easier to implement.

    b. Vaccination programs modify application programs to allow for a self-test mechanism within each program.

    c. The drawbacks to this implementation include the fact that the boot segment is very hard to vaccinate, and the malicious code might gain control before the vaccination program can warn the user.

    d. The majority of short-term infection detection products do not use vaccinations because they are very difficult to implement.

21. Which statement is correct about short-term infection detection products?

    a. The majority of short-term infection detection products use spectral analysis.

    b. The majority of short-term infection detection products use the snapshot technique because it is easier to implement.

    c. The majority of short-term infection detection products use vaccination because it is easier to implement.

    d. The majority of short-term infection detection products use heuristic analysis.

22. Which choice BEST describes the snapshot technique of virus detection?

    a. The snapshot technique is a long-term infection detection process.

    b. The snapshot technique identifies systems that have been infected for a long time.

    c. The snapshot technique uses educated guesses to find infections.

    d. Upon installation, a log of all critical information is made.

23. Which choice BEST describes long-term virus infection products?

    a. Long-term infection detection products detect an infection very soon after the infection has occurred.

    b. Long-term infection detection products identify specific malicious code on a system that has already been infected for some time.

    c. Long-term infection detection products can be implemented through vaccination programs and the snapshot technique.

    d. Long-term infection detection products generally address a small infected area of the system.

24. Which choice is an element of heuristic infection detection?

    a. Using heuristic analysis all data is examined and recorded for malicious code patterns.

    b. Heuristic analysis is used in short-term infection detection products.

    c. Heuristic analysis is much less scientific, using educated guesses.

    d. Heuristic analysis guarantees exact and hard evidence of infection.

25. Which statement about spectral analysis is not correct?

    a. Spectral analysis is a long-term infection detection product.

    b. Spectral analysis is a short-term infection detection product.

    c. All data is examined and recorded to discover automatically generated malicious code.

    d. When a pattern or subset of it appears, a counter is incremented.

26. Which description is the BEST definition of a Category 2 mobile code?

    a. Mobile code that has known security vulnerabilities with few or no countermeasures once it begins executing

    b. Mobile code supporting limited functionality, with no capability for unmediated access to workstation, host, and remote system services and resources

    c. Mobile code having full functionality, allowing mediated or controlled access to workstation, host, and remote system services and resources

    d. Mobile code exhibiting a broad functionality, allowing unmediated access to workstation, host, and remote system services and resources

27. Which choice is a property of immediate virus detection products?

    a. Immediate virus detection products are used to detect an infection very soon after the infection has occurred.

    b. Immediate virus detection products periodically scan the entire system to search out malicious code.

    c. Immediate virus detection is used to identify specific malicious code on a system.

    d. Immediate virus detection is not functional on Category 1 mobile code.

28. Which choice below is NOT a property of permanent virus detection products?

    a. Permanent virus detection usually removes malicious code after a scan and returns the system to its prior functionality.

    b. Permanent virus detection products detect an infection quickly after infection.

    c. Permanent virus detection periodically scans the entire system.

    d. Permanent virus detection can be used to identify specific malicious code on a system.

29. Which choice would NOT be an example of a proper enterprise-wide security procedure?

    a. Encourage the distribution of spam to increase the company's name recognition.

    b. Restrict users from bringing uncontrolled floppies from home to the office.

    c. Discourage blind downloading of software from unregulated Internet sites.

    d. Regulate access to Internet sites to reputable URLs only.

30. Why should an organization discourage users from forwarding email chain letters?

    a. The company does not want you wasting time on fun stuff.

    b. They waste computer system resources.

    c. They can contain false information to mislead people.

    d. They do not increase the company's name recognition.

Glossary

Many terms are defined within the chapter where they are initially discussed, so please use the index to locate them. In some cases, however, we felt a glossary definition should be added.

access   The ability and means to communicate with or otherwise interact with a system in order to use system resources to either handle information or gain knowledge of the information that the system contains.

access control   Protection of system resources against unauthorized access; a process by which use of system resources is regulated according to a security policy and is permitted by only authorized entities (users, programs, processes, or other systems) according to that policy.

access control list **(ACL)**   A mechanism that implements access control for a system resource by enumerating the identities of the system entities that are permitted to access the resource.

accountability   The property of a system (including all of its system resources) that ensures that the actions of a system entity can be traced uniquely to that entity, which can be held responsible for its actions.

adversary   An entity that attacks, or is a threat to, a system.

algorithm   A finite set of step-by-step instructions for a problem-solving or computation procedure—especially one that can be implemented by a computer.

assurance   (1) An attribute of an information system that provides grounds for having confidence that the system operates such that the system security policy is enforced. (2) A procedure that ensures a system is developed and operated as intended by the system's security policy.

assurance level   A specific level on a hierarchical scale representing successively increased confidence that a target of evaluation adequately fulfills the requirements.

asymmetric cryptography   A modern branch of cryptography (popularly known as public-key cryptography) in which the algorithms employ a pair of keys (a public key and a private key) and use a different component of the pair for different steps of the algorithm.

attack   An assault on system security that derives from an intelligent threat; in other words, an intelligent act that is a deliberate attempt (especially in the sense of a method or technique) to evade security services and violate the security policy of a system.

   active versus passive   An "active attack" attempts to alter system resources or affect their operation. A "passive attack" attempts to learn or make use of information from the system but does not affect system resources.

   insider versus outsider   An "inside attack" is an attack initiated by an entity inside the security perimeter (an "insider"); in other words, an entity that is authorized to access system resources but uses them in a way not approved by those who granted the authorization. An "outside attack" is initiated from outside the perimeter, by an unauthorized or illegitimate user of the system (an "outsider"). In the Internet, potential outside attackers range from amateur pranksters to organized criminals, international terrorists, and hostile governments.

automated information system   An organized assembly of resources and procedures; in other words, computing and communications equipment and services with their supporting facilities and personnel—that collect, record, process, store, transport, retrieve, or display information to accomplish a specified set of functions.

backup   A collection of data that is stored for a relatively long period of time for historical and other purposes, such as to support audit service, availability service, or system integrity service.

bandwidth   Commonly used to mean the capacity of a communication channel to pass data through the channel in a given amount of time; usually expressed in bits per second.

bastion host   A strongly protected computer that is in a network protected by a firewall (or is part of a firewall) and is the only host (or one of only a few hosts) in the network that can be directly accessed from networks on the other side of the firewall.

bind   To inseparably associate by applying some mechanism, such as when a CA uses a digital signature to bind together a subject and a public key in a public-key certificate.

biometric authentication   A method of generating authentication information for a person by digitizing measurements of a physical characteristic, such as a fingerprint, a hand shape, a retina pattern, a speech pattern (voiceprint), or handwriting.

block cipher   An encryption algorithm that breaks plain text into fixed-size segments and uses the same key to transform each plain-text segment into a fixed-size segment of ciphertext. For example, Blowfish, DEA, IDEA, RC2, and SKIPJACK.

brute force   A cryptanalysis technique or other kind of attack method involving an exhaustive procedure that tries all possibilities one-by-one. For example, for ciphertext where the analyst already knows the decryption algorithm, a brute-force technique to finding the original plain text is to decrypt the message with every possible key.

byte   A fundamental unit of computer storage; the smallest addressable unit in a computer's architecture. Usually holds one character of information and today usually means eight bits.

***Challenge Handshake Authentication Protocol* (CHAP)**   A peer entity authentication method for PPP, using a randomly generated challenge and requiring a matching response that depends on a cryptographic hash of the challenge and a secret key.

challenge-response   An authentication process that verifies an identity by requiring correct authentication information to be provided in response to a challenge. In a computer system, the authentication information is usually a value that is required to be computed in response to an unpredictable challenge value.

contingency plan   A plan for emergency response, backup operations, and post- disaster recovery in a system as part of a security program to ensure availability of critical system resources and facilitate continuity of operations in a crisis.

countermeasure   An action, device, procedure, or technique that reduces a threat, a vulnerability, or an attack by eliminating or preventing it, by minimizing the harm that it can cause, or by discovering and reporting it so that corrective action can be taken.

degauss   Apply a magnetic field to permanently remove, erase, or clear data from a magnetic storage medium, such as a tape or a disk.

Demilitarized Zone **(DMZ)**   A DMZ is a network created by connecting two firewalls. Systems that are exter-nally accessible but need some protection are usually located on DMZ networks.

denial of service **(DoS)**   The prevention of authorized access to a system resource or the delaying of system operations and functions.

electronic commerce **(e-commerce)**   General usage: Business conducted through paperless exchanges of information, using electronic data interchange, *electronic funds transfer* (EFT), e-mail, computer bulletin boards, facsimile, and other paperless technologies. SET usage: The exchange of goods and services for payment between the cardholder and merchant when some or all of the transaction is performed via electronic communication.

emanation   A signal (electromagnetic, acoustic, or other medium) that is emitted by a system (through radiation or conductance) as a conse-quence (in other words, byproduct) of its operation, and that might contain information

end-to-end encryption   Continuous protection of data that flows between two points in a network, provided by encrypting data when it leaves its source, leaving it encrypted while it passes through any intermediate computers (such as routers), and decrypting only when the data arrives at the intended destination. When two points are separated by multiple communication links that are connected by one or more intermediate relays, end-to-end encryption enables the source and destination systems to protect their communications without depending on the intermediate systems to provide the protection.

extranet   A computer network that an organization uses to carry application data traffic between the organization and its business partners.

fail safe   A mode of system termination that automatically leaves system processes and components in a secure state when a failure occurs or is detected in the system.

fail soft   Selective termination of affected non-essential system functions and processes when a failure occurs or is detected in the system.

failure control   A methodology used to provide fail-safe or fail-soft termination and recovery of functions and processes when failures are detected or occur in a system.

firewall   An internetwork gateway that restricts data communication traffic to and from one of the connected networks (the one said to be "inside" the firewall) and thus protects that network's system resources against threats from the other network (the one that is said to be "outside" the firewall). A firewall typically protects a smaller, secure network (such as a corporate LAN, or even just one host) from a larger network (such as the Internet). The firewall is installed at the point where the networks connect, and the firewall applies security policy rules to control traffic that flows in and out of the protected network. A firewall is not always a single computer. For example, a firewall may consist of a pair of filtering routers and one or more proxy servers running on one or more bastion hosts, all connected to a small, dedicated LAN between the two routers. The external router blocks attacks that use IP to break security (IP address spoofing, source routing, and packet fragments), while proxy servers block attacks that would exploit a vulnerability in a higher layer protocol or service. The internal router blocks traffic from leaving the protected network except through the proxy servers. The difficult part is defining criteria by which packets are denied passage through the firewall, because a firewall not only needs to keep intruders out, but usually also needs to let authorized users in and out.

gateway   A relay mechanism that attaches to two (or more) computer networks that have similar functions but dissimilar implementations and that enables host computers on one network to communicate with hosts on the other; an intermediate system that is the interface between two computer networks. (See: bridge, firewall, guard, internetwork, proxy server, router, and subnetwork.) In theory, gateways are conceivable at any OSI layer. In practice, they operate at OSI layer 3 (see: bridge, router) or layer 7 (see: proxy server). When the two networks differ in the protocol by which they offer service to hosts, the gateway might translate one protocol into another or otherwise facilitate interoperation of hosts. (See: Internet Protocol.)

guard   A gateway that is interposed between two networks (or computers, or other information systems) operating at different security levels (one level is usually higher than the other) and is trusted to mediate all information transfers between the two levels, either to ensure that no sensitive information from the first (higher) level is disclosed to the second (lower) level, or to protect the integrity of data on the first (higher) level. Many guards are referred to as high assurance guards (hags).

hash function   An algorithm that computes a value based on a data object (such as a message or file; usually variable-length; possibly very large), thereby mapping the data object to a smaller data object (the "hash result"), which is usually a fixed-size value.

honey pot   A system (for example, a Web server) or a system resource (for example, a file on a server) that is designed to be attractive to potential crackers and intruders (like honey is attractive to bears).

host   General computer network usage: A computer that is attached to a communication subnetwork or internetwork and can use services provided by the network to exchange data with other attached systems.

Internet   The Internet is the single, interconnected, worldwide system of commercial, government, educational, and other computer networks that share the set of protocols.

intranet   A computer network, especially one based on Internet technology, that an organization uses for its own internal and usually private purposes and that is closed to outsiders.

intruder   An entity that gains or attempts to gain access to a system or system resource without having authorization to do so.

intrusion detection   A security service that monitors and analyzes system events for the purpose of finding and providing real-time or near real-time warning of attempts to access system resources in an unauthorized manner.

ITU-T   International Telecommunications Union, Telecommunication Standardization Sector (formerly "CCITT"), a United Nations treaty organization that is composed mainly of postal, telephone, and telegraph authorities of the member countries and that publishes standards called "Recommendations". (See: X.400, X.500.)

Kerberos   A system developed at the *Massachusetts Institute of Technology* (MIT) that depends on passwords and symmetric cryptography (DES) to implement ticket-based, peer entity authentication service and access control service distributed in a client-server network environment.

***Lightweight Directory Access Protocol* (LDAP)**   A client-server protocol that supports basic use of the X.500 Directory (or other directory servers) without incurring the resource requirements of the full *Directory Access Protocol* (DAP).

MAC   See: mandatory access control, Message Authentication Code or Media Access Control.

***mandatory access control* (MAC)**   An access control service that enforces a security policy based on comparing (a) security labels (which indicate how sensitive or critical system resources are) with (b) security clearances (which indicate system entities are eligible to access certain resources). This kind of access control is called "mandatory" because an entity that has clearance to access a resource may not, just by its own volition, enable another entity to access that resource.

MD2   A cryptographic hash that produces a 128-bit hash result, was designed by Ron Rivest, and is similar to MD4 and MD5 but slower.

MD4   A cryptographic hash that produces a 128-bit hash result and was designed by Ron Rivest.

MD5 (N)   A cryptographic hash that produces a 128-bit hash result and was designed by Ron Rivest to be an improved version of MD4.

Multipurpose Internet Mail Extensions **(MIME)**   An Internet protocol [R2045] that enhances the basic format of Internet e-mail messages [R0822] to be able to use character sets other than US-ASCII for textual headers and text content and to carry non-textual and multi-part content. (See: S/MIME.)

National Information Assurance Partnership **(NIAP)**   An organization created by NIST and NSA to enhance the quality of commercial products for information security and increase consumer confidence in those products through objective evaluation and testing methods. NIAP functions include the following: Developing tests, test methods, and other tools that developers and testing laboratories may use to improve and evaluate security products.

National Institute of Standards and Technology **(NIST)**   A U.S. Department of Commerce agency that promotes U.S. economic growth by working with industry to develop and apply technology, measurements, and standards. Has primary government responsibility for INFOSEC standards for unclassified but sensitive information.

National Security Agency **(NSA)**   A U.S. Department of Defense intelligence agency that has primary government responsibility for INFOSEC for classified information and for unclassified but sensitive information handled by national security systems.

need-to-know   The necessity for access to, knowledge of, or possession of specific information required to carry out official duties.

proxy server   A computer process often used as, or as part of, a firewall, that relays a protocol between client and server computer systems, by appearing to the client to be the server and appearing to the server to be the client. In a firewall, a proxy server usually runs on a bastion host, which may support proxies for several protocols (for example, FTP, HTTP, and TELNET). Instead of a client in the protected enclave connecting directly to an external server, the internal client connects to the proxy server which in turn connects to the external server. The proxy server waits for a request from inside the firewall, forwards the request to the remote server outside the firewall, gets the response, then sends the response back to the client. The proxy may be transparent to the clients, or they may need to connect first to the proxy server, and then use that association to also initiate a connection to the real server. Proxies are generally preferred over SOCKS for their ability to perform caching, high-level logging, and access control. A proxy can provide security service beyond that which is normally part of the relayed protocol, such as access control based on peer entity authentication of clients, or peer entity authentication of servers when clients do not have that capability. A proxy at OSI layer 7 can also provide finer-grained security service than can a filtering router at OSI layer 3. For example, an FTP proxy could permit transfers out of, but not into, a protected network.

replay attack   An attack in which a valid data transmission is maliciously or fraudulently repeated, either by the originator or by an adversary who intercepts the data and retransmits it—possibly as part of a masquerade attack. (See: active wiretapping.)

repudiation   Denial by a system entity that was involved in an association (especially an association that transfers information) of having participated in the relationship. (See: accountability, non-repudiation service.)

role-based access control **(RBAC)**   A form of identity-based access control where the system entities that are identified and controlled are functional positions in an organization or process.

Secure/MIME **(S/MIME)**   Secure/Multipurpose Internet Mail Extensions, an Internet protocol to provide encryption and digital signatures for Internet mail messages.

Secure Sockets Layer **(SSL)**   An Internet protocol (originally developed by Netscape Communications, Inc.) that uses connection-oriented end-to-end encryption to provide data confidentiality service and data integrity service for traffic between a client (often a Web browser) and a server and that can optionally provide peer entity authentication between the client and the server.

Security   (1.) Measures taken to protect a system. (2.) The condition of a system that results from the establishment and maintenance measures to protect the system. (3.) The condition of system resources being free from unauthorized access and from unauthorized or accidental change, destruction, or loss.

security architecture   A plan and set of principles that describe (a) the security services that a system is required to provide to meet the needs of its users; (b) the system elements required to implement the services; and (c) the performance levels required in the elements to deal with the threat environment.

security audit   An independent review and examination of a system's records and activities to determine the adequacy of system controls, to ensure compliance with established security policy and procedures, to detect breaches in security services, and to recommend any changes that are indicated for countermeasures.

security mechanism   A process (or a device incorporating such a process) that can be used in a system to implement a security service that is provided by or within the system.

separation of duties   The practice of dividing the steps in a system function among different individuals so as to keep a single individual from subverting the process.

social engineering   A euphemism for the non-technical or low-technology methods and means, such as lies, impersonation, tricks, bribes, blackmail, and threats, used to attack information systems.

subnetwork   An OSI term for a system of packet relays and connecting links that implement the lower three protocol layers of the OSIRM to provide a communication service that interconnects attached end systems. Usually the relays operate at OSI layer 3 and are all of the same type (for example, all X.25 packet switches or all interface units in an IEEE 802.3 LAN).

Terminal Access Controller **(TAC)** *Access Control System* **(TACACS)**
A UDP-based authentication and access control protocol in which a network access server receives an identifier and password from a remote terminal and passes them to a separate authentication server for verification. TACACS was developed for ARPANET and has evolved for use in commercial equipment. TACs were a type of network access server computer used to connect terminals to the early Internet, usually using dial-up modem connections. TACACS used centralized authentication servers and served not only network access servers like TACs but also routers and other networked computing devices. TACs are no longer in use, but TACACS+ is.

TACACS+   A TCP-based protocol that improves on TACACS and XTA-CACS by separating the functions of authentication, authorization, and accounting and by encrypting all traffic between the network access server and authentication server. It is extensible to allow any authentication mechanism to be used with TACACS+ clients.

traffic analysis   Inference of information from observable characteristics of data flow(s), even when the data is encrypted or otherwise not directly available. Such characteristics include the identities and locations of the source(s) and destination(s), and the presence, amount, frequency, and duration of occurrence.

wiretapping   An attack that intercepts and accesses data and other information contained in a flow in a communication system. Although the term originally referred to making a mechanical connection to an electrical conductor that links two nodes, it is now used to refer to reading information from any sort of medium used for a link or even directly from a node, such as gateway or subnetwork switch. "Active wiretapping" attempts to alter the data or otherwise affect the flow; "passive wiretapping" only attempts to observe the flow and gain knowledge of information it contains.

work factor   In general, work factor is the estimated amount of effort or time that can be expected to be expended by a potential intruder to penetrate a system, or defeat a particular countermeasure, when using specified amounts of expertise and resources. In cryptography, work factor is the estimated amount of computing time and power needed to break a cryptographic system.

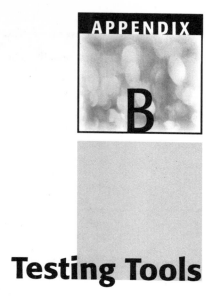

APPENDIX

B

Testing Tools

This appendix has been provided courtesy of NIST. The following sections show major tools to use for security testing in various areas. These tools can be used to help discover network or system assets, assist in vulnerability testing, or assist in determining effectiveness of controls that are in place.

File Integrity Checkers

Table B.1 shows the major file integrity checkers available and provides URLs for Web sites where you can find further information and download software.

Table B.1 File Integrity Checkers

TOOL	PURPOSE	OPERATING SYSTEMS	WEB SITE	COST
Advanced Intrusion Detection Environment (Aide)	File integrity checking. This is a free replacement for Tripwire.	Unix and Linux (a large number of platforms)	www.cs.tut.fi/ ~rammer/aide .html	Free

(continued)

Table B.1 *(continued)*

TOOL	PURPOSE	OPERATING SYSTEMS	WEB SITE	COST
LANGuard	Intrusion detection by checking whether files have been changed, added or deleted.	Windows 2000/NT	www.gfi.com /languard	Free
Tripwire	Monitors file changes, verifies integrity, and notifies the administrator of any violations of data on network hosts.	Windows, Unix, Linux, and Routers	www.tripwire security.com www.gfi.com /languard	Free

Network Sniffers

Table B.2 shows the major network sniffers and provides URLs for Web sites where you can find further information and download software.

Table B.2 Network Sniffers

TOOL	PURPOSE	OPERATING SYSTEMS	WEB SITE	COST
Dsniff	Dsniff is a collection of tools for network auditing and penetration testing.	Unix and Linux sniffer	www.monkey .org/~dygsibg /dsnff	Free
Ethereal	Ethereal is a free network protocol analyzer for Unix and Windows.	Unix, Linux and Windows sniffer with GUI	www.ethereal .com	Free
Sniffit	A general purpose sniffer.	Unix, Linux an Windows sniffer	reptile.rug.ac .be/~coder /sniffit/sniffit .html www.symbolic .it/Prodotti /sniffit.html (Windows)	Free
Snort	A freeware lightweight IDS and general purpose sniffer and IDS.	Unix, Linux and Windowns	www.snort.org	Free
TCPDump	A general purpose sniffer.	Unix and Linux sniffer	www.nrg.ee .lbl.gov	Free

Table B.3 Password Crackers

TOOL	OPERATING SYSTEMS	WEB SITE	COST
Crack 5	Unix (or other) password files.	www.sun.rhbnc.ac.uk /~phae107	Free
IMP 2.0	Novell Netware password cracker.	www.wastelands.gen.nz	Free
John the Ripper	Windows and Unix password cracker.	www.openwall.com/john	Free
L0pht	Windows password cracker.	www.securitysoftwaretech.com	$
Nwpcrack	Novell Netware password cracker.	www.nmrc.org/file	Free

Password Crackers

Table B.3 shows the major available password crackers and provides URLs for Web sites where you can find further information and download software.

Privilege Escalation and Back Door Tools

Table B.4 shows the major available privilege escalation and back door tools and provides URLs for Web sites where you can find further information and download software.

Table B.4 Privilege Escalation and Back Door Tools

TOOL	PURPOSE	WEB SITE	COST
Elitewrap	EliteWrap is an EXE wrapper, used to pack files into an archive executable that can extract and execute them in specified ways when the packfile is run.	www.megasecurity.org/	Free
Getadmin	Windows NT privilege escalation	www.nmrc.org/files/	Free
Hunt	TCP session hijacking	lin.fsid.cvut.cz/~kra/index.html	Free
Invisible Keystroke Logger	Keystroke logger	www.amecisco.com/iksnt.htm	$

(continued)

Table B.4 *(continued)*

TOOL	PURPOSE	WEB SITE	COST
Netcat	Back door		$
Port redirector		www.atstake.com/research/tools	
Pwdump2	Windows NT/2000 password collector	www.webspan.net/~tas /pwdump2	Free
Virtual Network Computing (VNC)	Remote control tool	www.uk.research.att.com/vnc/	Free

Scanning and Enumeration Tools

Table B.5 shows the major available scanning and enumeration tools and provides URLs for Web sites where you can find further information and download software.

Table B.5 Scanning and Enumeration Tools

TOOL	CAPABILITIES	WEB SITE	LINUX	WIN32	COST
DUMPSec	Windows enumeration tool	www.systemtools.com	N	Y	Free

Description: DumpSec is a security auditing program for Microsoft Windows. It dumps the permissions (DACLs) and audit settings (SACLs) for the file system, registry, printers and shares in a concise, readable listbox format, so that holes in system security are readily apparent. DumpSec also dumps user, group, and replication information.

Firewalk	Firewall filter rule mapper	www.packetfactory .net/firewalk/	Y	N	Free

Description: Firewalking is a technique that employs traceroutelike techniques to analyze IP packet responses to determine gateway ACL filters and map networks. Firewalk, the tool, employs the technique to determine the filter rules in place on a packet forwarding device.

Nmap	Port scanner and OS detection	www.insecure.org /nmap/	Y	Y	Free

Description: Nmap ("Network Mapper") is an open source utility for network exploration or security auditing. It was designed to rapidly scan large networks, although it also works against single hosts. Nmap uses raw IP packets to determine what hosts are available on the network, what services (ports) they are offering, what operating system (and version) they are running, what type of packet filters/firewalls are in use, and dozens of other characteristics.

Table B.5   *(continued)*

TOOL	CAPABILITIES	WEB SITE	LINUX	WIN32	COST
Solarwinds	Network enumeration	www.solarwinds.net/	N	Y	$
Description: A collection of network and management and discovery tools.					
SuperScan	Port scanner, OS detection, and Banner enumeration	www.foundstone.com/	Y	N	Free
Description: A GUI network mapper. It will rapidly scan large networks to determine what hosts are available on the network, what services they are offering, the version of these services and the type and version of the operating system. Will also perform reverse DNS lookup.					

Vulnerability Scanning Tools

Table B.6 shows the major available vulnerability scanning tools and provides URLs for Web sites where you can find further information and download software.

Table B.6   Vulnerability Scanning Tools

TOOL	CAPABILITIES	WEB SITE	LINUX	WIN32	COST
CyberCop Scanner	Vulnerability scanner	www.pgp.com /products	Y	Y	$
Description: CyberCop Scanner is a network-based vulnerability scanning tool that identifies security holes on network hosts.					
ISS Internet Scanner	Vulnerability scanner	www.iss.net	Y	N	$
Description: ISS Internet Scanner is a network-based vulnerability scanning tool that identifies security holes on network hosts.					
Nessus	Vulnerability scanner	www.nessus.org	Y	Y (client only)	Free
Description: A freeware network-based vulnerability scanning tool that identifies security holes on network hosts					
SAINT	Vulnerability scanner	www.wwdsi.com	Y	N	$
Description: SAINT is an updated and enhanced version of SATAN, designed to assess the security of computer networks.					

(continued)

Table B.6   *(continued)*

TOOL	CAPABILITIES	WEB SITE	LINUX	WIN32	COST
SARA	Vulnerability scanner	wwwarc.com/sara	Y	N	Free

Description: Sara is a freeware networkbased vulnerabilityscanning tool that identifies security holes on network hosts.

SATAN	Vulnerability scanner	www.fish.com/satan	Y	N	Free

Description: SATAN is a tool to help system administrators. It recognizes several common networking-related security problems, and reports the problems without actually exploiting them.

Table B.7   War Dialing Tools

TOOL	CAPABILITIES	WEB SITE	LINUX	WIN32	COST
Phonesweep	War Dialer	www.sandstorm.net/	N	Y	$

Description: A commercial wardialing program that supports multiple modems and attempts automated penetration.

Telesweep	War Dialer	www.securelogix.com /telesweepsecure/	N	Y	$

Description: A commercial war dialing application that supports multiple modems and attempts to automated penetration.

THC	War Dialer	http://packetstorm. decepticons.org /wardialers/	N	Y	Free

Description   Freeware DOS based war dialing program.

ToneLoc	War Dialer	www.hackersclub .com/km/files/	N	Y	Free

Description   Freeware DOS based war dialing program.

War Dialing Tools

Table B.7 shows the major available war dialing tools and provides URLs for Web sites where you can find further information and download software.

Port Scanning: Nmap

A commonly used port scanner for identifying active hosts and associated services (that is, open ports) is Nmap (see Table A.1 for website). Nmap allows for a variety of different types of port scans to be used in order to determine whether a port is open or closed. Nmap uses raw IP packets to identify the available hosts on a network, the services or ports that are open, type of operating system and version that hosts are running, type of packet filters and firewalls in use, and other characteristics.

The most basic form of port scanning supported by Nmap is the TCP connect() scan, using the *sT* option flag (Nmap is case sensitive). The connect() system call provided by the host operating system is used to attempt to open a connection to any or all ports (user selects) on a remote host. If the port is listening or open, then the connect() will succeed, otherwise the port is not listening or is in a closed state. No special privileges are needed in order to employ this kind of scan.

A more common scan that is not as easily detected as the TCP connect() scan is the TCP SYN scan, also known as a SYN Stealth scan or .halfopen. scan, since Nmap does not open a full TCP connection (see Figure B.1). This scan is implemented using the *sS* flag. On a Unix/Linux host running Nmap, root privileges are needed in order to create the custom SYN packets that are needed for this type of scan. First a SYN packet is sent as though the machine running Nmap is initiating a .genuine. TCP connection. The host running Nmap then waits for a response. A SYN|ACK response is indicative of a listening or open port. A response of RST is indicative of a nonlistening or closed port. If a SYN|ACK is received, a RST is immediately sent to cancel the connection. This final action is required to remove the possibility of causing a SYN flood DoS attack. This can occur because all pending connections are stored in a buffer. If a RST is not sent, the target host.s buffer may reach capacity. When this occurs legitimate requests will not be processed resulting in a DoS until either a RST is received or timeout occurs on the pending requests.

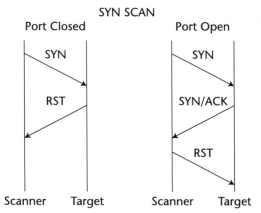

Figure B.1   SYN Stealth Scan.

When SYN scanning is not clandestine enough, Stealth FIN, XMAS Tree, or Null scan modes can be used. These scans are implemented using the *sF*, *sX*, and *sN* flags respectively. The FIN scan uses a bare FIN scan as the probe (see Figure B.2). The XMAS Tree scan turns on the FIN, URG, and PUSH flags (see Figure B.3). The Null scan turns off all flags (see Figure B.4). With all of these, a response of RST is indicative of a nonlistening or closed port while no response is indicative of a listening or open port. This response is based on the Request for Comments (RFC) 793. Microsoft does not implement these features therefore these scans will not work properly when scanning a Windows host. Root privileges are required to create custom packets needed for these scans.

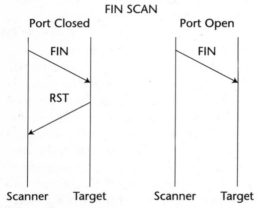

Figure B.2   FIN scan.

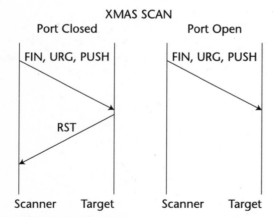

Figure B.3   XMAS scan.

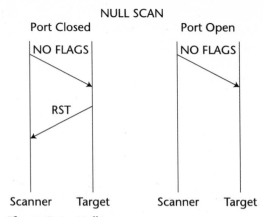

Figure B.4   Null scan.

Normally, a ping is used to determine if a host is up on a network before scanning. In a network environment that does not allow ICMP echo requests or responses, the *P0* flag can be used to prevent pinging hosts before scanning them. This is generally useful for scanning through firewalls.

Nmap allows other types of ping requests to be used also. These types include a .TCP. ping, connection request ping, and true ICMP ping or ICMP echo request. A .TCP. ping, flag of *PT*, sends out TCP ACK packets throughout the target network and waits for responses. Hosts that are up on the network should respond with a RST. A connection request ping, flag of *PS*, sends out connection request or SYN packets onto the target network. Hosts that are on the network should respond with a RST. A true ICMP ping, flag of *PI*, sends an ICMP echo request packet on to the network and waits for an ICMP echo response to validate hosts that are on the network. The default ping type, flag of *PB*, uses a combination of the .TCP. ping and the ICMP ping in parallel. This allows one to find hosts that are operating behind firewalls that filter one but not both types of pings.

Another feature of Nmap is the ability to remotely fingerprint the operating system and version that the scanned hosts are running. Nmap uses queries of the host.s TCP/IP stack and the knowledge that different operating systems and their respective versions have different responses. This feature can be implemented with the *O* flag.

The command line format for running Nmap is as follows:

```
nmap [Scan Type(s)] [Options] <host or net #1 ... [#N]>
```

An example SYN scan of a class C network is shown in Figure B.5.

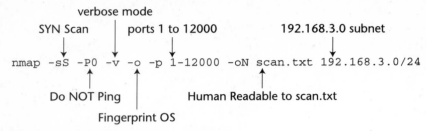

Figure B.5 Example Nmap configuration.

This scan would perform a SYN stealth scan without first pinging the hosts on the class C subnet 192.168.3.0. In addition, the scan will check ports 1 through 12,000 inclusive for open services. After mapping the ports, Nmap will attempt to fingerprint the operating system and version. All output from this scan will be in verbose mode (which provides more details on the scanned hosts) and this output will also be saved in human readable (plain text as opposed to binary) output to the file scan.txt. The output of Nmap on one of the scanned hosts is provided in Figure B.6 (the text file would list similar results for each active host found).

Nmap Command Summary

```
Usage:  Nmap [Scan Type(s)] [Options] <host or net list>



Host hp5.doahq.gov (192.168.3.10) appears to be up ... good.
Initiating SYN half-open stealth scan against hp5.doahq.gov
(192.168.3.10)
Interesting ports on hp5.doahq.gov (192.168.3.10):
(The 1516 ports scanned but not shown below are in state: closed)
Port         State    Service
21/tcp       open     ftp
23/tcp       open     telnet
80/tcp       open     http
280/tcp      open     http-mgmt
515/tcp      open     printer
631/tcp      open     unknown
9100/tcp     open     unknown
TCP Sequence Prediction: Class=trivial time dependency
                        Difficulty=1 (Trivial joke)
Sequence numbers: 6E1BC7 6E1BC8 6E1BC8 6E1BC9 6E1BCA 6E1BCB
Remote OS guesses: HP Print Server, HP LaserJet Printer
```

Figure B.6 Example Nmap output.

Scan Types

sT   TCP connect() scan   Most common form of TCP scanning. Because it completes the full TCP handshake it is the most detectable.

sS   TCP SYN scan   Often referred to as "halfopen" scanning, because this scan does not open a full TCP connection. Because this scan does not complete the TCP handshake, it is somewhat less detectable and is often referred to as a stealth scan. The user will need root privileges to conduct this type of scan.

sP   Ping scanning   Uses ICMP ping to detect active hosts. It does not conduct a port scan.

sF   Stealth FIN scan   Uses a bare FIN packet as the probe.

sU   UDP scan   This scan is used to determine which UDP ports are open on a host. UDP scanning can be slow due to the fact that some hosts limit the ICMP error message rate.

Options

P0   With this option enabled, nmap will not attempt to ping the host prior to starting a scan. This is useful for scanning through firewalls that block ICMP echo requests.

PT   This option enables the use of TCP "ping" to determine active hosts. To set the destination port of the probe packets use **.PT <port number>**. This option is similar to the .sP option in determining active hosts except that it does not rely on ICMP, which makes it useful for scanning through firewalls that block ICMP echo requests.

F   This option enables fast scan mode. With fast scan enabled, nmap will scan only for ports listed in the services file included with nmap.

O   This option activates remote host identification via TCP/IP finger-printing.

h   This option displays a quick reference screen of nmap usage options.

n/R   The option tells namp to never (**n**) or always (**R**) perform DNS resolution.

v   This option enables verbose mode. This mode provides additional information and can be used twice for greater effect (**v v**).

oN <logfilename>   Logs results of the scan in a .normal. (plain text) format to the file specified.

oM <logfilename>   Logs results of scan in a machine parsable form into the file specified.

resume <logfilename>   Resumes cancelled network scans. The log file-name must be either a normal or machine parsable log from the aborted scan. Nmap will start on the machine after the last one successfully scanned in the log file.

Nmap Usage Examples

The following are some common use examples for Nmap with various objectives for results.

nmap v target.example.com   This example scans all reserved TCP ports (11024) on the machine target.example.com. The v option activates verbose mode.

nmap sS O 192.168.10.1/24   This example launches a stealth SYN scan on all active hosts on the 192.168.10.x class 'C' network. This example will attempt to determine the operating system the scanned hosts are running. This scan will require root privileges due to the use of the SYN scan and the OS detection options.

nmap   .n .v .sS .O .oN nmapsSO_172.30.100.2031_230.N .oM nmap sSO_172.30.100.2031_230.M 172.30.100.2031,230

A stealth SYN scan of addresses 172.30.100.20 through 172.30.100.31 plus 172.30.11.230. Verbose mode, v and TCP/IP O fingerprinting modes are enabled. The n option configures Nmap not to attempt any DNS resolution. Output will be in both human readable format (oN) with filename nmapsSO_172.30.100.2031_230.N and machine-readable format (oM) with the filename nmapsSO_172.30.100.2031_230.M.

L0pht Crack

One of the most popular password crackers is L0pht Crack for Windows NT and 2000. For obtaining hashes, L0pht crack contains features that can be enabled to capture passwords as they traverse the network, copy them out of the Windows registry and retrieve them from Windows emergency repair disks.

When hashes are obtained, L0phtCrack first performs a dictionary attack. The dictionary used by L0phtCrack is selected by the user, or the included dictionary may be used (although more comprehensive dictionaries are available on the Internet). L0phtCrack hashes each word in the list and compares that hash to the hashes to be cracked. If the compared hashes match, L0phtCrack has found the password. After L0phtCrack completes the dictionary attack, it iterates through the word list again using a hybrid attack. Finally L0phtcrack resorts to a brute force attack to crack any remaining hashes, trying every possible combination of characters in a set. The set of characters used by L0phtCrack in a brute force attack can be controlled by the user. The larger the set selected the longer the crack will take. Figure B.7 shows a screen capture of L0pht Crack.

LANguard File Integrity Checker

There are numerous freeware, shareware and commercial file integrity checkers available. A popular freeware checker is LANguard File Integrity Checker for Windows NT/2000. It can be configured from either the command line or a GUI. It can also be configured to send email alerts when files are altered.

To configure LANguard from the start menu select .LANguard File Integrity Checker configuration. (See Figure B.8.)

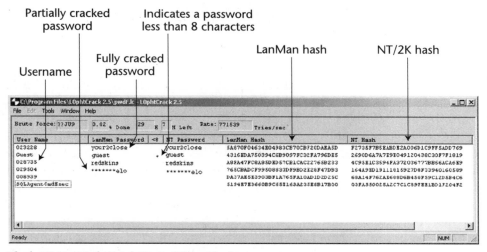

Figure B.7 L0phtCrack Brute Force Attack.

Figure B.8 Launching LANGuard File Integrity Checker configuration.

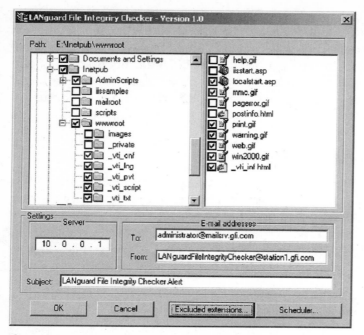

Figure B.9   LANGuard File Integrity Checker configuration.

This will open the LANguard configuration window. This window allows the user to select what files, folder (directories) and/or drives to have LANguard monitor. This should include operating system root directory and subdirectories (that is, winnt), antivirus program directory, critical boot files, and so on. It is important that the checksum be updated whenever files are updated. For example, when new antivirus signatures are downloaded. In addition, for email updates, the SMTP server IP address and recipient email address need to be configured. See Figure B.9 for more information.

When configured, an email will be sent to the address specified whenever a comparison is run and changes or additions are detected. This check can be run manually or scheduled to run automatically on a periodic basis. Figure B.10 shows an example LANGuard email.

Using Tripwire

Tripwire is a file system integrity-checking program for Unix operating systems. Before using Tripwire a configuration file needs to be created that designates the directories and files that are to be verified as well as the attributes verified for each. Tripwire is then run (with the initialize option) to create a database of cryptographic checksums that correspond to the files and directories specified in the configuration file.

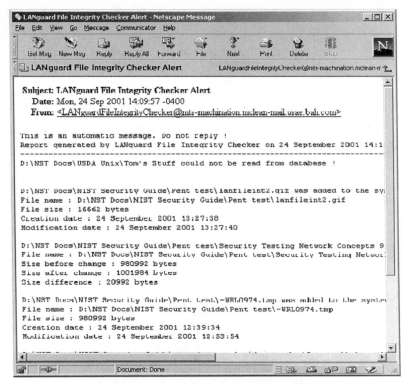

Figure B.10 LANGuard File Integrity Checker notification email.

To protect the Tripwire program, configuration file, and initialized database against corruption, they should be transferred to a medium that can be designated as physically write-protected, such as a disk or CD-ROM. This read-only version then becomes the authoritative reference program, configuration, and data, which can reliably be used to test the integrity of directories and files on the system.

In addition to one or more cryptographic checksums representing the contents of each directory and file, the Tripwire database also contains information that allows verification of:

- Access permissions and file mode settings, including effective execution settings
- Inode number in the file system
- Number of links
- User ID of the owner
- Group ID of the group of users to which access may be granted

- Size of the item
- Date and time the item was last accessed, the last modification made to the item, and the creation date and time associated with the item's inode

For most systems the administrator should configure Tripwire to verify the integrity of all critical operating system directories and files, plus any other directories and files that the administrator considers sensitive. Administrators should pay particular attention to executable programs, daemons, scripts, and the libraries and configuration files associated with them.

The default Tripwire configuration file for most operating systems is adequate, but administrators should carefully review and edit this file to reflect their particular requirements. When choosing which attributes of files and directories to verify, administrators should consider how files and directories are configured on their system. For example log files change as events cause records to be written, so verifying the constancy of the file size for these files is not generally useful. However, monitoring changes to the size of system binaries or to access permissions for log files is usually warranted.

The install process will itemize the steps required to install Tripwire on Unix and Linux systems. It will not cover Windows based systems although the install is relatively easy under Windows when using Tripwire's install program. Before downloading an installing Tripwire, administrators should confirm that the host(s) they are installing Tripwire on include the following software applications:

- An MD5 cryptographic checksum program
- GZIP to uncompress the downloaded file
- PGP to verify the authenticity of the software distribution
- A C compiler

Download or purchase (as appropriate) Tripwire from www.tripwiresecurity.com. Once Tripwire is downloaded verify the MD5 Checksum.

Installing Tripwire on Unix

Choose a storage location with sufficient space for the Tripwire distribution. Consult the Tripwire user manual before attempting installation. It contains troubleshooting suggestions and additional details that are beyond the scope of this implementation. After downloading Tripwire it will be necessary to unzip it:

$ gunzip Tripwire1_3_11_tar.gz

To unpack the Tripwire distribution, use the system tar command:

$ tar xvf Tripwire1.3.11_tar

This command creates a subdirectory named tw_ASR_1.3.1_src. Perform all operations within this subdirectory.

Several files exist in the created directory. One of these files is the Tripwire README file. It outlines the various strategies and settings for configuring and operating. Another file, Ported, lists the platforms and operating systems that Tripwire has been ported to. Find the appropriate operating system in the list and note the system settings. These will be required to build Tripwire successfully. After reviewing both the README and Ported files, an administrator should have a better understanding of how to configure Tripwire for his or her specific system.

Based on the appropriate system settings from the Ported file the administrator will have to change the Makefile to ensure that Tripwire will be correctly tuned for the specific operating system. Administrators will also have to edit the ./include/config.h file to tailor it for their specific system. Paths and names for Tripwire configuration files are specified in ./include/config.h. Administrators will need to decide where they are going to configure Tripwire to store its files. This should be readonly or removable media in order to adequately protect the data from unauthorized changes.

Next administrators will need to create an initial version of the Tripwire configuration files. Various templates for several operating systems are located in the ./config directory as part of the distribution. Administrators will need to copy the appropriate default file for their OS to the directory specified for the Tripwire configuration file location.

 # cp config/<appropriate OS config>/etc/tw.config

Next, Administrators will need to edit the /etc/tw.config file (consult the manual page) to include any local system binaries, other critical files, and any additional files that they wish to monitor. After the configuration is finished, the administrator should compile the Tripwire executable using the make command:

$ make

Starts the installation using the command **make install** to place the Tripwire binary and man pages into the correct system directories. This action will have to be performed using the root account. The administrator can also place all necessary files into the desired directory manually as follows:

 # cp man/siggen.8 /usr/local/man/man8/

 # cp man/tripwire.8 /usr/local/man/man8/

 # cp man/tw.config.5 /usr/local/man/man5/

 # cp src/tripwire /usr/local/bin/

 # cp src/siggen /usr/local/bin/

The Tripwire distribution includes a scriptdriven testing suite that checks the build process. To run the testing suite, type the following command:

$ make test

This starts a script that tests the build of Tripwire against a copy of the Tripwire database in the ./test directory. If all goes well, the output of the test matches the expected values that the script provides. For more information on the testing suite, consult the Tripwire User Manual.

For additional details on installation and configuration, consult the Tripwire User Manual, the README file, or the man pages.

Preparing to Use Tripwire

Once Tripwire has been compiled and tested, several additional topics need to be addressed. Not all files need the same level of protection. Tripwire comes with multiple cryptographic signature algorithms. Some execute more quickly than others and some are more secure than others. (See the Tripwire User Manual for a discussion of the individual algorithms.) Administrator will need to tailor their configuration files to reflect this tradeoff between security and performance. Tripwire's default setting is to use two algorithms to calculate cryptographic checksums; MD5 and Snefru. MD5 alone should be sufficient for most files and directories.

Tripwire can be run in one of four modes:

- Database generation
- Database update
- Interactive update mode
- Integrity checking

Generate the Tripwire Database

Integrity checking requires that a previously generated database to exist against which to compare. Such a database is created by the tw.config file. Once tw.config file is configured as desired, insert the prepared floppy disk (or other media as appropriate) and type the following commands:

 # mount n /dev/disk /floppy

 # tripwire initialize

The first command mounts the floppy. The second command creates a file named tw.db_<the local system's host name> within the directory /floppy/databases/. This file is the authoritative copy to which the Tripwire program refers when checking the file system's integrity for this host. Administrators can choose either the automatic or interactive update modes to maintain this database whenever changes are made to the system that need to be reflected in the Tripwire database.

After completing database generation, place a copy of the Tripwire program and its configuration file on the same disk as the database to protect the Tripwire software and critical files. Restrict access via the ownership and permissions settings on the files written to the disk so that only the root user can read them. Having all files on a write-protected floppy disk allows you to easily identify any changes by comparing versions on the disk to an authoritative reference copy. Once this step is complete, unmount and eject the floppy disk. The commands to execute this step are as follows:

> # cp /etc/tw.config /floppy

> # cp /usr/local/bin/tripwire /floppy

> # umount /floppy

Shift the write-protect tab on the disk to disable writing to it. This write-protected disk now represents the authoritative reference. Store this floppy in a physically secure location. Create an exact copy of the disk to work with so that original is not used on a daily basis.

Integrity Checking

Obtain the read-only medium containing the authoritative reference from its physically secured storage. Make sure that write protection is enabled and mount the floppy disk as shown below:

> # mount n /dev/disk /floppy

> # echo 'test' > /floppy/test

> /floppy/test: cannot create

If the file test exists after the last command, the floppy is not write-protected.

Compare each directory and file with its authoritative reference data. Identify any files whose contents or other attributes have changed. Execute Tripwire directly from the write-protected floppy, specifying which configuration (c option) and database (d option) files to use as follows:

> # cd /floppy

> # ./tripwire c ./tw.config d ./databases/tw.db_<the local system's host name>

Investigate any unexpected changes among those identified. Tripwire will identify the following:

- Files or directories that have changed
- Missing files or directories
- New files or directories

If any changes cannot be attributed to authorized activities, initiate incident response procedures immediately. Report the incident to the appropriate internal security point of contact. Provide the Tripwire report as additional data if applicable.

Return the authoritative reference data to its physically secured storage. If all changes reported by Tripwire are as expected, follow the organization's procedures for securely updating the authoritative reference copy of the Tripwire database.

When the Tripwire scan and update processes are complete, unmount the authoritative reference medium and return it to secure storage.

 # umount /floppy

Snort

Snort, called a lightweight network intrusion detection tool by creator Martin Roesch, is a network intrusion detection system (NIDS) that can be deployed to monitor small TCP/IP networks. Snort will detect a wide variety of suspicious traffic and attack attempts. Snort is publicly available under the GNU General Public License and is free for use in all types of environments. Rule based logging is used to perform content pattern matching and to detect a variety of attacks and probes. A simple language for the rule sets is used to expedite new rules as new attacks and exploits appear.

Snort Plugins

To allow for easy reporting, notification, and monitoring of log files and alerts generated by Snort, there are many additional programs that have been designed to work in conjunction with Snort. A partial listing of programs designed for use as analysis front ends would include:

- ACID, the Analysis Console for Intrusion Databases, is a PHP-based analysis engine that can search and process a database of incidents generated by Snort. Features for ACID include a query builder and search interface, a packet view to display packet information for layers 3 and 4, an alert management system, and a charting and statistics generator.
- ARIS Extractor is used to parse the Snort logs before sending the output to SecurityFocus's ARIS database for analysis. The ARIS database is a

service that allows network administrators to submit suspicious network traffic and intrusion attempts anonymously so that a detailed analysis and tracking can occur using the data from all contributors.

- Snort Report is a PHP-based front end for Snort that generates easy to read realtime reports from your MySQL or PostgreSQL database.

- SnortSnarf is a Perl program that converts files of alerts from Snort into HTML output. This program can be run on a schedule to generate HTML reports for use in diagnostic inspection and tracking down problems.

Snort Installation

Snort has been released or compiled successfully in multiple packages for different platforms, including:

- Linux
- OpenBSD
- FreeBSD
- NetBSD
- Solaris
- SunOS 4.1.X
- HPUX
- AIX
- IRIX
- Tru64
- MacOS X Server
- Win9x/NT/2000

The first step to installing Snort on a machine is to download all the appropriate files that will be needed. Depending on what plugins or addon programs are intended to be used, the list of downloads could vary. The main files that are necessary are:

- Snort
- Snort Rules
- WinPcap (for Windows)

Snort and the Snort rules can be found from the official Snort web page, www.snort.org.

Table B.8 Snort Rule Types

RULE TYPES	FUNCTION
Protocol	Protocols Snort analyzes for suspicious behavior: TCP/UDP/ICMP/IP
IP Address	Source and/or Destination IP address for matching
Direction	Direction of traffic
Port of Interest	Port traffic should be on to match
Option Fields	Additional options for use in matching rules to packets

WinPcap is a free packet capture architecture for Windows http://net-groupserv.polito.it/winpcap/install/default.htm). The packet filter is a device driver that adds the ability to capture and send raw data from a network card. With WinPcap, there is also the ability to filter and store the captured packets in a buffer. This ability to filter and store raw data packets from a network card is what makes WinPcap such a critical component of the Snort NIDS on the Windows Platform.

Snort Rules

Snort comes with a default rule set, snort.conf. While this file is a good start, many administrators will probably wish to modify it for their particular needs and requirements.

Snort rules are simple, yet effective in terms of detection capabilities. As shown in Table B.8, Snort rule sets can include the following rule types:

The option fields within the Snort rules allow for additional options to be included in the rules. The options for a rule are processed using a logical AND between them. This means that all options for a rule must be true for Snort to perform the rules action. A partial listing of these options is included in Table B.9.

Table B.9 Snort Rule Options

OPTION FIELD	FUNCTION
content	Search payload for specified pattern
flags	Test TCP flags for specified setting
ttl	Check IP header TTL field
itype	Match on ICMP type field

Table B.9 *(continued)*

OPTION FIELD	FUNCTION
icode	Match on ICMP code field
minfrag	Set threshold value for IP fragment size
id	Test the IP header for specified value
ack	Look for specific TCP header acknowledgement number
seq	Look for specific TCP header sequence number
logto	Log packets matching the rule to the specified filename
dsize	Match on the size of the packet payload
offset	Sets the offset into the packet payload to begin a content search
depth	Sets the number of bytes from the start position to search through
msg	Sets the message to be sent when a packet generates an event

There are five base action directives that Snort can use when a packet matches a specified rule pattern (see Table B.10).

Some example Snort rules, as found from www.snort.org/docs/ lisapaper.txt , are included below.

log tcp any any > 10.1.1.0/24 79

The above rule would record all traffic inbound for port 79 (finger) going to the 10.1.1 class C network address space.

Table B.10 Snort Rule Actions

RULE ACTION	FUNCTION
Pass	Ignore the packet and let it pass
Log	Write the full packet to the logging routine specified at run time
Alert	Generate an event notification using the selected alert method, then log the packet
Activate	Alert, and then turn on another dynamic rule
Dynamic	Remain idle until activated by an Activate rule, then act as a log rule

An example using an option field is as follows:

alert tcp any any > 10.1.1.0/24 80 (content: "/cgibin/phf"; msg: "PHF probe!";)

The rule above would detect attempts to access the PHF service on any of the local network's Web servers. When such a packet is detected on the network, an event notification alert is generated and the entire packet is logged using the logging mechanism selected at run time.

Additional Snort rules examples can be found within the document mentioned above or within the snort.conf file that is the default rule set included with Snort.

Snort Usage

There are three main modes for Snort:

- Sniffer Mode
- Packet Logger Mode
- Network Intrusion Detection Mode

The Snort sniffer mode is a basic way to write some or all of the intercepted TCP/UDP/ICMP/IP headers and/or packets to the screen. This is very similar in output to that of the tcpdump.

Table B.11 shows some simple flags to use in sniffer mode.

Flags can be combined for cumulative results. To record the packets to disk, the packet logger mode should be used. Table B.12 shows some simple flags to use in packet logger mode.

Table B.11   Snort Sniffer Mode Flags

FLAG	FUNCTION
v	Outputs the IP, TCP, UDP, and ICMP headers
d	Outputs the packet data for IP, TCP, UDP, and ICMP traffic
e	Outputs the data link layer headers for IP, TCP, UDP, and ICMP traffic

Table B.12   Snort Logger Mode Flags

FLAG	FUNCTION
l <log dir>	Packets specified by sniffer mode are placed into <log dir>
h <home network>	To log relative to home network, specify which network is home
b	Logs in binary mode, or tcpdump format
r <log file>	Read mode, plays back logfile to perform additional screening

Network intrusion detection mode can be configured in many ways. There are several alert output modes in addition to logging methods. The default alert method is to use full. alerts and to log in decoded ASCII format.

The alert output modes are described in Table B.13.

Packets can be logged using their default decoded ASCII format, to a binary file, or not at all. To disable packet logging, the .N command line switch should be used.

Additional command line flags and configurations can be found within Snort documentation. Table B.14 contains some links to sites with information and tools for use with Snort .

Table B.13   Snort IDS Mode Flags

ALERT	DESCRIPTION
A fast	Simple format with timestamp, alert message, source and destination IPs and ports
A full	Default mode, print alert message and full packet headers
A unsock	Send alerts to a Unix socket so another program can listen on
A none	Turn off alerting

Table B.14 Snort Web Resources

SITE/TOOL/INFO	WEBSITE
ACID	www.cert.org/kb/acid/
ARIS	http://aris.securityfocus.com
Incident.org Plugin	www.incident.org/snortdb/
Snort	www.snort.org
Snort Documentation	http://www.snort.org/documentation.html
Snort User Manual	www.snort.org/docs/writing_rules
Snort Downloads	www.snort.org/downloads.html
Snort Report	www.circuitsmaximus.com
Snorticus Shell Scripts	http://snorticus.baysoft.net/
SnortSnarf	www.silicondefense.com/software/snortsnarf/
Whitehats.com	http://www.whitehats.com
WinPcap	http://netgroupserv.polito.it/winpcap

References for Further Study

This appendix contains a list of the references that we used to compile this book, some additional references that you might want to refer to as you study, and the URLs of Web sites that have information regarding system security. We used all of these publications when researching for this book, and many of them will prove valuable to you also.

Books and Other Printed Materials

Austin, Tom. *PKI: A Wiley Tech Brief,* John Wiley & Sons, Inc., 2001.

Automated Tools for Testing Computer System Vulnerability, NIST Special Publication 800-6, December 1992.

Barr, Thomas H. *Invitation to Cryptology*, Prentice Hall, Inc., 2002.

Burnett, Steve and Paine, Stephen. *RSA Security's Official Guide to Cryptography*, McGraw-Hill, 2001.

Contingency Planning Guide for Information Technology Systems, NIST Special Publication 800-34, December 2001.

Engineering Principles for Information Technology Security (A Baseline for Achieving Security), NIST Special Publication 800-27, June 2001.

Establishing a Computer Security Incident Response Capability (CSIRC), NIST Special Publication 800-3, November 1991.

Federal Agency Use of Public Key Technology for Digital Signatures and Authentication, NIST Special Publication 800-25, October 2000.

Geier, Jim. *Wireless LANs (Second Edition)*, Sams Publishing, 2002.

Generally Accepted Principles and Practices for Securing Information Technology Systems, NIST Special Publication 800-14, September 1996.

Good Security Practices for Electronic Commerce, Including Electronic Data Interchange, NIST Special Publication 800-9, December 1993.

Guide for Developing Security Plans for Information Technology Systems, NIST Special Publication 800-18, December 1998.

Guidelines on Active Content and Mobile Code, NIST Special Publication 800-28, October 2001.

Guidelines on Electronic Mail Security, NIST Special Publication 800-45, March 2002.

Guidelines on Firewalls and Firewall Policy, NIST Special Publication 800-41, January 2002.

Draft Guideline on Network Security Testing, NIST Special Publication 800-42, February 2002. *A Guide to the Selection of Anti-Virus Tools and Techniques*, NIST Special Publication 800-5, December 1992.

Guidelines on Securing Public Web Servers, NIST Special Publication 800-44, February 2002.

Information Assurance Technology Framework Release 3.1, National Security Agency (NSA), September 2002.

"Information technology—Code of practice for information security management (ISO17799)," British Standards Publishing Limited, 2000.

Information Technology Security Training Requirements: A Role- and Performance-Based Model, NIST Special Publication 800-16, April 1998.

An Introduction to Computer Security: The NIST Handbook, NIST Special Publication 800-12, October 1995.

Introduction to Public Key Technology and the Federal PKI Infrastructure, NIST Special Publication 800-32, February 2001.

Intrusion Detection Systems (IDS), NIST Special Publication 800-31, November 2001.

Keeping Your Site Comfortably Secure: An Introduction to Internet Firewalls, NIST Special Publication 800-10, December 1994.

Krutz, Ronald L. and Vines, Russell Dean. *The CISSP Prep Guide: Gold Edition*, John Wiley & Sons, Inc., 2003.

Mitnick, Kevin D. and Simon, William. *The Art of Deception*, John Wiley & Sons, Inc., 2002.

Mobile Agent Security, NIST Special Publication 800-19, October 1999.

Neumann, Peter G. *Computer-Related Risks*, AMC Press, 1995.

Piper, Fred and Murphy, Sean. *Cryptography: A Very Short Introduction*, Oxford University Press, 2002.

Price, Brad, Yee, Erica, Price, John, and Hurley, Elizabeth (Eds.). *Networking Complete (Third Edition)*, Sybex, Inc., 2002.

Ramteke, Timothy. *Networks*, Prentice Hall Career and Technology, Inc., 1994.

Risk Management Guide for Information Technology System, NIST Special Publication 800-30, January 2002.

Rivest, Ronald L. *The RC5 Encryption Algorithm*, The MIT Laboratory for Computer Science, 1997.

Schneier, Bruce. *Secrets and Lies*, John Wiley & Sons, Inc., 2000.

Draft Security for Telecommuting and Broadband Communications, NIST Special Publication 800-46, December 2001.

Security Self-Assessment Guide for Information Technology Systems, NIST Special Publication 800-26, November 2001.

Stallings, William, *Computer Organization and Architecture (Second edition)*, Macmillan Publishing, 1990.

Stallings, William. *Cryptography and Network Security (Second Edition)*, Prentice-Hall, 1995 and 1999.

Stamper, David A. *Business Data Communications (Second Edition)*, Benjamin/Cummings, 1986 and 1989.

Systems Security Certified Practitioner (SSCP) Study Guide, (ISC)^2, 2001.

Telecommunications Security Guidelines for Telecommunications Management Network, NIST Special Publication 800-13, October 1995.

Tipton, Harold F. and Krause, Micki (Eds.). *Information Security Management Handbook*, CRC Press LLC, 2000.

Underlying Technical Models for Information Technology Security, NIST Special Publication 800-33, December 2001.

Wayner, Peter. *Disappearing Cryptography, Information Hiding (Second Edition)*, Morgan Kaufmann Publishers, 2002.

Web Sites

These sites might be of interest to the security practitioner:

www.rsasecurity.com

www.fts.gsa.gov/fts_mall/smartgovprog/infosec/rowlett.htm

www.ddj.com

www.emuseum.mnsu.edu/prehistory/egypt/hieroglyphics/rosettastone

www.nsa.gov/museum/

sra.org/glossary.htm

www.iacis.com

www.isc2.org

Web Sites of Interest to Security Administrators

www.isc2.org

csrc.nist.gov

www.nipc.gov

www.sans.org

www.cerias.purdue.edu

www.verisign.com

www.cisco.com

www.cai.com

www.cisecurity.org

www.3com.com

isc.incidents.org

www.gsa.gov

computer.org

www.sun.com

www.microsoft.com

linux.com

www.digicrime.com

xforce.iss.net

www.cert.org

grc.com

www.tripwire.com

www.gocsi.com

www.trusecure.com

nsi.org

www.fisrt.org

www.10pht.com

www.2600.com

www.hackernews.com

www.infosecnews.com

www.verisign.com

www.tigertesting.com

www.checkpoint.com

www.lordsomer.com

Answers to Sample Questions

Chapter 2—Domain 1: Access Controls

1. A user providing a password to a system is involved with:

    a. Evaluation

    b. Identification

    c. Authentication

    d. Authorization

    Answer: c

    The correct answer is c. A user presents a password to the system as an authenticator. Answer a is a distracter. Answer b is incorrect because a password is an authentication mechanism. Answer d is incorrect because it refers to the privileges that a user can have in accessing information.

2. The proactive approach to access control emphasizes which one of the following triples?

   a. Prevention, detection, confirmation

   b. Detection, correction, identification

   c. Prevention, detection, authentication

   d. Prevention, detection, reaction

   Answer: d

   The correct answer is d. The other answers are distracters.

3. Kerberos is an authentication scheme that uses which of the following technologies?

   a. Public key cryptography

   b. Digital signatures

   c. Private key cryptography

   d. Factoring of large numbers

   Answer: c

   The correct answer is c. Kerberos is a third-party authentication protocol that can also be used to implement single sign-on. Answers a, b, and d are incorrect because they refer to public-key cryptography and public-key cryptography is not used in the basic Kerberos protocol.

4. A *denial of service* (DoS) attack can be implemented by:

   a. Trying all possible combinations of words to break a password

   b. Sending large amounts of unsolicited messages

   c. Overwhelming the input of an information system to the point where it can no longer properly process the data

   d. Posing as a known, trusted source

   Answer: c

   The correct answer is c. Answer a refers to a brute-force attack, and answer b is spamming. Answer d is a masquerade attack.

5. The number of times that a password should be changed is a function of:

   a. The critical nature of the information to be protected

   b. The user's memory

   c. The strength of the user's cryptography

   d. The type of workstation used

   Answer: a

   The correct answer is a. Items b and c are distracters and answer d, the type of workstation used as the platform, is not the determining factor.

6. The three standard means of access control are:

   a. Physical, preventive, and logical (technical)

   b. Administrative, physical, and mandatory

   c. Administrative, logical (technical), and discretionary

   d. Physical, logical (technical), and administrative

   Answer: d

   The correct answer is d. The other answers are distracters.

7. A database View operation implements the principle of:

   a. Least privilege

   b. Separation of duties

   c. Entity integrity

   d. Referential integrity

   Answer: a

   The correct answer is a. Least privilege, in the database context, requires subjects to be granted the most restricted set of access privileges to the data in the database that are consistent with the performance of their tasks. Answer b, separation of duties, assigns parts of security sensitive tasks to several individuals. Entity integrity, answer c, requires that each row in the relation table must have a non-NULL attribute. Referential integrity, answer d, refers to the requirement that for any foreign key attribute, the referenced relation must have the same value for its primary key.

8. A synchronous password generator:

   a. Generates a password that must be used within a variable time interval

   b. Generates a password that must be used within a fixed time interval

   c. Generates a password that is not dependent on time

   d. Generates a password that is of variable length

   Answer: b

   The correct answer is b. Answer a is a distracter. Answer c is an asynchronous password—one that does not have to fit into a fixed time window for authentication, as is the case for a synchronous dynamic password. Answer d is a distracter.

9. Access control is concerned with:

    a. Threats, assets, and objectives

    b. Vulnerabilities, secret keys, and exposures

    c. Threats, vulnerabilities, and risks

    d. Exposures, threats, and countermeasures

    Answer: c

    The correct answer is c. Threats define sources of potential harm to an information system; vulnerabilities describe weaknesses in the system that might be exploited by the threats; and the risk determines the probability of threats being realized. All three items must be present to meaningfully apply access control. Therefore, the other answers are incorrect.

10. The type of access control that is used in local, dynamic situations where subjects have the ability to specify what resources certain users can access is called:

    a. Mandatory access control

    b. Rule-based access control

    c. Sensitivity-based access control

    d. Discretionary access control

    Answer: d

    The correct answer is d. Answers a and b require strict adherence to labels and clearances. Answer c is a made-up distracter.

11. Which of the following types of access control is preferred when there are frequent personnel changes in an organization?

    a. Mandatory

    b. Role-based

    c. Rules-based

    d. User-based

    Answer: b

    The correct answer is b. Role-based access control permits authorization to be assigned according to the individual's role or title in an organization. Answers a and c relate to mandatory access control that is based on labels, and answer d is a distracter.

12. Using symmetric key cryptography, Kerberos authenticates clients to other entities on a network and facilitates communications through the assignment of:

    a. Public keys

    b. Session keys

    c. Passwords

    d. Tokens

    Answer: b

    The correct answer is b. Session keys are temporary keys assigned by the KDC and used for an allotted period of time as the secret key between two entities. Answer a is incorrect because it refers to asymmetric encryption that is not used in the basic Kerberos protocol. Answer c is incorrect because it is not a key, and answer d is incorrect because a token generates dynamic passwords.

13. In a relational database, data access security is provided through:

    a. Domain

    b. Views

    c. Pointers

    d. Attributes

    Answer: b

    The correct answer is b. Answer a, a domain, is the set of allowable attribute values. Answer c is a distracter, and answer d denotes the columns in the relational table.

14. In a biometric system, the time that it takes to register with the system by providing samples of a biometric characteristic is called:

    a. Set-up time

    b. Log-in time

    c. Enrollment time

    d. Throughput time

    Answer: c

    The correct answer is c. Answers a and b are distracters. Answer d, throughput, refers to the rate at which individuals—once enrolled— can be processed and identified or authenticated by a biometric system.

15. Which one of the following statements is *true* concerning *Terminal Access Controller Access Control System* (TACACS) and TACACS+?

    a. TACACS supports prompting for a password change.

    b. TACACS+ employs tokens for two-factor, dynamic password authentication.

    c. TACACS+ employs a user ID and static password.

    d. TACACS employs tokens for two-factor, dynamic password authentication.

    Answer: b

    The correct answer is b. TACACS employs a user ID and static password and does not support prompting for password change or the use of dynamic password tokens.

16. An attack that can be perpetrated against call forwarding is which of the following types of access controls?

    a. Time stamping

    b. Digital certificate

    c. Timeout

    d. Callback

    Answer: d

    The correct answer is d. A cracker can have a person's call forwarded to another number to foil the callback system. Answer a is incorrect because it refers to tying a message to a time or time window. Answer b is incorrect and refers to a digital certificate vouching for a user's public key. Answer c is incorrect because it is a distracter.

17. In biometrics, a "one-to-one" search to verify an individual's claim of an identity is called:

    a. Authentication

    b. Audit trail review

    c. Accountability

    d. Aggregation

    Answer: a

    The correct answer is a. Answer b is a review of audit system data, usually done after the fact. Answer c is holding individuals responsible for their actions, and answer d is obtaining higher-sensitivity information from a number of pieces of information of lower sensitivity.

18. Which one of the following is a goal of integrity?

   a. Accountability of responsible individuals

   b. Prevention of the modification of information by unauthorized users

   c. Prevention of the unauthorized disclosure of information

   d. Preservation of internal and external consistency

   Answer: d

   The correct answer is d. Accounting is holding individuals responsible for their actions. Answer b is required by authorized users, and answer c refers to confidentiality.

19. A security kernel is:

   a. An abstract machine that mediates all accesses of subjects to objects

   b. The hardware, firmware, and software elements of a trusted computing base that implement the reference monitor concept

   c. The protected part of the operating system

   d. A means of controlling the administration of a database

   Answer: b

   The correct answer is b. Answer a is the reference monitor, and answer c is the trusted computing base. Answer d is a distracter.

20. Users who possess the ability to bypass most access controls are:

   a. Anonymous users

   b. Privileged users

   c. Guest users

   d. Trusted users

   Answer: b

   The correct answer is b. Privileged users are also known as super users or administrators. The other answers are distracters.

21. In finger scan technology:

   a. The full fingerprint is stored.

   b. Features extracted from the fingerprint are stored.

   c. More storage is required than in fingerprint technology.

   d. The technology is applicable to large one-to-many database searches.

   Answer: b

   The correct answer is b. The features extracted from the fingerprint are stored. Answer a is incorrect because the equivalent of the full fingerprint is not stored in finger scan technology. Answers c and d are incorrect because the opposite is true of finger scan technology.

22. Mandatory access control uses which of the following pairs to authorize access to information?

    a. Roles and identity

    b. Clearances and roles

    c. Classification and clearances

    d. Identity and roles

    Answer: c

    The correct answer is c. Mandatory access controls use the subject's clearance and the object's classification to determine whether subjects can have access to objects. The other answers are distracters.

23. An example of two-factor authentication is:

    a. A password and an ID

    b. An ID and a PIN

    c. A PIN and an ATM card

    d. A fingerprint

    Answer: c

    The correct answer is c. These items are something you know and something you have. Answer a is incorrect because, essentially, only one factor is being used (something you know; a password). Answer b is incorrect for the same reason. Answer d is incorrect because only one biometric factor is being used.

24. The *Crossover Error Rate* (CER) refers to which one of the following technologies?

    a. Employee history

    b. Databases

    c. Cryptography

    d. Biometrics

    Answer: d

    The correct answer is d. The CER is the percentage at which the False Rejection Rate and False Acceptance Rate are equal. The other items are distracters.

25. Biometrics is used for authentication in the logical controls and for identification in the:

    a. Detective controls

    b. Physical controls

    c. Preventive controls

    d. Corrective controls

    Answer: b

    The correct answer is b. The other answers are different categories of controls where preventive controls attempt to eliminate or reduce vulnerabilities before an attack occurs; detective controls attempt to determine that an attack is taking place or has taken place; and corrective controls involve taking action to restore the system to normal operation after a successful attack.

26. Which of the following is NOT an assumption of the basic Kerberos paradigm?

    a. Client computers are not secured and are easily accessible.

    b. Cabling is not secure.

    c. Messages are not secure from interception.

    d. Specific servers and locations cannot be secured.

    Answer: d

    The correct answer is d. Kerberos requires that centralized servers implementing the trusted authentication mechanism must be secured.

27. Logon notification, detection of user inactivity, and multiple log-on control are examples of what level of access control?

    a. System level

    b. Account level

    c. Data level

    d. Session level

    Answer: d

    The correct answer is d. Answer a, system-level controls, include mandatory and discretionary access controls. Answer b refers to privileged, individual, and group identification and authentication. Answer c involves database management systems and other applications as well as encryption.

28. A dynamic password is one that:

    a. Is the same for each logon

    b. Is a long word or phrase that is converted by the system to a password

    c. Changes at each logon

    d. Is unverifiable

    Answer: c

    The correct answer is c. Answer a defines a static password; answer b is a passphrase; and answer d is false.

29. Procedures that ensure that the access control mechanisms correctly implement the security policy for the entire life cycle of an information system are known as:

    a. Accountability procedures

    b. Authentication procedures

    c. Assurance procedures

    d. Trustworthy procedures

    Answer: c

    The correct answer is c. Accountability, answer a, refers to the ability to determine the actions and behavior of a single individual within a system and to identify that individual. Answer b, authentication, involves testing or reconciling of evidence of a user's identify in order to establish that identity. Answer d is a distracter.

30. CHAP is:

    a. A protocol for establishing the authenticity of remote users

    b. A protocol for authenticity of palm prints

    c. A protocol for authenticity of Kerberos exchanges

    d. A protocol for establishing TCP/IP connections

    Answer: a.

    The correct answer is a. The other answers are distracters.

Chapter 3—Domain 2: Administration

1. In the CIA triad, the tenet of confidentiality guarantees that:

   a. The data will not be altered by unauthorized means.

   b. The data will not be seen by unauthorized eyes.

   c. The data will be available to those who will need it.

   d. The data will be protected from lower security levels.

   Answer: b

   The CIA tenet of confidentiality guarantees that the data will not be seen by those who are not authorized to view it. Answer a describes the tenet of integrity, answer c describes availability, and answer d is a distracter.

2. The concept of data integrity assures that:

   a. The information will not be seen by those with a lower security clearance.

   b. The information will not be lost or destroyed.

   c. The information will be protected from fraudulent accounting.

   d. The information will be protected from unintentional or unauthorized alteration.

   Answer: d

   The CIA tenet of integrity assures that data will not be altered by unauthorized means, either intentionally or unintentionally. Answer a describes confidentiality, answer b describes availability, and answer c is a distracter.

3. In a system life cycle, information security controls should be:

   a. Part of the feasibility phase

   b. Implemented prior to validation

   c. Designed during the product implementation phase

   d. Specified after the coding phase

   Answer: a

   The correct answer is a. In the system life cycle, information security controls should be part of the feasibility phase. Information systems security controls should be implemented in the earliest phases of the software life cycle and not added later in the cycle or as an afterthought.

4. The software maintenance phase controls consist of:

   a. Request control, configuration control, and change control

   b. Request control, change control, and release control

   c. Request control, release control, and access control

   d. Change control, security control, and access control

   Answer: b

   The software maintenance phase controls consist of request control, change control, and release control by definition.

5. Place the following four information classification levels in their proper order, from the most-sensitive classification to the least sensitive:

   a. Top secret

   b. Unclassified

   c. SBU

   d. Secret

   Answer: b, c, d, and a

6. Place the following general information classification procedures in their proper order:

   a. Publicize awareness of the classification controls.

   b. Classify the data.

   c. Specify the controls.

   d. Specify the classification criteria.

   Answer: d, b, c, and a

7. Which statement describes "separation of duties"?

   a. Each user is granted the lowest clearance required for their tasks.

   b. Helps ensure that no single individual (acting alone) can compromise security controls.

   c. Requires that the operator have the minimum knowledge of the system to perform his task.

   d. Limits the time an operator performs a task.

   Answer: b

   Separation of duties requires assigning parts of tasks to different personnel. Answer a is "least privilege," where the user has the minimum security level required to perform his job function. Answer c is "need to know", which means that in addition to whatever specific object or role rights a user might have on the system, the user has also the minimum amount of information necessary to perform his job function, and no more. Answer d is "rotation of duties," wherein the amount of time an operator is assigned a security sensitive task is limited before being moved to a different task with a different security classification.

8. Which choice is NOT considered a defined role for information classification purposes?

   a. Data owner

   b. Data object

   c. Data user

   d. Data custodian

   Answer: b

   The other three answers are roles as defined for information classification.

9. Place the organizational data classification scheme in order from the most secure to the least:

   a. Private

   b. Sensitive

   c. Confidential

   d. Public

   Answer: c, b, a, and d

   This system would define the categories as follows:

   Confidential.   This classification applies to the most sensitive business information that is intended strictly for use within the organization. Its unauthorized disclosure could seriously and adversely impact the organization, its stockholders, its business partners, and/or its customers. This information is exempt from disclosure under the provisions of the *Freedom of Information Act* (FOIA) or other applicable federal laws or regulations.

   Sensitive.   This classification applies to information that requires special precautions to assure the integrity of the information, by protecting it from unauthorized modification or deletion. It is information that requires a higher-than-normal assurance of accuracy and completeness.

   Private.   This classification applies to personal information that is intended for use within the organization. Its unauthorized disclosure could seriously and adversely impact the organization and/or its employees.

   Public.   This classification applies to all other information that does not clearly fit into any of the preceding three classifications. While its unauthorized disclosure is against policy, it is not expected to impact seriously or adversely the organization, its employees, and/or its customers.

10. What does the data encapsulation in the OSI model do?

    a. Creates seven distinct layers

    b. Wraps data from one layer around a data packet from an adjoining layer

    c. Provides "best effort" delivery of a data packet

    d. Makes the network transmission deterministic

    Answer: b

    The correct answer is b. Data encapsulation attaches information from one layer to the packet as it travels from an adjoining layer. Answer b describes the OSI model, answer c describes the TCP/IP protocol UDP, and answer d is a property of token-passing networks.

11. Place these five system security life cycle phases in order of procedure:

    a. Development/acquisition phase

    b. Initiation phase

    c. Implementation phase

    d. Disposal phase

    e. Operation/maintenance phase

    Answer: b, a, c, e, and d

    Security, like other aspects of an IT system, is best managed if planned for throughout the IT system life cycle. There are many models for the IT system life cycle, but most contain five basic phases: initiation, development/acquisition, implementation, operation, and disposal.

12. Which term describes the concept of "separation of privilege"?

    a. A formal separation of command, program, and interface functions.

    b. Active monitoring of facility entry access points.

    c. Each user is granted the lowest clearance required for their tasks.

    d. A combination of classification and categories that represents the sensitivity of information.

    Answer: a

    Separation of privilege is the separation of functions, namely between the commands, programs, and interfaces implementing those functions, such that malicious or erroneous code in one function is prevented from affecting the code or data of another function.

    Answer c, least privilege, requires that each subject in a system be granted the most restrictive set of privileges (or lowest clearance) needed for the performance of authorized tasks.

Answer d is a security level, a combination of hierarchical classification and a set of non-hierarchical categories that represents the sensitivity of information.

Answer b is a distracter.

13. What is a *programmable logic device* (PLD)?

   a. A program resident on disk memory that executes a specific function

   b. An integrated circuit with connections or internal logic gates that can be changed through a programming process

   c. *Random Access Memory* (RAM) that contains the software to perform specific tasks

   d. A volatile device

   Answer: b

   Answer a is a distracter. Answer c is incorrect because RAM is volatile memory that is not a non-volatile logic device. Answer d is incorrect because a PLD is non-volatile.

14. Random access memory is:

   a. Non-volatile

   b. Volatile

   c. Programmed by using fusible links

   d. Sequentially addressable

   Answer: b

   RAM is volatile. The other answers are incorrect because RAM is volatile, randomly accessible, and not programmed by fusible links.

15. Which choice MOST accurately describes the difference between the role of a data owner versus the role of a data custodian?

   a. The custodian makes the initial information classification assignments, and the operations manager implements the scheme.

   b. The custodian implements the information classification scheme after the initial assignment by the owner.

   c. The custodian implements the information classification scheme after the initial assignment by the operations manager.

   d. The data owner implements the information classification scheme after the initial assignment by the custodian.

   Answer: b

   The data custodian implements the information classification scheme after the initial assignment by the data owner.

16. Primary storage is the:

    a. Memory that provides non-volatile storage, such as floppy disks

    b. Memory where information must be obtained by searching sequentially from the beginning of the memory space

    c. Memory for the storage of instructions and data that are associated with the program being executed and directly addressable by the CPU

    d. Memory used in conjunction with real memory to present a CPU with a larger, apparent address space

    Answer: c

    Answer a refers to secondary storage. Answer b refers to sequential memory, and answer d refers to virtual memory.

17. What is a control packet sent around a Token Ring network called?

    a. Secondary storage

    b. A computer bus

    c. A token

    d. A field in object-oriented programming

    Answer: c

    A token is a control message sent in a Token Ring network. Answer a refers to disk storage. Answer b, a computer bus, a group of conductors for the addressing of data and control. Answer d is a distracter.

18. Which of the following is NOT a VPN standard or protocol?

    a. UTP

    b. PPTP

    c. L2TP

    d. IPSec

    Answer: a

    UTP stands for unshielded twisted-pair wiring. The other three are common protocols used in *Virtual Private Networks* (VPNs).

19. Which choice describes the process of data destruction?

    a. Overwriting of data media intended to be reused in the same organization or area

    b. Degaussing or thoroughly overwriting media intended to be removed from the control of the organization or area

    c. Complete physical destruction of the media

    d. Reusing data storage media after its initial use

Answer: b

Answer a refers to data clearing, answer b describes data purging, and answer d describes object reuse.

20. Which choice is NOT an accurate statement about standards?

    a. Standards specify the use of specific technologies in a uniform way.

    b. Standards are not the first element created in an effective security policy program.

    c. Standards help describe how policies will be implemented within an organization.

    d. Standards are senior management's directives to create a computer security program.

    Answer: d

    Answer d describes high-level policy. Answers a, b, and c describe standards. Procedures, standards, and guidelines are used to describe how policies will be implemented within an organization.

21. Which TCP/IP protocol operates at the application layer?

    a. IP

    b. FTP

    c. UDP

    d. TCP

    Answer: b

    FTP operates at the application layer of TCP/IP, which is roughly similar to the top three layers of the OSI model: the Application, Presentation, and Session layers. Answer a, IP, operates at the network layer of the OSI model. Answer c and d, TCP and UDP, both operate at the OSI Transport layer.

22. What is the Data Link Layer of the OSI reference model primarily responsible for?

    a. Internetwork packet routing

    b. LAN bridging

    c. SMTP gateway services

    d. Signal regeneration and repeating

    Answer: b

    Bridging is a Data Link Layer function. Answer a, the OSI Network layer, is primarily responsible for routing. Answer c, gateways, most commonly function at the higher layers. Answer d, signal regeneration and repeating, is primarily a Physical layer function.

23. Which choice incorrectly describes the organization's responsibilities during an unfriendly termination?

    a. System access should be removed as quickly as possible after termination.

    b. The employee should be given time to remove whatever files he needs from the network.

    c. Cryptographic keys in the employee's property must be returned.

    d. Briefing on the continuing responsibilities for confidentiality and privacy.

    Answer: b

    The other choices are all examples of the organization's responsibilities during an unfriendly termination.

24. Which of the following is NOT a property of a packet-filtering firewall?

    a. Uses ACLs

    b. Susceptible to IP spoofing

    c. Intercepts all messages entering and leaving the network

    d. Examines the source and destination addresses of the incoming packet

    Answer: c

    A proxy server intercepts all messages entering and leaving the network, and is designed to hide true network addresses. The other three choices are all properties of packet-filtering firewalls.

25. Configuration management control refers to:

    a. The use of privileged-entity controls for system administrator functions

    b. The concept of "least control" in operations

    c. Implementing resource protection schemes for hardware control

    d. Ensuring that changes to the system do not unintentionally diminish security

    Answer: d

    Configuration Management Control ensures that any changes to the system are managed properly and do not inordinately affect either the availability or security of the system.

26. Which is NOT a layer in the OSI architecture model?

    a. Session

    b. Data Link

    c. Host-to-host

    d. Transport

Answer: c

The host-to-host layer is in the DoD TCP/IP architecture model, not the OSI model.

27. What choice is an example of a guideline?

   a. A recommendation for procedural controls

   b. The instructions on how to perform a quantitative risk analysis

   c. Statements that indicate a senior management's intention to support InfoSec

   d. Step-by-step procedures on how to implement a safeguard

   Answer: a

   Examples of guidelines are recommendations for controls or noncompulsory recommendation on how to achieve compliance with published standards. Answer b is a distracter. Answer c is high-level policies. Answer d is procedures.

28. Which of the choices is an OSI reference model Presentation Layer protocol, standard, or interface?

   a. Structured Query Language (SQL)

   b. Remote Procedure Call (RPC)

   c. AppleTalk Session Protocol (ASP)

   d. Musical Instrument Digital Interface (MIDI)

   Answer: c

   The MIDI standard is a Presentation Layer standard for digitized music. The other answers are all Session layer protocols or standards.

29. What is the definition of configuration identification?

   a. Identifying and documenting the functional and physical characteristics of each configuration item

   b. Controlling changes to the configuration items and issuing versions of configuration items from the software library

   c. Recording the processing of changes

   d. Controlling the quality of the configuration management procedures

   Answer: a

   Configuration identification is a process of configuration control consisting of identifying and documenting the functional and physical characteristics of each configuration item. Answer b is configuration control; answer c is configuration status accounting; and answer d is a definition of configuration audit.

30. Which of the following terms is NOT associated with Read Only Memory (ROM)?

    a. Firmware

    b. Static RAM (SRAM)

    c. Field Programmable Gate Array (FPGA)

    d. Flash memory

    Answer: b

    Static Random Access Memory (SRAM) is volatile and loses its data if power is removed from the system. Conversely, a ROM is nonvolatile in that it does not lose its content when power is removed. Answer a, firmware, is a program that is stored on ROMs Answer c, FPGA, is a type of *Programmable Logic Device* (PLD) that is programmed by blowing fuse connections on the chip or using an antifuse that makes a connection when a high voltage is applied to the junction. Answer d, flash memories, are a type of electrically programmable ROM.

Chapter 4—Domain 3: Auditing and Monitoring

1. Which one of the following statements is NOT true?

    a. Monitoring is an activity that takes place in real time and views current activity on a network.

    b. Monitoring retains detailed information for later review.

    c. Auditing captures network activity.

    d. Auditing retains information for later review.

    Answer: b

    The correct answer is b. Monitoring does not retain detailed information for later review.

2. Relative to information systems security auditing, which one of the following is NOT one of the reasons to conduct an audit?

    a. To reconstruct events that might have caused a security breach

    b. To identify a potential breach in security

    c. To reconstruct activities performed during a breach in security

    d. To develop techniques to prevent future breaches

    Answer: d

    The correct answer is d. It is not the responsibility of the auditing function to develop information security mechanisms to thwart future breaches.

3. Which of the following statements is TRUE?

    a. Most firewall systems do not provide logging functionality.

    b. Application-proxy gateway firewalls provide more comprehensive logging output than stateful inspection packet filter firewalls.

    c. Stateful inspection packet filter firewalls provide more comprehensive logging output than application-proxy gateway firewalls.

    d. Application-proxy gateway firewalls encompass a smaller portion of the OSI model than stateful inspection packet filter firewalls.

    Answer: b

    The correct answer is b because application-proxy gateway firewalls are aware of a larger portion of the OSI model.

4. The mechanism used to synchronize the time reference for installed intrusion detection systems and for logging across the network is:

    a. Network Time Protocol

    b. Synchronous Network Logging Protocol

    c. Time Synchronous Protocol

    d. Network Coordination Protocol

    Answer: a

    The correct answer is a, the NTP. The other answers are distracters.

5. One of the rules in a ruleset for a boundary router is given as follows:

RULE	SOURCE ADDRESS	SOURCE PORT	DESTINATION ADDRESS	DESTINATION PORT	ACTION
4	Any	Any	192.168.1.2	SMTP	Allow

Which one of the following items BEST describes the permissions specified by the rule?

    a. Prevents external users from directly addressing the firewall system

    b. Permits internal users to access external servers

    c. Permits inbound connections to the main firewall's SMTP port

    d. Instructs the router to pass SMTP traffic to the main firewall, which in turn will forward the message traffic to the respective application proxies

    Answer: d

    The correct answer is d. Incoming email is first directed to the main firewall, which in turn will pass along the email to an application proxy server located on an internal DMZ.

6. Which one of the following activities is NOT part of the process for establishing an audit trail?

    a. Defining your roadmap

    b. Developing your ruleset

    c. Auditing all violations

    d. Not auditing exceptions

    Answer: d.

    The correct answer is d. All exceptions should be audited.

7. The following activities are associated with auditing of what type of item?

    ■ Creation, alteration, or dropping of a table

    ■ Creation, alteration, or dropping of an index

    ■ Statements renaming an object

    ■ Performance statistics collection

    ■ Granting and revoking of system type privilege

    a. A network server

    b. A database server

    c. A mail server

    d. A Web server

    Answer: b

    The correct answer is b because the listed activities are associated with databases.

8. Which of the following resources that are impacted by the auditing process poses the most difficulty to management?

    a. Auditing systems' hardware

    b. Software to implement logging

    c. Human resources required for analyzing and interpreting data

    d. Offline storage for preserving the logs for a specified time period

    Answer: c

    The correct answer is c. Because of the large amount of data that is logged and has to be processed, labor costs can be significant. One solution is to supplement personnel resources with automated programs that correlate data, determine behavior patterns, and detect policy violations. The other answers, obviously, incur costs—but they are less relative to the labor costs associated with answer c.

9. Information about which one of the following activities is the LEAST important audit data to collect?

   a. The use of privileged commands

   b. Unsuccessful, unauthorized attempts to access files

   c. Permission modifications

   d. Successful, authorized accessing of files

   Answer: d

   The correct answer is d. Relative to the other answers, this action is normal and is not an enabler of unauthorized activities.

10. For events that are logged by the auditing process, which of the following data items is the LEAST important to collect?

    a. Date and time of each event

    b. Type of event

    c. Denial of access resulting from excessive logon attempts

    d. Non-system administrator functions

    Answer: d

    The correct answer is d. Functions performed by users who are not systems administrators include "normal" functions that are a lower priority than those listed in answers a, b, and c.

11. The main purpose of monitoring an information system is:

    a. Identifying a potential attack as it is occurring

    b. Reconstructing incidents after they have occurred

    c. Identifying incidents after they have occurred

    d. Preventing the occurrence of incidents

    Answer: a

    The correct answer is a. Monitoring is a pro-active approach that is aimed at identifying incidents as they are occurring. An *intrusion detection system* (IDS) is a form of automated monitoring. Answers b and c describe after the fact detective activities. Answer d is aimed at preventing an incident from occurring before the fact.

12. Which of the following items is NOT a type of network monitoring?

    a. Network management monitoring

    b. Mouse motion monitoring

    c. Security monitoring

    d. Key stroke monitoring

    Answer: b

    The correct answer is b, a distracter. Answer a refers to the monitoring of parameters such as network capacity, percent of usage, and so on.

    Answer c is concerned with network information security issues, such as detecting port scans, observing traffic to specific addresses, firewall status and so on. Keystroke monitoring, answer d, records an individual's keystrokes on a networked computer and the assorted responses. Keystroke monitoring might be considered an illegal activity and should not be implemented without paper authority.

13. SNORT is:

    a. An open-sourced audit system

    b. An open-sourced keystroke monitoring system

    c. A proprietary intrusion detection system

    d. An open-sourced intrusion detection system

    Answer: d

    The correct answer is d. SNORT is an open-sourced, free intrusion detection utility with a flexible and straightforward rules language. SNORT uses a promiscuous *network interface card* (NIC) to monitor packets traversing the network. The other answers are distracters.

14. A type of automated audit tool that provides the auditor with information concerning the network topology and assets is called:

    a. An intrusion detection tool

    b. A monitoring tool

    c. A documentation tool

    d. A discovery tool

    Answer: d

    The correct answer is d. Answers a and b refer to real-time monitoring of the network to detect irregularities and incidents. Documentation tools, answer c, provide support for recording the audit results and establishing a baseline for future audits.

15. Automated tools such as SATAN and CYBERCOP perform which of the following functions?

    a. Vulnerability analysis

    b. Intrusion detection

    c. Data mining

    d. Configuration management

    Answer: a

    The correct answer is a. Answer b, intrusion detection is the active monitoring of network or host-based events to discover incidents as they are occurring. Data mining, answer c, is the offline development of correlations among seemingly unrelated data items in large databases. Answer d, configuration management, refers to the process of tracking and approving changes to a system.

16. Which of the following items is NOT a correct, professional auditing standard?

    a. Due professional care is exercised in all aspects of the information systems auditor's work.

    b. If the information systems audit function is closely related to the area being audited, professional auditing practices must be enforced.

    c. The information systems auditor will provide a report, in appropriate form and content, to the intended recipients upon completion of the audit work.

    d. The responsibility, authority, and accountability of the information systems audit function must be appropriately documented in audit charters or an engagement letter.

    Answer: b

    The correct answer is b. The audit function should be significantly independent of the area being audited to permit objective completion of the audit. The standards cited in answer a, c, and d are taken from ISACA Standard Guidelines.

17. A level of diligence that a prudent individual would practice under given circumstances is called:

    a. Best effort

    b. Basic practices

    c. Due care

    d. Least privilege

    Answer: c

    The correct answer is c. It is a measure of what a prudent individual would do in similar circumstances. Answer a, best effort, is incorrect because the question does not ask for a measure of the best effort that possibly could be applied. Answer b is a distracter and answer d refers to giving an individual the minimum privileges to access information for that individual to perform his or her assigned tasks.

18. Which of the following statements is TRUE regarding a risk-based audit approach?

    a. The cost to implement controls should be evaluated relative to the potential for loss if no controls are applied.

    b. Residual risk can be eliminated by insurance coverage.

    c. The risk mitigation is independent of management's tolerance for risk.

    d. The means to eliminate risk through controls should be investigated.

    Answer: a

    The correct answer is a. Liability may exist if the cost to implement controls is less than the anticipated loss if the controls are not applied. Answer b and d are incorrect because risk can never be completely eliminated. Answer c is incorrect because management's tolerance for risk is very important in risk mitigation decisions.

19. Risk that is a result of the failure of the auditing process to discover important errors is called:

    a. Controls risk

    b. Preventive risk

    c. Inherent risk

    d. Detection risk

    Answer: d

    The correct answer is d. Answer a refers the risk associated with controls not mitigating risk as planned. Answer b is a distracter. Inherent risk, answer c, refers to risk without controls in place.

20. A control that is used to identify an area where an error has occurred is called:

a. Deterrent control

b. Detective control

c. Corrective control

d. Reactive control

Answer: b

The correct answer is b. Detective controls take place after the fact and are used to determine whether an incident has occurred. Answer a, a deterrent control, provides warning of a possible incident. Corrective controls, answer c, are applied after an incident has occurred in order to return the information system to its original state that existed prior to the incident. Answer d is a distracter.

21. Which of the following items is MOST important in identifying potential irregularities during the audit process?

a. Size of the payroll for the organization being audited

b. Determining whether information systems best practices are used

c. Existence of a vacation policy that requires employees to take vacation in one or two-week blocks

d. Identifying the type of gateway used by the organization

Answer: c

The correct answer is c. This item is the only one that will directly indicate that a potential for irregularities exist. The other answers may provide some relevant information, but none are direct indicators of possible problems.

22. Control objectives are important in audit engagements because they:

a. Define audit duration

b. Define the cost of audit

c. Identify the main control issues based on management input and risk

d. Define testing steps

Answer: c

The correct answer is c. The details listed in the other answers are not part of the control objectives.

23. Which one of the following terms BEST describes "defining the roles and responsibilities of the auditors?"

    a. Audit charter

    b. Audit scope

    c. Audit objectives

    d. Control objectives

    Answer: a

    The correct answer is a. The audit charter provides a clear mandate and authority for the auditors to perform their work. The other answers are related in that the scope of the audit should be limited to the topics outlined in the control objective.

24. Which one of the following BEST meets the requirements of audit evidence sampling?

    a. A confidence level higher than 90 percent based on repeated polling

    b. Sufficient, reliable, relevant, useful, and supported by appropriate analyses

    c. Should be conducted using the Delphi method

    d. Should be conducted using random sampling

    Answer: b

    The correct answer is b. The other answers are distracters.

25. What are the key items to consider relative to the reportable findings of an audit?

    a. Audit scope, materiality and audit charter

    b. Audit objectives, materiality, and management direction

    c. Audit objectives and management direction

    d. Audit objectives only

    Answer: b

    The correct answer is b. All three areas are key to the determination of reputable findings.

26. An analysis that ensures that the underlying problem and not the symptoms is addressed is called:

    a. Root cause analysis

    b. Cost benefit analysis

    c. Base problem analysis

    d. Linear causal analysis

Answer: a

The correct answer is a. The other answers are distracters.

27. The definition "determining whether the system is being operated in accordance with accepted industry practices" refers to:

    a. Monitoring

    b. Auditing

    c. Intrusion detection

    d. Vulnerability analysis

Answer: b

The correct answer is b. Answers a and c refer to real-time activities to detect an incident while it is occurring. Answer d refers to scanning and penetration testing to determine network vulnerability.

28. Which of the following BEST describes the given ruleset for a boundary router?

RULE	SOURCE ADDRESS	SOURCE PORT	DESTINATION ADDRESS	DESTINATION PORT	ACTION
4	Any	Any	192.168.1.0	>1023	Allow

    a. Allow external users to connect to the VPN server.

    b. Allow internal servers to connect to external servers.

    c. Allow external servers to send e-mail to the proxy.

    d. Allow return packets from established connections to return to the source systems.

Answer: d

The correct answer is d (see Table 4.2 in Chapter 4).

29. Which one of the following is NOT one of the processes for establishing an audit trail?

    a. Define your roadmap.

    b. Develop your ruleset.

    c. Audit all violations.

    d. Audit all normalizations.

Answer: d

The correct answer is d, a distracter. The additional process is to audit all exceptions.

30. Which of the following items is NOT an activity that should be logged on a relational database server?

    a. Creation, alteration, or dropping of a database table

    b. Enabling or disabling of the audit functionality

    c. Any user statement that does not return an error message because the object referenced does not exist

    d. Any user statement that renames a database object

    Answer: c

    The correct answer is c. If an error message does not occur, it cannot be logged. The correct answer should state, "Any user statement that *does* return an error message because the object referenced does not exist."

Chapter 5—Domain 4: Risk, Response, and Recovery

1. Which choice gives the BEST description of risk reduction?

    a. Altering elements of the enterprise in response to a risk analysis

    b. Removing all risk to the enterprise at any cost

    c. Assigning any costs associated with risk to a third party

    d. Assuming all costs associated with the risk internally

    Answer: a

    The correct answer is a. Answer b is not possible or desirable, c is risk transference, and d is risk acceptance.

2. Which choice is an example of an incident due to a human event, rather than a non-human incident?

    a. Sabotage

    b. Financial collapse

    c. Structure collapse

    d. Utility failure

    Answer: a

    Sabotage is an example of an intentional incident due to a human event; the other choices are examples of non-human incidents.

3. Place the following backup processing alternatives in order from the least-expensive solution to the most expensive:

   a. Warm site

   b. Hot site

   c. Cold site

   d. Mutual aid agreement

   Answer: d, c, a, and b

   A mutual aid agreement is likely to be the least expensive of the four because it does not necessarily entail any resource investment. As far as the capability of the alternatives to actually provide redundancy and processing in the event of a business-interrupting incident, the order is exactly the opposite—with mutual aid and cold sites providing the least and hot sites providing the highest level of processing redundancy assurance.

4. Which group represents the MOST likely source of an asset loss through inappropriate computer use?

   a. Crackers

   b. Employees

   c. Hackers

   d. Flood

   Answer: b

   The correct answer is b. Resource loss due to internal personnel constitute the largest amount of dollar loss due to inappropriate intentional or unintentional computer use.

5. Which statement about risk is not accurate?

   a. Risk is identified and measured by performing a risk analysis.

   b. Risk is controlled through the application of safeguards and countermeasures.

   c. Risk is managed by periodically reviewing and taking responsible actions based on the risk.

   d. Risk can be completely eliminated through risk management.

   Answer: d

6. Which statement most accurately describes contingency operations and recovery?

   a. The function of identifying, evaluating (measuring), and controlling risk

   b. Activities that are performed when a security-related incident occurs

   c. Planned activities that enable the critical business functions to return to normal operations

   d. Transferring risk to a third-party insurance carrier

   Answer: c

   Contingency operations and recovery are those planned activities that enable the critical business functions to continue under less-than-ideal circumstances and return to normal operations.

   Answer a describes Risk Management, the function of identifying, evaluating (measuring), and controlling risk.

   Answer b describes Incident Response—activities that are performed when a security-related incident occurs which has the potential for, or has caused, adverse effects to the system or enterprise.

   Answer d describes risk.

7. Which choice is NOT a commonly accepted definition for a disaster?

   a. An occurrence that is outside the normal computing function

   b. An occurrence or imminent threat to the entity of widespread or severe damage, injury, loss of life, or loss of property

   c. An emergency that is beyond the normal response resources of the entity

   d. A suddenly occurring event that has a long-term negative impact on social life

   Answer: a

   Answer a, an occurrence that is outside the normal computing function and does not fulfill the definition of a disaster, is correct.

   The disaster/emergency management and business continuity community consists of many different types of entities, such as governmental (federal, state, and local), nongovernmental (business and industry), and individuals. Each entity has its own focus and its own definition of a disaster. Answers, b, c, and d are examples of these various definitions of disasters.

8. Which choice MOST accurately describes a threat?

    a. Any weakness in an information system

    b. Protective controls

    c. Multi-layered controls

    d. Potential for a source to exploit a specific vulnerability

    Answer: d

    A threat is the potential for a threat-source to exploit (intentionally or accidentally) a specific vulnerability. Answer a describes a vulnerability, any weakness in an information system, system security procedures, internal controls, or implementation that could be exploited by a threat or threat agent. Answers c and d describe safeguards, controls in place that provide some amount of protection to the asset.

9. What is considered the major disadvantage to employing a "hot" site for disaster recovery?

    a. Exclusivity is assured for processing at the site.

    b. Annual testing is required to maintain the site.

    c. The site is immediately available for recovery.

    d. Maintaining the site is expensive.

    Answer: d

    A hot site is commonly used for those extremely time-critical functions that the business must have up and running to continue operating, but the expense of duplicating and maintaining all of the hardware, software, and application elements is a serious resource drain to most organizations.

10. Which choice MOST accurately describes a safeguard?

    a. Potential for a source to exploit a specific vulnerability

    b. Controls in place that provide some amount of protection for the asset

    c. Weakness in internal controls that could be exploited by a threat or threat agent

    d. A control designed to counteract an asset

    Answer: b

    Safeguards are those controls in place that provide some amount of protection to the asset. Controls can be operational, technical, or administrative. Answer a describes a threat—the potential for a threat-source to exploit (intentionally or accidentally) a specific vulnerability. Answer c describes a vulnerability—any weakness in an information system, system security procedures, internal controls, or implementation that could be exploited by a threat or threat agent. Answer d is a distracter.

11. Which choice is NOT an accurate statement about an organization's incident-handling response capability?

    a. It should be used to provide the ability to respond quickly and effectively to an incident.

    b. It should be used to prevent future damage from incidents.

    c. It should be used to detect and punish senior-level executive wrong-doing.

    d. It should be used to contain and repair damage done from incidents.

    Answer: c

    An organization incident-handling response capability should be used to:

    ▪ Provide the ability to respond quickly and effectively.

    ▪ Contain and repair the damage from incidents. When left unchecked, malicious software can significantly harm an organization's computing, depending on the technology and its connectivity. Containing the incident should include an assessment of whether the incident is part of a targeted attack on the organization or an isolated incident.

    ▪ Prevent future damage. An incident-handling capability should assist an organization in preventing (or at least minimizing) damage from future incidents. Incidents can be studied internally to gain a better understanding of the organization's threats and vulnerabilities.

12. Which choice is NOT a role or responsibility of the person designated to manage the contingency planning process?

    a. Providing direction to senior management

    b. Providing stress-reduction programs to employees after an event

    c. Ensuring the identification of all critical business functions

    d. Integrating the planning process across business units

    Answer: b

    Contingency planners have many roles and responsibilities when planning business continuity, disaster recovery, emergency management, or business resumption processes; however, providing stress-reduction programs to employees after an event is a responsibility of the human resources area.

13. Which choice MOST accurately describes a countermeasure?

    a. An event with the potential to harm an information system through unauthorized access

    b. Controls implemented as a direct result of a security analysis

c. The Annualized Rate of Occurrence multiplied by the Single Loss Exposure (ARO × SLE)

d. A company resource that could be lost due to an incident

Answer: b

Countermeasures are those controls put in place as a result of an analysis of a system's security posture. They are the same controls as defined in safeguards, but are implemented as a 'countermeasure' to reduce a specific identified and measured risk.

Answer a is a threat agent, any circumstance or event with the potential to harm an information system through unauthorized access, destruction, disclosure, modification of data, and/or denial of service. Answer c is a distracter, and answer d describes an asset.

14. Which disaster recovery/emergency management plan testing type is considered the most cost-effective and efficient way to identify areas of overlap in the plan before conducting more demanding training exercises?

a. Full-scale exercise

b. Walk-through drill

c. Table-top exercise test

d. Evacuation drill

Answer: c

In a table-top exercise, members of the emergency management group meet in a conference room setting to discuss their responsibilities and how they would react to emergency scenarios.

15. Which choice MOST closely depicts the difference between qualitative and quantitative risk analysis?

a. A quantitative RA does not use the hard costs of losses, and a qualitative RA does.

b. A quantitative RA makes a cost-benefit analysis simpler.

c. A quantitative RA results in a subjective (High, Medium, or Low) result.

d. A quantitative RA cannot be automated.

Answer: b

A quantitative risk analysis results in a result that shows quantity of some object. Typically, the results (quantity) are addressed in terms of dollars. A qualitative risk analysis results in a subjective result (quality rating). The results of qualitative analyses are addressed in terms of High, Medium, or Low, or on a scale from 0 to 5 (for example).

16. Which choice is an incorrect description of a control?

    a. Detective controls discover attacks and trigger preventative or corrective controls.

    b. Controls are the countermeasures for vulnerabilities.

    c. Corrective controls reduce the effect of an attack.

    d. Corrective controls reduce the likelihood of a deliberate attack.

    Answer: d

    Controls are the countermeasures for vulnerabilities. There are many kinds, but generally they are categorized into four types:

    - Deterrent controls reduce the likelihood of a deliberate attack.

    - Preventative controls protect vulnerabilities and make an attack unsuccessful or reduce its impact. Preventative controls inhibit attempts to violate security policy.

    - Corrective controls reduce the effect of an attack.

    - Detective controls discover attacks and trigger preventative or corrective controls. Detective controls warn of violations or attempted violations of security policy and include such controls as audit trails, intrusion detection methods, and checksums.

17. What is the main advantage of using a qualitative impact analysis over a quantitative analysis?

    a. Identifies areas for immediate improvement.

    b. Provides a rationale for finding effective security controls.

    c. Makes a cost-benefit analysis simpler.

    d. Provides specific measurements of the impacts' magnitude.

    Answer: a

    The main advantage of the qualitative impact analysis is that it prioritizes the risks and identifies areas for immediate improvement in addressing vulnerabilities. The disadvantage of the qualitative analysis is that it does not provide specific quantifiable measurements of the magnitude of the impacts, therefore making a cost-benefit analysis of any recommended controls difficult.

    The major advantage of a quantitative impact analysis is that it provides a measurement of the impacts' magnitude, which can be used in the cost-benefit analysis of recommended controls. The disadvantage is that, depending on the numerical ranges used to express the measurement, the meaning of the quantitative impact analysis may be unclear, requiring the result to be interpreted in a qualitative manner.

    Answer b is a distracter.

18. Which choice is NOT a common information-gathering technique when performing a risk analysis?

   a. Distributing a questionnaire

   b. Employing automated risk assessment tools

   c. Interviewing terminated employees

   d. Reviewing existing policy documents

   Answer: c

   Many information-gathering techniques can be used when performing a risk analysis, such as distributing questionnaires, on-site interviews, document reviews, and the use of automated scanning tools.

19. Put the following general steps in a qualitative risk analysis in order:

   a. The team prepares its findings and presents them to management.

   b. A scenario is written to address each identified threat.

   c. Business unit managers review the scenario for a reality check.

   d. The team works through each scenario by using a threat, asset, and safeguard.

   Answer: b, c, d, a

20. Which choice is usually the number-one-used criterion to determine the classification of an information object?

   a. Useful life

   b. Value

   c. Age

   d. Personal association

   Answer: a

   Value of the information asset to the organization is usually the first and foremost criteria used in determining its classification. Answer a refers to declassification of an information object due to some change in situation, and a and d are common value classification criteria.

21. What is the prime objective of risk management?

   a. Reduce the risk to a tolerable level.

   b. Reduce all risk regardless of cost.

   c. Transfer any risk to external third parties.

   d. Prosecute any employees that are violating published security policies.

   Answer: a

   Risk can never be eliminated, and risk management helps an organization find the level of risk that it can tolerate and still function effectively.

22. Which choice best describes a business asset?

    a. Events or situations that could cause a financial or operational impact to the organization

    b. Protection devices or procedures in place that reduce the effects of threats

    c. Competitive advantage, credibility, or goodwill

    d. Personnel compensation and retirement programs

    Answer: c

    Assets are considered the physical and financial assets that are owned by the company, such as revenues lost during the incident, ongoing recovery costs, fines and penalties incurred by the event, and competitive advantage, credibility, or goodwill damaged by the incident.

    Answer a is a definition for a threat. Answer b is a description of mitigating factors that reduce the effect of a threat, such as an *uninterruptible power supply* (UPS), sprinkler systems, or generators. Answer d is a distracter.

23. Which choice is the MOST accurate description of a "cold" site?

    a. A backup processing facility with adequate electrical wiring and air conditioning, but no hardware or software installed

    b. A backup processing facility with most hardware and software installed, which can be operational within a matter of days

    c. A backup processing facility with all hardware and software installed and 100-percent compatible with the original site, operational within hours

    d. A mobile trailer with portable generators and air conditioning

    Answer: a

    Answer a is an example of a "cold" site, which is a designated computer operations room with HVAC that might have few or no computing systems installed and therefore would require a substantial effort to install the hardware and software required to begin alternate processing. This type of site is rarely useful in an actual emergency.

    Answer b, a "warm" site, is a backup processing facility with most hardware and software installed, which would need a minor effort to be up and running as an alternate processing center. It might use cheaper or older equipment and create a degradation in processing performance but would be able to handle the most important processing tasks.

A "hot" site, answer c, has all required hardware and software installed to begin alternate processing either immediately or within an acceptably short time frame. This site would be 100-percent compatible with the original site and would only need an upgrade of the most current data to duplicate operations.

24. Which question is NOT accurate regarding the process of risk assessment?

    a. The likelihood of a threat must be determined as an element of the risk assessment.

    b. The level of impact of a threat must be determined as an element of the risk assessment.

    c. Risk assessment is the final result of the risk management methodology.

    d. Risk assessment is the first process in the risk management methodology.

    Answer: c

    Risk assessment is the first process in the risk management methodology. The risk assessment process helps organizations identify appropriate controls for reducing or eliminating risk during the risk mitigation process.

25. Which statement is NOT correct about safeguard selection in the risk analysis process?

    a. Maintenance costs need to be included in determining the total cost of the safeguard.

    b. The most commonly considered criteria is the cost effectiveness of the safeguard.

    c. The best possible safeguard should always be implemented, regardless of cost.

    d. Many elements need to be considered in determining the total cost of the safeguard.

    Answer: c

    Performing a cost-benefit analysis of the proposed safeguard before implementation is vital. The level of security afforded could easily outweigh the value of a proposed safeguard. Other factors need to be considered in the safeguard selection process, such as accountability, auditability, and the level of manual operations needed to maintain or operate the safeguard.

26. Which choice most accurately reflects the goals of risk mitigation?

    a. Analyzing the effects of a business disruption and preparing the company's response

    b. Analyzing and removing all vulnerabilities and threats to security within the organization

    c. Defining the acceptable level of risk that the organization can tolerate and assigning any costs associated with loss or disruption to a third party, such as an insurance carrier

    d. Defining the acceptable level of risk that the organization can tolerate and reducing risk to that level

    Answer: d

    The goal of risk mitigation is to reduce risk to a level that is acceptable to the organization. Therefore, risk needs to be defined for the organization through risk analysis, business impact assessment, and/or vulnerability assessment.

27. Which choice represents an application or system demonstrating a need for a high level of availability protection and control?

    a. The application contains proprietary business information and other financial information, which if disclosed to unauthorized sources, could cause unfair advantage for vendors, contractors, or individuals and could result in financial loss or adverse legal action to user organizations.

    b. Unavailability of the system could result in inability to meet payroll obligations and could cause work stoppage and failure of user organizations to meet critical mission requirements. The system requires 24-hour access.

    c. The mission of this system is to produce local weather forecast information that is made available to the news media forecasters and the general public at all times. None of the information requires protection against disclosure.

    d. Destruction of the information would require significant expenditures of time and effort to replace. Although corrupted information would present an inconvenience to the staff, most information, and all vital information, is backed up by either paper documentation or on disk.

    Answer: b

    Answer b is an example of a system requiring high availability. Answer a is an example of a system requiring a high level of confidentiality control, answer c is an example of a system that requires medium integrity control, and answer d is a system that requires only a low level of confidentiality.

28. Put the five disaster recovery testing types in their proper order, from the most extensive to the least:

    a. Full-interruption

    b. Checklist

    c. Structured walk-through

    d. Parallel

    e. Simulation

    Answer: a, d, e, c, and b

29. Which type of backup subscription service listed would require the longest recovery time?

    a. A hot site

    b. A mobile or rolling backup service

    c. A warm site

    d. A cold site

    Answer: d

    Warm and cold sites require more work after the event occurs to get them to full operating functionality. A "mobile" backup site might be useful for specific types of minor outages, but a hot site is still the fastest option.

30. Which of the following would best describe a "hot" backup site?

    a. A computer facility with electrical power and HVAC but with no applications or recent data installed on the workstations or servers prior to the event

    b. A computer facility available with electrical power and HVAC and some file/print servers, although the applications are not installed or configured and all of the needed workstations may not be on site or ready to begin processing

    c. A computer facility with no electrical power or HVAC

    d. A computer facility with electrical power and HVAC, all needed applications installed and configured on the file/print servers, and enough workstations present to begin processing

    Answer: d

    A hot site is a computer facility with electrical power and HVAC, all needed applications installed and configured on the file/print servers, and enough workstations present to begin processing in a very short time. It requires the least amount of preparation during recovery. Answer a, a cold site, is a computer facility with electrical power and HVAC, with workstations and servers available but no applications or current data installed. Answer b describes a warm site. Answer c is just an empty room.

Chapter 6—Domain 5: Cryptography

1. A strong hash function, H, and its output message digest, MD, have which of the following characteristics relative to a message, M, and another message, Ml?

   a. H(M) = MD, where M is of fixed length and MD is of fixed length

   b. H(M) = MD, where M is of variable length and MD is of fixed length

   c. H(M) = H(M1)

   d. H(M) = MD, where M is of variable length and MD is of variable length

   Answer: b

   The correct answer is b. A hash algorithm takes a message of variable length and produces a message digest of fixed length. Therefore, answers a and d are incorrect. Answer c is incorrect because two messages should not generate the same message digest in a strong hash function.

2. The *Secure Hash Algorithm* (SHA) is specified in the:

   a. Data Encryption Standard

   b. Digital Signature Standard

   c. Digital Encryption Standard

   d. Advanced Encryption Standard

   Answer: b

   The correct answer is b. Answer a refers to DES, a symmetric encryption algorithm; answer c is a distracter because there is no such term; and answer d is the Advanced Encryption Standard, which has replaced DES and is now the Rijndael algorithm.

3. What are MD4 and MD5?

   a. Symmetric encryption algorithms

   b. Asymmetric encryption algorithms

   c. Hashing algorithms

   d. Digital certificates

   Answer: c

   The correct answer is c. Answers a and b are incorrect because they are general types of encryption systems, and answer d is incorrect because hashing algorithms are not digital certificates.

4. What is the block length of the Rijndael Cipher?

   a. 64 bits

   b. 128 bits

   c. Variable

   d. 256 bits

   Answer: c

   The correct answer is c. The other answers with fixed numbers are incorrect.

5. What is the key length of the Rijndael Block Cipher?

   a. 56 or 64 bits

   b. 512 bits

   c. 128, 192, or 256 bits

   d. 512 or 1024 bits

   Answer: c

   The correct answer is c.

6. The hashing algorithm in the *Digital Signature Standard* (DSS) generates a message digest of:

   a. 120 bits

   b. 160 bits

   c. 56 bits

   d. 130 bits

   Answer: b

   The correct answer is b.

7. The *Wireless Application Protocol* (WAP) analog of SSL in the TCP/IP protocol is:

   a. *Wireless Transport Layer Security Protocol* (WTLS)

   b. *Wireless Session Protocol* (WSP)

   c. *Wireless Transaction Protocol* (WTP)

   d. *Wireless Application Environment* (WAE)

   Answer: a

   The correct answer is a. SSL performs security functions in TCP/IP. The other answers refer to protocols in the WAP protocol stack also, but their primary functions are not security.

8. Components of an IPSec *Security Association* (SA) are:

   a. Sockets security parameter and destination IP address

   b. *Authentication Header* (AH) and source IP address

   c. Security parameter index and destination address

   d. *Security Parameter Index* (SPI), *Authentication Header* (AH) or the *Encapsulation Security Payload* (ESP), and the destination IP address

   Answer: d

   The correct answer is d. The other answers are distracters.

9. Key clustering is:

   a. The identification of weak keys in symmetric key algorithms

   b. When two different keys encrypt a plain-text message into the same ciphertext

   c. When one key encrypts a plain-text message into different cipher-texts when the key is applied at different times

   d. When one key in a keyed hash function generates different message digests when applied at different times

   Answer: b

   The correct answer is b. The other answers are distracters.

10. The following table describes what cryptographic function?

INPUTS	OUTPUT
0 0	0
0 1	1
1 0	1
1 1	0

   a. Hash

   b. Keyed hash

   c. *Exclusive OR* (XOR)

   d. OR

   Answer: c

   The correct answer is c. An XOR operation results in a 0 if the two input bits are identical and a 1 if one of the bits is a 1 and the other is a 0.

11. In a block cipher, diffusion:

    a. Conceals the connection between the ciphertext and plain text

    b. Spreads the influence of a plain-text character over many ciphertext characters

    c. Is usually implemented by non-linear S-boxes

    d. Cannot be accomplished

    Answer: b

    The correct answer is b. Answer a defines confusion; answer c defines how confusion is accomplished; and answer d is incorrect because it can be accomplished.

12. The hard, one-way function that characterizes the elliptic curve algorithm is:

    a. Finding the prime factors of very large numbers

    b. The discrete logarithm problem

    c. RSA

    d. The knapsack problem

    Answer: b

    The correct answer is b. Modular exponentiation used in the elliptic curve algorithm, is the analog of the modular discreet logarithm problem. Answers a and c are incorrect because prime factors are involved with the RSA public key algorithm. Answer d is incorrect because the knapsack problem is not an elliptic curve problem.

13. What does the *Secure Sockets Layer* (SSL)/*Transaction Security Layer* (TSL) do?

    a. Implements confidentiality, authentication, and integrity above the Transport layer

    b. Implements confidentiality, authentication, and integrity below the Transport layer

    c. Implements only confidentiality above the Transport layer

    d. Implements only confidentiality below the Transport layer

    Answer: a

    The correct answer is a by definition. Answer b is incorrect because SSL/TLS operate above the Transport layer; answer c is incorrect because authentication and integrity are provided also, and answer d is incorrect because it cites only confidentiality and SSL/TLS operates above the Transport layer.

14. The Skipjack algorithm is used in:

    a. PGP

    b. The Clipper Chip

    c. DSS

    d. AES

    Answer: b

    The correct answer is b. Answer a refers to *Pretty Good Privacy* (PGP) that uses the IDEA symmetric key algorithm. Answer c refers to the Digital Signature Standard that employs public key cryptography, and answer d is the Advanced Encryption Standard that has replaced DES.

15. In most security protocols that support authentication, integrity, and confidentiality:

    a. AES is used to create digital signatures.

    b. Private key cryptography is used to create digital signatures.

    c. DES is used to create digital signatures

    d. Public key cryptography is used to create digital signatures.

    Answer: d

    The correct answer is d. Answers a, b, and c are incorrect because they refer to symmetric key algorithms and these algorithms are not used to create digital signatures.

16. Which of the following is an example of a symmetric key algorithm?

    a. Rijndael

    b. RSA

    c. Diffie-Hellman

    d. Knapsack

    Answer: a

    The correct answer is a. The other answers are examples of asymmetric key systems.

17. A polyalphabetic cipher is also known as a:

    a. One-time pad

    b. Vigenère cipher

    c. Steganography

    d. Vernam cipher

Answer: b

The correct answer is b. Answer a is incorrect because a one-time pad uses a random key with length equal to the plaintext message and is used only once. Answer c is the process of sending a message with no indication that a message even exits. Answer d is incorrect because it applies to stream ciphers that are XORed with a random key string.

18. Which one of the following is NOT a characteristic of a symmetric key algorithm?

    a. Secure distribution of the secret key is a problem.

    b. Most algorithms are available for public scrutiny.

    c. Work factor is a function of the key size.

    d. Is slower than asymmetric key encryption.

    Answer: d

    The correct answer is d. Symmetric key algorithms are approximately 1,000 times faster than asymmetric key algorithms. The other answers are all characteristics of symmetric key algorithms.

19. Which of the following is an example of an asymmetric key algorithm?

    a. IDEA

    b. DES

    c. 3 DES

    d. Elliptic curve

    Answer: d

    The correct answer is d. All the other answers refer to symmetric key algorithms.

20. Microdots, invisible ink, and hiding information in digital images is called:

    a. Hybrid cryptography

    b. Diffusion

    c. Steganography

    d. Confusion

    Answer: c

    The correct answer is c. Steganography hides the fact that a message even exists. Answer a, hybrid cryptography, uses public key cryptography to send the secret key and private key cryptography to encrypt the message. Answers b and d are used in symmetric key cryptography to hide the relationship between the plain text and ciphertext.

21. The classic Caesar cipher is a:

    a. Polyalphabetic cipher

    b. Monoalphabetic cipher

    c. Transposition cipher

    d. Code group

    Answer: b

    The correct answer is b. It uses one alphabet shifted three places. Answers a and c are incorrect because in a, multiple alphabets are used and in c, the letters of the message are transposed. Answer d is incorrect because code groups deal with words and phrases and ciphers deal with bits or letters.

22. The modes of DES do NOT include:

    a. Electronic Code Book

    b. Cipher Block Chaining

    c. Variable Block Feedback

    d. Output Feedback

    Answer: c

    The correct answer is c. There is no such encipherment mode in DES.

23. The Rijndael algorithm is also known as the:

    a. Advanced Encryption Standard (AES)

    b. Data Encryption Standard (DES)

    c. Digital Signature Algorithm (DSA)

    d. IDEA algorithm

    Answer: a

    The correct answer is a. Answer b, DES, was replaced by AES as the NIST standard. Answer c refers to the Digital Signature Algorithm used in the *Digital Signature Standard* (DSS). Answer d is another symmetric key algorithm.

24. Which of the following is true?

    a. The work factor of triple DES is the same as for double DES.

    b. The work factor of single DES is the same as for triple DES.

    c. The work factor of double DES is the same as for single DES.

    d. No successful attacks have been reported against double DES.

    Answer: c

    The correct answer is c. The meet-in-the-middle attack has been successfully applied to double DES with the work factor is equivalent to that of single DES. Thus, answer d is incorrect. Answer a is false because the work factor of triple DES is greater than that for double DES. In triple DES, three levels of encryption and/or decryption are applied to the message. Answer b is false because the work factor of single DES is less than for triple DES. In triple DES, three levels of encryption and/or decryption are applied to the message in triple DES.

25. In public key cryptography:

    a. Only the private key can encrypt, and only the public key can decrypt.

    b. Only the public key can encrypt, and only the private key can decrypt.

    c. The public key is used to encrypt and decrypt.

    d. If the public key encrypts, then only the private key can decrypt.

    Answer: d

    The correct answer is d. Answers a and b are incorrect, because if one key encrypts, the other can decrypt. Answer c is incorrect, because if the public key encrypts, it cannot decrypt.

26. Which of the following characteristics does a one-time pad have if used properly?

    a. It can be used more than once.

    b. The key does not have to be random.

    c. It is unbreakable.

    d. The key has to be of greater length than the message to be encrypted.

    Answer: c

    The correct answer is c. If the one-time-pad is used only once and its corresponding key is truly random, it is unbreakable. Answer a is incorrect, because if used properly, the one-time-pad should be used only once. Answer b is incorrect because the key should be random. Answer d is incorrect because the key is of the same length as the message.

27. The Clipper Chip is described by which of the following?

    a. The National Security Standard

    b. The Escrowed Encryption Standard

    c. Fair Public Key Cryptosystem

    d. Advanced Encryption Standard

    Answer: b

    The correct answer is b. Answer a is a made-up distracter. Answer c refers to another approach to key escrow proposed by Sylvio Micali. Answer d refers to the Rijndael symmetric key algorithm.

28. In a digitally signed message transmission using a hash function:

    a. The message digest is encrypted in the private key of the sender.

    b. The message digest is encrypted in the public key of the sender.

    c. The message is encrypted in the private key of the sender.

    d. The message is encrypted in the public key of the sender.

    Answer: a

    The correct answer is a. The hash function generates a message digest. The message digest is encrypted with the private key of the sender. Thus, if the message digest can be opened with the sender's public key that is known to all, the message must have come from the sender. The message, itself, is not encrypted with the sender's private key because the message is usually longer than the message digest and would take more computing resources to encrypt and decrypt. Since the message digest uniquely characterizes the message, it can be used to verify the identity of the sender. Answers b and d will not work because a message encrypted in the public key of the sender can only be read using the private key of the sender. Since the sender is the only one who knows this key, no one else can read the message. Answer c is incorrect because the message is not encrypted, but the message digest is encrypted.

29. A ciphertext attack where the selection of the portions of ciphertext for the attempted decryption is based on the results of previous attempts is known as:

    a. Known plain text

    b. Chosen ciphertext

    c. Chosen plain text

    d. Adaptive chosen ciphertext

    Answer: d

    The correct answer is d. In answer a, the attacker has a copy of the plain text corresponding to the ciphertext. In answer b, portions of the ciphertext are selected for trial decryption while having access to the corresponding decrypted plain text. Answer c describes the situation where selected plain text is encrypted and the output ciphertext is obtained.

30. A trap door is which of the following?

    a. A mechanism, usually in multilevel security systems, that limits the flow of classified information to one direction

    b. A mechanism in a database system that restricts access to certain information within the database

c. A method of sending a secret key

d. A secret mechanism that enables the implementation of the reverse function in a one-way function

Answer: d

The correct answer is d. Answer a refers to a data diode. Answer b is a database View; the View implements the principle of least privilege. Answer c is distracter. In a hybrid cryptographic system, public key cryptography is used to transmit the secret key used in private key cryptography.

Chapter 7—Domain 6: Data Communications

1. Which statement about the difference between analog and digital signals is correct?

a. Analog signals cannot be used for data communications.

b. A digital signal produces an infinite waveform.

c. An analog signal produces a sawtooth waveform.

d. An analog signal can be varied by amplification.

Answer: d

The other answers are incorrect properties of analog or digital signals.

2. Which answer is NOT true about the difference between TCP and UDP?

a. UDP is considered a connectionless protocol, and TCP is connection-oriented.

b. TCP is considered a connectionless protocol, and UDP is connection-oriented.

c. TCP acknowledges the receipt of packets, and UDP does not.

d. UDP is sometimes referred to as an unreliable protocol.

Answer: b

As opposed to the *Transmission Control Protocol* (TCP), the *User Datagram Protocol* (UDP) is a connectionless protocol. It does not sequence the packets, acknowledge the receipt of packets, and is referred to as an unreliable protocol.

3. Which choice is correct about the difference between conducted versus radiated transmission media?

   a. Microwave is a conducted transmission media.

   b. Infrared is a radiated transmission media.

   c. Fiber optic uses a radiated transmission media.

   d. UTP uses a radiated transmission media.

   Answer: b

   Conducted transmission media use copper wiring or fiber optics. Radiated transmission media use radio or light frequencies, such as microwave, infrared, broadcast, or satellite.

4. Which choice describes the range for Internet multicast addresses?

   a. 0.0.0.0. through 255.255.255.255

   b. 127.0.0.1 through 127.255.255.255

   c. 192.168.0.0 through 192.168.255.255

   d. 224.0.0.0 through 239.255.255.255

   Answer: d

   Internet multicast addresses range from 224.0.0.0 through 239.255.255.255.

5. Which UTP cable category is rated for 1Gbps?

   a. Category 4

   b. Category 6

   c. Category 5

   d. Category 7

   Answer: d

   UTP category 4 cabling is rated for 1Gbps. Answer a, UTP category 4 cabling is common in Token Ring networks and is rated for up to 16 Mbps. Answer b is rated for 155 Mbps. Answer c, category 5, is rated for 100Mbps.

6. Which choice BEST describes UTP cable?

   a. UTP consists of a hollow outer cylindrical conductor surrounding a single, inner conductor.

   b. UTP requires a fixed spacing between connections.

c. UTP consists of two insulated wires wrapped around each other in a regular spiral pattern.

d. UTP carries signals as light waves.

Answer: c

Unshielded twisted-pair (UTP) wiring consists of pairs of insulated wires wrapped around each other. Answers a and b describes properties of coax cabling. Answer d describes fiber-optic cable.

7. To what does 10Base-2 refer?

a. 10 Mbps thinnet coax cabling rated to 185 meters maximum length

b. 10 Mbps thicknet coax cabling rated to 500 meters maximum length

c. 10 Mbps baseband optical fiber

d. 100 Mbps unshielded twisted-pair cabling

Answer: a

Answer b is 10Base-5, answer c refers to 10Base-F; and answer d is 100Base-T.

8. FDDI uses what type of network topology?

a. Ring

b. Bus

c. Switched

d. Star

Answer: a

FDDI is a RING topology. Many fiber optic networks are implemented using RING topology. FDDI generally uses dual rings each having their own token with data flowing in opposite directions.

9. Which choice is NOT an element of IPSec?

a. *Encapsulating Security Payload* (ESP)

b. *Authentication Header* (AH)

c. *Security Association* (SA)

d. *Point Tunneling Protocol* (PPTP)

Answer: d

The *Encapsulating Security Payload* (ESP), *Authentication Header* (AH), and *Security Association* (SA) are all service elements of IPSec.

10. Which IEEE protocol defines wireless transmission in data rates up to 54 Mbps but is expected to be backward-compatible with existing 802.11b-based networks?

    a. IEEE 802.11g

    b. IEEE 802.11b

    c. IEEE 802.11a

    d. IEEE 802.15

    Answer: a

    IEEE 802.11g is a proposed standard that offers wireless transmission over relatively short distances at speeds from 20 Mbps up to 54 Mbps and operates in the 2.4 GHz range, and is expected to be backward-compatible with existing 802.11b-based networks. Answer b specifies high-speed wireless connectivity in the 2.4 GHz ISM band up to 11 Mbps. Answer c specifies high-speed wireless connectivity in the 5 GHz band using Orthogonal Frequency Division Multiplexing with data rates up to 54 Mbps, but is not naturally backward-compatible with existing 802.11b-based networks. Answer d, IEEE 802.15, defines *Wireless Personal Area Networks* (WPAN), such as Bluetooth, in the 2.4-2.5 GHz band.

11. Which LAN transmission method describes a packet sent from a single source to a single destination?

    a. Unicast

    b. Multicast

    c. Broadcast

    d. Anycast

    Answer: a

    Unicast describes a packet sent from a single source to a single destination. Answer b, multicast, describes a packet sent from a single source to multiple specific destinations. Answer c, broadcast, describes a packet sent to all nodes on the network segment. Answer d, anycast, refers to communication between any sender and the nearest of a group of receivers in a network.

12. Which choice BEST describes a property of UDP?

    a. Creates seven distinct layers

    b. Wraps data from one layer around a data packet from an adjoining layer

c. Provides "best effort" delivery of a data packet

d. Makes the network transmission deterministic

Answer: c

One of the properties of the TCP/IP protocol *User Datagram Protocol* (UDP) is that it provides unguaranteed, "best effort" packet delivery. Answer b describes Data Encapsulation in the OSI model, which is the process of attaching information from one layer to the packet as it travels from an adjoining layer. Answer a describes the OSI layered architecture model. Answer d describes a token-passing transmission scheme.

13. Which choice employs a dedicated, point-to-point technology?

   a. Frame Relay

   b. SMDS

   c. T1

   d. X.25

Answer: c

A T1 line is a type of leased line using a dedicated, point-to-point technology. The other answers employ packet-switched technologies.

14. Which TCP/IP protocol operates at the Transport layer?

   a. FTP

   b. IP

   c. TCP

   d. NFS

Answer: c

TCP and UDP both operate at the Transport layer, FTP and NFS operate at the Application layer, and IP operates at the Network layer.

15. Which is a property of fiber-optic cabling?

   a. Employs copper wire in the single, inner conductor

   b. Transmits at slower speeds than copper cable

   c. Harder to tap than copper cabling

   d. Consists of two insulated wires wrapped around each other

Answer: c

Fiber-optic cable is much harder to tap than copper cable. Answer a is a property of coax, answer b is incorrect, and answer d describes *unshielded twisted-pair* (UTP) cabling.

16. Which choice about L2TP is NOT true?

    a. L2TP is a predecessor to PPTP.

    b. PPTP is a predecessor to L2TP.

    c. L2TP does not include any mechanism for encryption or authentication of its traffic.

    d. L2TP is used by some IPSec VPNs.

    Answer: a

    PPTP is a predecessor to L2TP. L2TP enables the user to authenticate their identity directly to the network; however, L2TP does not include any mechanism for encryption or authentication of its traffic. L2TP is used by some IPSec VPNs to supplement nonstandard areas within IPSec, such as the exchange of policy or configuration information between a telecommuter and a security gateway.

17. Which process is an OSI Data Link layer function?

    a. Internetwork packet routing

    b. LAN bridging

    c. SMTP gateway services

    d. Signal regeneration and repeating

    Answer: b

    Bridging is a Data Link Layer function. Answer a, Internetwork packet routing, is a function of the Network layer. Answer c, gateways, most commonly function at the higher layers. Answer d, signal regeneration and repeating, is primarily a Physical layer function.

18. The protocol of the *Wireless Application Protocol* (WAP), which performs functions similar to SSL in the TCP/IP protocol, is called the:

    a. *Wireless Session Protocol* (WSP)

    b. *Wireless Application Environment* (WAE)

    c. *Wireless Transport Layer Security Protocol* (WTLS)

    d. *Wireless Transaction Protocol* (WTP)

    Answer: c

    WTSL performs security functions similar to SSL in TCP/IP. The other answers refer to protocols in the WAP protocol stack, also, but their primary functions are not security.

19. Which of the following is considered a property of Ethernet networks?

    a. These networks were originally designed to serve large, bandwidth-consuming applications.

    b. Workstations cannot transmit until they receive a token.

    c. All end stations are attached to a MSAU.

    d. These networks were originally designed to serve sporadic and only occasionally heavy traffic.

    Answer: d

    Ethernet networks were originally designed to work network transmitting lighter, more sporadic traffic than Token Ring networks. The other answers are properties of Token Ring networks.

20. Which IEEE standard defines wireless networking in the 2.4GHz band with speeds of up to 11Mbps?

    a. 802.5

    b. 802.11a

    c. 802.3

    d. 802.11b

    Answer: d

    IEEE 802.11b defines a wireless LAN in the 2.4GHz band with speeds up to 11Mbps. Answer a defines a token-passing ring access method. Answer b defines wireless networking in the 5GHz band with speeds of up to 54Mbps. Answer c describes a bus topology using CSMA/CD at 10Mbps.

21. Which choice most accurately describes S/MIME?

    a. It gives a user remote access to a command prompt across a secure, encrypted session.

    b. It uses two protocols: the Authentication Header and the Encapsulating Security Payload.

    c. It is a widely used standard of securing e-mail at the Application level.

    d. It enables an application to have authenticated, encrypted communications across a network.

    Answer: c

    The *Secure/Multipurpose Internet Mail Extension* (S/MIME) is a widely used standard of securing email at the Application level. Most major e-mail clients support S/MIME today. Answer a describes *Secure Shell* (SSH), answer b refers to IPSec, and answer d describes the *Secure Socket Layer* (SSL).

22. Which choice defines an interface to the first commercially successful connection-oriented packet-switching network?

    a. X.25

    b. Frame Relay

    c. SMDS

    d. ATM

    Answer: a

    X.25 was the first commercially successful connection-oriented packet-switching network, in which the packets travel over virtual circuits. Answer b, Frame Relay, was a successor to X.25, and offers a connection-oriented packet-switching network. Answer c describes *Switched Multi-megabit Data Service* (SMDS) is a high-speed, connectionless, packet-switching public network service. Answer d, *Asynchronous Transfer Mode* (ATM), was developed from an outgrowth of ISDN standards, and is fast-packet, connection-oriented, cell-switching technology.

23. Which standard defines copper cable as its physical media?

    a. 1000BaseLX

    b. 1000BaseSX

    c. 1000BaseCX

    d. 100BaseFX

    Answer: c

    1000BaseCX refers to 1000Mbps baseband copper cable and two pairs of 150 ohm balanced cable for CSMA/CD LANs. The other three choices define fiber-optic transmission media.

24. Which protocol is a management protocol for IP networks?

    a. ICMP

    b. RARP

    c. TFTP

    d. ARP

    Answer: a

    The *Internet Control Message Protocol* (ICMP) is a management protocol for IP and contains the PING utility. Answer b, the *Reverse Address Resolution Protocol* (RARP), is the reverse of ARP. It asks a RARP server to provide a valid IP address. Answer c, the *Trivial File Transfer Protocol* (TFTP), is similar to the *File Transfer Protocol* (FTP). Answer d, the *Address Resolution Protocol* (ARP), is used to resolve a known IP address to an unknown MAC address.

25. Which IEEE protocol specifies an Ethernet bus topology using CSMA/CD?

    a. IEEE 802.5

    b. IEEE 802.3

    c. IEEE 802.11

    d. IEEE 802.1D

    Answer: b

    IEEE 802.3 specifies an Ethernet bus topology using *Carrier Sense Multiple Access with Collision Detect* (CSMA/CD). Answer a specifies a token-passing ring access method for LANs. Answer c is the IEEE standard that specifies 1 Mbps and 2 Mbps wireless connectivity in the 2.4 MHz ISM (Industrial, Scientific, and Medical) band. Answer d defines the Spanning Tree protocol, an Ethernet link-management protocol that provides link redundancy while preventing routing loops.

26. Which type of cabling is referred to as "ThickNet"?

    a. 10Base2

    b. 10Base5

    c. Twinax

    d. UTP Cat5

    Answer: b

    ThickNet, also known as 10Base5, uses traditional thick coaxial (coax) cable at data rates of up to 10 Mbps. Answer a, 10Base2, is known as ThinNet. Answer c, Twinax was used in IBM Systems 36 and earlier AS/400 installations. Answer d, UTP Cat5, is the most common cabling for recent Ethernet installations.

27. Which choice is a Presentation layer specification for digital certificates?

    a. X.500

    b. X.509

    c. X.25

    d. X.400

    Answer: b

    X.509 is a Presentation layer specification for digital certificates. Answer a, X.500, is used in the Presentation layer for directory services. Answer c, X.25, is used in the first three layers, the Physical, Data Link, and Network layers. Answer d, X.400, is an email spec residing in the Presentation layer.

28. What could be a problem with Token Ring-type network topology?

    a. Lost tokens must be regenerated to re-enable network communications.

    b. Cabling termination errors can crash the entire network.

    c. A cable break can stop all communications.

    d. The network nodes are connected to a central LAN device.

    Answer: a

    In a Token Ring-type network topology, tokens control network access. The device with a token can use the network; a device without a token must wait until one is freed up by the device using the network. This process ensures that no collisions occur on the network; however, problems can exist when tokens are lost and must be regenerated to re-enable network communications. The other answers are incorrect.

29. Which statement about VPNs is incorrect?

    a. L2TP is used by some IPSec VPNs.

    b. Proprietary schemes restrict the user to a particular vendor's VPN products.

    c. Some VPN clients use proprietary technologies.

    d. Proprietary schemes benefit from testing by a wider community of users.

    Answer: d

    Proprietary schemes restrict the user to a particular vendor's VPN products and should be avoided wherever possible. Standardized schemes also benefit from security analysis and testing performed by a wider community of users and analysts.

30. Which choice is NOT a type of security testing?

    a. Penetration testing

    b. War gaming

    c. Vulnerability scanning

    d. Network mapping

    Answer: b

    Answer b is a distracter. The other three answers are common methods of testing network security.

Chapter 8—Domain 7: Malicious Code

1. Which one of the following characteristics is NOT associated with a computer virus?

   a. Malicious code that infects files and can infect the boot sector

   b. A program that replicates itself without the approval of the user

   c. Malicious code that attaches to a host program and propagates when the infected program is executed

   d. Malicious code that is hidden in a program that has a useful function or apparently useful function

   Answer: d

   The correct answer is d. Answer d describes a Trojan horse.

2. A malicious computer program that is activated when a particular state of the computer occurs, such as a particular date and time, is called a:

   a. Polymorphic virus

   b. Logic bomb

   c. Retro virus

   d. Keyed virus

   Answer: b

   The correct answer is b. Answer a refers to a type of virus in which the body of the virus is encrypted and a decryption routine is part of the virus. This routine decrypts the virus body and then the virus spreads to other programs. An encrypted virus can be identified by the signature of its decryption routine. In a polymorphic virus, the virus creates a new decryption routine each time it infects new executable code. Thus, the signature of the polymorphic virus decryption routine is always changing, making it much more difficult to identify. The virus uses a mutation engine to change its signature. Answer c is a virus program that attacks anti-virus software. Answer d is a distracter.

3. Code that can be downloaded from a network and executed on a local computer is known as:

   a. A virtual machine

   b. A dynamic machine

   c. Mobile code

   d. Pointer code

Answer: c

The correct answer is c. Answer a refers to a virtual computer, such as the Java virtual machine, that executes applets implemented in the virtual machine code. The virtual machine presents a standard "architecture" and can run on many types of hardware. Thus, the virtual machine concept is used to make the execution of code independent of the hardware platform. The Java virtual machine runs on the user computer's Web browser. Answer b is a distracter. Answer d is also a distracter, but pointers are used by programs to directly access memory locations. For security purposes, Java does not support pointers.

4. Which one of the following is NOT a characteristic of a worm virus?

   a. Can remain on an infected computer indefinitely

   b. Requires operating systems that support the execution of down-loaded programs

   c. Creates multiple replicas of itself on the infected computer until memory is used up and the infected computer crashes

   d. Requires a means to transmit itself to other networked computers

   Answer: a

   The correct answer is a. Because a worm "eats" memory until all memory space on a computer is used up, a worm must have a means to move to other networked computers (answer d) before it is destroyed on the host computer.

5. A virus that conceals the modifications that it makes to a computer's files is called a:

   a. Hidden virus

   b. Proxy virus

   c. Stealth virus

   d. Multipartite virus

   Answer: c

   The correct answer is c. Answers a and b are distracters. In answer d, the multipartite virus infects the computer in multiple locations such as in executable files and in the boot sector.

6. An individual that creates or uses programs to break into telephone systems to be able to access other computers is called a:

   a. Hacker

   b. Phreaker

   c. Cracker

   d. Social engineer

Answer: b

The correct answer is b. In its original sense, a hacker, answer a, was a person dedicated to using and promoting computers for the good of the public and exploring new ways of using computation to benefit mankind. Over the years, the popular press has imbued the term with the negative meaning of a person that breaks into computers and networks to cause harm or to perform unauthorized activities. That is the definition of a cracker, answer c. Answer d relates to the term social engineering wherein an individual uses social skills to acquire passwords or other information to gain unauthorized access to information systems.

7. Which of the following statements regarding malicious code is NOT true?

   a. Worms and viruses replicate themselves.

   b. Trojan horses and viruses replicate themselves.

   c. Trojan horses and viruses are associated with other programs.

   d. A worm does not need another program to serve as a host.

   Answer: b

   The correct answer is b. Trojan horses do not replicate themselves.

8. Malicious code that is set to execute when a user, A, logs on 110 times is a:

   a. Stealth virus

   b. Polymorphic virus

   c. Worm

   d. Logic bomb

   Answer: d

   The correct answer is d. Logic bombs are set to execute when a particular set of events occur. Answer a, stealth virus, refers to a virus that hides in presence in an infected file. A polymorphic virus, answer b, is a virus that changes its signature each time it infects a new file. Answer c, worm, is a program that "grows" and transmits itself to different computers on the network.

9. An attack script is which one of the following?

   a. A step-by-step procedure that a cracker follows to initiate attacks on networks

   b. Malicious code that can be downloaded from different sites on the Internet and used to mount an attack on computing resources

   c. A rehearsed social engineering ploy to gain access to passwords

   d. The product of applying a keyed hash function to a sensitive message

   Answer: b

The correct answer is b. Crackers that use this code are known as "script kiddies." The other answers are distracters.

10. Which one of the following procedures is NOT recommended for detecting malicious code and preventing malicious code attacks?

   a. Deploying virus scanning software

   b. Education of employees

   c. Downloading of software from the Internet

   d. Disable ports that are not required for the organization's business

   Answer: c

   The correct answer is c. Unless the downloading is from a confirmed, trusted source, the downloaded software might contain viruses or other types of malicious code.

11. An excellent approach to defending against malicious code is an access control layered defense. Which one of the following is NOT a component of this type of defense?

   a. Making backups of "clean" files

   b. Restricting who can physically gain entry to areas containing computing resources

   c. Controlling who has the ability to read, write and copy files

   d. Restricting the use of specific computing resources to those who require those resources to perform their assigned job functions

   Answer: a

   The correct answer is a. Creating backups of clean files is an excellent procedure, but it is not an access control procedure.

12. A virus that is associated with loading of the operating system into memory on startup is called a:

   a. Boot sector virus

   b. Companion virus

   c. Macro virus

   d. Source code virus

   Answer: a

   The correct answer is a. Answer b, companion virus, is a virus that has the same name as an executable file, but has a com extension. For example, if there is a valid file named Draw.exe, the virus can be hidden in a file named Draw.com. When the operating system finds the two files with the same name, it will execute the com file first. A macro virus, answer c, spreads by adding internal macro instructions to documents such as those created using Microsoft Word. Answer d is a virus that is appended to a source code file. When the source code is compiled, the virus is compiled into an executable file as is the valid source code.

13. Which one of the following items in the list best describes the accuracy of the following statement: "Only executable programs can contain viruses, therefore files that are not executable are not a concern relative to malicious code"?

    a. True

    b. True with one exception

    c. False

    d. False with one exception

    Answer: b

    The correct answer is b. The exception is a Word file that contains imbedded macros. These macros can be executed and, if they are self-duplicating, they are a virus.

14. Two general categories of stealth virus capabilities are:

    a. Write stealth and copy stealth

    b. Read stealth and write stealth

    c. Size stealth and write stealth

    d. Size stealth and read stealth

    Answer: d

    The correct answer is d. Size stealth is the capability of the virus to hide the increase in the file size caused by the appended virus code. Read stealth is the ability to intercept a request to read an infected file and, then, providing the requestor with an uninfected version of the file to conceal the existence of the virus. The other answers are distracters.

15. Which one of the following is NOT a reason that peer-to-peer networks are more vulnerable to file-resident virus attacks than network servers?

    a. Because every workstation on a peer-to-peer network can function both as a client and a server, the network is more resistant to file-resident virus attacks.

    b. Viruses can be transmitted from one workstation to another on a peer-to-peer network.

    c. Because every workstation on a peer-to-peer network can function both as a client and a server, the network is less resistant to file-resident virus attacks.

    d. Peer-to-peer network security is usually weaker than what exists on a network server.

Answer: a

The correct answer is a. Because every workstation on a peer-to-peer network can function both as a client and a server, there is more chance that one of them will become infected and spread the virus to other workstations on the network. This situation is true because the individual workstations are usually not as secure as a network server.

16. Which choice BEST describes a simple virus as opposed to a complex virus?

    a. Users who have little computer knowledge can use Internet programs to create simple viruses.

    b. Simple viruses attempt to conceal themselves from systems.

    c. A simple virus is divided into three parts: the replicator, the concealer, and the bomb.

    d. Knowledge of assembly language is required to manipulate interrupts so that simple viruses can remain hidden.

Answer: a

Simple viruses do not attempt to hide themselves and are easy to write. Users with little computer knowledge can use Internet programs to create these viruses. The other three answers are properties of complex viruses.

17. Which choice is NOT a common part of a complex virus?

    a. Replicator

    b. Macro

    c. Bomb

    d. Concealer

Answer: b

A complex virus is divided into three parts: the replicator, the concealer, and the bomb. The replicator part controls spreading the virus to other files, the concealer keeps the virus from being detected, and the bomb executes when the activation conditions of the virus are satisfied. After these parts are created and put together, the virus creator can infect systems with a virus that current antivirus software cannot detect. Answer b is a distracter.

18. Which choice is NOT a step in the polymorphic virus infection process?

   a. The decryption routine first gains control of the computer and decrypts both the virus body and the mutation engine.

   b. The decryption routine transfers control of the computer to the virus, which locates a new program to infect.

   c. The virus makes a copy of itself and the mutation engine in RAM.

   d. The virus creates a network backdoor to allow unauthorized entry at a later date.

   Answer: d

   Answer d is an example of a Trojan horse. The other three are all steps in the polymorphic virus infection process.

19. Which choice is an incorrect statement about pre-infection prevention?

   a. Pre-infection prevention products are used as the first level of defense against malicious code.

   b. Email filtering products that do not allow executable programs or certain file types to be transferred.

   c. Options in browsers that limit the use of and/or disable Java and ActiveX plug-ins.

   d. Pre-infection prevention products are much less scientific than post-infection products because they use educated guesses.

   Answer: d

   Answer d is a distracter; the other three answers are all properties of pre-infection prevention.

20. Which choice is NOT true about virus vaccination programs?

   a. The majority of short-term infection detection products use vaccination because it is easier to implement.

   b. Vaccination programs modify application programs to allow for a self-test mechanism within each program

   c. The drawbacks to this implementation include the fact that the boot segment is very hard to vaccinate, and the malicious code may gain control before the vaccination program can warn the user.

   d. The majority of short-term infection detection products do not use vaccinations because they are very difficult to implement.

   Answer: d

   The majority of short-term infection detection products use vaccination because it is easier, not difficult to implement. The other three answers are all correct properties of vaccination programs.

21. Which statement is correct about short-term infection detection products?

    a. The majority of short-term infection detection products use spectral analysis.

    b. The majority of short-term infection detection products use the snapshot technique because it is easier to implement.

    c. The majority of short-term infection detection products use vaccination because it is easier to implement.

    d. The majority of short-term infection detection products use heuristic analysis.

    Answer: c

    The majority of short-term infection detection products use vaccination because it is easier to implement. Answer b is incorrect because the snapshot technique is difficult to implement and not widely used. Answers a and d are incorrect because they refer to long-term infection detection products.

22. Which choice BEST describes the snapshot technique of virus detection?

    a. The snapshot technique is a long-term infection detection process.

    b. The snapshot technique identifies systems that have been infected for a long time.

    c. The snapshot technique uses educated guesses to find infections.

    d. Upon installation, a log of all critical information is made.

    Answer: d

    A log of all critical information is made, then during routine system inspections the user is prompted for appropriate action if any traces of malicious code are found. These system inspections occur when the system changes: disk insertion, connection to different Web sites, and so on. The other answers are incorrect. The snapshot technique is a short-term infection detection process. Answer c refers to heuristic analysis.

23. Which choice BEST describes long-term virus infection products?

    a. Long-term infection detection products detect an infection very soon after the infection has occurred.

    b. Long-term infection detection products identify specific malicious code on a system that has already been infected for some time.

    c. Long-term infection detection products can be implemented through vaccination programs and the snapshot technique.

    d. Long-term infection detection products generally address a small infected area of the system.

Answer: b

Long-term infection detection products identify specific malicious code on a system that has already been infected for some time. They usually remove the malicious code and return the system to its prior functionality. The other three answers are properties of short-term virus infection products.

24. Which choice is an element of heuristic infection detection?

a. Using heuristic analysis all data is examined and recorded for malicious code patterns.

b. Heuristic analysis is used in short-term infection detection products.

c. Heuristic analysis is much less scientific, using educated guesses.

d. Heuristic analysis guarantees exact and hard evidence of infection.

Answer: c

The underlying principle that governs heuristic analysis is that new malicious code must be identified before it can be detected and subsequently removed. Heuristic analysis does not guarantee optimal or even feasible results. Answer a describes a property of short-term infection detection products. Answer b and d are incorrect.

25. Which statement about spectral analysis is not correct?

a. Spectral analysis is a long-term infection detection product.

b. Spectral analysis is a short-term infection detection product.

c. All data is examined and recorded to discover automatically generated malicious code.

d. When a pattern or subset of it appears, a counter is incremented.

Answer: b

Spectral analysis is a long-term infection detection product. The other three answers are all examples of spectral analysis.

26. Which description is the BEST definition of a Category 2 mobile code?

a. Mobile code that has known security vulnerabilities with few or no countermeasures once it begins executing

b. Mobile code supporting limited functionality, with no capability for unmediated access to workstation, host, and remote system services and resources

c. Mobile code having full functionality, allowing mediated or controlled access to workstation, host, and remote system services and resources

d. Mobile code exhibiting a broad functionality, allowing unmediated access to workstation, host and remote system services and resources

Answer: c

Category 2 mobile codes have full functionality, allowing mediated or controlled access to workstation, host, and remote system services and resources. Category 2 mobile code may have known security vulnerabilities but also have known fine-grained, periodic, or continuous countermeasures or safeguards. Category 2 mobile code technologies can pose a moderate threat to information systems. The use of Category 2 mobile code technologies, when combined with prudent countermeasures against malicious use, can afford benefits that outweigh their risks. Where possible, web browsers and other mobile code enabled products shall be configured to prompt the user prior to the execution of Category 2 mobile code. Where feasible, protections against malicious Category 2 mobile code technologies shall be employed at end user systems and at enclave boundaries.

Answer a describes category one mobile code. Category 1 mobile code exhibits a broad functionality, allowing unmediated access to workstation, host and remote system services and resources. Category 1 mobile code has known security vulnerabilities with few or no countermeasures once they begin executing. Execution of Category 1 mobile code typically requires an all or none decision, either execute with full access to all system resources or don't execute at all. To the extent possible, all systems (for example, hosts), workstations, and applications capable of executing mobile code shall be configured to disable the execution of Category 1 mobile code obtained from outside the protection layers of the organization.

Answer b describes category three mobile code. Category 3 mobile code support limited functionality, with no capability for unmediated access to workstation, host, and remote system services and resources. Category 3 mobile code technologies may have a history of known vulnerabilities, but also support fine-grained, periodic, or continuous security safeguards. Category 3 mobile code technologies pose a limited risk to systems. When combined with vigilance comparable to that required to keep any software system configured to resist known exploits, the use of Category 3 mobile code affords benefits that outweigh the risks.

Answer d is a property of category one mobile code.

27. Which choice is a property of immediate virus detection products?

    a. Immediate virus detection products are used to detect an infection very soon after the infection has occurred.

    b. Immediate virus detection products periodically scan the entire system to search out malicious code.

c. Immediate virus detection is used to identify specific malicious code on a system.

d. Immediate virus detection is not functional on Category 1 mobile code.

Answer: a

Immediate detection products are used to detect an infection very soon after the infection has occurred by, for example, scanning a floppy when inserted. Answers b and c are properties of permanent virus detection products. Answer d is a distracter.

28. Which choice is NOT a property of permanent virus detection products?

a. Permanent virus detection usually removes malicious code after a scan and returns the system to its prior functionality.

b. Permanent virus detection products detect an infection quickly after infection.

c. Permanent virus detection periodically scans the entire system.

d. Permanent virus detection can be used to identify specific malicious code on a system.

Answer: b

Permanent infection detection products periodically scan the entire system to identify specific malicious code on a system, usually removing it and returning the system to its prior state. Answer b describes a property of immediate virus detection.

29. Which choice would NOT be an example of a proper enterprise-wide security procedure?

a. Encourage the distribution of spam to increase the company's name recognition.

b. Restrict users from bringing uncontrolled floppies from home to the office.

c. Discourage blind downloading of software from unregulated Internet sites.

d. Regulate access to Internet sites to reputable URLs only.

Answer: a

Junk email, spam, or email chain letters should never be encouraged or permitted.

30. Why should an organization discourage users from forwarding email chain letters?

    a. The company does not want you wasting time on fun stuff.

    b. They waste computer system resources.

    c. They can contain false information to mislead people.

    d. They do not increase the company's name recognition.

    Answer: b

    Email chain letters or virus hoax mass mailings use up large amounts of computer resources, including SMTP server storage space and network bandwidth. In the worst case, an email chain letter may contain malicious code.

What's on the CD-ROM

This appendix provides you with information on the contents of the CD that accompanies this book. For the latest and greatest information, please refer to the ReadMe file located at the root of the CD. Here is what you will find:

- System Requirements
- Using the CD with Windows
- What's on the CD
- Troubleshooting

System Requirements

Make sure that your computer meets the minimum system requirements listed in this section. If your computer doesn't match up to most of these requirements, you may have a problem using the contents of the CD.

For Windows 9*x*, Windows 2000, Windows NT4 (with SP 4 or later), Windows Me, or Windows XP:

- PC with a Pentium processor running at 120 Mhz or faster
- At least 32 MB of total RAM installed on your computer; for best performance, we recommend at least 64 MB
- Ethernet network interface card (NIC) or modem with a speed of at least 28,800 bps
- A CD-ROM drive

Using the CD with Windows

To install the items from the CD to your hard drive, follow these steps:

1. Insert the CD into your computer's CD-ROM drive.
2. A window appears with the following options: Install, Explore, Links and Exit.

   Install: Gives you the option to install the supplied software and/or the author-created samples on the CD-ROM.

   Explore: Enables you to view the contents of the CD-ROM in its directory structure.

   Links: Opens a hyperlinked page of Web sites.

   Exit: Closes the autorun window.

If you do not have autorun enabled, or if the autorun window does not appear, follow these steps to access the CD:

1. Click Start ➪ Run.
2. In the dialog box that appears, type *d*:**setup.exe**, where *d* is the letter of your CD-ROM drive. This brings up the autorun window described in the preceding set of steps.
3. Choose the Install, Browse, Links, or Exit option from the menu. (See Step 2 in the preceding list for a description of these options.)

What's on the CD

The following sections provide a summary of the software and other materials you'll find on the CD.

Author-Created Materials

All author-created material from the book, including code listings and samples, are on the CD in the folder named Author.

- A complete interactive self-test using all the questions and answers from the book, powered by the Boson test engine
- The Risk Management Guide for Information Technology Systems (from NIST)
- The Advanced Encryption Standard and the Secure Hash Standard (from FIPS Pubs)
- A list of links to security Web sites

Experience with the question-and-answer Boson test engine will enable you to become familiar with the type of testing that you will see in the exam.

Questions are the same as the ones that appear in the book; they apply to all eight domains covered in the book.

Upon answering each question, the test engine will let you know whether you are correct or not. It will also provide an explanation of *why* the answer is right or wrong. Thus, you can use it for both exam experience and as a tutorial aid as well.

Troubleshooting

If you have difficulty installing or using any of the materials on the companion CD, try the following solutions:

Turn off any anti-virus software that you may have running.   Installers sometimes mimic virus activity and can make your computer incorrectly believe that it is being infected by a virus. (Be sure to turn the anti-virus software back on later.)

Close all running programs.   The more programs you're running, the less memory is available to other programs. Installers also typically update files and programs; if you keep other programs running, installation may not work properly.

If you still have trouble with the CD, please call the Customer Care phone number: (800) 762-2974. Outside the United States, call 1 (317) 572-3994. You can also contact Customer Service by e-mail at techsupdum@wiley.com. Wiley Publishing, Inc. will provide technical support only for installation and other general quality control items; for technical support on the applications themselves, consult the program's vendor or author.

Index

A

abuse, threat type, 155
acceptable use policy, 65
acceptance, risk handling method, 163
access control lists (ACLs), 20, 40
access controls
  accountability assurance, 23
  account-level, 35–44
  asset and resource protection, 22–23
  attack types, 24–28
  availability support, 22
  biometrics, 31
  characteristics-based, 32–33
  confidentiality support, 22
  data-level, 40–44
  defined, 20
  Exclude All-Include by Exception principle, 29
  integrity support, 22
  knowledge methods, 31
  layered security protection, 11–13
  logical controls, 30–31
  malicious code countermeasure, 351
  OSI model
  physical controls, 29–30
  possession methods, 31
  principles, 21–28
  risk countermeasure, 156
  role-based, 39
  session-level, 39–40
  system level, 33–34
  token-based, 32
  transaction-level, 40
  Trusted Computing Base (TCB), 34
  unauthorized access prevention, 23–28
  VPN protection, 275
accessibility, logical control methods, 31
accountability, 6, 23
account-level access controls, 35–41
accounts, privileged, 35
ACLs (access control lists), 20, 40
actions, threat identification, 170–173
activation
  contingency plan (CP), 204
  virus lifecycle phase, 337
administration
  awareness training, 99–101
  compartmented mode, 72
  conceptual analysis phase, 56–57
  configuration management (CM), 76–77
  data/information storage, 59–63
  dedicated security mode, 72
  defined, 52
  employment policies, 63–64
  firewall environment, 91–93
  firewall functions, 91
  firewall platform access, 88–89
  firewall platform builds, 89–99
  firewall policy, 93–97
  guidelines, 68
  information classification, 69–71
  logging functionality, 90
  mechanism implementation, 80–88
  multilevel mode, 72
  OSI layer model, 74–75

Wiley Publishing, Inc.
End-User License Agreement

READ THIS. You should carefully read these terms and conditions before opening the software packet(s) included with this book "Book". This is a license agreement "Agreement" between you and Wiley Publishing, Inc. "WPI". By opening the accompanying software packet(s), you acknowledge that you have read and accept the following terms and conditions. If you do not agree and do not want to be bound by such terms and conditions, promptly return the Book and the unopened software packet(s) to the place you obtained them for a full refund.

1. **License Grant.** WPI grants to you (either an individual or entity) a nonexclusive license to use one copy of the enclosed software program(s) (collectively, the "Software" solely for your own personal or business purposes on a single computer (whether a standard computer or a workstation component of a multi-user network). The Software is in use on a computer when it is loaded into temporary memory (RAM) or installed into permanent memory (hard disk, CD-ROM, or other storage device). WPI reserves all rights not expressly granted herein.

2. **Ownership.** WPI is the owner of all right, title, and interest, including copyright, in and to the compilation of the Software recorded on the disk(s) or CD-ROM "Software Media". Copyright to the individual programs recorded on the Software Media is owned by the author or other authorized copyright owner of each program. Ownership of the Software and all proprietary rights relating thereto remain with WPI and its licensers.

3. **Restrictions On Use and Transfer.**

   (a) You may only (i) make one copy of the Software for backup or archival purposes, or (ii) transfer the Software to a single hard disk, provided that you keep the original for backup or archival purposes. You may not (i) rent or lease the Software, (ii) copy or reproduce the Software through a LAN or other network system or through any computer subscriber system or bulletin- board system, or (iii) modify, adapt, or create derivative works based on the Software.

   (b) You may not reverse engineer, decompile, or disassemble the Software. You may transfer the Software and user documentation on a permanent basis, provided that the transferee agrees to accept the terms and conditions of this Agreement and you retain no copies. If the Software is an update or has been updated, any transfer must include the most recent update and all prior versions.

4. **Restrictions on Use of Individual Programs.** You must follow the individual requirements and restrictions detailed for each individual program in the About the CD-ROM appendix of this Book. These limitations are also contained in the individual license agreements recorded on the Software Media. These limitations may include a requirement that after using the program for a specified period of time, the user must pay a registration fee or discontinue use. By opening the Software packet(s), you will be agreeing to abide by the licenses and restrictions for these individual programs that are detailed in the About the CD-ROM appendix and on the Software Media. None of the material on this Software Media or listed in this Book may ever be redistributed, in original or modified form, for commercial purposes.

5. **Limited Warranty.**

   (a) WPI warrants that the Software and Software Media are free from defects in materials and workmanship under normal use for a period of sixty (60) days from the date of purchase of this Book. If WPI receives notification within the warranty period of defects in materials or workmanship, WPI will replace the defective Software Media.